Three
Days at
Gettysburg

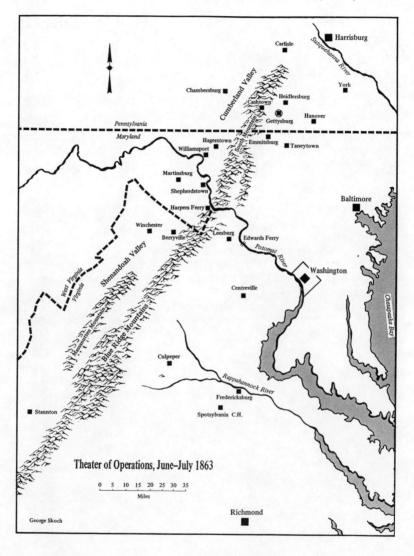

Theater of Operations, June–July 1863

0 5 10 15 20 25 30 35
Miles

George Skoch

Three

ESSAYS ON CONFEDERATE

Days at

AND UNION LEADERSHIP

Gettysburg

EDITED BY GARY W. GALLAGHER

THE KENT STATE UNIVERSITY PRESS

Kent, Ohio, & London

©1999 by The Kent State University Press, Kent, Ohio 44242
Library of Congress Catalog Card Number 98-55436
ISBN 0-87338-629-9
Manufactured in the United States of America

08 07 06 05   5 4 3 2

Parts One and Two were originally published as *The First Day at Gettysburg: Essays on Confederate and Union Leadership* (1992) and *The Second Day at Gettysburg: Essays on Confederate and Union Leadership* (1993) by The Kent State University Press.

Library of Congress Cataloging-in-Publication Data
Three days at Gettysburg : essays on Confederate and Union leadership
/ edited by Gary W. Gallagher.
p.   cm.
Includes The first day at Gettysburg (1992)
and The second day at Gettysburg (1993) with new essays.
Includes bibliographical references and index.
ISBN 0-87338-629-9 (cloth : alk. paper)∞
1. Gettysburg (Pa.), Battle of, 1863.   2. Command of troops—Case
studies.   I. Gallagher, Gary W.   II. The first day at Gettysburg.
III. The second day at Gettysburg.   IV. Title: 3 days at Gettysburg.
E475.53.T57   1999
973.7'349—dc21   98-55436

British Library Cataloging-in-Publication data are available.

For

Karen A. Ebeling, Darla A. Franks, W. Lynn Moyer,

Linda Kay Nihart, Judith L. Shawley, and Karin H. Weaver—

splendid friends and coworkers

Contents

Introduction

THIS BOOK BRINGS TO COMPLETION A PROJECT BEGUN in 1992. *The First Day at Gettysburg: Essays on Confederate and Union Leadership* appeared that year, followed in 1993 by *The Second Day at Gettysburg: Essays on Confederate and Union Leadership*. A third volume covering July 3, 1863, which was to have been published soon after the second book, languished because of my tendency to take on too many commitments. After the passage of several years and reflection about how best to present material on the battle's third day following so long a hiatus, I proposed offering in a single volume the nine original essays together with four new ones devoted to leadership on July 3. John T. Hubbell at The Kent State University Press, exhibiting admirable patience regarding this project, agreed that a single book covering the entire battle made sense. The result is *Three Days at Gettysburg: Essays on Confederate and Union Leadership*.

No Civil War military campaign has inspired as much controversy relating to leadership as Gettysburg. The debates began almost immediately after the battle, and they continue today. After the war, Confederates engaged in fierce arguments over who was to blame for their defeat. Following the lead of Lost Cause writers who sought to absolve Lee of all responsibility (Lee himself had taken full responsibility during the war), most white Southerners fixed on James Longstreet as their principal villain. For his part, Longstreet suggested that Lee's actions invited critical scrutiny. Less vitriolic discussion focused on the actions of Richard S. Ewell and A. P. Hill, Lee's other two corps commanders, as well as on cavalry chief James E. B. Stuart, division leader Jubal A. Early, and various others. On the Union side, supporters of the Army of the Potomac's commander George G. Meade and Third Corps chief Daniel E. Sickles waged a bitter battle of words about events on July 2. Northern veterans also wrangled about who should receive credit for establishing the splendid defensive position on high ground south of Gettysburg on July 1. In one way or another, corps commanders Oliver Otis Howard, Winfield Scott Hancock, and Henry W. Slocum, as well as the brilliant artillerist Henry J. Hunt, figured in postwar bickering about what had transpired on July 1–3, 1863.

Many of the principals defended their actions at Gettysburg in memoirs, reminiscences, articles, essays, and published speeches. Some of the leading outlets for Gettysburg-related material included *Century Magazine*'s "Battles and Leaders" series, the *Philadelphia Weekly Times*'s similar "Annals of the War," and the Southern Historical Society's *Papers*. By the end of the nineteenth century the literature on Gettysburg already was extensive, and throughout the twentieth century historians have labored to increase its imposing mass. In 1982, Richard A. Sauers's *The Gettysburg Campaign, June 3–August 1, 1863: A Comprehensive, Selectively Annotated Bibliography* listed more than 2,750 items, and the decade and a half since that book appeared has witnessed an explosion of new scholarship. Much of this recent work has dealt, at least in part, with Confederate and Union leadership on the battlefield.

Although the size of the existing literature has prompted many historians to wonder whether military leadership at Gettysburg has been exhausted as a topic for fruitful study, the contributors to this volume believe that there is room for scholarship of at least two types. The first entails revisiting the sources on which earlier accounts have been based, submitting them to rigorous evaluation and testing widely accepted interpretations of key officers' performances. The second approach involves training the investigative lens on relatively neglected officers—some at the corps level and some of lower rank—with an eye toward illuminating not only what happened at Gettysburg but also the nature of command at different levels. Because Gettysburg was a defining moment for both the Army of the Potomac and the Army of Northern Virginia (neither organization was ever quite the same afterward), the contributors believe that commanders and their decisions that influenced the course of the battle—and by extension the later histories of the armies—retain validity as subjects of scholarly exploration.

The book is divided into three parts, opening with four essays on leadership during the first day's battle. Alan T. Nolan leads off with an evaluation of Lee's strategy and tactics, finding the Confederate chieftain wanting in both areas. The movement across the Potomac invited unnecessary risk for the Army of Northern Virginia, insists Nolan, and Lee's decision to press the tactical offensive shortly after he arrived on the battlefield needlessly diminished his limited pool of precious manpower. Fighting on July 1 provided the first major test for the Confederate army's three-corps structure instituted following the death of "Stonewall" Jackson; it also marked the debut in corps command of Richard S. Ewell and A. P. Hill, who suffer invidious comparisons with Jackson in much of the literature on Gettysburg. In the second essay I suggest that Lee more than anyone else controlled Confederate tactical decisions on July 1 and that he, rather than either of his new corps commanders, should be the focus of analysis for those who choose to criticize the handling of the Southern army on that fateful day.

In the third essay, A. Wilson Greene shifts the spotlight to Oliver Otis Howard and the officers of the Union Eleventh Corps. Maligned at the time and usually slighted as second-rate soldiers thereafter, Howard and his subordinates played a crucial part in the collapse of Northern resistance about midafternoon on July 1. Greene argues that Howard and his lieutenants, as well as the men they led, deserve better treatment than they typically have received. Three notable debacles among Lee's brigadiers are the subject of Robert K. Krick's essay. Sour notes in an apparent symphony of Confederate success, the failures of Joseph R. Davis, Edward A. O'Neal, and Alfred Iverson, Jr., foreshadowed weakness at this level of leadership that would haunt Lee during the campaigning of 1864.

Part Two takes up command on the second day. In the first of five essays in this section I examine key questions concerning Lee's decision to resume the tactical offensive on July 2. Did he have better options? Did he give too free a rein to his naturally aggressive personality? And is it fair to look at Gettysburg in isolation, or should Lee's actions there be judged within the context of the history of the Army of Northern Virginia? William Glenn Robertson then reviews Daniel Sickles's controversial decision to occupy an advanced position embracing the high ground at the Peach Orchard. He analyzes the case against Sickles, taking into account the importance of reputation and clashes of personality as well as such military factors as the nature of the terrain and perceptions about the tactical situation. In the third of the second-day essays, Robert K. Krick draws on wartime testimony (unstained by Lost Cause propaganda) to reassess Longstreet's much-maligned actions. Finding a consistent pattern in Longstreet's behavior throughout the war, Krick reaches conclusions that are certain to provoke additional debate.

The final pair of essays in Part Two depart from such hotly contested historiographical ground. A. Wilson Greene looks at Henry W. Slocum and the Union Twelfth Corps. The senior Northern corps leader, Slocum has received relatively little attention in the enormous literature on Gettysburg. Greene offers a convincing portrait of a general unwilling or unable to act decisively and of a corps that fell far short of achieving its full potential at

Gettysburg. In the last essay, D. Scott Hartwig moves the spotlight to the division level, where he reconstructs the chaotic experience of directing large numbers of men in mid-nineteenth-century combat. Cast as attackers in a Union drama dominated by the tactical defensive, John C. Caldwell and his men performed admirably before factors beyond their control overwhelmed them. Hartwig suggests why good tactical plans often went astray—and why modern students should exercise care in criticizing Civil War commanders for failures on the battlefield.

Part Three of the volume offers four essays on July 3. Many writers have suggested that George G. Meade contributed relatively little direction to the Union effort at Gettysburg, while other critics (including Abraham Lincoln) believed he frittered away a major opportunity to counterattack in the wake of Pickett's Charge. Richard A. Sauers presents a different portrait of the Union commander, arguing that he made the crucial decision to fight on the third day, took an active hand in placing troops where they could do the most good, and would have had to overcome daunting challenges to mount a quick counterattack after Lee's great assault failed. Carol Reardon then explores the postwar jousting among former Confederates regarding James Longstreet's role on July 3. She highlights the survivors of George E. Pickett's division, explaining why their opinions, which usually supported "Old Pete's" actions, did not achieve the same degree of authority as those of Longstreet's critics.

The role of artillery on the third day dominates the last two essays. Peter S. Carmichael dissects the reasons behind the Confederate failure to provide better artillery support for their infantry during the climactic assault. He finds an absence of coordination that reflects poorly on artillery chief William Nelson Pendleton, an officer who he argues contributed nothing positive to the Southern effort. But Lee must also bear part of the blame, believes Carmichael, for granting too much responsibility to Pendleton and for largely ignoring preparations for the artillery bombardment that preceded Pickett's Charge. Gary M. Kross closes the book with an essay on the gifted gunner Henry Jackson Hunt and the Federal artillery. Hunt's work on July 3 helped preserve Union victory; he nonetheless believed his guns should have been more decisive. Kross explores the tension between Hunt and Second Corps chief Winfield Scott Hancock, who clashed over both control and employment of artillery along Cemetery Ridge. Bitter about his failure to receive what he considered due credit for his accomplishments on July 3, Hunt nourished a grudge against Hancock for the rest of his life.

The essays in this book reflect research in both easily accessible sources and a range of unpublished materials. The authors hope their interpretations will challenge readers to look again at old questions, while at the same time they offer new evidence that enhances our understanding of the campaign. The essayists sometimes contradict one another—even when relying on the same evidence. This is a strength that points to the potential for continued investigation into the problems of command at Gettysburg.

Peter Carmichael, Will Greene, Scott Hartwig, Bob Krick, Gary Kross, Alan Nolan, Carol Reardon, and Glenn Robertson are talented historians whose cheerful cooperation made editorial tasks much easier than usually is the case with cooperative scholarly efforts. George Skoch, a widely respected mapmaker, responded to various requests for changes and still met every deadline. John Hubbell offered consistent support and encouragement, exceeding in his relations with me the patience Lee exhibited regarding William Nelson Pendleton. I will not speculate about whether John's patience was as misguided as Lee's, but I thank him and all the others for their stalwart assistance.

Day One

R. E. Lee and July 1 at Gettysburg

Alan T. Nolan

ALTHOUGH PRESIDENT JEFFERSON DAVIS APPROVED OF THE
Army of Northern Virginia's moving into Maryland and Pennsylvania in
1863, the Gettysburg campaign was Gen. Robert E. Lee's idea. In 1914,
Douglas Southall Freeman wrote that Lee's "army . . . had been wrecked
at Gettysburg."[1] This catastrophic consequence was the result of leadership failures on the part of the army commander. The first of these was
strategic; the second involved a series of errors in the execution of the
campaign.

In regard to strategy, it is apparent that the drama of Gettysburg and
the celebrated controversies associated with the battle have obscured the
primary question about the campaign: Should it have been undertaken;
should Lee have been in Pennsylvania in 1863? When questioning Lee's
campaigns and battles, one is frequently confronted with the assertion that
he had no alternative. Accordingly, before addressing the question of the
wisdom of Lee's raid into Pennsylvania, one must consider whether he had
an alternative.

On the eve of the campaign, during the period following Chancellorsville, Lee's army remained near Fredericksburg on the Rappahannock
facing Joseph Hooker's Army of the Potomac, located on the north side of
that river. In this situation, Lee had at least three possible options: to attack

Hooker across the river, which surely would have been problematical; to assume the defensive as he had at Fredericksburg in December 1862 and was to do again in 1864; or to undertake a raid into the North. The most likely of these choices was surely the middle course—to assume the defense and force the Army of the Potomac to come after him. Lee apologists, committed to the "no alternative" thesis, would exorcise this option. The analysis of Col. Charles Marshall, Lee's aide-de-camp and military secretary, is illustrative. In an effort to justify the campaign, Marshall carefully constructed the no alternative argument. He identified the same three choices for Lee set forth above. Rejecting the choice of Lee's attacking across the river, he eliminated the defensive option by the naked assertion that had Lee stood on the defensive south of the river he "was bound to assume . . . the enemy would abandon his effort to dislodge him from his position at Fredericksburg, and would move his army to Richmond by water." This, Marshall insisted, would have required Lee to retreat to defend Richmond. Based on this assumption, Marshall eliminated the defensive option and, as if by magic, concluded that there was no alternative to the Gettysburg raid. That the Federals would not have moved against Lee but would, instead, have proceeded directly to Richmond by water is simply Marshall's hypothesis. In fact, the evidence since the 1862 withdrawal from the Peninsula pointed to the North's commitment to the overland route.[2]

The Southern army's need for food is the premise of another no alternative justification for Lee's moving into Maryland and Pennsylvania. The South's supply problems were severe, as Robert K. Krick has graphically stated.[3] Collecting supplies and living off the Northern country was surely a motive for the campaign. But the Army of Northern Virginia was sustained in Virginia from July 1863 until April 1865, so it was not necessary to go North for food and forage. If supplying the army had really been the motive for the campaign, a raid by small, mobile forces rather than the entire army would have had considerably more promise and less risk.

Since there was an alternative, we may return to the primary question: Should Lee have undertaken the campaign at all? This question cannot be meaningfully considered in the abstract. It must be considered within the context of the larger question of the appropriate grand strategy of the war from the standpoint of the Confederacy. In this larger respect, the concern is not military strategy in the sense of a campaign or battle, that is, operational strategy. Rather, it is grand strategy, that is, to paraphrase Carl von Clausewitz, the art of employing military forces to attain the objects of war, to support the national policy of the government that raises the military forces. In evaluating a general's performance, the only significant in-

Robert E. Lee, sketched in the field by Frank Vizetelly in late 1862. From *Harper's Weekly*, March 14, 1863.

quiry is whether the general's actions related positively or negatively to the war objective and national policy of his government.

The statements of two Confederate leaders describe quite different theories of the South's grand strategy to win the war. E. Porter Alexander, chief of ordnance of the Army of Northern Virginia and later chief of artillery of Longstreet's First Corps, has described the South's appropriate grand strategy in this way:

> When the South entered upon war with a power so immensely her superior in men & money, & all the wealth of modern resources in machinery and transportation appliances by land & sea, she could entertain but one single hope of final success. That was, that the desperation of her resistance would finally exact from her adversary such a price in blood & treasure as to exhaust the enthusiasm of its

population for the objects of the war. We could not hope to conquer her. Our one chance was to wear her out.[4]

This fairly describes a defensive grand strategy—to wear the North out instead of trying to defeat the North militarily.

The second view was Lee's. It may be found in two letters to President Davis. The first, written en route to Gettysburg, is dated June 25, 1863, at Williamsport, Maryland. Lee states: "It seems to me that we cannot afford to keep our troops awaiting possible movements of the enemy, but that our true policy is, as far as we can, so to employ our own forces as to give occupation to his at points of our selection." He further argues that "our concentration at any point compels that of the enemy." It is important that this letter was concerned with Confederate military forces on a wide range of fronts, including Virginia, North Carolina, and Kentucky. Since it contemplates drawing Federal armies to Confederate points of concentration to "give occupation" to the Federals, the letter is a prescription for military confrontation. It is therefore a statement of an offensive grand strategy, whether the confrontation at the "point of concentration" was to take the form of the tactical offensive or defensive on the part of the South. The second letter to Davis is dated July 6, 1864, shortly after the siege of Petersburg began. Lee wrote: "If we can defeat or drive the armies of the enemy from the field, we shall have peace. All our efforts and energies should be devoted to that object."[5]

This, then, was Lee's view of the way, as Clausewitz defined grand strategy, for the Confederacy "to attain the objects of [the] war." The South was to pursue the military defeat of the North. Lee's offensive grand strategic sense is reiterated again and again in his dispatches to Davis, the War Department, and his fellow general officers. These dispatches, in the *Official Records* and *The Wartime Papers of R. E. Lee*, bristle with offensive rhetoric and planning: "striking a blow," "driving the enemy," "crushing the enemy."[6]

Any doubt that Lee was committed to the offensive as the South's appropriate grand strategy is presumably eliminated when one considers the most obvious source for identifying his grand strategic thinking, the campaigns and battles of the Army of Northern Virginia. Consistent with the grand strategy that he said he believed in and repeatedly planned and advocated, Lee from the beginning embraced the offensive. Appointed to command the Army of Northern Virginia on June 1, 1862, he turned at once to the offensive, beginning with major engagements on the Peninsula— Mechanicsville, Gaines' Mill, Frayser's Farm, and Malvern Hill. Following on the heels of the Seven Days, the Second Bull Run campaign was strategically offensive in an operational sense although, except for Longstreet's counterattack on August 30, it may be classified as defensive from a tactical standpoint. At Antietam Lee stood on the defensive, but the Maryland campaign was strategically offensive; his moving into Maryland assured a major battle in that state. At Chancellorsville, he chose not to retreat when confronted by the Federal pincer movement. Instead, he repeatedly attacked, and the Federals retreated back across the river.

The point is not that each of these campaigns and battles represented an error by Lee. Driving the Federals away from Richmond in 1862, for example, may have been required to maintain Southern morale and to avoid the practical consequences of losing the capital. The point is that the offensive pattern is plain. Lee believed that the South's grand strategic role was offensive.

Lee's grand strategy of the offensive, to defeat the North militarily as distinguished from prolonging the contest until the North gave it up, created a profound problem. It was not feasible and, indeed, was counterproductive to the Confederacy's "objects of war." Curiously, that Lee's attack grand strategy was misplaced is suggested by his own awareness of factors that argued against it. The primary reason the attack grand strategy was counterproductive was numbers, and Lee was sensitive to the South's manpower disadvantage and its implications. A letter of January 10, 1863, to Secretary of War James A. Seddon, between his victory at Fredericksburg and Ambrose E. Burnside's abortive Mud March, reflects this awareness. "I have the honor to represent to you the absolute necessity that exists . . . to increase our armies, if we desire to oppose effectual resistance to the vast numbers that the enemy is now precipitating upon us," Lee wrote. "The great increase of the enemy's forces will augment the disparity of numbers to such a degree that victory, if attained, can only be achieved by a terrible expenditure of the most precious blood of the country."[7]

Further recognition of the numbers problem appears in Lee's letter of June 10, 1863, to Davis, after Chancellorsville and at the outset of the Gettysburg campaign:

While making the most we can of the means of resistance we possess . . . it is nevertheless the part of wisdom to carefully measure and husband our strength, and not to expect from it more than in the ordinary course of affairs it is capable of accomplishing. We should not therefore conceal from ourselves that our resources in men are constantly diminishing, and the disproportion in this respect between us and our enemies, if they continue united in their effort to subjugate us, is steadily augmenting. The decrease of the aggregate of this army as disclosed by the returns affords an illustration of this fact. Its effective strength varies from time to time, *but the falling off in its aggre-gate shows that its ranks are growing weaker and that its losses are not supplied by recruits.* (Emphasis added)[8]

The *Official Records* are full of Lee's analyses of his strength problems. These communications predict that unless his army was reinforced, "the consequences may be disastrous" and include such statements as "I cannot see how we are to escape the natural military consequences of the enemy's numerical superiority."[9]

Consciousness of his numerical disadvantage, of the ever-increasing Federal disproportion, did not mute Lee's commitment to the grand strategic offensive. Nor did that grand strategy permit his army to "husband our strength." During the Seven Days' battles on the Peninsula, George B. McClellan lost approximately 9,796 killed and wounded, 10.7 percent; Lee's casualties were 19,739 men, 20.7 percent of his army. Although Federal casualties in killed and wounded at Second Bull Run exceeded Lee's by approximately 1,000 men, the Army of Northern Virginia lost in excess of 9,000, almost 19 percent as compared to 13.3 percent for the Federals. In spite of McClellan's ineptitude, Lee lost almost 12,000 men, 22.6 percent, at Antietam, immediately following losses in excess of 1,800 at South Mountain on September 14. McClellan's Antietam casualties were 15.5 percent. At Chancellorsville, Lee lost almost 11,000 of 57,000 effectives, in excess of 18 percent, a much higher proportion than Joseph Hooker's 11.4 percent.[10]

These statistics show the serious attrition of Lee's limited numbers. In addition, Lee's losses were mostly irreplaceable, as he was aware. Finally, his losses also seriously affected his army's leadership. "The Confederates' ability to operate as they moved northward was affected by the loss of much mid-level command," Robert K. Krick has written. "The heart of the Confederate Army was starting to feel this difficulty for the first time just *before* Gettysburg. To the tremendous losses of the successful but costly campaign in the summer of 1862 . . . were added the victims of the dreadful bloodshed at Chancellorsville" (emphasis added).[11] Clearly, the Federals' increasingly disproportionate strength was the result of Northern reinforcements, but it was also exacerbated by Lee's heavy, disproportionate, and irreplaceable losses. Had Lee taken the defensive, the increasing Federal manpower advantage would have been slowed.

It is appropriate to contrast the alternative grand strategy of the defensive. In 1986, historians Richard E. Beringer, Herman Hattaway, Archer Jones, and William N. Still, Jr., noted that "no Confederate army lost a major engagement because of the lack of arms, munitions, or other essential supplies." These authors then summarized the case as follows:

> By remarkable and effective efforts the agrarian South did exploit and create an industrial base that proved adequate, with the aid of imports, to maintain suitably equipped forces in the field. Since the Confederate armies suffered no crippling deficiencies in weapons or supply, their principal handicap would be their numerical inferiority. But to offset this lack, Confederates, fighting the first major war in which both sides armed themselves with rifles, had the advantage of a temporary but very significant surge in the power of the tactical defensive. In addition, the difficulties of supply in a very large and relatively thinly settled region proved a powerful aid to strengthening the strategic defensive. Other things being equal, if Confederate military leadership were competent and the Union did not display Napoleonic genius, the tactical and strategic power of the defense could offset northern numerical superiority and presumably give the Confederacy a measure of military victory adequate to maintain its independence.[12]

British observers sensed the feasibility of the grand strategy of the defensive as the war began. Harking back to their own experience in America, they did not see how the South could be conquered. The War of Independence analogy is not perfect, but it is illustrative. The military historian Col. George A. Bruce has pointed out that George Washington "had a correct insight into the minds of his own people and that of the enemy, the strength of resolution of each to endure heavy burdens, looking forward with certainty to the time when the public sentiment of England, led by Chatham and Burke, would be ready to acknowledge the Colonies as an independent nation. With these views he carried on the war for seven years, all the way from Boston to Yorktown, on a generally defensive plan, the only one pointing to the final goal of independence."[13] The Americans, on the grand strategic defensive, lost many battles and retreated many times, but they kept forces in the field to avoid being ultimately defeated, and they won because the British decided that the struggle was either hopeless or too burdensome to pursue.

A Confederate defensive grand strategy would have been premised on E. Porter Alexander's conservative principle "to wear her [the North] out," to "exact . . . such a price in blood & treasure as to exhaust the enthusiasm of its population." To contribute to this wearing out, it was essential for Lee to maintain the viability of his army, to keep it in the field as a genuine force. That viability depended on his retaining sufficient relative strength for mobility and maneuver so as to avoid a siege and also to undertake timely and promising operationally strategic offensives and the tactical offensive. Lee could have accomplished these things had he pursued a defensive grand strategy. And despite Southern manpower disadvantages, this grand strategy was at the outset feasible because of the North's logistical task and the relative power that the rifled gun afforded the defense.

It is to be emphasized that the grand strategy of defense would not have required Southern armies always to be on the strategic operational or tactical defensive. As the British military historian Maj. Gen. J. F. C. Fuller points out, "It is possible to develop an offensive tactics from a defensive strategy."[14] Thus, if Lee's grand strategic sense of the war had been defensive, he could nevertheless on appropriate occasions have pursued offensive campaigns and offensive tactics in the context of that defensive grand strategy. The Revolution again provides an illustration. Although pursuing a grand strategy of defense, the Americans were sometimes aggressive and offensive, for example, at Trenton, Saratoga, and Yorktown.

The Federal manpower superiority would also have been less significant had Lee assumed the defensive in 1862–63, as evidenced by what happened in the overland campaign in 1864–65. Despite his prior losses and the great Northern numerical superiority, Lee's defense in 1864, again in Alexander's words, exacted "a price in blood" that significantly affected "the enthusiasm of [the North's] population" for continuing the war.[15] Indeed, Lee demonstrated in 1864 the feasibility of the grand strategy of the defense. Had he adopted the defensive earlier he would have had available a reasonable portion of the more than one hundred thousand officers and men that he lost in the offensives in 1862 and 1863, including Gettysburg. With these larger numbers he could have maintained mobility and avoided a siege.

It is in the context of grand strategy that one must view the primary issue regarding Gettysburg, that is, whether Lee should have been there at all. The Gettysburg campaign, Lee's most audacious act, is the apogee of his grand strategy of the offensive. The numerous reasons for the campaign offered by Lee and the commentators are well known: the necessity to upset Federal offensive plans, avoidance of a siege of the Richmond defenses, alleviation of supply problems in unforaged country, encouragement of the peace movement in the North, drawing the Federal army north of the Potomac in order to maneuver, even the relief of Vicksburg. Some or all of these reasons may have contributed to the decision, but fighting a battle was plainly inherent in the campaign because of the foreseeable Federal reaction and because of Lee's intent regarding a battle.

In his outline report dated July 31, 1863, Lee stated that "It had not been intended to fight a general battle at such a distance from our base, unless attacked by the enemy." The foreseeable Federal reaction to Lee's presence in loyal states suggests that the "unless attacked" provision was meaningless. As Hattaway and Jones point out: "Lee could have been under no illusion that he could bring off such a protracted campaign without a battle. . . . If he raided enemy territory, it would be politically if not strategically imperative for the Union army to take the offensive."[16] And on June 8, 1863, in a letter to Secretary of War Seddon, he spoke of the "difficulty & hazard in taking the aggressive with so large an army in its front, entrenched behind a river where it cannot be advantageously attacked" and of drawing the enemy out into "a position to be assailed." In the outline report, the same report in which he stated that "it had not been intended to fight a general battle at such a distance from our base," he wrote of his intent to "transfer the scene of hostilities north of the Potomac": "It was thought that the corresponding movements on the part of the enemy to which those contemplated by us would probably give rise, might offer a fair opportunity to *strike a blow* at the army then commanded by General Hooker, and that in any event that army would be compelled to leave Virginia" (emphasis added).[17]

The point is that the Gettysburg campaign involved substantial and unacceptable risks for Lee's army. His northernmost base in Virginia was to be Winchester, after it was taken by Richard S. Ewell. Winchester was ninety miles from Staunton, the available rail terminus. For this reason, and simply because of the distances involved, the extended lines of communication, and the necessity to recross the Potomac, these risks extended to the loss of the Army of Northern Virginia. In any event, assuming victory, the Gettysburg campaign was bound to result in heavy Confederate casualties, as Lee surely knew because of his losses in previous victories and at Antietam. Such foreseeable losses at Gettysburg were bound to limit his army's capacity to maneuver, to contribute to the risk that his army would be fixed, and to increase the risk of his being driven into a siege in the Richmond defenses. Lee had repeatedly said that a siege would be fatal to his army.[18]

Colonel Charles Marshall, whose writings originated many of the still-current rationalizations of Lee's generalship, set forth what he called "Lee's Military Policy." Having identified the critical importance of the defense of Richmond, Marshall wrote that Lee sought "to employ the enemy at a distance and prevent his near approach to the city." The Maryland campaign and Gettysburg fit this purpose, according to Marshall. But having identified the Confederacy's inherent strength problem, Marshall states that Lee was "unwilling to incur the risks and losses of an aggressive war having for its object the destruction of the enemy." Indeed, wrote Marshall: "General Lee thought that to expose our armies to the sacrifices of great battles the object of which was only to disperse or destroy those of the enemy would soon bring the Confederacy to the verge of exhaustion. Even victory in such engagements might prove disastrous. The North could readily raise new armies, while the means of the South were so limited that a few bloody victories might leave it powerless to continue the struggle."[19]

These are fine words, a prescription for a defensive strategy, but surely they do not describe Lee's military policy. For an accurate description of Lee's leadership one may again consult Major General Fuller, who in 1929 characterized Lee's strategy: "He rushed forth to find a battlefield, to challenge a contest between himself and the North."[20] This is why Lee went north in 1863. It was a continuation of his offensive grand strategy, to "defeat or drive the armies of the enemy from the field." Win, lose, or draw, the Gettysburg campaign was a strategic mistake because of the inevitable casualties that the Army of Northern Virginia could not afford.

In regard to defective execution, it is plain that if an army commander is to undertake a high-risk, strategically offensive maneuver, he had better do it with great care, especially if he is moving into enemy territory with extended lines of communication and endemic relative manpower problems. The fact is that Lee proceeded at Gettysburg without essential control of his army in three crucial respects—reconnaissance, the onset of the battle, and the renewal of the battle on the afternoon of July 1.

In his detailed report of January 1864, Lee made the following statements relating to the reconnaissance: "It was expected that as soon as the Federal Army should cross the Potomac, General Stuart would give notice of its movements, and nothing having been heard from him since our entrance into Maryland, it was inferred that the enemy had not yet left Virginia." This report also recounts Lee's learning from a scout on the night of June 28 that the Army of the Potomac had crossed the river and was approaching South Mountain. Colonel Marshall, who drafted the relevant orders as well as Lee's reports, also states that Lee "had not heard from him [Stuart] since the army left Virginia, and was confident from that fact, in view of the positive orders that Stuart had received, that General Hooker had not yet crossed the Potomac."[21] The facts challenge both the candor of

Lee's report and the assumption that Stuart's silence meant that the Army of the Potomac was not following Lee.

In the first place, Lee should have assumed that the Federal army would place itself between him and Washington, by that time a well-developed pattern in the Virginia theater. In addition, dictating the movements of the Army of the Potomac was one of the premises of Lee's movement north. In his outline report of July 31, 1863, Lee stated as an objective of the campaign "the transfer of the scene of hostilities north of the Potomac." He intended, he wrote, that his movement north would provoke "corresponding movements on the part of the enemy . . . and that in any event that army would be compelled to leave Virginia." Lee reiterated the substance of these expectations in his detailed report of January 1864.[22] And as he proceeded, Lee knew considerably more than he admitted in his January 1864 report.

On June 18, Lee advised Davis that "the enemy has been thrown back from the line of the Rappahannock, and is concentrating, as far as I can learn, in the vicinity of Centreville. The last reports from the scouts indicate that he is moving over toward the Upper Potomac." Centreville is about halfway to the Potomac from Fredericksburg. Thus Lee was aware that the Federals were on the move. On June 19, in another communication to Davis, Lee reported that "indications seem to be that his [the enemy's] main body is proceeding toward the Potomac, whether upon Harper's Ferry or to cross the river east of it, is not yet known." On the following day from Berryville, Virginia, having reported the location of the parts of his own army—Ewell was by this time across the river—Lee again reported what he knew of the Federals: "The movement of the main body . . . is still toward the Potomac, but its real destination is not yet discovered." Three days later, on June 23, another dispatch went to Davis: "Reports of movements of the enemy east of the Blue Ridge cause me to believe that he is preparing to cross the Potomac. A pontoon bridge is said to be laid at Edward's Ferry, and his army corps that he has advanced to Leesburg and the foot of the mountains, appear to be withdrawing." This letter also reported that Ewell was "in motion toward the Susquehanna" and that A. P. Hill's and James Longstreet's corps were nearing the Potomac.[23]

Two more dispatches bear on Lee's expectations. On June 22, in the first of his controversial dispatches to Stuart, he stated that "I fear he [the enemy] will steal a march on us, and get across the Potomac before we are aware." And on June 25, he advised Davis from opposite Williamsport, "I think I can throw General Hooker's Army across the Potomac."[24] From these statements it is apparent that Lee knew that his plan was working—the enemy was following him across the Potomac and out of Virginia. He would have the opportunity to "strike a blow."

On June 22 the much-debated issue of Stuart's orders arose. Lee's cavalry force included, in addition to horse artillery, six brigades under Stuart: Wade Hampton's, Beverly H. Robertson's, William E. "Grumble" Jones's, Fitzhugh Lee's, A. G. Jenkins's, and W. H. F. Lee's, the last-named temporarily commanded by Col. John R. Chambliss, Jr. Jenkins moved with Ewell, screening the front of the advance, while Robertson and Jones were to guard the mountain passes behind the army. Hampton, Fitz Lee, and Chambliss were to ride with Stuart. Also with the Army of Northern Virginia was Brig. Gen. John D. Imboden's command of four regiments.[25]

Setting aside postwar recollections of conversations and concentrating on the contemporaneous written word, Lee's June 22 communication to Stuart is the first relevant document. This letter, written at Berryville, begins with a direct inquiry regarding the enemy: "Do you know where he is and what he is doing?" The letter then identifies specific assignments for the cavalry brigades with Stuart: "If you find that he [the enemy] is moving northward, and that two brigades can guard the Blue Ridge and take care of your rear, you can move with the other three into Maryland, and take position on General Ewell's right, place yourself in communication with him, guard his flank, keep him informed of the enemy's movements, and collect all the supplies you can for the use of the army."[26]

Lee's June 22 letter to Stuart was sent to General Longstreet for forwarding to Stuart. Lee's letter to Longstreet that accompanied it is lost, but Longstreet's letter of transmittal to Stuart, dated 7:00 P.M. on June 22, refers to Lee's writing of Stuart's "passing by the rear of the enemy" and included advice from Longstreet: "If you can get through by that route, I think that you will be less likely to indicate what our plans are than if you should cross by passing to our rear."[27]

On the following day, June 23, another directive went from Lee to Stuart. Written at 5:00 P.M., it contained the following relevant provisions:

> If General Hooker's army remains inactive, you can leave two brigades to watch him, and withdraw with the three others, but should he not[28] appear to be moving northward I think you had better withdraw this side of the mountain tomorrow night, cross at Shepherdstown the next day, and move to Fredericktown.
>
> You will, however, be able to judge whether you can pass around their army without hindrance, doing them all the damage you can, and cross the river east of the mountains.

In either case, after crossing the river, you must move on and feel the right of Ewell's troops, collecting information, provisions, etc.[29]

This order, like that of June 22, included the instruction to the cavalry-man to feel Ewell's right and give Lee information. Since Lee knew his plan was working and the Federals were following him and were to cross the Potomac, information should have been his concern. In the circumstances, any commander in control of his army would have issued instructions to Stuart that were short, single-minded, and not discretionary. In the June 22 communication, Lee had asked a question regarding the enemy: "Do you know where he is and what he is doing?" He should have told Stuart that this question needed a prompt answer and that Stuart's one task was to keep him constantly informed of the enemy's movements. Lee did not do this, and taken together the orders contain the following problems :

1. No time sequences were specified; no deadlines were stated by which time Stuart was to perform his tasks or make reports.

2. Four missions for the brigades with Stuart were identified in the two orders—guarding Ewell's flank, keeping Ewell informed of the enemy's movements, collecting supplies for the army, and inflicting all possible damage on the Federals.

3. Stuart was to "judge whether you can pass around their army without hindrance." Even Colonel Marshall acknowledges that it was left to "Stuart to decide whether he can move around the Federal army."

4. The reference to Stuart's then "cross[ing] the river east of the moun-tains" is not specific as to location. Sir Frederick Maurice says that "Lee certainly meant that Stuart was to cross *immediately* east of the mountains, so as to be close to the right flank of the army," but that is not what the communication says.[30]

What fair and reasonable conclusions may be drawn in view of these problems with the orders? In the first place, the orders were ambiguous and uncertain with regard to such critical matters as the times and places of Stuart's movements. Second, contrary to the assertion of some writers, in riding around the Federal army Stuart was manifestly not acting on his own. That ride was expressly contemplated by Lee and was expressly left to Stuart's judgment. Third, regardless of other problems of interpretation, Stuart could not perform reconnaissance adequately with so many other tasks to perform. Two of these tasks indeed contradicted the reconnais-sance function and minimized the likelihood of success in the perfor-mance of that function. Collecting provisions and doing damage to the enemy were sure to draw the cavalry away from the intelligence task and delay its progress, which they did. These collateral missions diminished

Maj. Gen. James E. B. Stuart at the head of his cavalry, sketched in the field by Frank Vizetelly. From *Illustrated London News*, November 4, 1862.

the intelligence function and diluted the significance of that function. Their existence was bound to have contributed to Stuart's judgment that the ride around the Federals was a reasonable thing to do. Fourth, pushing east around the Union army was inconsistent with protecting the Confederate army's right. Stuart could not effectively protect Ewell's right and at the same time place eighty-five thousand Federals between himself and Ewell.

A fifth conclusion may be drawn regarding the orders to Stuart. Those orders are usually considered in the context of Lee's need for information concerning the movements of the Federal army. They are not analyzed in reference to the movements of the Confederate army after the orders were issued to Stuart. Such an analysis is appropriate.

Lee's entire army was on the move in June 1863. The army commander moves an army and knows where all of its parts are or are supposed to be. The individual parts do not necessarily know where the rest of the army is. A commander in control of his army may not rationally leave the movement of a detached unit up to that unit's commander, in this case Stuart, and then proceed to move the rest of the army and hope that the detached unit will be able to find its way to the moved or moving main body. The army commander is responsible for keeping the detached unit informed.

Lee made no plan or timely effort to do this. In his June 22 communication to Stuart, Lee told the cavalry leader that the army's advance, Ewell's corps, was to move toward the Susquehanna River via Emmitsburg and Chambersburg. The June 23 order stated that "the movements of Ewell's corps are as stated in my former letter. Hill's first division will reach the Potomac to-day, and Longstreet will follow tomorrow."

These messages were the last Stuart received from Lee before the cavalry moved out on the night of June 24 to begin the fateful ride around the Federals. Thus there was justice to Stuart's complaint in his defensive official report that when he started east he understood that the rest of the army was moving toward the Susquehanna. Accordingly, he stated that when he swung north he moved toward York to rendezvous, only to discover that the Confederates had left that area. His sole source of information regarding the Confederate army's location was Northern newspapers. Finally, on the night of July 1, he received a dispatch from Lee telling him that the army was at Gettysburg.

There is a final conclusion that may be drawn regarding reconnaissance. Stuart had been given the discretion to "pass around their army," with no time or distance limitations. Having in mind that Lee knew the Federal army was following him, a reconnaissance contingency plan was surely in order. There was also justification for Stuart's statement in his report that if cavalry "in advance of the army the first day of Gettysburg" was wanted, "it must be remembered that the cavalry [Jenkins's brigade] specially selected for advance guard to the army by the commanding general on account of its geographical location at the time, was available for this purpose." Kenneth P. Williams's observation is fair: "There were still three cavalry brigades near at hand that he [Lee] could have called upon for mounted service: Imboden's operating toward the west, and those of B. H. Robertson and W. E. Jones guarding the passes below the Potomac that soon needed little or no guarding. There seems to be no excuse for Lee's finding himself at Chambersburg on the 28th without a single regiment of cavalry."[31]

This, then, was the Confederate reconnaissance failure as the armies moved toward July 1, 1863, and this failure was essentially Lee's.

The second leadership error in execution on July 1 concerns the onset of the battle. Coddington states that "to say that Stuart's late arrival was a major cause of Lee's defeat is a little too pat an answer to the question of why the Confederates lost the battle." There were other command failures. Colonel Marshall speaks of the Gettysburg campaign as involving the "risk [of] the battlefield which chance might bring us during a movement northward."[32] As it turned out, it was simply a chance battlefield.

In his July 31, 1863, outline report, part of which has been previously quoted, Lee states: "It had not been intended to fight a general battle at such a distance from our base, unless attacked by the enemy, but, finding ourselves unexpectedly confronted by the Federal Army, it became a matter of difficulty to withdraw through the mountains with our large trains. At the same time, the country was unfavorable for collecting supplies while in the presence of the enemy's main body. . . . A battle thus became in a measure unavoidable."[33]

In their essentials, these words bear little resemblance to what Lee in fact intended or what in fact occurred. In the same report, he stated that his movement was intended to require Hooker to move with him and that this "might offer a fair opportunity to strike a blow" at the Federals. With regard to the "unless attacked" condition of the report, Lee was not attacked. His forces initially attacked and were the aggressor for three days. As a result of the initial attack, a battle occurred on July 1, not by plan but by chance.

Had Lee seriously intended to avoid a chance battle, he could have so instructed his corps commanders. The Official Records contain no such circular. Lee's reports do not say that he had issued any such order. Nor do the reports of Hill, Ewell, or Longstreet. Even after he learned on the night of June 28 that the Army of the Potomac had, as he expected, crossed the river, there is no evidence of warning orders. No such orders were forthcoming before July 1, and the battle and the battlefield were left to chance until it was too late because he had not asserted control over his army. This was his second failure of control.

Lee provided a laconic account of the start of the battle in his official report dated July 31, 1863. "The leading division of Hill met the enemy in advance of Gettysburg on the morning of July 1," he wrote. "Driving back these troops to within a short distance of the town, he there encountered a larger force, with which two of his divisions became engaged. Ewell, coming up with two of his divisions by Heidlersburg road, joined in the engagement." The battle thus began without Lee's knowing the location of other elements of the Federal army and without the Confederate army's being closed up. On June 30 Henry Heth had sent James J. Pettigrew's brigade from Cashtown to Gettysburg and discovered the enemy, principally cavalry, there. Lee was at Chambersburg. Hill's November 1863 report states: "A courier was then dispatched with this information to the general commanding . . . ; also to General Ewell, informing him, and that I intended to advance the next morning and discover what was in my front." As Coddington notes, Hill's "announcement seemed not to have disturbed the commanding general."[34]

As that fateful July 1 began, conservative instincts came over Lee, and he briefly and belatedly asserted himself to control events. Thus Ewell's 1863 report of the campaign recites that at Heidlersburg on the night of June 30 he received Lee's order to proceed to Cashtown or Gettysburg "as circumstances might dictate," together with a note from Hill saying that he was at Cashtown. On July 1, Ewell reported that he started for Cashtown and Hunterstown. Receiving a note from Hill telling of his advance on Gettysburg, Ewell ordered Robert E. Rodes's and Jubal A. Early's divisions toward that place. Ewell notified Lee of these movements and was informed by Lee that, "in case we found the enemy's forces very large, he did not want a general engagement brought on till the rest of the army came up." Ewell's report continued: "By the time this message reached me, General A. P. Hill had already been warmly engaged with a large body of the enemy in his front, and Carter's artillery battalion, of Rodes' division, had opened with fine effect on the flank of the same body, which was rapidly preparing to attack me, while fresh masses were moving into position in my front. It was too late to avoid an engagement without abandoning the position already taken up, and I determined to push the attack vigorously."[35] In short, Lee's attempt at control came too late because of his failure to react to Hill's June 30 communication and because of the onrush of events.

Lee's renewal of the battle on July 1 constitutes the third error in execution. He apparently did make a second effort at control when he became aware of the fighting at Gettysburg. This awareness, Coddington states, occurred while Lee rode from Chambersburg to Cashtown, where he and his party heard the sound of cannon fire to the east. Walter H. Taylor adds that at Cashtown Lee received a communication from Hill and that he then sent instructions to Heth to avoid a general engagement but to ascertain the enemy's force and report immediately. A. L. Long confirms the Cashtown report from Hill but states that it was a request for reinforcements and that Lee rushed Richard H. Anderson's division forward. General W. N. Pendleton, who was with Lee, mentions the sound of cannon fire. He reports further that the command party hastened toward Gettysburg and that, "arriving near the crest of an eminence more than a mile west of the town . . . we took positions overlooking the field. It was, perhaps, 2 o'clock, and the battle was raging with considerable violence. . . . Observing the course of events, the commanding general suggested whether positions on the right could not be found to enfilade the valley between our position and the town and the enemy's batteries next the town."[36]

Pendleton's account suggests that if Lee, aware of Heth's morning attack, instructed Heth to avoid a general engagement, he abandoned this caution when he reached the field. And Coddington, relying on Heth's postwar account, confirms Lee's decision to commit the Confederates to the afternoon attack. Coddington tells of Heth's observation of Rodes's becoming engaged and states: "[Heth] took the trouble to find Lee and seek his permission to attack in coordination with Rodes. Lee refused the request on the grounds that Longstreet was not up. Returning to his division, Heth saw the enemy shifting his weight to meet Rodes's attack. He again sought Lee's consent to give assistance, and this time received it. These meetings of the two generals occurred before the grand assault all along the Union line."[37]

Thus did Lee permit the renewal of the battle in the afternoon of July 1 in spite of his lack of knowledge of the Federal army's whereabouts and the absence of his own First Corps, which meant that he did it without having reason to believe that he had sufficient manpower to deprive the Federals of the high ground south of the town. Laxness with respect to reconnaissance and his lack of control of Hill's movements had caused him to stumble into a battle. The renewal of the battle represents Lee's third failure with respect to the events of July 1. It committed him to a major confrontation on this particular ground. The need for food and forage did not require his renewal of the battle on July 1 any more than they did on the days following July 1. Porter Alexander, referring to July 2 and the retreat to the Potomac, notes that the Confederates foraged successfully for more than a week in a restricted area of Pennsylvania. He also states that it was feasible for the Confederates to have abandoned Seminary Ridge on the night of July 1 or on July 2: "The onus of attack was upon Meade. . . . We could even have fallen back to Cashtown & held the mountain passes . . . & popular sentiment would have forced Meade to take the aggressive."[38] This was even more true in the early afternoon of July 1, when Lee authorized the all-out Confederate attack on Seminary Ridge, without sufficient troops of his own on hand to keep going and without knowledge of the whereabouts of the rest of the Federal army.

At the close of the day, the net effect of his command failure was that Lee was on the battlefield and in the battle that chance had brought him. As a consequence, he was significantly disadvantaged: he confronted an enemy that occupied what Porter Alexander called a "really wonderful position," with interior lines; Lee's line was a long exterior line, a difficult one from which to organize a coordinated attack; and four of his divisions, as Lee reported, were "weakened and exhausted by a long and bloody struggle."[39]

Committed to the Lee tradition, a number of commentators in the *Southern Historical Society Papers* and elsewhere have attempted to rationalize his command failures in regard to July 1. As has been indicated, Stuart's absence is a major thrust of these efforts. Blaming Hill, in spite of Lee's knowledge on June 30 of Hill's planned movements on July 1, is another. Lee's advocates also attempt to moot the issue of his command failures by placing blame on Ewell. They argue that these failures would have been irrelevant if only Ewell had pushed on late on July 1 and seized Cemetery Hill or Culp's Hill. It is argued that this could have been readily accomplished. A number of Confederate officers said so—after the war and when the Lee tradition of invincibility was being formed.[40] A good lawyer may reasonably be skeptical of the *Southern Historical Society Papers* as evidence. Written after the facts during the creation of the Lost Cause tradition, their value as history is surely limited. Like the patriarchal stories of the Old Testament, such accounts have ideological rather than historical value. They nevertheless require a response.

An initial difficulty in regard to the controversy about Ewell's conduct concerns identification of the issue. The advocates on both sides insist on debating whether or not Ewell would have been successful. This is inevitably a hypothetical question and therefore inappropriate for historical inquiry. Properly framed, the issue historically can only be whether Ewell made a reasonable decision in the circumstances. There is a second problem. Those who criticize Ewell frequently resort to a contention that is also inappropriate: regardless of the facts, Ewell "should have tried." They forget that Ewell was not a Civil War student. He was a general officer responsible for the consequences of his acts and for the lives of his soldiers. Finally, the partisans frequently overlook the fact that there was more involved for the Confederates than simply getting on the heights. There was also the question of whether they would be able to stay if the Federals were to mount a prompt effort to drive them off.

With the foregoing considerations in mind, one may pursue the question of whether Ewell made a rational decision. This is a matter of the evidence with respect to four factors: the nature of the terrain, the Federal forces opposed, the manpower available to Ewell, and the orders given to Ewell by Lee.

The terrain confronting Ewell may be seen today looking up from the area of the Culp House and the low ground immediately to the west of that house. The heights are precipitous, irregular, and complex, marked by hollows and ravines. An attacking force would have been advancing uphill against defenders with ample places from which to effect an ambush.

In considering the Federal forces opposed—and the troops Ewell could have used—the identification of precise times of day is an impossible task. Any discussion of the issue is limited by inability to state exactly when either Federal or Confederate units were available. Nevertheless, Federals to oppose an attack were on the heights or very close by during the general time period in which Ewell was considering the question:

1. One brigade of Adolph von Steinwehr's division and Michael Wiedrich's battery had been on Cemetery Hill since the arrival of the Eleventh Corps.

2. The remnant of the Iron Brigade, approximately seven hundred men, had been sent from Cemetery to Culp's Hill and was entrenching there in a strong position.

3. The 7th Indiana of Lysander Cutler's brigade, five hundred rifles, which had not been engaged, had arrived and had been sent to Culp's Hill with the members of that brigade who had come through the day's fighting.

4. The remaining effectives from the First Corps and Eleventh Corps, "basically intact" according to Harry W. Pfanz, were present. There were skirmishers in the town at the base of Cemetery Hill.

5. The Federals had a total of forty guns and ample ammunition on the heights.

6. Henry W. Slocum's Twelfth Corps was close by, approximately one mile from the scene. John W. Geary's division was on the Federal left by approximately 5:00 P.M.; the First Division was on the Federal right at about the same time.[41]

Confederate perceptions of this opposition are illuminating. In his 1863 report, Rodes stated that before "the completion of his defeat before the town, the enemy had begun to establish a line of battle on the heights back of the town, and by the time my line was in a condition to renew the attack, he displayed quite a formidable line of infantry and artillery immediately in my front, extending smartly to my right, and as far as I could see to my left, in front of Early." Ewell's 1863 report was similar: "The enemy had fallen back to a commanding position known as Cemetery Hill . . . and quickly showed a formidable front there. . . . I could not bring artillery to bear on it."[42] There were, in short, substantial forces opposed to Ewell, infantry and artillery, placed on imposing terrain.

With regard to the manpower available for the attack, each of the Confederate corps on hand was missing a division. In the case of Ewell, Edward "Allegheny" Johnson's division was not present. It arrived at a late hour. From Hill's corps, Anderson's division did not come up until after the day closed. Lee's detailed report describes the four divisions that had participated in the July 1 fight as "already weakened and exhausted by a long and bloody struggle." Hill reported that his two divisions were "exhausted by some six hours hard fighting [and that] prudence led me to be content with what had been gained, and not push forward troops exhausted and necessarily disordered, probably to encounter fresh troops of the enemy." Ewell's report similarly noted that "all the troops with me were jaded by twelve hours' marching and fighting."[43] And the Confederate reports uniformly state that the Southern units had lost formation at the conclusion of the movement that drove the Federals from Seminary Ridge. Ewell's task was not simply to continue an organized assault that was ongoing. He would have been required to marshal forces and undertake a new movement against the heights.

Douglas Southall Freeman, Lee's great advocate, is always anxious to rationalize Lee's failures at the expense of his lieutenants. In *Lee's Lieutenants*, he criticizes Ewell for not mooting Confederate problems on the first day by taking the heights. He describes in detail Ewell's communications at this hour and his efforts to organize the forces with which to attack. Having recounted Lee's advising Ewell that none of Hill's troops were available on Ewell's right, Freeman states: "All of this meant that if Cemetery Hill was to be taken, Ewell must do it with his own men." Noting then that Early had detached two brigades under John B. Gordon to operate on Ewell's left, Freeman says: "Still again, the force with which Ewell could attack immediately was small. . . . Two Brigades of Early, then, and the tired survivors of Rodes's confused charges—these were all Ewell had for the attack till Johnson arrived. Nor would this force . . . have any support from the right."[44] Even Freeman concedes that Ewell did not have significant numbers for the attack.

Finally, what were Ewell's orders? Lee's detailed report identifies them and also their logic:

> It was ascertained . . . that the remainder of that army [the Federal army] . . . was approaching Gettysburg. Without information as to its proximity, the strong position which the enemy had assumed could not be attacked without danger of exposing the four divisions present, already weakened and exhausted by a long and bloody struggle, to an overwhelming number of fresh troops. General Ewell was, therefore, instructed to carry the hill occupied by the enemy, if he found it practicable, but to avoid a general engagement until the arrival of the other divisions of the army. . . . He decided to await Johnson's division, which . . . did not reach Gettysburg until a late hour.[45]

In *Lee's Lieutenants*, Freeman covers this issue in a chapter titled "Ewell Cannot Reach a Decision."[46] Surely this is nonsense. Pursuant to Lee's order, Ewell decided that it was not "practicable" to attack. Lee was on Seminary Ridge and available. The plain fact is that he did not issue a peremptory order to Ewell for the reasons he states in his report: the Federal army was approaching, but its proximity was unknown; the "strong position" of the enemy; the worn condition of the Confederate forces available; the risk of the presence of overwhelming and fresh Federal troops; and the desire to avoid a general engagement.

It is unhistoric to conclude that Ewell was necessarily wrong in his judgment. His decision was reasonable in the circumstances, and that responds to the only historically appropriate question concerning Ewell's conduct.

One can only conclude that Lee's movement across the Potomac was a grave strategic error. In addition, in reference to the first day of the battle, there were significant command failures on Lee's part that were destructive to the Confederate chances of victory at Gettysburg.

Confederate Corps Leadership on the First Day at Gettysburg

A. P. Hill and Richard S. Ewell in a Difficult Debut

Gary W. Gallagher

FORMER CONFEDERATES PURSUED THE QUESTION OF responsibility for the defeat at Gettysburg with almost religious zeal in the years following Appomattox. Accusations about the culpability of Lee's principal lieutenants had surfaced well before the end of the war, but not until the mid-1870s did the debate take on the character of an inter-necine brawl. At the heart of the controversy lay an attempt on the part of Jubal A. Early, Fitzhugh Lee, J. William Jones, and others to refute James Longstreet's suggestion, first given wide circulation in William Swinton's history of the Army of the Potomac, that Lee had erred badly at Gettysburg. Early and the others sought to absolve Lee of responsibility for any military failures during the war and singled out Longstreet as their primary villain. Longstreet had ignored orders to launch an assault against the Federal left at dawn on July 2, they argued, thereby denying the South a victory at Gettysburg and probably its independence. Although Longstreet stood at the vortex of this war of words, other ranking Confederates also received substantial criticism during and after the war—"Jeb" Stuart for a ride around the Union army that prevented his keeping Lee informed of Federal movements, A. P. Hill for precipitating the battle against Lee's orders and then mounting a weak pursuit of routed Federals, and Richard Stoddert Ewell for failing to seize Cemetery Hill and Culp's Hill late in the first day's fighting.[1]

Lost opportunities on July 1 loomed large because the troops of Hill and Ewell had gained a decided advantage over their opponents north and west of Gettysburg by midafternoon. To many Southern observers it seemed that one more round of assaults would have carried Cemetery Hill and Culp's Hill and sealed a major victory. Loath to engage the enemy in the first place, Lee had reached the field in time to recognize the opening presented by Hill's earlier decision to commit two divisions and had sought to press the Confederate advantage. But first Hill and then Ewell declined to renew the offensive, observed their critics, affording the desperate Federals time to patch together a strong line on high ground below the town. Their failure set the stage for two more days of bloody battle during which the commanders of the Second and Third corps became little more than bystanders in a drama dominated on the Confederate side by Lee and Longstreet.

Hill and Ewell entered Pennsylvania in June 1863 burdened with the legacy of "Stonewall" Jackson. Between them they commanded the four divisions of the old Second Corps. Lee's reorganization of the army after Jackson's death had assigned three of Jackson's divisions to Ewell as chief of a smaller Second Corps, while Hill's Light Division, long a bulwark of Jackson's corps, supplied six of the thirteen brigades in "Little Powell's" new Third Corps.[2] Perhaps inevitably, estimates of the performances of Hill and Ewell on July 1 frequently included invidious comparisons to Jackson—always to the "Mighty Stonewall" of the Valley and Chancellorsville rather than to the eminently fallible "Old Jack" of the Seven Days or Cedar Mountain.

Less than a month after Gettysburg, surgeon Spencer Glasgow Welch of the 13th South Carolina complained to his wife that Hill had mishandled his troops on July 1. Had he not done so, the Third Corps could have captured "the strong position last occupied by the enemy . . . and the next day when Ewell and Longstreet came up the victory completely won." "If 'Old Stonewall' had been alive and there," suggested Welch (whose regiment had served in the Second Corps before being moved to the Third), "it no doubt would have been done. Hill was a good division commander, but he is not a superior corps commander. He lacks the mind and sagacity of Jackson." Henry Heth's division led the Third Corps toward Gettysburg and suffered severe casualties during the fighting on July 1. Writing about the battle in 1877, Heth refrained from making direct comments about Hill's actions but did mention the public's questioning "whether if Stonewall Jackson had been in command of Hill's corps on the first day— July 1st—a different result would have been obtained."[3]

Other critics focused on Hill's decision to send Heth's division into Gettysburg despite Lee's orders to avoid a general engagement. In his his-

Lt. Gen. A. P. Hill. From
*Battles and Leaders of the
Civil War* 2:626.

tory of Virginia during the war, Jedediah Hotchkiss observed that "A. P.
Hill, always ready and anxious for a fight, but so far as known without
orders from General Lee, sent the divisions of Heth and Pender toward
Gettysburg. . . . [He thus] brought on an engagement with two corps of
Meade's army." The careful Porter Alexander averred that "Hill's movement to Gettysburg was made of his own motion, and with knowledge that
he would find the enemy's cavalry in possession." "Lee's orders were to
avoid bringing on an action," continued Alexander, who added that Hill's
"venture is another illustration of an important event allowed to happen
without supervision." No postwar critic savaged Hill more completely than
John S. Mosby. In an extended apology for Jeb Stuart's absence from the
army, the famous guerrilla insisted that Hill miscalculated in sending
Heth's division toward Gettysburg on the morning of July 1. "Hill and Heth
in their reports, to save themselves from censure, call the first day's action
a reconnaissance; this is all an afterthought," wrote Mosby. "They wanted
to conceal their responsibility for the final defeat. Hill said he felt the need
of cavalry—then he ought to have stayed in camp and waited for the cavalry." No one ordered Hill to advance, concluded Mosby, and Lee "never
would have sanctioned it."[4]

Modern historians have joined this chorus. For example, in his massive
chronicle of the artillery in Lee's army, Jennings C. Wise observed that
Hill's "orders were specific not to bring on an action, but his thirst for

battle was unquenchable, and . . . he rushed on, and . . . took the control of the situation out of the hands of the commander-in-chief." Warren W. Hassler's *Crisis at the Crossroads*, the first general monograph devoted to the action on July 1, stated unequivocally that "Hill certainly erred, as evidenced by Lee's later painful surprise, in permitting Heth to march on Gettysburg for forage and shoes." Hassler believed that Hill should have exercised greater caution "in developing the situation in the event that Federal troops were present there in numbers." Even Edwin B. Coddington, whose admirable study of the campaign set a standard for meticulous scholarship, speculated that Hill expected to find a fight as well as some shoes and provisions on the morning of July 1. Mosby may have been correct, stated Coddington, "when he charged Hill with planning a 'foray' and calling it a 'reconnaissance.'" Douglas Southall Freeman labeled the manner in which the Army of Northern Virginia stumbled into a confrontation on the first day "incautious," apportioning most of the responsibility to Jeb Stuart. "Obvious blame, also, would be charged against Powell Hill," remarked Freeman, "if he had not been sick on the 1st." That illness prevented his monitoring Heth's advance more closely and, in Freeman's view, absolved him of criticism.[5]

Richard S. Ewell's decision not to attack Cemetery Hill and Culp's Hill on the afternoon of July 1 inspired more heated discussion—and more direct comparisons with Jackson—than did Hill's conduct. Maj. Gen. Isaac Ridgeway Trimble held no command on July 1 but found himself in Gettysburg with Ewell about midafternoon. "The fighting ceased about 3 P.M.," Trimble noted in his diary, "Genl. Ewell saying he did not wish to bring on a hurried engagement without orders from Lee. This was a *radical error*, for had we continued the fight, we should have got in their rear & taken the Cemetery Hill & Culps Hill." Trimble expanded on his diary entry in a speech prepared after the war and published in the 1870s. He described a tense confrontation between himself and Ewell, during which he told Ewell that Culp's Hill held the key to the Federal position and advised that a brigade be sent to occupy it. Ewell asked if Trimble was certain the hill commanded the town, prompting Trimble to reply that the general could see for himself that it did and ought to be seized at once. "General Ewell made some impatient reply," remembered Trimble, "and the conversation dropped."[6]

Junior officers also sensed a passing opportunity. J. A. Stikeleather of the 4th North Carolina, a regiment in S. Dodson Ramseur's brigade of Robert E. Rodes's division, entered Gettysburg on the heels of the retreating Federals and estimated that five hundred troops could have captured

Cemetery Hill at that point. "The simplest soldier in the ranks felt it," he wrote his mother soon after the battle. "But, timidity in the commander that stepped into the shoes of the fearless Jackson, prompted delay, and all night long the busy axes from tens of thousands of busy hands on that crest, rang out clearly on the night air, and bespoke the preparation the enemy were making for the morrow." Another Confederate witness, writing twenty-two years after the battle, professed to have heard Brigadier General Harry Hays urge Jubal Early to strike Culp's Hill with his entire division. Early agreed that the eminence "should be occupied on the spot" but felt constrained by Ewell's orders not to advance beyond the town. Turning away from Hays and the writer, Early then muttered, "more to himself than Hays, 'If Jackson were on the field I would act on the spot.'"[7]

Influential postwar accounts by Henry Kyd Douglas and John B. Gordon were equally damning. Douglas recalled in his memoirs written shortly after the war (but not published until 1940) that Ewell's staff lost heart when the general failed to follow his initial success with an assault against Cemetery Hill. According to Douglas, chief of staff Sandie Pendleton, when just out of Ewell's hearing, said "quietly and with much feeling, 'Oh, for the presence and inspiration of Old Jack for just one hour!'" Gordon characteristically placed himself at center stage in a dramatic account. His brigade, which belonged to Early's division, had pursued the broken Federals into Gettysburg; looking southward toward the high ground, Gordon saw an opening and believed that in "less than half an hour my troops would have swept up and over those hills, the possession of which was of such momentous consequence." Two times, claimed Gordon, he ignored instructions to halt: "Not until the third or fourth order of the most peremptory character reached me did I obey." "No soldier in a great crisis ever wished more ardently for a deliverer's hand," stated Gordon, "than I wished for one hour of Jackson when I was ordered to halt. Had he been there, his quick eye would have caught at a glance the entire situation, and instead of halting me he would have urged me forward and have pressed the advantage to the utmost."[8]

Though he gave no hint of it in his official report or correspondence with President Davis, R. E. Lee apparently also felt keen disappointment in Ewell. He told former Second Corps chief of ordnance William Allan in April 1868 that he could not get Ewell "to act with decision." "Stuart's failure to carry out his instructions *forced the battle of Gettysburg*," Allan paraphrased Lee in notes written immediately after their conversation, "*& the imperfect, halting way in which his corps commanders* (especially Ewell) *fought the battle, gave victory . . . finally to the foe.*" Nearly two years later, Lee confided to

Allan that he often thought that "if Jackson had been there [at Gettysburg] he would have succeeded."[9] Three months before he died Lee discussed Gettysburg with his cousin Cassius Lee, again saying that Jackson's presence would have brought victory. "Ewell was a fine officer," Lee commented, "but would never take the responsibility of exceeding his orders, and having been ordered to Gettysburg, he would not go farther and hold the heights beyond the town."[10]

In the face of such an array of evidence (and these examples only hint at its extent), it is scarcely surprising that most historians have taken Ewell to task for his decision not to assault Cemetery Hill. Douglas Southall Freeman's handling of this phase of Gettysburg in *Lee's Lieutenants* appears in a chapter titled "Ewell Cannot Reach a Decision." Granting Ewell every extenuating circumstance, concluded Freeman, the "impression persists that he did not display the initiative, resolution and boldness to be expected of a good soldier." Clifford Dowdey, whose gracefully written books on Lee and his army gained wide popularity, portrayed Ewell as a man frozen by irresolution, dependent upon Jubal Early's counsel, and fearful of Lee's adverse opinion. By the evening of July 1, argued Dowdey, Lee realized that "paralysis of will marked Ewell like a fatal disease. . . . [He] saw that Jackson's great subordinate had failed in his hour of decision." Hill had drawn Lee into a battle he did not want, believed Dowdey; then "the commander of the mobile Second Corps had robbed the army of its chance to win the field." Warren Hassler hedged on the issue of Cemetery Hill and Culp's Hill: "Ewell—a new corps commander—proved that he was by no means up to stepping into Jackson's shoes and filling them, though he was perhaps correct in not launching an attack on these eminences, as the Unionists, by 5 o'clock, were well on their way toward rendering the elevations impregnable." Coddington defended Ewell's decision not to order an assault more directly, though he, too, could not resist adding that if "Ewell had been a Jackson he might have been able to regroup his forces quickly enough to attack within an hour after the Yankees had started to retreat through the town."[11]

Any judgments about the conduct of Hill and Ewell on July 1 necessarily rest on an imperfect body of evidence. It is important to evaluate the individuals who kept diaries, wrote letters or memoirs, or reported on conversations they overheard. Did they have motivations that colored their accounts? For example, it is possible that Trimble, a major general without portfolio, resented Ewell's offhand dismissal of his counsel and consequently exaggerated the lieutenant general's confusion. It is also pertinent to inquire whether soldiers who had fought under Jackson in the glory days of the Second Corps too quickly assumed that their old chief might have acted differently and accomplished more. Finally, did writers unintention-ally (or intentionally) allow postwar interpretations to shape their testi-mony as eyewitnesses?

Among the leading examples of participants whose postwar writings must be used with great care is John B. Gordon. Few witnesses matched Gordon in his egocentrism or his willingness to play loose with the truth, and his recollections leave unwary readers with a distinct impression that the South would have triumphed if only misguided superiors such as Ewell and Early had acted on his advice. Henry Kyd Douglas displayed similar tendencies to magnify his own role and opt for the embellished anecdote rather than mundane fact—a circumstance that has led some to suggest that his book should be titled "Stonewall Rode with Me" rather than "I Rode with Stonewall." Yet each of these men saw so much and wrote so well that their books are cited with great frequency in the literature. Modern judgments based on such testimony necessarily reflect the flaws of the originals.[12]

It is especially important to employ discrimination in using literature that embraces the myth of the Lost Cause, much of which sought to can-onize Lee. As a rough yardstick, students may assume that the later the account by a soldier, the less likely it will be to offer dispassionate analy-sis of Lee (there are exceptions to this rule, E. Porter Alexander's writings being the most obvious). Jubal Early anticipated this trend in postwar literature with the publication of his address on Lee delivered at Washing-ton and Lee University on the general's birthday in 1872. After catalog-ing great captains through the ages, Early assured his listeners that "it is a vain work for us to seek anywhere for a parallel to the great character which has won our admiration and love. Our beloved Chief stands, like some lofty column which rears its head among the highest, in grandeur, simple, pure and sublime, needing no borrowed lustre; and he is all our own." This vision of Lee precluded serious criticism lest an author raise doubts about his own Southern loyalty, a fact not lost on those who wrote about the cam-paigns of the Army of Northern Virginia. This is not to say that the dozens of articles published in the *Southern Historical Society Papers*, in which Early and others orchestrated a massive examination of Gettysburg, and the vast body of other postwar testimony cannot be used with profit. Indeed, some of the most valuable information on the Confederate side of the campaign resides in such sources. But readers should be aware that they contain much special pleading, selective recall, and outright falsehood.[13]

Just as the evidence relating to Hill and Ewell on July 1 must not be ac-cepted uncritically at face value, so also must modern students resist the temptation to judge the generals outside of their historical context. Both men made decisions based on available intelligence about the Union army and an imperfect understanding of the terrain. What they did not know should not be used against them. For example, many writers have buttressed their case against Ewell by quoting a letter written in January 1878 by Winfield Scott Hancock to Fitzhugh Lee. "In my opinion," stated Hancock in response to a query from Lee, "if the Confederates had continued the pursuit of General Howard on the afternoon of the 1st July at Gettysburg, they would have driven him over and beyond Cemetery Hill." Such a statement from the man who commanded the Federal defense late on the first day seemingly carried great weight. But should it? Hancock knew how weak the Federal defenders were at that point in the battle; Ewell did not and should not be criticized for failing to understand the situation on high ground he could not see.[14]

Factors such as the nature of Lee's orders, the condition of Hill's and Ewell's troops following their midafternoon success, problems of communication, and the normal chaos of a large battlefield also should be weighed. Finally, the fair question is whether Hill and Ewell discharged their duties reasonably well on July 1—not whether they matched the standard of excellence set by Stonewall Jackson in the campaigning from Second Manassas through Chancellorsville.

Hill almost certainly went into the Gettysburg campaign with his commanding general's full confidence. As early as October 1862, Lee had told Jefferson Davis that next to Jackson and Longstreet, "I consider A. P. Hill the best commander with me. He fights his troops well, and takes good care of them." "At present," added Lee, "I do not think that more than two commanders of corps are necessary for this army." Eight months later, in the wake of Jackson's death, Lee opted to add a third corps. "I have for the past year felt that the corps of this army were too large for one commander," Lee explained to the president (contradicting his statement of October 1862). "Nothing prevented my proposing to you to reduce their size and increase their number but my inability to recommend commanders." Now he reaffirmed his belief that Hill was "the best soldier of his grade" with the army and asked Davis to agree to his heading the new Third Corps.[15] Hill took his famous Light Division, less two brigades and led by William Dorsey Pender, with him from the Second to the Third Corps; there it joined Richard H. Anderson's division, shifted over from Longstreet's First Corps, and a new division under Henry Heth composed of two brigades from the Light Division and a pair of others transferred to the army from Mississippi and North Carolina.

As the bulk of the Army of Northern Virginia prepared to march toward the Potomac during the first week in June, Lee instructed Hill to watch and react to the Army of the Potomac along the Rappahannock River line. "You are desired to open any official communications sent to me," the commanding general told his lieutenant, "and, if necessary, act upon them, according to the dictates of your good Judgment." Reminiscent of the freedom previously accorded Jackson, this grant of wide discretion suggests that Lee harbored few doubts about Hill's ability to restrain the headlong impulse to fight that had been so obvious in his conduct at Mechanicsville and elsewhere.[16]

Hill's first substantial test in his new position came on July 1 and raised questions about his impetuosity as well as his broader capacity to command a corps. Did he needlessly trigger a battle Lee hoped to avoid? And once on the verge of sweeping success late in the afternoon, did he fail to use his men to best advantage? Affirmative answers to these questions not only constitute an indictment of Hill's generalship, but they also affect any assessment of Lee's role in shaping the ultimate Confederate defeat.

Lee learned from Longstreet's scout Harrison on the night of June 28 that the Federal army had crossed the Potomac. In the absence of more substantial intelligence from his own cavalry—and fearing a Union movement against his supply line in the Cumberland Valley—Lee aborted a planned movement toward Harrisburg and issued orders on June 29 for the reconcentration of the Army of Northern Virginia on the east side of the South Mountain range. Hill and Longstreet were "to proceed from Chambersburg to Gettysburg," toward which point Ewell's divisions would march from their positions to the north and east.[17]

A surgeon on James Longstreet's staff remembered a relaxed Lee talking to a group of officers at his headquarters shortly after dispatching these orders: "To-morrow, gentlemen, we will not move to Harrisburg as we expected, but will go over to Gettysburg and see what General Meade is after." Heth's division of Hill's corps led the way eastward from Chambersburg to Cashtown, a hamlet eight miles west of Gettysburg, on the twenty-ninth; Pender and the Light Division followed the next day, and Anderson's orders called for his division to take the same route on July 1.[18]

On the morning of June 30, Heth sent his largest brigade, four North Carolina regiments under James Johnston Pettigrew, to Gettysburg in search of shoes and other supplies. A nonprofessional soldier who had compiled a dazzling record as a student at the University of North Carolina, Pettigrew spotted Northern cavalry as he neared the western edge of Gettysburg and elected to withdraw rather than risk battle against a foe of unknown size and composition. He subsequently told Heth about the Federal cavalry, adding that some of his officers also had heard drums on the far side of Gettysburg, indicating the presence of Union infantry. Hill soon joined Heth and Pettigrew, and the brigadier repeated his story. Hill doubted that Pettigrew had seen more than a small detachment (he had in fact seen part of John Buford's two full brigades): "I am just from General Lee, and the information he has from his scouts corroborates that I have received from mine—that is, the enemy are still at Middleburg [some sixteen miles from Gettysburg], and have not yet struck their tents."[19]

There may have been some of the West Pointer's disdain for civilian soldiers manifest in this discussion—a professional questioning a talented amateur's observations. Perhaps sensing this, Pettigrew asked Captain Louis G. Young of his staff, who knew Hill from their service together during the Seven Days, to speak to the corps commander. Young insisted that the troops he saw were veterans rather than Home Guards; however, Hill "still could not believe that any portion of the Army of the Potomac was up; and in emphatic words, expressed the hope that it was, as this was the place he wanted it to be." Heth reiterated that he wanted the shoes. "If there is no objection," he said to Hill, "I will take my division to-morrow and go to Gettysburg and get those shoes!" "None in the world," came the nonchalant reply. "A courier was then dispatched with this information to the general commanding," noted Hill in his official report, "and with orders to start Anderson early; also to General Ewell, informing him, and that I intended to advance the next morning and discover what was in my front."[20]

Hill's message to Ewell and Young's postwar recollection indicate that Hill considered Heth's movement on July 1 a reconnaissance in force. Young's account might also be construed to mean that Hill hoped to find the Federals at a disadvantage so that he could strike a blow; however, Heth stated categorically after the war that his chief stressed the importance of not precipitating an engagement. Whatever Hill's full intention, he ordered Pender to support Heth while he awaited Anderson in Cashtown.[21]

When Heth's division took the pike eastward from Cashtown just after daylight on July 1, Hill lay at his headquarters contending with an unknown malady.[22] Heth collided with Buford's cavalry about 8:00 A.M. and soon committed two brigades. The fighting swelled rapidly as Confederate artillery went into action. Back at Cashtown, Hill listened to the distant rumble and discussed its import with Lee, who had arrived shortly after the battle commenced. Hill informed Lee that Heth's instructions called for him to report the presence of any Union infantry immediately "without forcing an engagement."[23] After a short conversation with his chief, Hill rode to the front, where he arrived about noon to find that Heth had stirred a hornet's nest of Union cavalry and infantry and withdrawn to a position on Herr Ridge west of Willoughby Run. Lee joined Hill before long, and

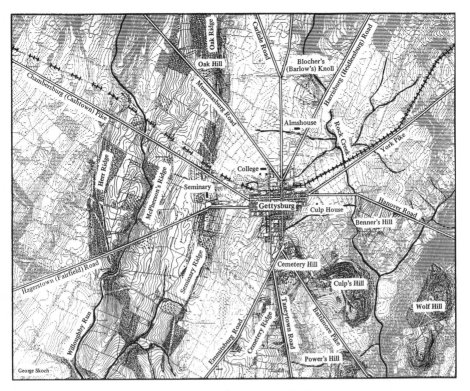

Area Contested by the Confederate Second and Third Corps on July 1

shortly after 2:00 P.M. the two men watched an artillery duel between Hill's guns and those of the Federal First Corps east of Willoughby Run.[24]

Once Lee was on the field, responsibility for the battle passed to him. In his postwar memoirs, Walter H. Taylor of Lee's staff wrote that when Lee reached the battlefield he "ascertained that the enemy's infantry and artillery were present in considerable force. Heth's division was already hotly engaged, and it was soon evident that a serious engagement could not be avoided." Actually, at that juncture only the infantry brigades of James J. Archer and Joseph Davis in Heth's division had seen serious action. The Army of Northern Virginia had thus not been drawn into a general battle, and it was Lee rather than Hill who subsequently decided when the other brigades of Heth's division and Pender's division would be sent forward.[25]

In sum, the charge that Hill brought on a major battle against Lee's orders simply does not hold up under careful scrutiny. He did approve a heavy reconnaissance in force for the morning of July 1—a movement that would have been unthinkable had Jeb Stuart been performing his duties.

The need for such an action certainly is open to debate; however, Hill informed Lee and Ewell of his intentions, cautioned Heth to be careful, and arranged for Pender to be within supporting distance of Heth. Had Lee wished for Hill to exercise more restraint, he could have communicated with him on the night of June 30. He chose not to do so; neither did he shrink from battle when the tactical situation seemed propitious on July 1. Stuart's absence set in motion the sequence of events that erupted in fighting on July 1, and Lee gave the orders that turned a meeting engagement into a full-scale battle.

What of Hill's responsibility for failing to press the Southern assault late in the afternoon? Between 3:00 and 4:30 P.M., Heth's division and three brigades of Pender's division, together with Rodes's division on their left, forced the Federal First Corps toward Gettysburg and finally to Cemetery Hill. To the northeast, Jubal Early's division of the Second Corps enjoyed similar success against the Union Eleventh Corps. Fortune had guided Lee's infantry to the battlefield in precisely the right places to achieve tactical success; now, as he watched the Union retreat from atop Seminary Ridge, Lee sensed a great opportunity if the Army of Northern Virginia took the high ground below Gettysburg. Still hamstrung by a lack of intelligence concerning the enemy's location and strength, however, he worried about "exposing the four divisions present, already weakened and exhausted by a long and bloody struggle, to overwhelming numbers of fresh troops."[26]

Hill and Lee were together on Seminary Ridge about 4:30 P.M. Some four hours of daylight remained. Despite his vaunted reputation as an offensive fighter, Hill evinced little enthusiasm for renewed assaults on his front. He told Col. A. J. L. Fremantle, a British observer, that the Federals had fought with unusual determination all day. Heth had been wounded, many field officers were down, and casualties in some units approached critical levels. "Under the impression that the enemy were entirely routed," noted Hill in his official report, "[and with] my own two divisions exhausted by some six hours' hard fighting, prudence led me to be content with what had been gained, and not push forward troops exhausted and necessarily disordered, probably to encounter fresh troops of the enemy."[27] Hill undoubtedly shared these views with Lee, who had seen with his own eyes the condition of Hill's men. Apparently persuaded that no more could be expected of Heth's and Pender's divisions, Lee turned his attention to Ewell's corps.

Neither Lee's allusion to "four divisions present" nor Hill's description of his "exhausted" divisions acknowledged the presence near the battlefield of R. H. Anderson's five brigades. Third Corps surgeon Welch wrote about a month after the battle that Heth and Pender "should have been immediately reinforced by Anderson with his fresh troops." Col. Abner Perrin, who led a brigade in Pender's division, complained bitterly to Governor Luke Bonham of South Carolina on July 29, 1863, that Anderson's division (the largest in the Third Corps) took no part in the action on the afternoon of July 1. Whether Anderson or Hill was to blame, conceded Perrin, he could not say, but he considered this to be "*the cause of the failure of the campaign.*" Captain Young of Pettigrew's brigade related a conversation with Anderson after the war in which the latter stated that Lee ordered his division to halt some two miles west of Gettysburg. Puzzled by these instructions when sounds of heavy fighting were audible nearby, Anderson sought out Lee for clarification. "General Lee replied that there was no mistake made," Anderson told Young, "and explained that his army was not all up, that he was in ignorance as to the force of the enemy in front, that . . . [Anderson's] alone of the troops present, had not been engaged, and that a reserve in case of disaster, was necessary."[28]

Hill and Lee both knew of Anderson's presence. Hill also must have known that James H. Lane's and Edward L. Thomas's brigades of Pender's division had suffered relatively light casualties. Together these troops likely could have mounted a strong assault in the available daylight. Why did Hill choose not to advocate their deployment for another attack? Perhaps Lee had told him he considered Anderson's division a reserve. Or, as William Woods Hassler has suggested, Hill may have thought that "since [he] and Lee were together . . . it was up to Lee to decide whether Anderson's division should be employed."[29] Whatever the explanation, Lee's presence on Seminary Ridge and knowledge of the pertinent facts rendered him rather than Hill primarily responsible for the decision not to press the Federals along Hill's front after 4:30 P.M.

Hill's withdrawal from the fighting shifted the spotlight to Richard S. Ewell. Before the death of Jackson, Ewell had served only briefly under Lee. The commanding general knew that soldiers in the Second Corps liked and respected "Old Bald Head" and may have heard rumors that on his deathbed Jackson expressed a preference for Ewell as his successor.[30] Convinced that Ewell had recovered from the loss of a leg at Groveton the previous August, Lee settled on him to receive a revamped Second Corps containing Ewell's old division, under Jubal A. Early, the division once commanded by Jackson himself, now under Edward "Allegheny" Johnson, and Robert E. Rodes's division, formerly directed by D. H. Hill. In sending Ewell's name to Jefferson Davis for promotion to lieutenant general, Lee termed him "an honest, brave soldier, who has always done his duty well"—far fainter praise than that accorded Hill in the same letter. He sent Ewell's name forward, said Lee to Colonel Allan after the war, with full knowledge of "his

Lt. Gen. Richard Stoddert Ewell. Courtesy of the Library of Congress.

faults as a military leader—his quick alternations from elation to despondency[,] his want of decision &c." Lee talked frankly with Ewell when he made him a lieutenant general, stressing that as a corps commander Ewell would have to exercise independent judgment. As the army embarked on the Gettysburg campaign, Lee remarked to Allan, he hoped Ewell no longer needed minute supervision.[31]

As with Hill, Ewell's first moment of truth as a corps chief came on July 1. Recalled from his advance against Harrisburg on June 29, he placed his divisions on roads whence they might march toward Chambersburg. The next day another directive named Gettysburg as the point of concentration. By that time, Johnson's division was well on the road to Chambersburg. On the morning of July 1, Rodes's division was a few miles north of Gettysburg at Heidlersburg, and Early's brigades were some three miles east of Rodes. Allegheny Johnson's division was far to the west, just outside Chambersburg near Scotland. Ewell's orders for July 1 permitted him to march to Cashtown or Gettysburg. When Hill informed Ewell on the morning of July 1 that Heth was moving toward Gettysburg, Ewell instructed Rodes and Early to march there as well. "I notified the general commanding of my movements," wrote Ewell in his official report, "and was informed by him that, in case we found the enemy's force very large, he did not want a general engagement brought on till the rest of the army came up." By the time Lee's message reached him sometime after noon, Ewell knew that Hill's corps was in a fight. Indeed, some of Rodes's artillery had reached Oak Ridge and opened on the Federals in Hill's front. "It was too late to avoid an engagement without abandoning the position already taken up," Ewell later explained, "and I determined to push the attack vigorously."[32]

Rodes's infantry went into action against the Union First Corps north and northwest of Gettysburg shortly after 2:30 P.M., followed by Early's division, which approached from the north and northeast and struck the Union Eleventh Corps about an hour later. Outnumbered Federals offered stiff resistance for a time, then fell back to Cemetery Hill in the face of relentless Confederate pressure. Several thousand prisoners and some artillery fell into Southern hands as Ewell's triumphant infantry surged into Gettysburg. Ewell's decision to press the attack after receiving Lee's cautionary orders had been vindicated. To the west, Hill's brigades also had advanced and taken position on Seminary Ridge. It was between 4:30 and 5:00 P.M. Ewell's critics would insist that he lost a fabulous opportunity during the next hour—the time when Hancock later told Fitzhugh Lee that the Federals were vulnerable on Cemetery Hill.[33]

Perhaps the most meticulous account of Ewell's movements after he entered Gettysburg came from the pen of Campbell Brown. As Ewell's stepson and staff officer, Brown had direct knowledge of the events. It is true that by the time he wrote in December 1869, he believed that his stepfather had been wronged by those who said he vacillated at the decisive moment. Nonetheless, his version of what transpired accords with most of the known facts. "I shall set down facts as well & truly as I can," he wrote, "remembering them more distinctly because [they were] discussed & seem[ed] to be important at the time & soon after."[34]

Brown met Ewell as the latter entered Gettysburg amid the divisions of Rodes and Early, which "were mingling in their advance." Early soon appeared and joined Ewell. Riding forward, they "surveyed the ground & examined the position & force on Cemetery Hill. Having concluded to attack, if Hill concurred, Gen'l Ewell ordered Early & Rodes to get ready." Just then a messenger arrived from William "Extra Billy" Smith, one of Early's brigadiers, with news of Federals in the Southern left rear. Early doubted the accuracy of this intelligence but suggested that he suspend his movements long enough to make certain the flank was secure. Ewell told him to do so: "Meantime I shall get Rodes into position & communicate with Hill."[35]

A staff officer galloped in search of Hill, eventually returning with word that he had not advanced against Cemetery Hill and that Lee, who was with

Hill on Seminary Ridge, "left it to Gen'l Ewell's discretion, whether to advance alone or not." The enemy on the high ground looked formidable, continued Brown; any assault would entail moving Rodes's and Early's divisions around either end of town and reuniting them in the open ground in front of Cemetery Hill. There the troops would be "within easy cannon shot & in open view of an enemy superior in numbers & advantageously posted." Hill clearly intended to offer no support, and Johnson's division had not yet reached the battlefield. Moreover, Rodes reported that just three of his brigades were in good condition, while Early also had just three within easy distance.

"It was, as I have always understood, with the express concurrence of both Rodes & Early," concluded Brown, "& largely in consequence of the inactivity of the troops under Gen'l Lee's own eye . . . that Gen'l Ewell finally decided to make no direct attack, but to wait for Johnson's coming up & with his fresh troops seize & hold the high peak [Culp's Hill] to our left of Cemetery Hill." The notion that Ewell's decision lost the battle was, in Brown's opinion, "one of those frequently recurring but tardy strokes of military genius, of which one hears long after the minute circumstances that rendered them at the time impracticable, are forgotten."

Brown's narrative has no mention of dramatic confrontations with Trimble or Gordon. Early and Ewell are the principals, and it is thus instructive that Early's official report agrees in essentials with Brown. As he rode into town in the wake of retreating Federals, Early took in a chaotic scene. Ahead, to the south, loomed Cemetery Hill, presenting a "very rugged ascent" and defended by enemy artillery that disputed the Confederate advance. Union prisoners were so numerous as "really to embarrass" the Southern infantry. Far from a dramatic rout (as many postwar writers would describe it), the Federal withdrawal, especially to the west, was carried out in "comparatively good order." Still, Early believed an immediate advance would expand on the success already won, and he set out to find Ewell or Hill.

Before he located either lieutenant general a message arrived from Extra Billy Smith telling of a Federal threat approaching on the York road. Early doubted the veracity of this report but thought it "proper to send General Gordon with his brigade to take charge of Smith's also, and to keep a lookout on the York road, and stop any further alarm." He also sent word to Hill, by a member of Pender's staff he met in the town, that "if he [Hill] would send up a division, we could take the hill to which the enemy had retreated." Shortly thereafter, Early found Ewell, conveyed his views, and was "informed that Johnson's division was coming up, and it was determined with this division to get possession of a wooded hill to the left of Cemetery Hill, which it commanded."[36]

Both Brown's and Early's accounts suggest that Ewell and Early discussed the situation and concluded that a successful assault against Cemetery Hill would require help from A. P. Hill; failing in that, Culp's Hill should be the target once Allegheny Johnson's division arrived.

Robert Rodes's report provides additional information relating to the situation about 4:30 P.M. Even before the Federals had been cleared from Gettysburg, asserted Rodes, "the enemy had begun to establish a line of battle on the heights back of the town, and by the time my line was in a condition to renew the attack, he displayed quite a formidable line of infantry and artillery immediately in my front, extending smartly to my right, and as far as I could see to my left, in front of Early." To have assaulted that line with his division, which had suffered more than twenty-five hundred casualties, "would have been absurd." With no Confederates in evidence on Rodes's right—where Hill's corps held the Southern line—and no specific orders to continue the advance, Rodes assumed that Lee's previous instructions to avoid a general engagement still held and began to place his troops in a defensive posture.[37] Brown's observation that Ewell instructed Rodes to "get ready" to advance does not necessarily contradict Rodes's statement that he received no "specific orders" to do so. The division leader might well have received an initial directive to prepare his men, concluding later, when no follow-up order came, that there would be no renewal of the assault.

Three last pieces of evidence suggest that the Federals presented a daunting front along Cemetery Hill as soon as the Confederates took possession of Gettysburg. Ewell's own report mentioned that the "enemy had fallen back to a commanding position known as Cemetery Hill, south of Gettysburg, and quickly showed a formidable front there." Moreover, an absence of favorable positions for artillery prevented Ewell's bringing cannon to bear on the Federals. Second Corps topographer Jedediah Hotchkiss's entry in his journal for July 1 noted "complete success on our part": "The pursuit was checked by the lateness of the hour and the position the enemy had secured in a cemetery." Even John Gordon offered testimony radically at odds with his postwar posturing. In a letter to his wife written six days after the fighting, Gordon observed that his brigade "drove [the Federals] before us in perfect confusion; but night came on [and] they fell back to a strong position & fortified themselves."[38]

While James Power Smith of Ewell's staff rode in search of Lee and Ewell and his subordinates continued to gather the scattered Second Corps units, the commanding general had sent Walter Taylor to find Ewell. The two messengers undoubtedly passed each other somewhere on the field. Taylor soon reached Ewell with word that Lee had "witnessed the flight of the Federals through Gettysburg and up the hills beyond. . . . It was only necessary to press 'those people' in order to secure possession of the heights, and that, if possible, he wished him to do this." Ewell expressed no objection, remembered Taylor after the war, thereby conveying the impression that he would seek to implement Lee's order. "In the exercise of that discretion, however, which General Lee was accustomed to accord to his lieutenants," added Taylor, "and probably because of an undue regard for his admonition, given early in the day, not to precipitate a general engagement, General Ewell deemed it unwise to make the pursuit. The troops were not moved forward, and the enemy proceeded to occupy and fortify the position which it was designed that General Ewell should seize."[39]

Taylor's account is notable for its distortion of the conditions on Ewell's end of the field. It described a Federal "flight" when most of the Union troops maintained some order to their lines; it claimed that Ewell failed to execute Lee's order to take the heights when Lee had only suggested an attack against the high ground if the situation seemed favorable; and it spoke of Federals "occupying and fortifying ground" as a result of Ewell's dereliction that they already held and were fortifying. Overall, Taylor's narrative illustrates nicely the degree to which officers not present on the Confederate left, including Lee in his postwar statements, minimized the obstacles faced by Ewell and exaggerated the Second Corps chief's indecision.

Ewell confronted a very difficult choice on the late afternoon of July 1. Lee manifestly wished for him to capture Cemetery Hill. Accomplishment of this object would have entailed not a continuation of the previous assaults, as so many of Ewell's critics blithely claimed, but the preparation and mounting of an entirely new assault using portions of Rodes's and Early's divisions. With enough time to gather the troops and stage them south of town, Ewell might have brought to bear six brigades—at most six to seven thousand men. Numerous factors militated against a rapid deployment of such a striking force: the streets of Gettysburg were clogged with men, and units were intermixed; the soldiers were tired after a long day of marching and fighting; thousands of Union prisoners demanded attention; Extra Billy Smith's warning of Federals on the York pike and later cavalry reports of menacing Union troops were potentially ominous. Most important, Union strength on the heights was unknown, though clearly growing, and Allegheny Johnson's division had yet to reach a position from which it might support an assault.

Douglas Southall Freeman wrote that Ewell could not reach a decision. But Ewell did reach a decision—not to attack Cemetery Hill. Although it was not the decision that Lee wished him to make, it certainly was reasonable given the situation. All of which does not prove Ewell experienced no loss of nerve that eventful afternoon. Perhaps he did. Perhaps, as Lee and other critics of Ewell later suggested, the general's old inability to function without specific orders paralyzed him. If that was the case, Lee must shoulder much of the responsibility for Ewell's failure. For if, as he told Colonel Allan after the war, Lee knew that Ewell lacked decisiveness, he should have applied a stronger hand. Lee realized that Ewell was not Jackson or Longstreet and should have modified his method of command accordingly. If he issued a discretionary order when he really wanted to convey a desire that Ewell take those heights (as Taylor's testimony implied), Lee should have known that an indecisive Ewell might react as he did. Direct instructions would have avoided any confusion.

Both A. P. Hill and Richard S. Ewell have suffered more than a century's carping about their conduct on July 1, 1863. Neither of them performed brilliantly; each worked in the immense shadow of Stonewall Jackson, whose greatest triumph remained vividly present in the minds of their fellow soldiers in the Army of Northern Virginia. Hill did not cause the battle to be fought, nor did he or Ewell cost the South a more impressive victory. At every crucial moment, Lee was on the field and able to manage events. In the end, he more than any of his lieutenants controlled the first day's action. Anyone seeking to apportion responsibility for what transpired on the Confederate side on the opening day at Gettysburg should look first to the commanding general.

From Chancellorsville to Cemetery Hill

O. O. Howard and Eleventh Corps Leadership

A. Wilson Greene

CAPTAIN FREDERICK OTTO VON FRITSCH SPOKE FOR MANY of his comrades in characterizing the Battle of Chancellorsville. "On the sixth day of May orders came for the Eleventh Corps to march to United States Ford to recross the Rappahannock River on pontoon bridges . . . and to march back to the old camps," wrote von Fritsch. "I recrossed with a heavy heart, and . . . I felt tears rolling down my cheeks. I was ashamed of this battle, and deplored the sad experience of the Eleventh Corps." "The army, at least our corps, is demoralized," concurred Frederick C. Winkler of the 26th Wisconsin. "Officers talk of resigning and a spirit of depression and lack of confidence manifests itself everywhere." Maj. Gen. Oliver Otis Howard, the Eleventh Corps commander, agreed that "there was no gloomier period during our great war than the month which followed the disasters at Chancellorsville."[1]

A combination of factors made that month grim for the unlucky Eleventh, the most prominent of which was a negative perception of the outfit's performance on May 2, 1863. A portion of "Stonewall" Jackson's command had driven the Eleventh from its vulnerable position on the right flank of the Army of the Potomac in an action more tactically and logistically impressive than strategically decisive. The corps had generally acquitted itself well in a nearly hopeless situation and delayed Confederate progress until dark. Four days later, the Union forces retreated to Stafford

County in ignominious defeat, and the army and the press began to search for culpable parties.[2]

The burden of responsibility for the disaster at Chancellorsville settled quickly, if unjustly, on the Eleventh Corps. Nearly 50 percent of the unit hailed from Germany, and this ethnic composition made the entire corps a natural target for persecution. "The troubles of the corps arose," wrote historian Edwin B. Coddington, "from the prejudice of the Americans and the defensive attitude of the Germans." Well might the German-Americans and their compatriots who wore the crescent badge of the Eleventh Corps bridle when greeted in camp by cruel jokes calculated to humiliate and offend. "[You] fights mit Sigel but runs mit Schurz, you tam cowards," ran the typical refrain.[3] The effects of such bigotry were exacerbated because many veterans of George B. McClellan's time as army commander refused to accept the Eleventh Corps as a meritorious member of the Army of the Potomac (they identified the Eleventh with John Pope's Army of Virginia), an attitude that contributed to their propensity for scorn.[4]

Northern journalists carried this theme to all corners of the country. Many newspapers spoke of the "unexampled misconduct" of the Eleventh Corps and how "the whole failure of the Army of the Potomac was owing to [its] scandalous poltroonery." Such criticism, particularly when without foundation in fact, had a predictably ill effect on the men in question.[5]

A brigade commander in the Eleventh Corps approached his superior after Chancellorsville with an unmistakable message:

> The officers and men of this brigade . . . filled with indignation, come to me, with newspapers in their hands, and ask if such be the reward they may expect for the sufferings they have endured and the bravery they have displayed. . . . It would seem as if a nest of vipers had but waited for an auspicious moment to spit out their poisonous slanders upon this heretofore honored corps. . . . I have been proud to command the brave men in this brigade; but I am sure that unless these infamous falsehoods be retracted and reparation made, their good-will and soldierly spirits will be broken. . . . I demand that the miserable penny-a-liners who have slandered the division, be excluded . . . from our lines, and that the names of the originators of these slanders be made known to me and my brigade, that they may be held responsible for their acts.[6]

Maj. Gen. Carl Schurz, the recipient of this petition, expressed his concerns to Joseph Hooker, the commander of the Army of the Potomac, in a May 9 communique. "I would . . . respectfully observe," stated Schurz, "that the measureless abuse and insult which is heaped upon the Eleventh Corps by the whole army and the press, produces a state of mind among the soldiers, which is apt to demoralize them more than a defeat."[7] Schurz sought to publish his Chancellorsville report to relieve the corps of its odious stigma. When this effort failed, he printed a letter in the *New York Times* demanding an immediate congressional investigation, a request that also fell on deaf ears. Schurz concluded that "a scapegoat was wanted for the remarkable blunders which had caused the failure of the Chancellorsville Campaign," and the Eleventh Corps fit the bill.[8]

As a result, the corps seethed with resentment in mid-May 1863. General Howard did little to mitigate the bruised egos of his troops, accepting practically no personal responsibility for the debacle on May 2. His attitude aggravated ill feelings among German soldiers already upset that Howard had replaced the immensely popular Franz Sigel in late March. "It is said that General Sigel is coming back to the Army of the Potomac to have an enlarged command, his old corps included," wrote a Wisconsin soldier on May 11. "I hope it is so. He is the man to command this corps, all have confidence in him, while very little confidence is felt in General Howard." Charles Wickesburg of the 26th Wisconsin spoke in more extreme terms: "In time the truth will come out," he observed. "It was all General Howard's fault. He is a Yankee, and that is why he wanted to have us slaughtered, because most of us are Germans. He better not come into the thick of battle a second time, then he won't escape."[9]

Sigel had resigned on February 12 and been replaced temporarily by officers of German extraction promoted from within the corps.[10] Howard, a deeply religious abolitionist from Maine, came from the Second Corps and had compiled a creditable combat record as a brigade and division commander. The New Englander's pious personality won scant favor among soldiers of the Eleventh Corps, who apparently paid minimal attention to their new chief's martial abilities. "Tracts now, instead of sauerkraut," complained the soldiers, who disliked Howard's emphasis on Christian warfare. Had Republicans in Maine convinced Howard to run for governor in early June, most members of the corps would have been happy to see him go.[11]

Howard's command consisted of three divisions. Brig. Gen. Francis Channing Barlow, who replaced the wounded Charles Devens, Jr., after Chancellorsville, led the two brigades of the First Division. Slender, pale, beardless, and not yet thirty years old, Barlow was a Harvard graduate and New York lawyer who had demonstrated bravery under fire on the Peninsula and at Antietam.[12] The boyish-looking general ruled his division with a martinet's hand, prompting a member of the 153d Pennsylvania to label

Maj. Gen. Oliver Otis
Howard. From Miller's
Photographic History 10:76.

his tenure "an epoch in our history, which will never be forgotten by those who had the misfortune to serve under him. As a taskmaster he had no equal. The prospect of a speedy deliverance from the odious yoke of Billy Barlow filled every heart with joy." Barlow reciprocated his men's distrust. "You can imagine my disgust & indignation at the miserable behavior of the 11th Corps," he wrote on May 8. "You know how I have always been down on the 'Dutch' & I do not abate my contempt now." Although not apparent from this statement, the native-born regiments of the corps also attracted Barlow's contempt.[13]

The commander of Barlow's First Brigade, Col. Leopold von Gilsa, learned firsthand about his chief's unforgiving style of leadership. Admired by a comrade as "one of the bravest of men and an uncommonly skillful officer," von Gilsa would be arrested by Barlow during the march to Gettysburg for allowing more than one man at a time to leave ranks to fetch water.[14]

Brig. Gen. Nathaniel C. McLean led the Second Brigade of the First Division at Chancellorsville, but Howard found McLean's battlefield performance lacking and banished the former Cincinnati lawyer to a staff job in the Ohio Valley. Twenty-seven-year-old Adelbert Ames replaced McLean. Ames had graduated fifth in the West Point class of 1861 and risen to command the 20th Maine. His promotion to brigadier general on May 20, 1863, qualified him as one of the "boy generals" of the Union.[15]

Brig. Gen. Francis
Channing Barlow.
From Miller's
Photographic History 2:237.

Baron Adolph Wilhelm August Friedrich von Steinwehr continued at the head of the Second Division after Chancellorsville. This forty-one-year-old scion of an Old World military family came to America in the 1840s seeking a commission in the United States Army. Failing in this, he settled for marriage to an Alabama woman and eventually moved to a farm in Connecticut. One of Pope's division commanders in the Army of Virginia, von

Steinwehr impressed a Pennsylvania soldier as "accomplished and competent, and deserv[ing] of more credit than he ever received."[16]

Neither of von Steinwehr's brigade commanders at Chancellorsville retained his post during the Gettysburg campaign. Col. Adolphus Buschbeck of the First Brigade became ill in early June, and Col. Charles Robert Coster of the 134th New York filled his place. Coster had begun the war as a private; Gettysburg would be his only battle in brigade command. Col. Orland Smith of the 73d Ohio assumed control of the Second Brigade, which had been Barlow's at Chancellorsville, and soon won the affection of his men and praise from the difficult Barlow.[17]

The most renowned of Howard's subordinates was Carl Schurz, who led the Third Division and stood second only to Sigel himself in the estimation of German-Americans. Politics figured more prominently than the military in Schurz's European background, and upon arriving in Wisconsin he had immersed himself in antislavery activities. Lincoln rewarded Schurz for his work in the 1860 presidential canvass with the Spanish portfolio, but in 1862 Schurz returned from Madrid seeking a commission in the army. Lincoln accommodated his influential friend; Schurz responded by displaying some promise in the field. More important, the Germans of the Eleventh Corps considered him their spiritual leader and a deserving candidate for corps command.[18]

The brigade-level leadership of the Third Division remained intact after Chancellorsville. Alexander Schimmelfennig, thirty-eight years old and a native of the Prussian province of Lithuania, headed the First Brigade. According to an oft-told fable, Lincoln commissioned Schimmelfennig a brigadier general in November 1862 because he found the immigrant's name irresistible. Short, thin, and customarily dressed in old uniforms, Schimmelfennig cut a figure less memorable than his multisyllabic surname. He suffered from chronic dyspepsia, diarrhea, and bad ankles, and as might be imagined, his disposition left something to be desired.[19] Schimmelfennig's counterpart in the Third Division also had a name most Americans found unpronounceable. Wladimir Krzyzanowski emigrated from Poland in 1846, settling in New York. He organized the 58th New York in 1861 and served in Pope's army as a brigade commander. "Kriz," as he was known in the ranks, proved to be an inspirational officer who led by example.[20]

On balance, the Eleventh Corps possessed a solid stable of officers on the eve of Gettysburg. Schurz, von Gilsa, Schimmelfennig, Krzyzanowski, and von Steinwehr had exhibited reasonably impressive military skills, while Ames and Barlow boasted excellent credentials. The temporary brigade

Maj. Gen. Carl Schurz. From Miller's *Photographic History* 10:23.

commanders, Smith and Coster, entered the campaign with question marks beside their names, as did Howard, whose experience at Chancellorsville had diminished an otherwise enviable record.[21]

Back in its camps near Brooke Station on the Richmond, Fredericksburg & Potomac Railroad by May 8, the Eleventh Corps began a period of restoration. Efficient logisticians soon replaced the equipment and supplies sacrificed south of the Rappahannock. "This attended to, things began to look more cheerfully," wrote a soldier from Pennsylvania. "The despondency of the men gradually vanished, and soon all traces of our late disaster were obliterated."[22] On June 12 the corps folded its tents and began to follow R. E. Lee's northward-marching Army of Northern Virginia. According to Carl Schurz, the Federals were "ready and eager to march and fight."[23]

The Eleventh Corps evinced that eagerness perhaps more than any other unit in Hooker's army. Its maligned men harbored disappointment, anger, and hostility. Already outsiders in the Army of the Potomac by virtue of their military pedigree and ethnicity, the soldiers of the crescent tramped north hoping for an opportunity to shed their dishonorable post-Chancellorsville reputation. "May we meet Lee somewhere soon," wrote an officer to von Gilsa on June 15, "and may the Eleventh Corps prove that it is as good and brave as any other."[24]

The corps followed a route through Hartwood Church and Catlett's Station, where it joined Maj. Gen. John F. Reynolds's newly constituted right wing of the army. Howard's troops then moved to Manassas, Centreville, and Goose Creek, just south of Leesburg, marching, according to Howard, "in a very orderly style" and obeying his orders "with great alacrity." After barely escaping capture at the hands of John S. Mosby's cavalry, Howard left Goose Creek on June 24 and crossed the Potomac at Edwards Ferry.[25]

All question of morale disappeared when the corps entered Maryland. The verdant countryside and warm greetings from loyal citizens invigorated the soldiers. Lt. Albert Wallber of the 26th Wisconsin vividly recalled June 24: "Having tramped around northern Virginia . . . and viewed nothing but those melancholy pine forests, barren, impoverished fields . . . and old dilapidated homes . . . where a deathlike stillness prevailed," wrote Lieutenant Wallber, "our feelings may be imagined when we stepped on Maryland's shore and beheld the fertile fields, rich pastures, [and] well-kept gardens . . . all showing the prosperity of the inhabitants. The contrast between the two shores was so conspicuous that we really feasted on the landscape." "What a sudden change had overcome the men!" exclaimed a member of the 153d Pennsylvania. "How easy their steps and how cheerful their countenances." A soldier in the 33d Massachusetts gave similar testimony on June 27, writing that the "fate of Maryland and Washington is about to be decided. . . . Our boys have fought well heretofore and we believe that they will now fight better than ever."[26]

George G. Meade's ascension to command of the army on June 28 had a positive, if muted, effect on the leaders of the Eleventh Corps. Howard considered Hooker to be morally impure, and his distrust of "Fighting Joe" had deepened when he learned that Hooker held the Eleventh Corps responsible for the defeat at Chancellorsville. Schurz testified that the army was pleased with Meade's appointment because "everybody respected him." Capt. Alfred E. Lee of the 82d Ohio recognized that a change in command on the eve of battle had potentially serious implications for morale: "But fortunately, a feeling had taken hold of the army that it had suffered disasters enough, and that the time had now come whatever leader and at whatever cost. This sentiment fired every breast and reduced the matter of change of commanders to the dimensions of a mere passing incident."[27]

On June 29, the Eleventh Corps entered Emmitsburg, Maryland, a village near the Pennsylvania border. As the corps made camp, the soldiers knew that a major battle loomed on the horizon, but their attitude had come full circle since May 6. "General Lee had advertised that his 'troupe' will perform in Pennsylvania for a short time," wrote a man in the 33d Massachusetts, "but I think he will have to dance to just such tunes as we see fit to play for him." According to Lt. Col. Edward Salomon of the 82d Illinois, "every man felt that . . . a complete victory here meant the beginning of the end of the Rebellion."[28]

After a march of nearly twenty miles over muddy roads on the twenty-ninth, the Eleventh Corps rested around St. Joseph's College near Emmitsburg. Howard ordered his troops to move a short distance northwest of the town on June 30, a day that otherwise provided the men a welcome respite from marching. Howard, Schurz, and other officers found comfortable lodging at the college, which they variously described as a nunnery or seminary.[29]

Meade assigned the left wing of the army, composed of the First, Third, and Eleventh corps, to Reynolds on June 30. That same day, Howard dispatched reconnaissance parties from several regiments to investigate reports of Confederates in nearby villages.[30] A relatively quiet day had nearly passed when Howard received a request from Reynolds, his immediate superior, to ride to Reynolds's headquarters near Marsh Run some five miles north on the road to Gettysburg. Accompanied by his brother Charles and staff member Lt. F. W. Gilbreath, Howard arrived at the Moritz Tavern just in time for a pleasant supper with Reynolds. The wing commander showed Howard communications indicating that Meade believed "a general engagement was imminent [and] the issues involved immense." The officers expected instructions from Meade for the next day, but when nothing had arrived by 11:00 P.M., Howard departed for his own headquarters at St. Joseph's.[31]

Howard spent two hours picking his way to Emmitsburg in the dark along a rough, muddy road. Awakened by a courier an hour after his return, Howard received a copy of Meade's orders for General Reynolds. Reading the dispatch, as was the custom, he learned that Meade had called for the First Corps to move immediately to Gettysburg and for the Eleventh Corps to follow "in supporting distance." Howard forwarded the orders to Reynolds and awaited official authority from his wing commander before placing his corps in motion.[32]

July 1 dawned with a promise of rain. Howard issued a preparatory order for the morning's march, designating two parallel routes to expedite the movement to Gettysburg. Barlow's division would use the direct road from Emmitsburg, which would take the First Division to the Adams County seat eleven miles away. Schurz and von Steinwehr would take a route to the east leading to Horner's Mill and the Taneytown Road, adding about two miles to the trek. The anticipated marching orders arrived from Reynolds between 8:00 and 8:30 A.M., and the corps took to the roads with reasonable efficiency. By 9:30 A.M., all the men of the crescent were on the move.[33]

Some of the regiments left their knapsacks in Emmitsburg to quicken their gait, and officers allowed their troops little rest. Barlow's men encountered a muddy track marred by deep ruts left by Reynolds's trains and found a few wagons of the First Corps blocking the roadway. Nevertheless, the First Division covered about two and one-half miles per hour, a respectable pace. Schurz and von Steinwehr, accompanied by four of the five artillery batteries in the corps, moved more quickly on an unobstructed route and promised to arrive near Gettysburg simultaneously with Barlow. As the corps crossed the Mason-Dixon Line in midmorning, "the Pennsylvania regiments saluted their state with cheers, dipped colors and ruffled drums."[34]

Howard and his staff rode through fields bordering the Emmitsburg-Gettysburg road to avoid Barlow's columns. Charles Howard remembered meeting a staff officer dispatched by Reynolds who pointed out a camping place for the Eleventh Corps consistent with Meade's original conception of placing Howard's troops within supporting distance of the First Corps. The younger Howard stated that the sounds of battle to the north and west persuaded his brother to ignore the directive to halt and to instruct his troops instead to hurry toward the roar of the guns.[35] General Howard confirmed this episode in his official report, adding that he sent several couriers to find Reynolds to determine the nature of the combat. The general's postwar writings, however, say nothing about this initial communication from Reynolds. Howard recalled instead that by 10:30 A.M. he "was in sight of the village of Gettysburg, when the staff officer which Reynolds had dispatched on his arrival met me. He gave me information . . . of the battle."[36]

What happened next forms the basis for one of several lingering controversies regarding the Eleventh Corps leadership on July 1. Howard's conference with Reynolds's courier, whether the first or second such meeting of the morning, occurred near Sherfy's peach orchard less than a mile south of Gettysburg. Howard's recollection of the conversation is clear and consistent. Reynolds's aide told the corps commander to "come quite up to Gettysburg." Howard inquired as to precisely where Reynolds wished him to go. "Encamp anywhere about here according to your judgment at present" was the reply.[37]

Howard dispatched Capt. Daniel Hall, and perhaps other members of his staff, to locate Reynolds so he could consult with his superior in person.

Meanwhile, sounds of battle and concern about where best to deploy his men prompted Howard to ride first to Seminary Ridge and then back across the Emmitsburg road to parallel high ground that reached a northern terminus at the town cemetery. Noticing another elevation to the right and recognizing the natural value of the eminence on which he stood, Howard turned to his adjutant general, T. A. Meysenburg, and said, "This seems to be a good position, Colonel." Meysenburg responded, "It is the only position, General."[38]

Some writers credit Reynolds with selecting Cemetery Hill as the anchor for the Union line at Gettysburg. At least one account attributes the decision to von Steinwehr.[39] The evidence seems clear, however, that O. O. Howard was the initial architect of the defensive position that would prove so strong during the next fifty-four hours. Howard himself wrote in 1884 that there "is no official communication or testimony from any quarter whatever . . . which even claims that any orders . . . to occupy Cemetery Hill or Ridge were delivered to me." Captain Hall confirmed that he did find Reynolds, who instructed him to tell Howard to bring the Eleventh Corps forward as rapidly as possible but "gave no order whatever in regard to occupying Cemetery Hill, nor did he make any allusion to it." Hall returned to Howard, encountered him hurrying into Gettysburg, and relayed Reynolds's message. "Riding into the town at your side," stated Hall, "I remember that . . . you pointed to the crest of Cemetery Ridge on our right and said: 'There's the place to fight this battle,' or words to similar effect."[40]

No military genius was required to recognize the obvious defensive qualities of Cemetery Hill. Stone fences formed natural breastworks for infantry; gentle slopes provided outstanding locations for artillery. Culp's Hill and Cemetery Ridge offered strong protection on the flanks, and the position's convex shape would allow reinforcements to move quickly to any point along the line.[41]

Not entirely satisfied with his view of the distant battlefield from Cemetery Hill, Howard rode into town to obtain a better vantage point. He first tried to ascend the belfry of the courthouse but found no ladder or stairway. A young man named D. A. Skelly directed the general to a building across the street, at the intersection of Baltimore and Middle streets, known as Fahnestock's Observatory. Howard climbed a flight of stairs and emerged onto a small railed balcony from which he and a few staff officers gained a clear view of the surrounding terrain. Employing field glasses and maps, Howard carefully studied the landscape where his men likely would be deployed when they arrived to support the beleaguered First Corps.[42]

While Howard made these observations, a young cavalry officer named George Guinn reported that General Reynolds had been wounded. Moments later, about 11:30 A.M., another officer, perhaps Captain Hall or Maj. William Riddle of the First Corps, announced that Reynolds had died and that Howard now commanded the field. "Is it confessing weakness to say that when the responsibility of my position flashed upon me I was penetrated with an emotion never experienced before or since?" asked Howard in a postwar account. "My heart was heavy and the situation was grave indeed but I did not hesitate and said: 'God helping us, we will stay here till the army comes.'"[43]

Reynolds's death sent changes rippling through the command of the Eleventh Corps. Schurz succeeded Howard and passed his division to Schimmelfennig, who in turn assigned the First Brigade to Col. George von Amsberg of the 45th New York.[44]

These events at Eleventh Corps headquarters transpired while the rank and file toiled up the highways leading to Gettysburg. In addition to muddy roads and stray wagons from the First Corps, the troops negotiated streams and marshes, climbed fences, and endured drenching thunderstorms during the morning. The skies eventually cleared, but the humidity remained and men unburdened themselves of accoutrements to lighten their loads. Some soldiers in Krzyzanowski's brigade marched barefoot, having worn out their shoes during the march from Brooke Station.[45]

By 10:30 A.M., the division commanders had received Howard's instructions to increase the pace in response to Reynolds's request for help. Schurz read this order while at Horner's Mill and rode forward to meet Howard. He reached East Cemetery Hill before noon and learned from Howard of Reynolds's demise.[46] The Third Division, now under Schimmelfennig, arrived in Gettysburg between 12:30 and 1:00 P.M., swinging up the Taneytown road after a rapid march of several miles without a rest. Barlow's division came next, probably thirty minutes later, while von Steinwehr's men labored to join their comrades.[47]

Howard's three divisions numbered fewer than nine thousand effectives, making his command the second smallest corps in the army.[48] Twenty-six guns under Maj. Thomas W. Osborn supported the infantrymen. Sixteen of Osborn's pieces were Napoleons and the remainder longer-range 3-inch rifles. Lieutenants Bayard Wilkeson and William Wheeler and Captains Hubert Dilger, Lewis Heckman, and Michael Wiedrich commanded Osborn's batteries.[49]

Upon learning of his ascension to overall command, Howard had returned to Cemetery Hill and established army headquarters. He notified Maj. Gen. Daniel E. Sickles, chief of the Third Corps, of the situation and urged him to move his troops from near Emmitsburg to Gettysburg as expeditiously as possible. A similar message went to Twelfth Corps commander Maj. Gen. Henry W. Slocum at Two Taverns near Taneytown, and a summary of events soon was on its way to General Meade. Howard then made a series of decisions based on the realization that he must rely for a time on the troops at hand—decisions that form the crux of the debate over Eleventh Corps leadership on July 1. He responded initially to information supplied by Brig. Gen. Abner Doubleday, Reynolds's replacement at the head of the First Corps, that the Union right flank west of Gettysburg faced great danger. Schurz should take the First and Third divisions, instructed Howard, "to seize and hold a prominent height on the right of the Cashtown road and on the prolongation of Seminary Ridge," an eminence known as Oak Hill.[50]

Two problems rendered these orders obsolete almost immediately. Howard and Reynolds had learned the night before that a portion of the Confederate army had appeared north of Gettysburg at Heidlersburg and that a Rebel division had crossed the mountains at Carlisle. It thus could not have surprised Howard when Brig. Gen. John Buford of the cavalry reported at 12:30 P.M. that gray-clad units were massing three or four miles north of Gettysburg between the York and Carlisle roads.[51] Howard sent modified orders for Schurz "to halt his command, to prevent his right flank being turned, but to push forward a thick line of skirmishers, to seize the point first indicated [Oak Hill] as a relief and support to the First Corps." As Schurz soon discovered, however, Confederates already had occupied his objective, forcing the Eleventh Corps to form at right angles to Doubleday facing north rather then extending the original Union line.[52]

Several analysts have argued that Howard's decision to advance Schimmelfennig and Barlow north of town sealed the fate of the Eleventh Corps before a Confederate shot had been fired at them. General Howard, wrote one critic, "recognized the fact that the 1st Corps would soon be taken in the flank, and that he would soon be confronted with two confederate army corps. Why he should not at once have withdrawn the 1st corps to Cemetery Ridge, the strength of which he had recognized . . . and there formed his line of battle . . . is not understood." Captain Lee of the 82d Ohio averred that "instead of advancing we should have fallen back as soon as the approach of the enemy from the right was developed . . . with our right well refused upon the town, and our left connecting . . . with the . . . First Corps. We could then have punished the enemy more severely, and, perhaps, have held the town until dark." A staff officer serving with Schurz found Howard culpable not for failing to fall back but for failing to send von Steinwehr to provide direct support for the rest of the corps.[53]

John Reynolds had selected the Union battlefield in the morning, and Doubleday continued to maintain this ground in the early afternoon. "I immediately determined to hold the front line as long as possible," explained Howard, "and when compelled to retreat from the Seminary Line, as I felt I would be, to dispute the ground obstinately; but to have all the time a strong position at the Cemetery . . . that I could hold until at least Slocum and Sickles, with their eighteen thousand reinforcements, could reach the field."[54]

Edwin B. Coddington assails Howard's reasoning on two counts. First, he argues that Howard was under no obligation to maintain Reynolds's line after the midday lull in the fighting and should have withdrawn Doubleday to Seminary Ridge. Second, Coddington terms Howard's reliance on the timely arrival of reinforcements "unrealistic."[55]

Even Howard's most severe detractors do not suggest that the First and Eleventh corps had the strength on July 1 to defeat A. P. Hill and R. S. Ewell on the fields west and north of Gettysburg. Howard's only course was to delay the enemy. Legitimate debate, therefore, must revolve around whether Howard most effectively slowed Confederate progress until help arrived from the south (the timing of the arrival of such help is a subject for another inquiry). The Cemetery Hill–Culp's Hill–Cemetery Ridge position clearly offered the best terrain for a tactical defensive. Did Howard do everything possible to secure that ground until the bulk of the Army of the Potomac could reach the field? A review of the evidence suggests that his reasons for acting as he did were sound despite the protestations of his critics.

Schurz determined the initial dispositions of the Eleventh Corps. "I ordered General Schimmelfennig . . . to advance briskly through the town, and to deploy on the right of the first corps in two lines," reported the German general. "This order was executed with promptness and spirit." Howard personally accompanied Barlow's division through Gettysburg, beyond which it formed near the Almshouse on Schimmelfennig's right.[56] When the corps appeared on the battlefield, Doubleday's men saluted it with ringing cheers.[57]

Schurz had two immediate missions: to protect Doubleday's right and to guard against the anticipated arrival of Confederates from the northeast. To meet these responsibilities, Schurz's line stretched some fifteen hundred yards across the fields north of Gettysburg between the Mummasburg and York roads. A gap of about a quarter-mile separated Schimmelfennig's left from Doubleday's right, creating a natural target for attack. Schurz's six thousand soldiers formed the equivalent of a strong skirmish line along their broad front, completing their first dispositions about 2:00 P.M.[58]

At approximately that time, von Steinwehr arrived atop Cemetery Hill, executing Howard's decision to make it the reserve position for the corps.

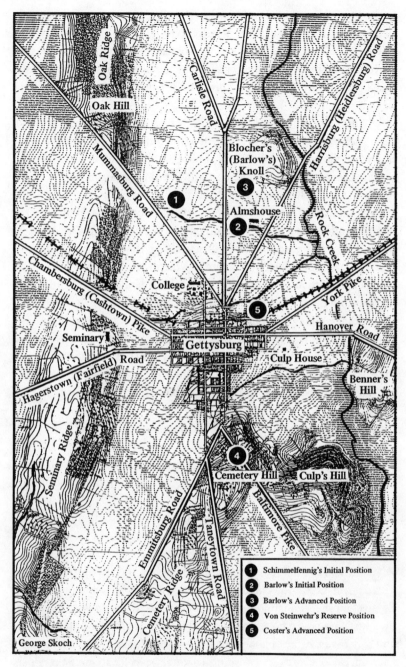

1 Schimmelfennig's Initial Position
2 Barlow's Initial Position
3 Barlow's Advanced Position
4 Von Steinwehr's Reserve Position
5 Coster's Advanced Position

Area Contested by the Eleventh Corps on July 1

Von Steinwehr placed Coster's brigade on the northeast end of the hill in support of Wiedrich's battery. Smith's brigade moved to the northwest in support of Heckman's guns. The rest of Osborn's artillery had accompanied Schurz—Wilkeson with Barlow, and Dilger and Wheeler with Schimmelfennig.[59]

Howard reported his actions to Meade and repeated his plea for support from Slocum and Sickles about 2:00 P.M. He also ordered his brother to consult with Buford about the approach of Confederates from the north and personally inspected the Eleventh Corps line from right to left. Continuing on to Doubleday's part of the field, Howard found the First Corps commander about a quarter-mile beyond the seminary. After examining the First Corps front, Howard accepted Doubleday's assurance that McPherson's woods would shield the Federal left and told the New Yorker to maintain his position as long as possible before retiring to the designated rallying point on Cemetery Ridge. These instructions were consistent with Howard's strategy of delay; so too was his denial of Doubleday's request for help from von Steinwehr—a movement of troops off of Cemetery Hill, he thought, would compromise the integrity of the Federal reserve.[60]

Shortly after Schurz had deployed the Third Division, Confederate artillery on Oak Hill began to shell his exposed troops in the valley below. To Schurz's left, Rebel infantry pressed against elements of the First Corps, and Schurz noticed enemy soldiers maneuvering to his front. When the acting corps commander looked to his right, however, he witnessed a more ominous sight. "I had ordered General Barlow to refuse his right wing, that is to place his right brigade, Colonel Gilsa's, a little in the right rear of his other brigade, in order to use it against possible flanking movement by the enemy," observed Schurz. "But I now noticed that Barlow, be it that he had misunderstood my order, or that he was carried away by the ardor of the conflict, had advanced his whole line and lost connection with my third division on his left, and . . . he had instead of refusing, pushed forward his right brigade, so that it formed a projecting angle with the rest of the line."[61]

Barlow had committed the tactical error that, more than any other Eleventh Corps command decision of the day, dictated the course of combat on that part of the field. Why did he do it? Did he act on his own accord, or did he respond to orders? What potential advantage might have been gained by advancing from the Almshouse line?

The evidence seems conclusive that Barlow made this decision of his own volition.[62] Howard had accompanied him when the First Division marched through Gettysburg on its initial deployment, then departed to inspect Schurz's and Doubleday's positions once Barlow halted at the

Almshouse. Howard had ordered Barlow and Schimmelfennig to seize Oak Hill; "but as soon as I heard of the approach of Ewell and saw that nothing could prevent the turning of my right flank if Barlow advanced," wrote Howard, "the order was countermanded."[63] The attempt to occupy Oak Hill ended as soon as Schimmelfennig's division reached the ground between the Mummasburg and Carlisle roads and discovered Confederates on the heights. It is thus difficult to ascribe Barlow's advance at 2:30 P.M. to orders that had ceased to apply practically and explicitly more than an hour earlier.

Schurz's postwar writings charitably allow that a misunderstanding of his directive to refuse the right flank might explain Barlow's actions. Schurz made no such allowance, however, in his official report. Barlow informed his mother after the battle that he had "formed as directed," but it is hard to imagine that he could so badly misconstrue an order. Even if he did, his culpability remains. Other testimony portrays Barlow in an aggressive mood. Captain von Fritsch remembered that the general ordered skirmishers toward Blocher's Knoll, a hillock overlooking Rock Creek to Barlow's right front. Shortly thereafter, recalled E. C. Culp of the 25th Ohio, Barlow sent his division to support the skirmishers with the words, "What is that skirmish line stopping for?"[64]

If it may be agreed that Barlow was the author of his division's development, what might have prompted this fatal decision? Blocher's Knoll did rise slightly higher than the ridge occupied by the division near the Almshouse, and its cleared summit offered reasonable positions for artillery. But thick woods began about one hundred feet below the crest toward Rock Creek, severely limiting the field of fire in the direction of the anticipated Confederate advance.[65] Most likely, Barlow saw the unprotected left of Brig. Gen. George Doles's Georgia brigade, which was maneuvering opposite Schimmelfennig's position, and could not resist the temptation to take Doles in flank and rear.[66]

Caught off guard by the shift on his right, Schurz ordered Schimmelfennig to conform with Barlow's dispositions so as to maintain contact between the First and Third divisions. Krzyzanowski's brigade moved out, lengthening the Eleventh Corps line. Schurz also sent couriers to Howard renewing his request that one of von Steinwehr's brigades advance through town and take position on Barlow's right and rear to mitigate the impact of an attack against that exposed flank.[67]

Potential danger became reality about 3:00 P.M. Barlow had moved some twenty-one hundred men on or near Blocher's Knoll when the Federals received fire from Confederate artillery to the northeast along the Harrisburg road. "Then came one of the most warlike and animated spectacles I ever looked upon," stated a Confederate staff officer. "Gordon &

Hays charged across the plateau in their front, at double-quick, sweeping everything before them, and scattering the extreme right of the enemy."[68]

In fact, only Brig. Gen. John B. Gordon's Georgia brigade of fifteen hundred effectives and Doles's fourteen hundred men launched the initial infantry assault against the Eleventh Corps. Doles's presence probably explained why Barlow had advanced northward in the first place. Gordon's appearance, remarkably, came as a surprise. The Federals had known of a Confederate threat from the north since the previous evening; Rodes's division had occupied Oak Hill and undertaken offensive operations against the right of the First Corps; and the Southern guns along the Harrisburg road had begun to pound Barlow's soldiers. Still, when Gordon's men boiled out of the woods skirting the bed of Rock Creek, they caught the Eleventh Corps unprepared.[69]

Gordon struck Barlow's vulnerable right flank held by von Gilsa's little brigade—the same men who had absorbed Jackson's initial blow on May 2. According to a Confederate participant, "it was a fearful slaughter, the golden wheat fields, a few minutes before in beauty, now gone, and the ground covered with the dead and wounded in blue."[70] When von Gilsa gave way, Gordon focused on the exposed right flank of Ames's brigade. Contending with both Doles and Gordon, Ames's outnumbered troops also collapsed. Barlow attempted to rally his soldiers but fell wounded with a bullet in his left side. Ames assumed command of the division and sought to form a new line near the Almshouse. "We ought to have held the place easily, for I had my entire force at the very point where the attack was made," wrote Barlow shortly after the battle. "But the enemies [sic] skirmishers had hardly attacked us before my men began to run. No fight at all was made."[71]

Most accounts disagree with Barlow. Brigadier General Henry J. Hunt, the Union chief of artillery, portrayed the fight between Barlow and the Georgians as "an obstinate and bloody contest. The fighting here was well-sustained." Pvt. G. W. Nichols of the 61st Georgia reported that the Confederates "advanced with our accustomed yell, but they stood firm until we got near them. They then began to retreat in fine order, shooting at us as they retreated. They were harder to drive than we had ever known them before. . . . Their officers were cheering their men and behaving like heroes and commanders of the 'first water.'" The finest tactical study of this engagement calls it "a bruising, violent struggle."[72]

Krzyzanowski's brigade had not reached Ames's left when Gordon and Doles began their attacks. By the time the troops arrived at the Carlisle road, Barlow's men already were withdrawing. Doles centered his attention on Krzyzanowski, and another fierce combat erupted. "Bullets hummed about our ears like infuriated bees, and in a few minutes the meadow was strewn with . . . the wounded and the dead," testified an Ohio officer. "The combatants approached each other until they were scarcely more than seventy-five yards apart, and the names of battles printed on the Confederate flags might have been read, had there been time to read them."[73]

Both of Krzyzanowski's flanks received enfilading fire, and the brigade fell back across the Carlisle road toward an orchard on the north side of Gettysburg. Most of von Amsberg's brigade manned the skirmish line facing Oak Hill or supported Dilger's and Wheeler's batteries on the Eleventh Corps left; Schimmelfennig thus could send only one regiment to Krzyzanowski's aid. This unit, the 157th New York, bravely advanced toward Doles's right flank but met a tremendous fire and suffered 75 percent casualties.[74]

The entire Union line at Gettysburg faced disaster by 3:20 P.M. As the Confederates renewed their attacks against Doubleday, John Buford informed Meade that in his opinion "there seems to be no directing person," an artless indictment of O. O. Howard.[75]

In fact, Howard, Schurz, and Doubleday did attempt to salvage a situation that had quickly become desperate. All three men needed reinforcements, and each of them requested help. Howard asked again that Slocum hurry the Twelfth Corps forward, while Schurz and Doubleday begged Howard for assistance. Howard authorized Schurz to detach a regiment or two to support Doubleday, an option the beleaguered German lacked the manpower to satisfy.[76] Still hoping for the arrival of one of von Steinwehr's brigades, Schurz enjoyed the only reasonable expectation of aid. Howard would claim that before Barlow's advance he had ordered three regiments from Coster's brigade to occupy the north end of town, but other sources mention no such directive. "I feared the consequences of sparing another man from the cemetery," explained Howard. "It was not time to lose the nucleus for a new line that must soon be formed."[77]

About 3:45 P.M., the tenuous rallying point near the Almshouse collapsed. Gordon's men swept forward despite the best efforts of von Gilsa and Ames, and two fresh Confederate brigades menaced the right of the makeshift line. By this time, Howard had definitely instructed von Steinwehr to dispatch Coster's brigade to cover Schurz's withdrawal.[78]

Coster pulled some eleven hundred men off Cemetery Hill before 3:30 P.M., entered Baltimore Street, and marched through town, leaving one regiment at the railroad depot.[79] The remaining eight hundred soldiers filed through the north side of Gettysburg, receiving artillery fire from Oak Hill and passing the wounded and fugitives from both Federal corps. "I led [the brigade] out of the town," said Schurz, "and ordered it to deploy on the right of the junction of the roads . . . which the enemy was fast approaching." Schurz placed Heckman's Ohio battery on the brigade's left, as Coster's men strode toward the impending maelstrom with perfect order and discipline. John F. Sullivan of the 154th New York believed that had his "regiment been on dress parade it could not have done better."[80]

Unfortunately, some of Coster's troops halted below rising ground that obstructed their field of fire. Before they could adjust their position, the brigades of Brig. Gen. Harry Hays and Col. Isaac E. Avery had closed to within two hundred yards. "I shall always remember how the Confederate line of battle looked as it came into full view and started down toward us," wrote Pvt. Charles W. McKay of the 154th New York. "It seemed as though they had a battle flag every few rods, which would indicate that their formation was in solid column."[81]

Coster's men, as much as any other unit in the Eleventh Corps, belied their reputation as demoralized cowards. Fighting against tremendous odds, the blue line held long enough for "the first division to enter the town without being seriously molested on its retreat." "Our fire did good execution," boasted McKay, "and their line was stopped in our front." Heckman's gunners pulled their lanyards 113 times before pressured to withdraw. The fierce engagement lasted only a short time before Coster, whose losses would total 250 killed and wounded and another 300 captured, ordered his men to disengage.[82]

Schimmelfennig's division also fell back, fighting as it went. Schurz reported that his old command retreated toward Gettysburg "in good order, contesting the ground step by step with the greatest firmness."[83]

Coster's brigade contributed significantly to the extrication of the Eleventh Corps north of Gettysburg. Might it have accomplished more had Howard acted on Schurz's requests to move it forward sooner? Did Howard's hesitation ensure dire consequences once the army reached the streets of Gettysburg?

It takes a great leap of faith to argue that Coster's tiny regiments could have saved the First Division's vulnerable position at Blocher's Knoll. Had Barlow remained at the Almshouse line, however, and Coster moved up on his right rear as Schurz preferred, the Eleventh Corps might well have held its ground somewhat longer. In Howard's defense, it must be recalled that the Union strategy that afternoon revolved around standing firm on Cemetery Hill until the Third and Twelfth corps came up. To detach one-half of the small reserve holding that key ground and risk it in the open fields north of Gettysburg would have entailed a tremendous gamble promising doubtful dividends.

By 4:00 P.M., Confederate attacks against Doubleday's line and Schurz's left threatened to overrun organized Union resistance west and north of

Gettysburg. "If you cannot hold out longer," Howard told Doubleday, "you must fall back to the cemetery." At 4:10 P.M., Howard sent both corps commanders instructions to retire fighting to Cemetery Hill, the First Corps to take position on the left and the Eleventh Corps on the right of the Baltimore Pike. Howard ordered Buford to cover Doubleday's left flank during the withdrawal and sent his brother to urge Slocum yet again to move up to Cemetery Hill.[84]

It is difficult to determine whether von Amsberg's brigade or the right flank of the First Corps gave way first. "We of Robinson's division have a very vivid remembrance of a division of the Eleventh Corps throwing away its guns and manifesting intense anxiety to regain the charming shelter of Cemetery Hill," wrote a veteran of the 12th Massachusetts (of the First Corps).[85] A soldier of the 45th New York stated the case for the Eleventh Corps: "We made preparations to defend the college . . . although we saw the left of the First Corps broken to pieces and pursued by overwhelming numbers of the enemy making for the left of the town."[86]

Conflicting evidence likewise exists regarding the nature of the retreat. Many Confederate accounts support the notion that both Union corps fled the field in disarray.[87] "This is far from the truth," claimed Carl Schurz. "There was no element of dissolution in it." The men of the 33d Massachusetts of Smith's brigade watched from Cemetery Hill as blue-clad soldiers "stubbornly retreated, turning every few rods to fire a volley, facing in every direction." E. C. Culp of the 25th Ohio concluded that "there was no organization as far as I could see. Neither was there any great hurry."[88]

Most witnesses do agree that confusion reigned once the troops reached the confines of Gettysburg. Soldiers from the Eleventh and First corps collided in the narrow streets, some of which were dead ends in more ways than one for unfortunate Federals. "The enemy's brigades poured in like . . . ceaseless . . . waves and threatened to overwhelm . . . all that did not flee before them," remembered a Bay State soldier. Skulkers, stragglers, and the panic-stricken from both corps added to the chaos.[89]

General Schimmelfennig crafted his most enduring Civil War legacy by effecting a hairbreadth escape from capture. Climbing a tall fence while sustaining blows from pursuing Confederates, he played dead until the Rebels passed by, his identity masked by his customary private's garb. He then sought shelter in what has been variously described as a water tank, lumberyard, or woodshed but was most likely a pigsty. There the acting division commander would remain undetected for two more days of battle.[90]

Not all of the Eleventh Corps shared the general's luck. Confederates captured more than fourteen hundred soldiers of the crescent in

Gettysburg—a total smaller than the number of killed and wounded suffered by the corps during the afternoon's fighting.[91]

A lack of leadership contributed to the disaster in Gettysburg. Although Schurz and Doubleday "were in front of the town till the last minute, doing everything to inspirit their troops," both Eleventh Corps division commanders were indisposed. Howard remained on Cemetery Hill, where smoke and trees obscured his view of the withdrawal. Moreover, no one had designated specific routes of retreat despite Howard's knowledge that the army eventually would be forced to retire under pressure.[92]

No such lapse marred the effort to rally fugitives on Cemetery Hill. "In whatever shape the troops issued from the town, they were promptly reorganized, each was under the colors of his regiment, and in as good a fighting trim as before," reported Schurz. By 4:30 P.M., Howard had firm command of the situation. An aide from Barlow's staff who reported to the field commander remembered with pride "that interview which, in two or three minutes, taught me what a cool and confident man can do. No hurry, no confusion in his mind."[93]

Smith's two thousand troops supported by Wiedrich's battery of three-inch rifles provided the anchor around which the rest of the Union army would form. A crestfallen von Amsberg reached the heights first; Howard personally positioned his brigade by carrying the corps flag to the designated location. Ames arrived next, reporting, "I have no division: it is all cut to pieces." Howard exhorted him to try to extend the line eastward, and Ames "succeeded better than he had feared." Krzyzanowski, now in charge of the Third Division, appeared about 4:45 P.M. and placed his soldiers on the left flank of the corps behind a stone wall near the cemetery's gate.[94]

Doubleday's veterans supported the Eleventh Corps left, except for one division that occupied Culp's Hill. Osborn selected advantageous ground for his batteries as they arrived, while Buford's cavalry gamely sought to protect the left flank of the First Corps during the retreat. Some of the troops on Cemetery Hill strengthened their lines by constructing breastworks.[95]

The two Union corps had assumed a formidable defensive posture by 5:00 P.M., one which the Confederates chose not to assault. In Carl Schurz's opinion, Ewell and Hill made wise decisions: "[Our] infantry was indeed reduced by . . . one-half its effective force, but all that was left, was good. . . . It is therefore at least doubtful whether they could have easily captured Cemetery Hill before the arrival of . . . reinforcements on our side."[96] Thus did the combat on July 1 conclude with Howard's soldiers holding fast on the crest of Cemetery Hill.

Although fighting had ended, Howard's performance before nightfall inspired further controversy. Meade had learned of Reynolds's death at 1:00 P.M. and immediately sent Maj. Gen. Winfield Scott Hancock, commander of the Second Corps, to take control of the field at Gettysburg. Both Howard and Sickles ranked Hancock, but Meade trusted the brave Pennsylvanian more than his other two subordinates. Moreover, General in Chief Henry W. Halleck had specifically granted Meade the authority to elevate anyone he wished to field command, regardless of seniority. Hancock left Taneytown about 1:30 P.M. and reached Cemetery Hill a little before 4:30 P.M. All sources agree that the soldiers responded enthusiastically to the popular officer's appearance, but what transpired between Howard and Hancock is the subject of historical debate.[97]

Capt. Eminel P. Halstead of Doubleday's staff witnessed Hancock's arrival. Halstead stated that Hancock sought out Howard, who was sitting alone at the time, and declared that Meade had placed him in overall command: "General Howard woke up a little and replied that he was the senior . . . 'I am aware of that, General, but I have written orders in my pocket from General Meade which I will show you if you wish to see them.'" Howard replied that he did not doubt Hancock's word, adding with a certain illogic, "You can give no orders here while I am here." Hancock accepted this arrangement, agreeing to second any order Howard issued rather than debate military protocol in such an emergency. He also told Howard that Meade had instructed him to select the battleground on which the army would make its stand. "But I think this is the strongest position by nature upon which to fight a battle that I ever saw," said Hancock, "and if it meets your approbation I will select this as the battlefield." Howard observed that he also thought "this a very strong position." "Very well, sir, I select this as the battlefield," stated Hancock, who, according to Halstead, "immediately turned away to rectify our lines."[98]

Howard described this incident no fewer than four times in writings spanning a generation. Nowhere did he mention the exchange quoted by Halstead. Instead, Howard characterized Hancock's role as Meade's "temporary chief of staff" and claimed that Hancock reported himself merely as the army commander's representative on the field—although in his official report Howard confessed that Meade had given Hancock orders "while under the impression that he was my senior." Howard asserted that he told Hancock that "this was no time for talking" and instructed him to deploy troops on the left of the Baltimore Pike; Howard himself would place men on the right of the road. "I noticed that he sent Wadsworth's division, without consulting me . . . to Culp's Hill," wrote Howard, "but as it was just the thing to do, I made no objection."[99]

Hancock mentioned nothing of the conversation with Howard in his official report. After the war, Hancock explained that "as soon as I arrived on the field . . . I rode directly to the crest of the hill where General Howard stood, and said to him that I had been sent by General Meade to take command of all the forces present; that I had written orders to that effect with me, and asked him if he wished to read them." "He replied that he did not," concluded Hancock, "but acquiesced in my assumption of command."[100]

Someone's account of this episode is at variance with the truth, and it would appear that Howard had more reason to misrepresent the record than Hancock or the disinterested Halstead.[101] Without doubt, Meade's lack of confidence wounded Howard, as he made clear later that day.

The real issue is not Howard's effort to save face but how the Howard-Hancock controversy affected Union military leadership on Cemetery Hill. Here the verdict is unanimous. Both officers did their utmost to secure the Federal defense; questions of seniority and authority had no effect on the efficiency of Union operations. "Howard, in spite of his heart-sore, co-operated so loyally with Hancock that it would have been hard to tell which of the two was the commander and which the subordinate," testified Schurz.[102] What pettiness Howard displayed came primarily from his pen after the war rather than on the battlefield itself.

As the sun disappeared behind Seminary Ridge and South Mountain, Howard received Meade's written orders relieving him of command, presumably the same orders Hancock carried in his pocket that Howard had declined to examine. Deeply "mortified" by this directive, Howard asked Hancock to tell Meade that he had discharged his duties faithfully. At the same time, he officially turned the command over to Slocum, the de facto senior officer, who finally had arrived on Cemetery Hill. Howard expressed his evaluation of the day's fighting in a heartfelt dispatch to Meade later that night:

I believe I have handled these two corps to-day from a little past 11 until 4, when General H[ancock] assisted me in carrying out orders which I had already issued, as well as any of your corps commanders could have done. . . . [Our] position was not a good one, because both flanks were exposed, and a heavy force approaching from the northern roads rendered it untenable, being already turned, so that I was forced to retire the command to the position now occupied, which I regard as a very strong one. The above has mortified me and will disgrace me. Please inform me frankly if you disapprove of my conduct to-day, that I may know what to do.[103]

The distracted general received an indication of Meade's opinion before dawn on July 2 when the two men and some staff officers examined the army's dispositions south of town. "Well, Howard," asked the army commander, "what do you think; is this the place to fight the battle?" Howard naturally replied that he regarded the position he had chosen as the strongest available. "I am glad to hear you say so," agreed Meade, "for I have already ordered the other corps to concentrate here and it is too late to change."[104]

That night Howard and a few of his staff slept in the gatekeeper's house at the cemetery. What remained of the Eleventh Corps bedded down among the graves, wrapped in their blankets. "There was a profound stillness in the graveyard," remembered Schurz, "broken by no sound but the breathing of the men . . . the tramp of a horse's foot; and sullen rumblings mysteriously floating on the air from a distance all around."[105]

So ended another bloody day of combat for the Eleventh Corps and its leaders, the second in less than two months in which the corps had been driven from a battlefield. Writers for generations would point to May 2 and July 1, 1863, as twin disgraces for a unit deemed to be the weakest in the Army of the Potomac. Is this image deserved? Does the caricature of General Schimmelfennig hiding in a filthy hog's hovel until all danger had passed typify a cowardice and incompetence of the corps as a whole?

Casualty figures suggest otherwise. The Eleventh Corps lost roughly 2,900 men on July 1, and the number of prisoners exceeded killed and wounded in only four regiments in the First and Third divisions.[106] Confederate fire felled every regimental commander in Krzyzanowski's brigade. The 82d Ohio lost 150 of its 258 men; fifteen minutes of savage fighting cost the 75th Pennsylvania more than half its strength. John Gordon called the Federal performance on July 1 "a most obstinate resistance," and a veteran of the 157th New York proclaimed after the war that when any "person brands the Eleventh Corps as a corps of cowards, he is falsifying the record."[107]

Francis Barlow leveled the harshest criticism against the corps in the days following the battle. "These Dutch won't fight," he told a friend in August. "Their officers say so & they say so themselves & they ruin all with whom they come in contact." On July 7, Barlow assured his mother, "This is the last of my connection with the division. . . . I would take a brigade in preference to such a division." Barlow may have revealed a jaundiced perspective in his evaluation when he added, "Except among those on our side who are fighting this war upon anti-slavery grounds, there is not much earnestness nor are there many noble feelings and sentiments involved."[108] Barlow's ill-advised occupation of the knoll that now bears his name lends irony to his fault-finding.

Modern students of the battle point out that the Eleventh Corps suffered 50 percent casualties among its units engaged while inflicting only 14 percent casualties on its opponent.[109] But such statistics do not necessarily demonstrate that the Federals fought less courageously than the soldiers of Ewell's corps. The discrepancy may be explained by the patently hopeless Union position on the afternoon of July 1. This last premise, in turn, raises a different question. If the Eleventh Corps had a forlorn mission on the first day at Gettysburg, could its leadership have done anything to ameliorate the situation?

Apart from Barlow's tactical blunder, an analysis of Eleventh Corps generalship on July 1 boils down to an evaluation of O. O. Howard. Howard wrote his wife on July 16 that at "Gettysburg I am awarded much credit & fear that this excess of praise will excite the unkind criticisms of some of my brother officers." As he predicted, articles soon appeared that took him to task for various indiscretions on the first day's field. A soldier from the 25th Ohio reflected the tenor of the denunciations: "I always blamed Howard for that day's work as well as for our defeat at Chancellorsville, and he ought to be praying today for forgiveness for the lives he sacrificed in these two battles, instead of being a preacher and holding a Major-General's commission." Nevertheless, Congress passed a resolution of thanks dated January 28, 1864, praising Howard for his role in selecting the Union position at Gettysburg.[110]

What conclusions should be drawn regarding Howard's leadership on July 1? Events during the next two days vindicated his choice of the Cemetery Hill–Culp's Hill–Cemetery Ridge line as the Union strong point. "Howard fought the first day's battle from the time Reynolds fell to its close," wrote his brother, "with the purpose and plan of securing Cemetery Ridge as the military position from which the great battle with the whole army should be fought."[111]

Howard's tactical execution is a thornier matter. Writers assail him for locating his headquarters on Cemetery Hill, where his view of the battlefield would be obscured; for declining to withdraw Doubleday's corps to Seminary Ridge during the midday lull in the fighting; for failing to erect extensive breastworks along the Union line; and for neglecting to designate specific routes of march through Gettysburg to eliminate confusion during the retreat. Howard's critics insist that he exercised little tactical control over the battle after the initial deployment, allowed both flanks of the Eleventh Corps to hang suspended in the air, and delayed the advance of von Steinwehr's division north of town until it was too late to stem the Confederate tide.[112]

This impressive list of particulars possesses some merit. A more compact defensive position west and north of Gettysburg would have stood up better to Confederate assaults. Howard's notion of occupying Oak Hill would have strengthened Doubleday's right immeasurably had Rodes not already held that high ground, but it would not have secured the Carlisle and Harrisburg road corridors along which Jubal A. Early's division approached the field. During his early afternoon inspection of the Eleventh Corps, Howard should have eliminated the gap between Schimmelfennig's and Robinson's divisions at the hinge of the Eleventh and First corps. He might have acted on Schurz's suggestion that von Steinwehr advance a brigade in support of Barlow before Gordon launched his attack, but von Steinwehr's entire command could not have redeemed the situation after the First Division went forward to Blocher's Knoll. Finally, though circumstances dictated a certain degree of confusion in Gettysburg during the Federal retreat, Howard must bear partial responsibility for the disastrous flight through town that resulted in so many Union prisoners.

Would correction of all these tactical oversights have enabled the Army of the Potomac to hold off the Confederates and conduct an orderly withdrawal through Gettysburg after dark? Few historians think so. But because the Union defense on July 1 contributed to the enemy's inability to occupy key ground south of town, Howard did succeed in achieving his overall objective.[113]

Better generalship might have reduced casualties in the Eleventh Corps, especially the number of missing and captured. Some writers suggest that Howard could have accomplished this by retreating earlier to Cemetery Hill, yet such a maneuver might have cost the Federals their final position. As Carl Schurz asked, "Would not the enemy, if we had retreated . . . even one hour earlier, have been in better condition, and therefore more encouraged to make a determined attack upon the cemetery that afternoon,— and with a better chance of success?" Howard himself summed up the first day's fighting by saying that his troops "did wonders: held the vast army of General Lee in check all day; took up a strong position; fought themselves into it, and kept it for the approaching army of the Potomac to occupy with them, so as to meet the foe with better prospects of victory."[114]

The Eleventh Corps performed with honor on July 1, 1863, and deserves a better reputation. Its soldiers, recovered from the reversals if not the recriminations of Chancellorsville, contributed materially to eventual Northern victory at Gettysburg. Except for the personally courageous Barlow's egregious tactical error, brigade and division commanders, including the maligned Alexander Schimmelfennig, handled their units with skill and gallantry. Although he was in charge of the entire field during most of the day, Oliver Otis Howard's performance remains central to an analysis of Eleventh Corps leadership. Hancock, Slocum, and Meade all endorsed Howard's strategic view of the battle and his choice of ground. Howard's tactical leadership in executing his policy of delay may have been flawed, but no one can gainsay his pivotal contribution to the three-day struggle.

Three Confederate Disasters on Oak Ridge

Failures of Brigade Leadership on the First Day at Gettysburg

Robert K. Krick

ANY LISTING OF THE MOST VICTORIOUS DAYS IN THE tactical annals of the Army of Northern Virginia must include May 2, 1863, and several days at the end of August 1862. Fredericksburg leaps to mind as a thoroughly triumphant day, but the simplicity and ease of General Ambrose E. Burnside's destruction leaves little room for talk of Confederate prowess. Gettysburg hardly stands high on any register of Southern successes—but July 1, 1863, taken alone, was unquestionably one of the best days Lee's army ever enjoyed. Late that afternoon, as Federals scampered through the town in desperate flight, leaving thousands of casualties behind and losing thousands more as prisoners, their prospects were bleak indeed. Some forty hours later the Northern army would be able to claim an immensely important victory that forever dimmed the memory of the Confederate triumph on July 1.

The newly reorganized Army of Northern Virginia that approached Gettysburg at the end of June 1863 seemed an unlikely candidate for quick and sweeping conquests. It had unbounded confidence in its commander, and it rode the momentum imparted by familiarity with success; but it also had a disturbingly large increment of leaders new to their posts and units new to the army—and it did not have the mighty arm of "Stonewall" Jackson to execute Lee's designs. As fate would have it, the entire command structure of the army component that opened the battle was new to its role:

A. P. Hill was in his first combat day as corps commander; Henry Heth in his first battle as division commander; and Joseph R. Davis in his first battle as brigade commander.

Under the circumstances, it is not cause for astonishment that four Confederate brigades suffered dreadful disasters west of Gettysburg on July 1. Three of them came to grief within a small piece of Oak Ridge north of the Chambersburg Pike. Their troubles, which displayed an unhappy mixture of poor leadership, inexperience, and bad luck, serve as a case study of failure in the midst of victory. The remarkable part of the story is that even in the face of the three fiascoes on Oak Ridge, Lee's great victory ultimately developed in that sector of the field. Not surprisingly, the eventual victory was compounded of good leadership, experience, and good luck.

Although he could not have foreseen the trend, Gettysburg was the first of many campaigns in which Lee would find himself obliged to exert an ever-stronger personal control on events at the corps and even the division level. Nearly a year later, in May 1864, deterioration in his support would leave Lee with the virtually impossible task not only of directing the army but also literally commanding each of its three corps in person. As July 1863 dawned, however, Lee doubtless presumed that he would be able to continue, at least to a degree, the laissez-faire form of army command that had proved so spectacularly successful in the Jackson era.

Lee faced his increased burdens at Gettysburg in his worst physical condition of the war. Though now in his fifty-seventh year, the army commander was accustomed to bringing phenomenal endurance to his tasks. That spring, however, an attack had floored Lee so thoroughly that it caused concern around headquarters. Whether or not that ailment was—as has been conjectured—the onset of the angina pectoris that ultimately contributed to his death, he had recovered from the episode by mid-April.[1] No evidence of any affliction hampered Lee at Chancellorsville, and the next notable onset of his visceral discomfort that is of record occurred during the fall of 1863. At Gettysburg, though, the general suffered from a debilitating attack of intestinal upset that certainly impaired his strength and probably reduced his ability to bear the added load that befell him. The oft-quoted source for information about Lee's famous and ill-timed malady was a member of "Jeb" Stuart's staff who could not have seen the army commander until late on the second day at Gettysburg, so whether he was afflicted by July 1 remains uncertain. A Louisiana staff officer reported the etiology of Lee's malady as an overdose of "old Virginia flapjacks. . . . Thin as a wafer and big nearly as a cart wheel . . . served hot with fresh butter and maple molasses and folded and folded, layers thick."[2]

Maj. Gen. Henry Heth.
From Miller's *Photographic History* 10:109.

Lee's stalwart right arm near the scene of the opening engagement on Oak Ridge should have been the commander of his new Third Corps, Ambrose Powell Hill. The newly minted lieutenant general had just finished a year as the leader of a splendid division with a solid record. Hill would be mysteriously invisible at Gettysburg and would prove a disappointment as a corps commander, but on July 1 there seemed ample reason to trust him. The unbridled aggressive spirit that had made Hill and his division a terror to the enemy while they were in the employ of Stonewall Jackson did not suit his new role so well. James Johnston Pettigrew's brigade of Heth's division had ventured toward Gettysburg on the last day of June and run afoul of John Buford's seasoned Federal cavalry. When Hill expressed his intention to repeat the process on July 1, Pettigrew sent a member of his staff who had served under Hill around Richmond to warn the corps commander to be prepared for opposition, thinking that the familiar face "might have some weight with him." Hill told his former subordinate that he "could not believe that any portion of the Army of the Potomac was up; and, in emphatic words, expressed the hope that it was, as this was the place we wanted it to be."[3] In that incautious spirit, Hill launched Henry Heth's division down the Chambersburg Pike and into the battle at Gettysburg.

As Henry Heth led the movement to Gettysburg with his division, he faced a number of new challenges. Although he had commanded A. P Hill's division for a time at Chancellorsville because of wounds suffered by his superiors, Heth had been a major general only since late May and this was his first real experience as division commander. He had come to the army quite recently bearing the clear imprimatur of R. E. Lee, who, Heth wrote, "has always been my personal friend."[4]

During February 1863, Lee and Stonewall Jackson exchanged correspondence about criteria for promotion, with Jackson eager to use some judicious weighting on behalf of officers who had fought successfully with him for a long time. Lee rejected that notion firmly, saying that merit alone must apply without any hint of credit for propinquity. General Heth deserved a brigade, and Lee wanted to give him one under Jackson. The lieutenant general eventually acquiesced gracefully in the face of higher authority and wrote hopefully to Lee: "From what you have said respecting General Heth, I have been desirous that he should report for duty."[5]

A strong tradition that reveals Lee's high regard for Heth states that the young officer was the only one of his generals—some two hundred of them, first and last—"whom Lee called by his first name." The army commander's regard cannot have been based on any substantive achievements by Heth, whose antebellum career and war experiences had been similarly unremarkable. Conventional wisdom suggested that Heth was an officer dogged by bad luck.[6]

Before he fell prey to bad Civil War luck, Heth had suffered the stigmata of honestly earned bad grades at the United States Military Academy. During his first year at West Point, the young Virginian somehow managed to finish ahead of seven of his forty-five passing comrades. The next year he plummeted to dead last in his class, however, and he clung tenaciously to that rung all the way to graduation. Heth's thirty-seven classmates who graduated ahead of him in 1847 included close friends A. P. Hill, who ranked fifteenth, and Ambrose E. Burnside, who ranked eighteenth. In conduct—which was rated across all four classes—Heth stood 198th out of 218 cadets; Burnside's demerit total was even worse and Hill's barely better.[7]

The young army officer's prewar experience in the old army was as generally quiet as that of hundreds of other West Point graduates in the peacetime establishment. He performed credibly in an 1855 fight with Sioux Indians but enjoyed particular distinction because of his interest in marksmanship systems for both muskets and rifles. While the army and most of its leaders ignored the need for accuracy with shoulder arms and some officers even ridiculed the concept as corrupting the principles of volley firing, Henry Heth methodically translated French marksmanship texts and gathered information on the most successful systems. The War Department eventually accepted the manual that Heth had prepared, and it was published in 1858. The author included a self-deprecating introduction insisting that he could claim no credit for anything new, offering only "a digest of what has already been practised." The U.S. War Department did Heth the honor of reprinting the manual in 1862, identical down to cover color and illustration—but, of course, wiping the Rebel's name off the cover and substituting Edwin M. Stanton's suitably patriotic name on an inner page as sponsor.[8]

For most of the war's first two years Heth served in western Virginia. The same tangled mountain terrain and shifting loyalties that had bedeviled R. E. Lee in that region in 1861 frustrated most of Heth's efforts. Confederates in the mountains hoped for great things from the professional soldier sent to lead them and suffered proportionate dismay when affairs continued to be uneasy and confused. On May 23, 1862—the same day that Stonewall Jackson was winning a famous victory in the Shenandoah Valley—Heth launched a surprise attack on Federals under George Crook at Lewisburg. The raw Confederate troops could not execute the apparently sound plan their general put into operation, and they suffered a bitter defeat in consequence. A century later one historian wrote that in that region, "even today you can find people who blame him for the failure to recapture the town." A young girl who lived in Lewisburg at the time recorded with wry amusement the general's fall from grace in local eyes: "Up to this time my father had been much struck with General Heth's resemblance to Napoleon, but after this affair we heard no more of this fancied resemblance. General Heth was [now] short, rotund, and square-faced."[9]

None of this cooled support for Heth from R. E. Lee and Jefferson Davis, although a wary Confederate Senate rejected the president's nomination of Heth for rank of major general during the fall of 1862. When the disgruntled brigadier joined the famed Army of Northern Virginia early in 1863, he must have hoped that this new arena would offer a fresh set of opportunities. His arrival cannot have pleased his peers in brigade command in the excellent division commanded by A. P. Hill because Heth outranked all of them, including such seasoned and successful men as J. J. Archer and W. Dorsey Pender. In Hill's absence, the strange newcomer would take command over the able veterans; that circumstance developed during the next battle under difficult conditions.

There is no strong evidence that Heth either embarrassed or distinguished himself when catapulted to division command vice Hill at Chancellorsville. Several of the division's brigades led the way on May 3, but they accomplished what they did without clear indications of the temporary division commander's hand on the helm. Later in the month, with the army turned upside down for reorganization because of Jackson's death, Heth stood in line to take over a division because his rank as brigadier was markedly senior. Since Hill had earned promotion to corps command, his oversized division was an obvious choice for gerrymandering into a new configuration. The six brigades and two others new to the army became two divisions when split in half.

Not surprisingly, Heth's half consisted of the two new brigades (Pettigrew's and Joseph R. Davis's) and the two veteran brigades (Archer's and John M. Brockenbrough's) that had—and still have today—the least distinguished reputations among Hill's original six. Pender's new division would contain Hill's four best brigades, which had fought shoulder-to-shoulder through a spectacularly successful year of victories. Although he must have recognized that it compounded his difficult adjustment, Heth, as the outsider, can hardly have grumbled at this arrangement. Everyone knew that Archer could not serve under Pender, whom he loathed. At Fredericksburg, one of Archer's colonels had been with Pender when a bullet hit the North Carolinian in the hand. After he questioned his colonel about the incident, Archer sputtered nastily, "I wish they had shot him in his damn head." In narrating the incident the colonel added, entirely unnecessarily, "He didn't like him."[10]

As the brand-new division commander advanced his uneven brigades toward Gettysburg on July 1, Archer wound up in the front line just south of the Chambersburg Pike while Davis moved to Archer's left and just north of the pike. Heth's orders were simply "to feel the enemy." As the two brigades pushed across Willoughby Run to open the battle, neither quite knowing where they were going, both of them ran into serious difficulty. Because his field of battle lay south of the road, Archer's disaster falls outside the immediate scope of this study. To summarize Archer's nearby misfortune, he surged forward into an untenable situation without adequate reconnaissance (if any at all) and found Federals in great strength and in advantageous position. One of Archer's Alabamians captured near him expressed the situation vividly when he wrote that suddenly "there were 20,000 Yanks down in among us hollowing surrender." The unfortunate Archer was the first general officer ever taken prisoner from Lee's army. The general and his men stumbled under guard through Gettysburg, a "little town full of red headed women that were bulldozing and cursing us." His captors marched Archer so mercilessly that he "fainted and fell by the roadside." The effects of captivity on the general left him so weak that

Brig. Gen. Joseph Robert
Davis. From Miller's
Photographic History 10:277.

he died in October 1864 not long after being exchanged to return to Virginia. Although Archer could not have known of the event until long after it occurred, it was the division of his bête noir, Dorsey Pender, that finally swept victorious through the bottom of Willoughby Run that had been so troublesome at the outset of the battle.[11]

Joseph R. Davis led his mixed Mississippi–North Carolina brigade into battle on Archer's left with even less experience to his credit as a commander in combat than Heth had. His promotion to the rank of brigadier general seems to be as unadulterated an instance of nepotism as the record of the Confederacy offers. Joe Davis's uncle was president of the Confederate States; there seemed little else to commend him (if indeed the relationship deserved commendation). The promotion to brigadier general might be unparalleled in the annals of such things because it shows the tightest imaginable grouping of dates, which usually stretched over many months. Davis was promoted on October 8, 1862, to rank from September 15; won confirmation on the date of promotion on October 8; and accepted on November 1. That unusual sequence probably reflects the political nature of the transaction at a time when the president still had some clout to use. The army found Joe Davis to be "a very unpretending and pleasant gentleman," despite his connections.[12]

No one serving on Joe Davis's staff showed strong signs of having the background, experience, and ability that might help the brigadier meet his responsibilities. The staff member with the most tenure, in fact, suffered from a reputation so bad in both Civil War armies that Gen. Zachary Taylor's grandson (a Federal) thought that "he ought to be kicked out of the Confederacy." Jeb Stuart suggested that the staff officer—thirty-seven-year-old William Thomas Magruder—should have his commission revoked. Stuart encouraged G. W. C. Lee, Jefferson Davis's aide, "to lay this matter before the Prest."[13]

The nine field officers who led the brigade's regiments were similarly bereft of background and skills needed to help Davis cope with the coming battle. Only one of the nine men claimed professional military education or experience before the war (and that one colonel had gone to the U.S. Naval Academy, which of course did not have much to do with infantry training). The three field officers of the 42d Mississippi at Gettysburg, for instance, were a physician, a judge, and a saddler. The colonel commanding the 2d Mississippi admitted after the war to General Davis with refreshing honesty that one of his "most serious difficulties" was that "I almost always lost my bearings."[14]

Davis also came to battle minus one-fourth of his strength because one of his regiments, the 11th Mississippi, had been left behind to guard the division's trains. The 11th would be particularly missed because it was one of two regiments in the brigade with experience in Lee's army. The absence of that unit probably affected the brigade's fate dramatically. The sudden, almost bizarre, turn of events that boxed the brigade in an unusual terrain feature might well have been overcome with a line one-third longer. That raises the question, Why did Heth send forward his weakest brigade as the leading element north of the pike? The answer remains conjectural, but presumably he simply uncoiled the division in the manner it had marched.[15] The order of march traditionally rotated daily, or at least regularly, to spread out the privileges and disadvantages of marching first or eating dust and dodging road debris. Whatever his reasons, if any, Heth made a bad choice when he sent Davis's understrength brigade off to open the battle.

Joe Davis deployed his scant three regiments north of the pike and perpendicular to it—the 2d Mississippi, the 42d Mississippi, and the 55th North Carolina. By this stage of the war, Southern brigades with units from more than one state were decidedly anomalous. By coincidence, Archer's nearby command was the only other mixed brigade out of thirteen in the Third Corps. (The other two infantry corps had just one mixed brigade each.) This Confederate homogeneity by state, which was by no means the

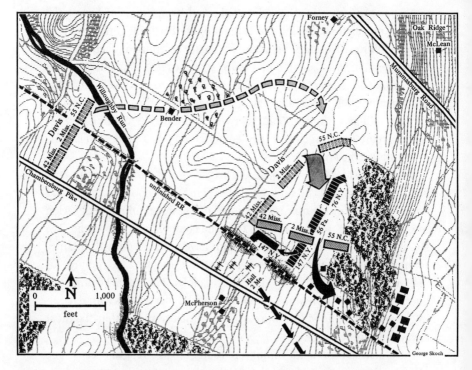

Assault of Davis's Brigade, July 1

rule in the Federal army, was one of Jefferson Davis's organizational fe-
tishes. Finding his handpicked nephew-brigadier in command of one of
the very few exceptions to the presidential rule is surprising.

By about 10:30 A.M., General Davis had formed his line of battle on the
eastern slopes of Herr Ridge, just west of Willoughby Run. He put his
North Carolinians on the left, with their left extended about twelve hundred
feet north of the pike. The 2d Mississippi formed battle line to the right
of the 55th North Carolina, and the 42d Mississippi prepared to advance
on the brigade right, with its flank right on the pike.[16] Perhaps Davis positioned the 2d Mississippi in the middle to provide a leavening of experience
to the new regiments on either side. The 2d and the unfortunately absent
11th had served with distinction in Evander M. Law's brigade before they
fell victim to the shuffling demanded by Joe Davis's uncle in the interest of
tidy tables of organization. The 2d had spent the entire preceding night on
picket so the men can hardly have been fresh and ready.[17] Poor Davis deserved the chance to start this day in reserve, but Heth directed otherwise.

The 55th North Carolina began the advance with its left touching the run,
so it faced the chore of getting through the wet bottom almost at once. The

two Mississippi regiments soon crossed too, though the course of the run put it farther to their front. Their comrades under Archer across the pike had found the run thick with both nettles and armed foemen, but if Davis's men experienced any difficulty none of them reported it. Almost at once the 55th began to swing out leftward in an arc that took it farther north as well as east, past the Bender house and into the adjacent orchard. The left of the 2d Mississippi also stretched into the edge of the orchard. After the war the colonel commanding the 55th returned to the field and showed the battlefield's leading contemporary historian, John B. Bachelder, exactly where his regiment had passed through the northeast corner of Bender's orchard. Emmor B. Cope, a surveyor and mapper who became famous for his work at both Gettysburg and Sharpsburg, marked the spot, which proved to be fully two thousand feet from the pike.[18] The leftward drift of the 55th would turn out to be tactically advantageous, but loosening the line by eight hundred feet during a short advance gave evidence of some uncertainty, and two thousand feet was an extremely broad front for three regiments to cover.

Because of the nature of the ground and its leftward loop, the 55th North Carolina drew the first fire from the Federals, who were themselves newly arrived on the field. The initial round struck two men of the 55th's color guard, as though in forecast of a day in which the men around the colors would suffer even more heavily than was customary. The 2d Mississippi, to the 55th's right, could see the Federal line at the far edge of the broad field of wheat. "They were in the wheat . . . lying down, though plainly seen," one of the Mississippians wrote, "while their officers rode up and down their lines." The 42d, down next to the pike, reached the diagonal path of the run after the other two regiments. "The enemy's skirmish line was posted along this brooklet, and we soon began to hear the peculiar hiss of the minnie ball," a soldier of the 42d recalled.[19] The advancing Confederates, all under fire and with their target in view, gathered momentum as they swept through the wheat on their broad front.

The distance from Davis's line of departure to the hurriedly formed Federal line measured about one thousand yards. The Federals preparing to receive them included three regiments, from north to south the 76th New York, 56th Pennsylvania, and 147th New York. Given the pronounced advantage of the defensive and the inexperience of most of the Confederates, three Federal regiments ought to have been able to repulse three attacking regiments without inordinate strain. In the event, however, Davis's brigade swept its foe off the ridge and won what seemed for a time to be a crucial victory to open the fighting in that sector.

Davis's surprising initial success was by no means easily achieved. The 2d Mississippi moved steadily "up the slope to within good shot of their line," when the Federals "jumped to their feet" out of the wheat and opened fire. The 42d "advanced steadily and rapidly up the hill" but only by braving a fire that rapidly sent two score of its men back with wounds to a forward hospital set up under some trees near Willoughby Run. The stalwart advance of those two regiments could hardly have produced any positive results, however, without the 55th North Carolina's fortunate positioning on the far left. As the regimental historian noted: "The left of our regiment extended considerably beyond the right of the enemy's line—and at the proper time our left was wheeled to the right. The enemy fled from the field with great loss."[20] The extended left of the 55th, a circumstance more than likely coincidental rather than designed, decided the result of the engagement.

The color guard of the 55th, which had suffered the loss of first blood at long range, drew more fire as it closed with the 76th New York. The sergeant carrying the flag went down about one hundred yards from the New Yorkers' line and Col. John Kerr Connally grabbed the falling flag. Connally—the erstwhile Naval Academy sailor—had provoked Gen. W. Dorsey Pender's unequivocal wrath earlier in the war, prompting the North Carolina general to call the colonel "very ridiculous . . . a most conceited fellow." On this July morning, Colonel Connally performed under fire up to any standard that Pender or anyone else could desire. As he waved aloft his unit's flag and wheeled it around to the right in the pivotal tactical maneuver, the colonel fell severely wounded in two places. Major Alfred H. Belo rushed over to the fallen regimental commander and asked anxiously if Connally was badly wounded. "Yes," the colonel answered through his pain, "but do not pay any attention to me; take the colors and keep ahead of the Mississippians." Connally fell 315 feet from where the 76th New York monument now stands, at a point in the southwestern corner of the modern battlefield tour road.[21]

Although the 55th's sweeping wheel determined the result, keeping ahead of the Mississippians would take some doing. Lt. A. K. Roberts of the 2d led a dash forward near the seam between the two Mississippi regiments that broke into the 56th Pennsylvania's front and captured a flag, at the cost of the lieutenant's life. As the Federal line came unhinged and streamed away to its left rear, the Mississippians swarmed into their midst and took about three hundred prisoners. The 42d, from its position closest to the focus of the retreat, netted the largest haul. Some men of the 2d thought they saw cavalry in the woods behind the Northern position and fired a volley that knocked down several men and horses; they later decided that they had fired on mounted officers and their staff members.[22]

The Confederate success and the Federal collapse did not unfold evenly, of course. Knots of Federals continued to make what Davis called "a stubborn resistance," and a substantial number (mainly of the 147th New York) rallied on the Confederate right near an unfinished railroad that soon would bring grief to the Southerners. Northern gunners of Hall's 2d Maine Battery, firing from just beyond the railroad line, contributed valiantly to the efforts to delay Davis's victorious troops. Some Federal infantry also mustered a brief threat to what was now the left rear of the Confederate line, after it had swung toward the railroad.[23]

Even as Davis and his regiments were enjoying the delirium of a sweeping and well-earned victory, the instruments of their destruction were gathering in a random grouping just across the pike. The 6th Wisconsin of the famed Iron Brigade had angled northwestward toward the pike, diverging from its sister regiments as they headed approximately due west well south of the pike. The two northernmost regiments (84th and 95th New York) of the force that had been facing Archer also began to move toward what obviously was a threatened point. The two New York regiments had not been much involved in Archer's easy repulse; had the Southern attack south of the pike been better managed, the 84th and 95th would not have had the leisure to figure in Davis's sector.

The completion of the Confederate reorientation through ninety degrees, from an advance due east to a facing of due south, came about according to one North Carolinian in response to the sight of the Wisconsin regiment moving across the fields toward the pike. The 147th New York viewed the Wisconsin men as their saviors, which confirms the close timing. Many other Southerners probably faced toward the Maine battery position. While some of the Mississippians and Carolinians had advanced beyond the railroad and others had not, that commanding feature soon lured them like a malignant magnet into its deceptively protective shelter. Joe Davis had neither the experience nor the grasp to recognize this deadfall for what it was. Col. John M. Stone, commanding the 2d Mississippi, wrote to Davis after the war about the events of this day and included with unconscious irony one of the general's favorite stories about the difficulty of achieving a large perspective in battle: "General, I was very much like the French Soldier of whom you sometimes told us, who never saw anything while the battle was going on except the rump of his fat file leader. In battle I rarely knew anything that occured beyond the immediate vicinity of my own command." That honest admission of a universal combat truth doubtless applied to the original storyteller, Joe Davis, in the chaotic moments when his men clustered in a deep cut of the railroad line, binding themselves up in sheaves for delivery to Northern prison camps.[24]

The railroad line ran through the countryside west of Gettysburg on a mixture of grades and cuts resulting from the usual engineering efforts to flatten the route. As was the case with several other unfinished lines made famous by the Civil War (at Second Manassas, Chancellorsville, and the Wilderness, for instance), the nascent railroad industry had accomplished much of its work but had not quite gotten into operation when the war interrupted such civilian endeavor. The unfinished line west of Gettysburg, in the words of a Carolinian under Davis, "had been graded but not ironed." A very deep and steeply walled cut that proved Davis's undoing was not very long, west to east, and could have been readily avoided with a modicum of intelligent leadership. As the Confederates flocked into the cut, the 42d Mississippi on the right and some of the 2d Mississippi found its illusory deep shelter. The color guard of the 2d, though, was far enough east that "the ditch was not more than two feet deep" and thus formed ideal shelter without restricting movement or firing positions. The entire 55th North Carolina on the left (east) of the position was free from the hampering aspect of the deep cut. A carefully surveyed stake placed after the war at the eastern end of the Carolinians' line was 109 yards from the center of the bridge over the cut.[25]

The three Southern regiments at the railroad line suffered from the disorganization inherent in victory nearly as much as in defeat. They had covered a long distance under fire and stress and were, Davis reported, "all much exhausted by the excessive heat." An alarming number of their regimental leaders had gone down wounded or killed. Seven of the nine field officers would be casualties by noon. Although it is impossible to time each of those losses, many of them had fallen before the crisis at the railroad. The 55th, for instance, had already lost not only Colonel Connally opposite the 76th New York but also its lieutenant colonel, Maurice Thompson Smith. Smith, a thirty-five-year-old planter educated at Chapel Hill, suffered a mortal wound while beyond the railroad. The commander of the 2d Mississippi had been shot off the top rail of a fence as he climbed over.[26] Disorganization spawned by movement and victory, by exhaustion, and by loss of command and control through regimental leadership all contributed to the disaster stalking Davis, but none of them mattered as much as the dreadful limitations of the railroad cut position.

The Federals opposite Davis—especially the 6th Wisconsin and its stalwart commander, Lt. Col. Rufus R. Dawes—soon launched an attack, the valor of which made possible a victory that reaped the opportunities presented by the railroad cut. Three Northern regiments faced two hundred yards of naked turf, interrupted only by fences that help set up men climbing over them as slow-moving targets. From west to east the Federal attackers included the 84th New York, the 95th New York, and the 6th Wisconsin. From west to east the Confederates faced them with the 42d Mississippi, 2d Mississippi, and 55th North Carolina. The alignment was not as crisp as that enumeration suggests, of course.

As Dawes pushed his men through swarms of bullets toward the railroad, the two New York regiments closed on his left and somewhat behind him. The appearance of a nicely coordinated attack was misleading; cooperation was all but accidental at the outset. One of Dawes's aides had the good idea of sending a fifty-man detachment out to the east to close that route of escape from the cut to the Confederates and put his notion into operation without any delay during the attack across the deadly field.[27]

The Northerners lost heavily in the attack, but a considerable part of the line that they approached was all but silent because the deep part of the cut left its defenders unable to see out and fire at their assailants. Much later that day another Confederate brigade occupied the same line (in enough strength to stretch wide beyond the cut so it came to no grief), and one of its men described vividly the difficulties of firing from the deep point toward the field and its fences:

Taking up a musket, I managed with difficulty to crawl to the top of the embankment, and saw the enemy drawn up in line . . . behind an old Virginia worm fence. They soon began to advance, but with no alacrity for the work. Seeing a field officer in front, urging them on whilst waving his hat, the thought occurred that his loss might be of considerable advantage to us in checking the advance. He fell on the instant . . . and letting myself aloose at the top, [I only] recovered an upright position at the bottom, but in a dilapidated plight. A jutting root or jagged rock caught in my breeches' leg and tore it from the bottom, to the top, losing [my] hat also in the fall.[28]

Enough Southern muskets east of the cut could bear on the Wisconsin men to hit them hard, but they crossed the interval in the face of their losses and struck the Confederates in a brief flurry of hand-to-hand fighting. G.W. Bynum of the 2d Mississippi "was so close on the enemy when wounded that the paper attached to the . . . cartridge was forced into his leg." The color guard of that regiment "were all killed and wounded in less than five minutes"; more than a dozen bullets perforated their flag, and the staff was hit and splintered two or three times. A squad of blue-clad

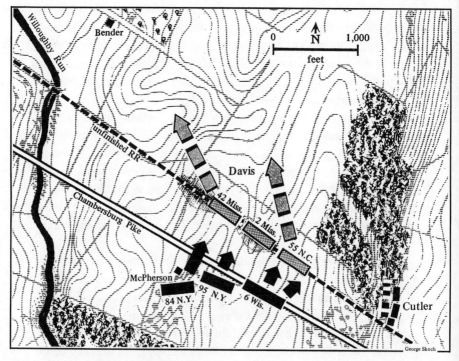

Bender

Willoughby Run

unfinished RR

0   N   1,000
feet

Davis

Chambersburg Pike

42 Miss.

2 Miss.

55 N.C.

McPherson

84 N.Y.   95 N.Y.   6 Wis.

Cutler

George Skoch

Repulse of Davis's Brigade, July 1

enemies closed on the Mississippi colors, but a volley knocked them all down. More came behind them. A lieutenant reaching for the trophy collapsed with a bullet in the shoulder. One Mississippian killed a Wisconsin soldier, then fell to a rifle butt wielded by another attacker. After a dozen Northerners had been shot down, a large soldier gathered up both the flag and its last defender, who had torn the colors from the splintered staff.[29]

Federals coming up opposite the 55th North Carolina saw Maj. Alfred H. Belo—a particularly feisty officer who fought a famous wartime duel against the Confederate Englishman John Cussons—and identified him as the soul of the defense in that sector. A Federal officer hurled his sword like a javelin at Belo, missing the major but striking a man behind him. The swordless Northerner shouted, "Kill that officer, and that will end it," but Confederate rifles silenced him instead.[30] Farther west, where the cut was a deep deathtrap, the attackers quickly ended the fighting when they lined the southern lip of the chasm and pointed their weapons down into it. The blocking force of Northerners sent to the east end of the cut added to the scope of the Confederate disaster, although apparently this cork in Davis's bottle slipped into place west of most of the North Carolinians, who streamed north unhampered by the level railroad grade there.

Davis had lost perhaps 600 men, and the Federal forces that faced him in both halves of his battle lost about 850. The first phase of the fight north of the pike had produced a striking success for Davis that turned quickly into a bitter disaster. As an extended lull settled on the field, masses of Federal prisoners moved westward and about the same number of Confederate prisoners were herded eastward. One unwounded Mississippian seethed for the rest of his life about his treatment as a prisoner. One of the guards "punched me in the side," he grumbled, and made the luckless Confederate give up "the finest field glasses that I ever saw." Thirty-seven years later on the anniversary of the battle the robbed prisoner still cherished a fantasy: "I would like very much to meet up with him now." A wounded Confederate who remained on the field until July 5 had better luck with his captors. Within thirty minutes after Lee's rear guard passed, Union cavalry came past the railroad cut with the task of smashing abandoned Confederate weapons. A Federal picked up a rifle next to the wounded man by its muzzle, raised it high over his head, and smashed it on a nearby rock. The concussion fired the weapon by some freak, and the bullet dropped the Northerner dead on the ground, leaving the wounded prisoner to yearn, "O for a thousand such guns!"[31]

The railroad cut saw more fighting later on July 1, hours after Davis's collapse. Confederates would occupy it and then sweep through the area in triumph. Federals used the railroad line as a corridor of retreat when the day went against them. One of Davis's men watched artillery falling on the retreating foe and thought that "every shell seemed to bring down a dozen men." A North Carolinian who saw the same retreat from the vicinity of the cut thought the Confederate artillery firing down the railroad line was so horribly effective that he "could almost hear their bones crunch under the shot and shell." A Virginian marching down the railroad toward town that evening with Edward Johnson's division—the last military use of the now-famous unfinished railroad—was shocked by the "gruesome sights in the railroad cut," where bodies were torn apart to a degree astonishing even to a veteran.[32]

When Davis's brigade scattered in various directions just after noon on July 1, perhaps the more thoughtful of its leaders began asking the questions that persist to this day. No doubt in the painful aftermath of their ordeal they would have been more inclined to grimace than to smile sadly over the unintentional drollery of General Heth's official summary of the joint disasters that befell Davis and Archer. "The enemy had now been felt," Heth wrote with accidental irony, "and found to be in heavy force in and around Gettysburg."[33]

Several questions that Heth did not address, and that we still cannot answer, stand out starkly under what we must admit is the somewhat unfairly pitiless glare of hindsight. Why was Pender's strong and all-veteran division not at the front for this delicate operation, rather than Heth's weak and largely untested force? If Heth must take the point, why put Davis in the front line instead of Pettigrew's larger brigade, or even Brockenbrough's? It is difficult to imagine the fiasco at the railroad cut developing against a four-regiment front, such as a normal brigade would show: the deadly deep spot in the cut is not that extensive. A line one-third longer than Davis's likely would have lacerated the flanks of the Wisconsin and New York attackers unbearably from the railroad and perhaps even advanced on one flank or the other to make the Federal position entirely untenable.

Where were the Southern division and corps commanders who might have been expected to superintend green commanders and green troops at a critical moment? Heth was far enough to the rear that he had no impact whatsoever on Davis's defeat, and A. P. Hill was nearly ten miles away at Cashtown, totally insulated from the action. By contrast, Hill's Union counterpart, John F. Reynolds, hurried to the front, where he was able to inspirit the defense and throw troops into the decisive zone. Reynolds paid with his life for being in the thick of things, but not before he had done his job successfully. Hill did not do his job at all, and Heth did not do his competently.

After the wrong Confederate troops went into action, without adequate high-level supervision, events raised a surprising new tactical question: Why did three Confederate regiments succeed in a direct attack against three Federal regiments, despite the advantages of the defensive, then succumb—while on the defensive—to an attack by three more Federal regiments? Conventional wisdom would suggest that the defenders would win in both instances and could hardly countenance a complete double reversal of form. Two obvious circumstances help to explain Davis's reverse while defending the cut: the abysmal position where the cut deepened and the cumulative effect of two battles, the second against a fresh set of foes. Two other factors also deserve consideration: good colonels and the advantages of the offensive side in choosing its ground and exploiting momentum. Colonels Connally and Dawes played important roles from opposite sides of the line in Davis's initial success and in his eventual disaster. Removing Connally from the 55th North Carolina and introducing Dawes into the scene at the railroad cut helped tip the scales. Both successful attacking forces had the freedom of the aggressor to choose the setting at the moment of decision, and each did so to good effect. The 55th swung left to make the position of the 76th New York and its companions untenable, and the Federals later corked the end of the railroad cut to good effect. Both successful attackers then sealed their triumph by exploiting momentum that turned into victories greater than the sum of their parts would have suggested.

For an hour after Davis's collapse, the battlefield north of the Chambersburg Pike lay quiet under the midday sun. Then, from the north, Confederates from Richard S. Ewell's Second Corps began to filter into the area. They were the advanced guard of Robert E. Rodes's division, and they represented a stroke of good fortune that would win July 1 for the Army of Northern Virginia. While Federals facing west had soundly rebuffed Heth, Rodes was moving toward their rear on an axis perpendicular to the Federal line of fire. The fortuitous arrival of Rodes and the rest of Ewell's force behind him doomed the Federal position where Archer and Davis had come to grief, despite two further Confederate disasters on the new front some thousand yards northeast of the railroad cut.

Ewell's Second Corps of the Army of Northern Virginia had been brilliantly successful on many fields under the leadership of the late lamented Stonewall Jackson. Although the new corps commander had missed nine extremely active months of the army's history, his return to command had seemed brightly auspicious during the movement north. Ewell had thrashed Federals under Robert H. Milroy at Winchester about as well as Jackson ever had done, and in Stonewall's own Shenandoah Valley, too. On the morning of July 1, Ewell rode with Rodes's division as it moved south toward Gettysburg. The troops that followed them exhibited an élan forged from good leadership and an unbroken string of successes. An experienced Second Corps officer wrote: "One thing is certain: Lee's army was never in better spirits or morale than it exhibited at Gettysburg. It never seemed to me as invincible as on the 1st July 1863."[34]

Robert E. Rodes advanced toward the open flank of the Federal First Corps at Gettysburg facing not only a golden tactical opportunity but also his first battle as a major general commanding a division. At Chancellorsville, Rodes had commanded the same division (it had been D. H. Hill's for the preceding year) as its ranking brigadier general, and with marked success. Now it belonged to him permanently.

Rodes would craft a fine record at the division's head during the fourteen months of life left to him. In fact, he stands among the best division commanders—I think the very best—in an army full of famous units and famous men. Not least among his talents was the ability to inspire subordinates. Young James Power Smith of Jackson's staff wrote of Rodes early in

Maj. Gen. Robert Emmett Rodes. From *Battles and Leaders of the Civil War* 2:580.

1863: "I like him so much. He is very much admired by all and very popular." Perhaps his appeal grew in part from a striking martial appearance; a member of Jeb Stuart's staff called Rodes and Pender "the most splendid looking soldiers of the war." Another element of Rodes's popularity was based on a bluff personality featuring "blunt speech" and a tincture of "blarney." The new major general's wry style shone through an episode from the winter after Gettysburg, when corps commander Ewell was steadily succumbing to a combination of physical and domestic ailments. Rodes "laughingly" asked a visiting chaplain, "Who commanded the Second Corps, whether Mrs. Ewell, General Ewell, or Sandy Pendleton, hoping it was the last."[35]

On July 1, 1863, Ewell's decline was not yet obvious and Rodes's rise in esteem had only just begun. The pivotal individuals in the opening round of the division's fight on Oak Ridge were of lower rank, however, and Rodes had the misfortune to be ill-served by both brigade commanders who led—or were supposed to lead—the forward units. Junius Daniel, S. Dodson Ramseur, and George Doles fought superbly at the head of Rodes's brigades at Gettysburg and would do so on many future fields; but Alfred Iverson and Edward A. O'Neal opened the July 1 fight for Rodes in execrable fashion.

As Rodes drew near the booming guns west of Gettysburg, he discovered in Oak Ridge a convenient ally: "I found that by keeping along the wooded ridge, on the left side of which the town of Gettysburg is situated, I could strike the force of the enemy with which General Hill's troops were engaged upon the flank, and that, besides moving under cover, whenever we struck the enemy we could engage him with the advantage in ground." The situation seemed ideal. Rodes was pointed squarely at a vulnerable Federal point, he had a wooded ridge to cover his approach, and the height of his protecting ridge assured him of a commanding position whenever he established hostile contact. Rodes initially advanced south down Oak Ridge on a narrow front just one brigade wide, but as the ground permitted he widened the front until it included, from right to left, Iverson, O'Neal, and Doles. All of this wheeling and realigning imposed added exertion on the troops, especially in those regiments serving as outriders for the wheels. The 5th Alabama, for instance, covered the last one and one-half miles at an uncomfortable pace—"frequently at a run"—across "very rough" ground that included mature wheat fields, freshly plowed ground, orchards, gardens, and wood and stone fences. The regimental commander reported that the ordeal fatigued every soldier and caused "many of them to faint from exhaustion."[36]

As the Confederates reached the edge of the woods north of the Forney farm, a vista south and west of them unfolded as though on a massive relief map. The coup d'oeil so often sought (and so rarely found) on confusing Civil War battlefields took away the breath of officers and soldiers alike. A member of the 6th Alabama wrote that they could plainly see A. P. Hill's troops "away to our right across broad fields of ripe wheat . . . moving slowly but steadily on the long blue lines." This novel vantage point "was the only time during the war that we were in position to get such a view of contending forces. It seemed like some grand panorama with the sounds of conflict added." Rodes, with the responsibility for exploiting the chance in mind, reported that "the whole of that portion of the force opposing General Hill's troops could be seen."[37]

Rodes at once ordered his supporting artillery up to occupy the commanding knob that overlooked the Forney farm and the fields sloping toward the railroad and the Chambersburg Pike just beyond it. The division's outstanding artillery chief, Lt. Col. Thomas Hill Carter, sent his own old battery, the King William Artillery, together with Capt. Charles W. Fry's Orange Artillery, to open on the enemy below the knob and "to enfilade the enemy's lines and batteries." The time by now was about 1:00 P.M. Less than an hour had passed since the curtain fell on Davis's disaster at the railroad cut.[38]

Carter's fire hurt the Federals opposite him, but it also brought down on his position a storm of counter-battery fire. The colonel reported that his two batteries "fired with very decided effect, compelling the infantry to take shelter in the railroad cut"—that cut so deadly a trap in the face of infantry attack but so wonderfully useful for protection against artillery rounds. For its good shooting, the King William company paid with a dozen casualties, or about 20 percent of its engaged strength. Shells exploding "fiercely" among the men of the Alabama brigade took their toll. One killed a captain in the 12th Alabama while that regiment waited in the woods; another badly wounded two men. Colonel O'Neal styled the artillery exchange "a severe engagement" and estimated its duration as a full hour. Col. Samuel Bonneau Pickens of the 12th (a Citadel graduate still a few days short of his twenty-fourth birthday) echoed O'Neal on both the severity and duration of the artillery affair. Rodes eventually ordered his Alabamians back into the woods for better shelter from Northern shells.[39]

As Rodes prepared to send his troops into battle, covering his activity with Carter's artillery fire, the vacuum in front of him began to turn into a more substantial, if still chaotic, Federal presence. The Union Eleventh Corps began to come onto the field to Rodes's left by 1:00 P.M., and the two brigades of Gen. John C. Robinson's First Corps division took up positions on the Forney farm right in front of the Confederates. The brigades of Generals Gabriel R. Paul and Henry Baxter hurried into line behind stone and wood fences approximately at right angles to Rodes's proper line of advance. Their awkward location should have made Paul and Baxter ready targets for Rodes, but they would inflict grievous losses from their flawed position on maladroitly led Southern brigades under O'Neal and Iverson.

From his elevated post of observation Rodes could see what seemed to be enemy units closing in on him: "The enemy began to show large bodies of men in front of the town, most of which were directed upon the position which I held, and almost at the same time a portion of the force opposed to General Hill changed position so as to occupy the woods on the summit of the same ridge I occupied . . . directly opposite my center." The troops to his left—the Eleventh Corps—Rodes would hold at bay by the expedient of putting George Doles's sturdy Georgia brigade out in that direction, even though it meant that a gap would exist between Doles's right and O'Neal's left. That should suffice "until General Early's division arrived," Rodes thought, which he knew would happen soon and to good effect.[40]

That left O'Neal to advance southward down the steep eastern slopes of the ridge, in tandem with Iverson's parallel move down the crest of the ridge. Daniel's big but new brigade would advance en echelon be-

hind Iverson's right. Ramseur's excellent regiments would be in close reserve to exploit the first opportunity.

This straightforward and eminently workable plan ran afoul of poor reconnaissance, which was Rodes's fault (recognition of the precise Federal alignment would have suggested weighting his left more heavily); it stumbled upon sturdy Federal resistance; but more than anything else the advance foundered on the nicely matched incompetence of O'Neal and Iverson. O'Neal's advance began somewhat before Iverson's—therein lay some of the tale—and it led directly to Iverson's difficulty so it requires the initial review.

Edward Asbury O'Neal was an Alabama lawyer who dabbled in politics, not always successfully before the war, though he became governor after the war. He was forty-four years old at Gettysburg. Nothing O'Neal had studied or experienced before 1861 had prepared him for military command at any level. He was an ardent secessionist and extraordinarily well connected with powerful leaders. On that basis O'Neal won early rank, which put him in position for advancement by seniority later in the war.

Rodes apparently maintained cordial relations with O'Neal (Edward A. O'Neal, Jr., served Rodes as a volunteer aide-de-camp at Chancellorsville and Gettysburg), but the division commander did not think that his subordinate had the potential for advancement. Although O'Neal was senior colonel in his brigade, Rodes formally recommended another officer for promotion in a letter to the corps commander in mid-May 1863. Rodes mentioned O'Neal but clearly did not want him promoted. Neither of the two colonels whom Rodes did want—John B. Gordon and John T. Morgan, both of whom became general officers in due course—was known to R. E. Lee, nor was O'Neal. Complications also intervened with the other two so Lee suggested that seniority should be followed. O'Neal, wrote Lee to Jefferson Davis, "has been identified with his regiment and the brigade by long service as Lieut. Col. and Colonel."[41] Richmond accordingly forwarded to the army a commission as brigadier general for O'Neal, dated June 6, 1863.

Immediately after Gettysburg the army high command began taking steps to ensure an arrangement that would keep O'Neal from both brigade command and general's rank. Lee returned O'Neal's commission to Richmond and had it canceled, but for most of the rest of the war the issue continued to haunt the army commander, to his considerable disgust. Three weeks after Gettysburg most of the officers of the Alabama brigade signed a circular letter to Jefferson Davis lauding O'Neal's valor and expressing appreciation for the way he had treated them. Perhaps significantly, the letter did not tout O'Neal's skill noticeably. Cullen A. Battle, who would be O'Neal's eventual replacement, signed first. This letter was framed under the impression that O'Neal would be leaving the Army of Northern Virginia immediately. On August 1, Rodes wrote to Lee through Walter H. Taylor, reiterating his opposition to having O'Neal in high authority. Having given up on getting Gordon or Morgan, Rodes now endorsed Battle with the earnest hope that "his appointment . . . will be made promptly, because until the Brigade has a permanent commander, and a better one in a disciplinary character than it has had lately it is likely to continue in a condition that is not at all satisfactory to any one concerned."[42]

Colonel O'Neal expended considerable energy and vast pools of ink in pressing his claim that his commission as brigadier general was withdrawn illegally. He mustered in support a mighty array of political correspondence. The governor of Alabama wrote repeatedly to Jefferson Davis in that vein. Letters signed by dozens of state legislators reached the War Department attesting to such of O'Neal's virtues as being the best orator in Alabama and owning a striking appearance. The net volume of political material in O'Neal's records (and typically not all of such manuscripts survive) is at least twice as extensive as the logrolling political paperwork in any other Confederate service record I have ever seen.[43]

In the spring of 1864, as Lee prepared for a death struggle with Grant, he still faced grumbling from O'Neal and his political friends. The commanding general wrote to Jefferson Davis that O'Neal's complaint "has been presented to me several times" but that the accession to command of Rodes's old brigade had been made on the basis of pressing "military considerations." Lee's usually calm style showed some hairline cracks when he wrote: "I feel aggrieved at this repeated charge of injustice, & but that we are upon the eve of a campaign . . . I should ask for a court of Inquiry into the matter." A few weeks later O'Neal marshaled a new argument in his struggle for promotion when he forwarded the novel notion that his salary as colonel was inadequate for his family's financial needs and he therefore must have a general's pay. Whether or not Lee saw that letter, there is no record of any comment, but he doubtless would have joined most others who read it in marveling at the precedent proposed by a man who outranked all but a few score of the hundreds of thousands of individuals in Confederate service. Two weeks after O'Neal wrote his low-salary letter, Lee washed his hands of the matter with finality. The army commander wrote bluntly that he had lately "made more particular inquiries into his capacity to command the brigade and I cannot recommend him to the command." O'Neal remained a colonel.[44]

What O'Neal did at Gettysburg on July 1 that led to cancellation of his commission was to lose control of his brigade at a crucial moment; perhaps he never had control from the beginning. He compounded this felony by failing to lead—or even to follow—his troops in their important attack. O'Neal put a finishing touch on his performance by grumbling in his official report weeks after the battle that he had not figured out what happened to his various regiments, even though the reports of his subordinates showed that they had grasped events with easy clarity.

The attack of O'Neal's brigade down the eastern slope of Oak Ridge toward the Mummasburg Road included only three of its five regiments. The reduction in numbers and the resultant reduction in width of the brigade front drastically hampered the attack. Rodes himself pulled one of the regiments—the 5th Alabama—out of line and sent it down the ridge behind the rest of the brigade as a makeshift measure to protect the yawning gap that stretched eastward to Doles's right. The 3d Alabama failed to advance with its mates because of O'Neal's disorientation. That came about when Rodes pushed the brigade back into the woods for protection during the artillery duel. He carefully aligned the 3d Alabama (on O'Neal's far right) with Daniel's left unit (the Second North Carolina Battalion), to be sure that his weak brigade commander knew what to do, then ordered O'Neal to use that as his point of reference for the rest of the Alabama regiments. When the temporary expedient for dodging artillery ended, O'Neal evidently concluded that since Rodes had placed the 3d once, it no longer was his own to direct. No one told Daniel that the orphaned 3d Alabama

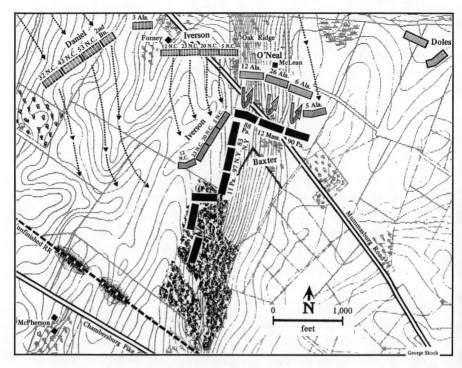

Assault of Rodes's Division along Oak Ridge, July 1

was his to run because no one but O'Neal had that in mind. The colonel of the regiment tried to stay aligned with Daniel, but the North Carolinian reasonably enough responded to a request for instructions with word that the Alabama regiment should operate independently.[45]

The 3d Alabama felt its forlorn lot keenly. An officer in the regiment wrote that Daniel "said he did not have room for us. All this time firing going on and we losing men could not leave the field and had nothing to fight." Although the official reports by officers of both the 3d and the 5th (two for the latter) were written soon after the battle and reported clearly on the circumstances affecting the regiments on July 1, O'Neal's report, written on July 24, insisted querulously: "Why my brigade was thus deprived of two regiments, I have never been informed."[46]

At about 2:15 P.M., Rodes, cognizant of O'Neal's need for special attention, gave the Alabama lawyer the order to attack and indicated to him "precisely the point to which he was to direct the left of the four regiments then under his orders." At that tense moment, O'Neal announced that for some reason (none is of record, and it is hard to imagine a persuasive excuse) he and his entire staff were without horses. The subject came up when Rodes discovered that the 3d Alabama was missing because of O'Neal's confusion, and it became necessary for Rodes to send a lieutenant of his own staff far to the right in what proved to be a vain attempt to attach the lost regiment to Daniel's brigade.[47]

Even the pared-down three-regiment Alabama attack might have met with success had it been properly coordinated with Iverson's advance and, equally important, had it moved far enough east to enfilade the Federal position. As Rodes reported disgustedly: "The three . . . regiments moved with alacrity (but not in accordance with my orders as to direction) and in confusion into the action." The Union commanders whose soldiers had been faced nominally westward had recognized the vulnerability of their right flank and rear along the Mummasburg Road and swung regiments out to provide some protection. The resulting line came to be known from its shape as the Hook. One of the regiments in the refused portion of the line was the 12th Massachusetts. Its adjutant remembered that the Alabama troops relished the protection of the big red barn of the McLean farm. From "behind this, and under its cover the enemy . . . deployed in several columns to the right (our left) we firing upon them as best we could."[48] Fortunately for the 12th Massachusetts and its companions in arms, the Alabama troops were moving away from the Federal weakness and into the Federal strength.

Given the misdirection of the feeble attack, its repulse by the Federals is hardly surprising. A member of the 88th Pennsylvania positioned near the Hook reported the easy victory almost nonchalantly: "Their line of battle, covered by a cloud of busy skirmishers, came driving through the woods from the right of the Mummasburg Road. Waiting until they were in easy range, the order was given, 'Commence firing.' With the sharp crack of the muskets a fleecy cloud of smoke rolled down the front of the brigade and the Minie balls zipped and buzzed with a merry chorus toward the Southern line, which halted, and after a brief contest, retired to the shelter of the woods."[49]

The view from the other end of the firing range was, of course, far less comfortable. Rodes wrote, "It was soon apparent that we were making no impression upon the enemy." Colonel Pickens of the 12th Alabama thought that the "desperate fight" lasted only "about fifteen minutes." Robert E. Park of that regiment lay down flat and urged his men to keep cool and continue firing while he tended to wounded comrades. "Balls were falling thick and fast around us, and whizzing past and often striking some one near." A round finally hit Park in the hip. He later recalled, "It was a wonder, a miracle, I was not afterward shot a half dozen times." Not surprisingly, Park thought his ordeal consisted of "long exposure" rather than just fifteen minutes. Through the whole frightful episode, Major Adolph Proskauer of the 12th inspired everyone within visual range. The twenty-four-year-old German-born officer was the "best dressed man in the regiment . . . very handsome" and clearly very brave too. The wounded Park marveled at how "our gallant Jew Major smoked his cigars calmly and coolly in the thickest of the fight."[50]

While Major Proskauer waxed calm at the eye of the storm, General Rodes discovered to his astonishment that O'Neal had not accompanied his troops into action. When the plight of the three misdirected Alabama regiments became apparent to him, Rodes hurried back to the 5th Alabama, guarding the gap in the direction of Doles's brigade, intending to use the regiment in this emergency. Rodes reported officially, with a mixture of restraint and blunt apportionment of blame: "To my surprise, in giving this command to its colonel (Hall), I found that Colonel O'Neal, instead of personally superintending the movements of his brigade, had chosen to remain with his reserve regiment. The result was that the whole brigade . . . was repulsed quickly, and with loss."[51]

The 5th Alabama did move forward in an attempt to ease the plight of its three sister regiments. The sharpshooter battalion of the brigade, commanded by the major of the 5th, served as a gauzy screen providing tenuous linkage between O'Neal's shivered left and the right of Doles while the main body of the 5th moved south. The 5th formed an obtuse angle for a time, part of the regiment facing east and part of it south toward O'Neal's difficulties. When the main body of the brigade fell back, the 5th returned to its starting point and resumed its original mission guarding the chasm between the ridge and Doles. The 5th received an invaluable boost in both of its roles—guarding the gap toward Doles and assisting its stricken comrades—from fire poured out by the Virginia artillery battery commanded by Capt. R. C. M. Page. The Virginians went into position at the eastern foot of the ridge behind the McLean farm, at a considerable elevation disadvantage, and hurled shells into the Federals facing O'Neal as well as southeastward toward enemy units opposite the gap. Page lost the enormous total, for a single battery, of thirty casualties, and he lost seventeen horses as well.[52]

The break in O'Neal's front began, predictably, at his misplaced left flank. The regiment there, the 6th Alabama, should have been farther east beyond the Federal point at the Hook according to Rodes's design and in keeping with every tactical rule. The collapse of the 6th spread steadily westward. All of the regiments could have echoed the colonel of the 12th when he wrote: "My regiment suffered severely in this attack." He concluded that "it was impossible for us to hold the position we had gained any longer without being cut to pieces or compelled to surrender, the enemy

having advantage of us in numbers and position." O'Neal used almost the same language (his "we had gained" being the royal or editorial "we" apparently because he had not participated in the advance); much of the body of O'Neal's report is paraphrased noticeably from Colonel Pickens's report for the 12th Alabama.[53]

O'Neal's premature start and the all-too-brief duration of his attack combined to leave a dreadful situation facing Iverson's brigade, just to O'Neal's right. With no support on the left, and with the vulnerable Federal flank opposite O'Neal out of danger, the four North Carolina regiments that made up Iverson's command needed judicious and competent leadership. Instead, they had Alfred Iverson. The result was a disaster so awful that one survivor wrote feelingly: "Deep and long must the desolate homes and orphan children of North Carolina rue the rashness of that hour."[54]

Alfred Iverson, Jr., was thirty-four years old at Gettysburg. He had served as a lieutenant during the Mexican War while still in his teens, under a commission probably secured by the political influence of his father, a newly seated United States congressman. In 1855 the younger Iverson received a commission in the regular army directly from civilian life (by now his father was a United States senator, seated the same day as the son's commissioning date). In 1861, Alfred Iverson participated in raising the 20th North Carolina Infantry and became its first colonel.

The North Carolina regiment apparently never enjoyed the empathy with its first commander that developed under like circumstances in so many other units. The officers of the 20th spent the entire winter before Gettysburg at loggerheads with Iverson, who had recently been promoted to command the brigade. The field officers of Iverson's old regiment did not like him, and he reciprocated the feeling. A captain in the 20th wrote in January, "Genl Iverson now and all ways did hate Major [Nelson] Slough." When the brigadier sought to import a friend from outside the regiment to take the colonelcy that he himself had vacated, twenty-six officers of the 20th signed a protest to Confederate Adjutant and Inspector General Samuel Cooper. Iverson refused to forward the document. The rebellious officers sent it on anyway, "over hiss head"; perhaps the "hiss" served as editorial comment, rather than just indicating an anomalous Carolinian spelling.

On December 27, 1862, Iverson sent an aide to the camp of his old regiment to arrest all twenty-six of its officers. One of them, Captain (later major and lieutenant colonel) John Stanley Brooks, wrote an outraged letter home insisting that resistance to Iverson was every reasonable man's duty and asserting that he would oppose him again "with grate pleasure" if occasion offered. Brooks considered resigning, and perhaps others did as well. The arrested men retained a high-powered bevy of counsel, including Col. (later brigadier general) Alfred Moore Scales and Col. William P. Bynum, who would become a member of the state supreme court.

Iverson failed in his attempt to import an outside favorite to command the 20th, but he took revenge on his irreverent subordinates by convening a "diabolical board" (Brooks's phrase, from two separate letters) that rejected promotions of all who had opposed him.[55] The suffering officers of the 20th would find relief from Iverson when he was exiled from the army, but first they faced their worst ordeal of the war at Gettysburg, where their misgivings about their chief found ample validation.

Rodes intended that Iverson should attack simultaneously with O'Neal and along the same axis. Neither of those intentions bore fruit. Iverson later reported that when he received his advance orders, he at once sent a staff officer to watch for O'Neal's movement so as to conform to it. Almost immediately the aide returned with the startling word that O'Neal already was moving. The poor timing resulted in O'Neal's repulse "just as we came up," according to one of the North Carolinians. Division commander Rodes reported bluntly that Iverson's heavy loss came because of his "left being thus exposed." Although Iverson's official declaration that the Alabamians had been "almost instantaneously driven back" was an exaggeration, the brevity of O'Neal's ill-aimed effort did ensure a failure of collaboration. Even misdirected and understrength as it was, the Alabama brigade's attack would have served to ease Iverson's plight had it been pressed with ordinary tenacity.[56]

The four North Carolina regiments—5th, 20th, 23d, and 12th, from left to right—began their advance heading more south than east. Nearly fifteen hundred officers and men marched with the doomed brigade. Losses at Chancellorsville had left some regiments short on officers. The 5th, for instance, had no field officers present and lost the captain commanding and the other three captains on duty on July 1 to wounds. The major and lieutenant colonel of the 20th were hit "soon" after the advance began, each wounded in his left arm, leaving that hard-pressed regiment critically short of leadership.[57] (The scarcity of officers with Iverson and the frightful losses among those who were present show up in a historiographical fashion as clearly as on the battlefield: accounts of the regiment's actions by officers are uncommonly scarce.)

The most critical leadership shortfall in the Forney fields is chargeable to Alfred Iverson. A member of the 23d wrote pointedly: "But our brigade commander (Iverson) after ordering us forward, did not follow us in that advance, and our alignment soon became false. There seems to have been utter ignorance of the [enemy] force crouching behind the stone wall." A soldier of Ramseur's brigade, the division reserve, declared that Iverson "was drunk, I think, and a coward besides," and that the general "was off hiding somewhere." Lieutenant General Ewell's favorite staff officer (his stepson) wrote that he learned from Rodes, Daniel, and others of "the well-known cowardly behavior of Iverson."[58] For whatever reason, Iverson emulated O'Neal by remaining behind while his men attacked. He was not far enough to the rear to warrant the description "off hiding somewhere," though, because he soon found opportunity to embarrass himself by a humiliating misinterpretation of the behavior of his men as they closed with the enemy.

The field across which "unwarned, unled as a brigade, went forward Iverson's deserted band to its doom" was completely devoid of cover. Farmer Forney later described his crop on the field as "a luxuriant growth of Timothy." A member of the 97th New York who watched the approach of the unsuspecting North Carolinians wrote of a "crop of wheat" on an area that "was all open meadow in my front." The Carolinians aimed at the southeast corner of the field, where Federals were visible in the woods, unaware of the more potent enemy lurking closer to them, on their left front. The Northern brigades of Baxter and Paul in the Hook occupied a position that should have been very vulnerable to O'Neal; but to a force advancing as Iverson's was, Baxter and Paul held impregnable ground. A stone fence ran down the front about two-thirds of the distance from the Mummasburg Road to the woods. For part of the way, a wooden fence augmented the stones. The steep-edged ridge that made their right and rear so easily turned also made the front of the Federal regiments strong and secure. Between the rock fence and the steep ridge edge, the Federals found complete cover. "Not one of them was to be seen," a member of the 12th North Carolina recalled ruefully.[59]

Iverson's men marched southeastward "as evenly as if on parade," one of them insisted. A Pennsylvanian waiting for orders to shoot at them agreed that "Iverson's men, with arms at a right shoulder, came on in splendid array, keeping step with an almost perfect line . . . as orderly as if on brigade drill, while behind the stone wall the Union soldiers, with rifles cocked and fingers on the triggers, waited and bided their time, feeling confident."[60] The men behind the stones had ample reason for confidence: the Carolinians were marching steadily, without skirmishers and without reconnaissance, into one of the most devastating deadfalls of the entire war.

The savage shock that awaited Iverson's men doubtless is beyond imagining for anyone who did not experience it. "When we were in point blank range," one of the victims later wrote, "the dense line of the enemy rose from its protected lair and poured into us a withering fire." At a range of little more than one hundred yards the Federals hurled "a sheet of fire and smoke . . . from the wall, flashing full in the faces of the Confederates, who at once halted, and, though their men were falling like leaves in a storm . . . attempted to make a stand and return the bitter fire." Situated as they were, the Carolinians could not stand for long. Most of them huddled under the fragile shelter of a shallow swale running irregularly through the field about eighty yards from the wall (a forward marker to the 88th Pennsylvania stands there today). They kept up what a Federal called "a rapid fusilade," but with scant success.[61]

The deadly effects of the initial surprise seemed to onlookers to be the worst part of the ordeal. One of Ramseur's men watching from back up the ridge wrote that when "Iverson's men charged . . . the Yankees raised up and fired and the death rate was terrible." Down near the wall, the initial horror soon developed into an even more gruesome scene as the helpless Confederates fell in long windrows. "I believe every man who stood up was either killed or wounded," an officer in the 20th North Carolina wrote. Not far to his right, an officer of the 23d saw so much carnage that he later insisted to a comrade "that it was the only battle—and he was in all in which the command was engaged from Williamsburg to Appomattox—where the blood ran like a branch. And that too, on the hot, parched ground."[62]

A Virginia artillerist who passed the Forney fields just a few hours later noticed with surprise and shock that the butchered Carolinians had fallen so thickly and quickly that they lay in perfect alignment. The gunner counted, within "a few feet . . . seventy-nine (79) North Carolinians laying dead in a straight line." The ghastly formation "was perfectly dressed. Three had fallen to the front, the rest had fallen backward; yet the feet of all these dead men were in a perfectly straight line." The "perfectly sickening and heart-rending" sight prompted the Virginian to exclaim: "Great God! When will this horrid war stop?"[63]

Alfred Iverson watched this bloody horror from some point well to the rear and understood it so imperfectly that he committed what Ewell in his official report called "the unfortunate mistake of . . . at this critical juncture . . . sending word to Major-General Rodes that one of his regiments had raised the white flag and gone over to the enemy." Iverson described the incident as resulting from seeing his men lying down in front of the Federal wall. In his official report the general backed away earnestly from his confused judgment of July 1, writing: "When I found afterward that 500 of my men were left lying dead and wounded on a line as straight as a dress parade, I exonerated, with one or two disgraceful exceptions, the survivors. . . . No greater gallantry and heroism has been displayed during this war."[64]

Absolution from their far-distant brigadier cannot have been of any current interest to the Carolinians bleeding in the swale, if in fact any of them ever considered Iverson in a position to pass judgment on anything they did. The historian of the 23d characterized their plight: "Unable to advance, unwilling to retreat, the brigade lay down in this hollow or depression in the field and fought as best it could." In the process, he noted, every one of the 23d's commissioned officers fell, with a single exception. So totally were the Confederates overwhelmed that they could put up little resistance when Federals swarmed out of the cover of their strong position and rushed through the swale gathering prisoners "with bayonets and clubbed muskets." As an enlisted man in the 23d put it, he and his comrades moved into battle "just in time for them to forge us in the rear of the line. We left the battle ground with only 60 men." Another member of the 23d explained the result in a letter home: "We fought like tigers and [made the] bravest stand I ever saw but the Yankees cross fired on us a good while and then . . . the Yankees ran up and captured very nearly all of them."[65]

Northerners firing their rifles down into the swale began shouting to one another about the need to charge out and gather in prisoners after Confederates began waving handkerchiefs tied to their guns as tokens of surrender. As the Federals scurried out to the swale and beyond, "several hundred of the rebs left their arms on the ground and rushed through our lines and they were directed to run out of range as quick as possible which they did without much urging." The momentum of their lunge into the swale carried some of the Federals on beyond into range of the Confederate brigades that soon would win the day on Oak Ridge. General Baxter—unlike Iverson and O'Neal, he was with his troops—shouted orders "to give them the cold steel," but a "scorching fire" quickly extinguished that notion.[66]

The only sizable piece of Iverson's brigade that escaped with any organizational integrity was the 12th North Carolina. Because the brigade line was angled away from the Federal position, the 12th on the far right suffered least from the deadfall and enjoyed the best opportunity to defend itself and to pull back from the trap. It suffered fewer than half as many casualties as any of the other three regiments. Capt. Don P. Halsey of Iverson's staff—the same aide who had arrested twenty-six officers of the 20th North Carolina for his chief the preceding December—stood in for the absent brigade commander and rallied the 12th and other such fragments as he could find. When Confederate reinforcements under competent leaders appeared, as they did very promptly, Halsey seized a battle flag and led Iverson's pathetic remnant in the victorious pursuit that had seemed impossible when the brigade blundered into the swale. Ewell went so far as to declare that Captain Halsey had "assumed command" in place of Iverson.[67]

The soldiers of Iverson's brigade immediately heard and repeated the prevalent account that their general "not only remained in the rear but that a big chestnut log intervened between him and the battle and that more than once he reminded his staff that for more than one at the time to look over was an unnecessary exposure of person." The brigade's regimental officers shared the feelings of the men about Iverson. Col. Daniel Harvey Christie of the 23d North Carolina, suffering from a mortal wound and accordingly immune to concerns about rank or discipline, "had the surviving handful of the 23d" brought to the front yard of the house where he lay. From the porch the dying colonel "with much feeling assured them that he might never live to again lead them [into] battle but he would see that 'The Imbecile Iverson never should.'"[68]

In the aftermath of Gettysburg, participants and commentators reached an easy consensus on Iverson's disaster: they blamed the general and exonerated the men, accepting Rodes's verdict that the soldiers "fought and died like heroes." A staff officer repeating what he had heard from Rodes and others wrote soon after the war with disgust that although Iverson "was relieved at once & sent back to await trial," he fell into the hands of politicians when "forwarded to Richmond, got off scot free & had a brigade of reserves given him in Georgia." Thomas F. Toon, a colonel of the 20th who won promotion to brigadier general late in the war, bitterly summarized Iverson's disaster at Gettysburg in a succinct phrase opening his sketch of the regiment: "initiated at Seven Pines, sacrificed at Gettysburg, surrendered at Appomattox."[69]

The historian of the 12th North Carolina recorded the sorrowful burial of the dead who strewed the swale in number far too large and an equally melancholy visit to the scene years after the war:

In the lowest part of the depression, in the rear of the battleground of Iverson's Brigade, four shallow pits were dug by the prisoners, in which were buried the dead of that brigade. The surface of these pits is to be easily distinguished [to] this day [ca. 1900] from surrounding ground on account of the more luxuriant growth of the grass and crops over them. Mr. Forney, who owned the ground on which the battle was fought, and who still owns it, and the writer of this sketch, two years ago, with pointers in their hands, traced with ease and certainty the edges of these pits as they walked around them. Mr. Forney said that the place was then known, throughout the neighborhood, as the "Iverson Pits," and that for years after the battle there was a superstitious terror in regard to the field, and that it was with difficulty that laborers could be kept at work there on the approach of night on that account.[70]

Iverson's disaster ended Confederate fumbling on Oak Ridge. In quick aftermath, Junius Daniel and Dodson Ramseur skillfully led their North Carolina brigades to triumph on precisely the same ground. George Doles held onto his stanchion firmly and well until Jubal A. Early's division poured down on his left and sealed a Confederate victory that swept the fields west of Gettysburg with irresistible force.

The three Confederate brigades that had suffered so badly on July 1 faced continued buffeting from fate during the rest of the campaign. When O'Neal's 3d Alabama sought to accompany Ramseur, he responded, "Yes, N.C. will stay with you"; an Alabamian discouraged by recent events replied, "They haven't been a doing it." The 3d and Ramseur soon stood together in the triumphant moment near where Iverson and O'Neal had failed so signally. On July 2 the Alabama brigade moved into the confused fighting around Culp's Hill and played a secondary role that is apparently impossible to decipher in detail at this late date. Its difficult outing in

Pennsylvania continued during the retreat from Gettysburg. In a frustrating anticlimax to the bitter main event, the brigade's quartermaster trains fell prey to Yankee cavalry at 2 A.M. on July 5. Among the losses was a money chest holding some $11,235 scheduled for paying the troops and feeding them.[71]

Joseph Davis's shattered brigade was included for some reason in the assault on Cemetery Ridge on July 3. Perhaps the arrival of the full-strength 11th Mississippi contributed to the decision to subject the brigade to further battering. Iverson's brigade was beyond further service. Rodes's division as a whole cut a surprisingly faint figure after leaving Oak Ridge. O'Neal's son and namesake, who served on Rodes's staff at Gettysburg (but doubtless felt his father's humiliation deeply), declared that the division "could easily have taken possession of the hill which afterward sent such havoc through our Army, but [was] prevented by our Division Commander." A field officer of the Alabama brigade commented pointedly about the poor coordination of Confederate efforts at Gettysburg. "From the first day reason seemed to have deserted our generals," he wrote. Each division general seemed bent on "acting on his own hook" and "without the smallest concert of action with the other Division Commanders." "So lamentably conspicuous was this want of concert," he insisted, "that the privates noticed it and when ordered to charge did so with misgivings as to the result."[72]

The affairs on Oak Ridge constituted a series of extraordinarily dark tactical failures in the midst of a Confederate strategic bonanza. They supplied renewed evidence of the military truth that leaders must lead, rather than rely on direction from ivory towers. The disasters also established some trends only clearly visible with hindsight: Ewell was not Stonewall Jackson in fact or even in simulacrum, the Robert Rodes of July 1863 was not the Robert Rodes of 1864; Iverson, O'Neal, and Davis were not competent and never would be. The aftermath of the disasters gave further evidence that Ramseur was as able as he had seemed to be and new evidence that Daniel brought solid competence to the army he had recently joined.

When he reflected on Gettysburg a few years later, R. E. Lee doubtless had July 1 clearly in mind when he commented on the absence—for very different reasons—of two crucial officers. "Stuart failed to give him information," Lee told a former staff officer, "and this deceived him into a general battle." And, Lee mused, he "often thinks that if Jackson had been there he would have succeeded."[73]

Day Two

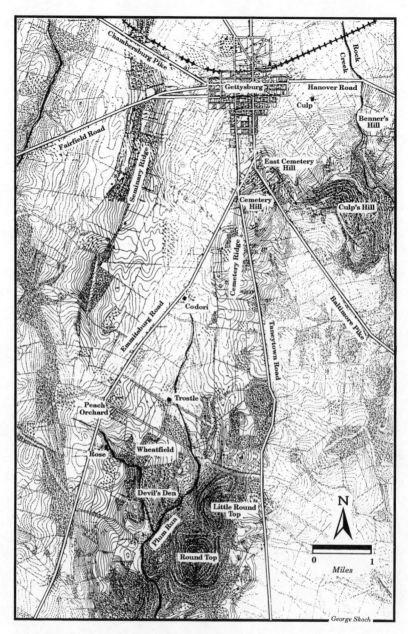

Battlefield of the Second Day at Gettysburg

"If the Enemy Is There, We Must Attack Him"

R. E. Lee and the Second Day at Gettysburg

Gary W. Gallagher

NO ASPECT OF R. E. LEE'S MILITARY CAREER HAS SPARKED more controversy than his decision to pursue the tactical offensive at Gettysburg. Lee's contemporaries and subsequent writers produced a literature on the subject notable for its size and discordancy. Unwary students can fall victim to the hyperbole, dissembling, and self-interest characteristic of many accounts by participants. The massive printed legacy of the "Gettysburg Controversy," with its blistering critiques of James Longstreet and "Old Pete's" clumsy rejoinders, demands special care. Even many modern writers unfurl partisan banners when they approach the topic. Despite the size of the existing literature, Lee's decision to resume offensive combat on July 2 remains a topic worthy of study. Before passing judgment on his actions, however, it is necessary to assess the merits of earlier works—an exercise that underscores the contradictory nature of the evidence and the lack of interpretive consensus among previous writers.

The Army of Northern Virginia went into Pennsylvania at its physical apogee, supremely confident that under Lee's direction it could triumph on any battlefield. LeRoy Summerfield Edwards of the 12th Virginia Infantry struck a common note in a letter written near Shepherdstown on June 23: "[T]he health of the troops was never better and above all the *morale* of the army was never more favorable for offensive or defensive operations . . . victory will inevitably attend our arms in any collision with the enemy."

British observer A. J. L. Fremantle detected a similar outlook when he spoke to a pair of officers from Louisiana on that same day. Recuperating from wounds suffered in fighting at Winchester during the march northward, these men gave Fremantle "an animated account of the spirits and feeling of the army. At no period of the war, they say, have the men been so well equipped, so well clothed, so eager for a fight, or so confident of success. . . ."[1]

Two weeks and more than twenty-five thousand casualties later the picture had changed considerably. The soldiers still believed in Lee, but they had lost their almost mystical faith in certain victory. Randolph H. McKim, a young Marylander in Richard S. Ewell's Second Corps, betrayed such sentiment in his diary shortly after Gettysburg: "I went into the last battle feeling that victory *must* be ours—that such an army could not be foiled, and that God would certainly declare himself on our side. *Now* I feel that unless He sees fit to bless our arms, our valor will not avail." Stephen Dodson Ramseur, a brigadier in Robert E. Rodes's division, reacted similarly to the shock of Gettysburg. "Our great campaign," wrote Ramseur a month after the battle, "admirably planned & more admirably executed up to the fatal days at Gettysburg, has failed. Which I was not prepared to anticipate." Although insisting that Gettysburg did not spell the doom of the Confederacy, he believed it foreshadowed other crises the South must overcome to gain independence. Ramseur looked "the thing square in the face" and stood ready "to undergo dangers and hardships and trials to the end."[2]

Staggering losses and a shift in morale thus grew out of Lee's decision to press for a decisive result on the field at Gettysburg. Some Southerners immediately questioned his tactics. "Gettysburg has shaken my faith in Lee as a general," Robert Garlick Hill Kean of the War Department wrote in his diary on July 26, 1863. "To fight an enemy superior in numbers at such terrible disadvantage of position in the heart of his own territory, when the freedom of movement gave him the advantage of selecting his own time and place for accepting battle, seems to have been a great military blunder. . . . and the result was the worst disaster which has ever befallen our arms—." Brig. Gen. Wade Hampton used comparably strong language in a letter to Joseph E. Johnston less than a month after the battle. The Pennsylvania campaign was a "complete failure," stated Hampton, during which Lee resorted to unimaginative offensive tactics. "The position of the Yankees there was the strongest I ever saw & it was in vain to attack it." Hampton had expected the Confederates to "choose our own points at which to fight" during the expedition, but "we let Meade choose his position and then we attacked."[3]

More restrained in his disapproval was James Longstreet, who informed his uncle Augustus Baldwin Longstreet confidentially in late July 1863 that the "battle was not made as I would have made it. My idea was to throw ourselves between the enemy and Washington, select a strong position, and force the enemy to attack us." Through such a defensive stance, thought Longstreet, the Confederates might have "destroyed the Federal army, marched into Washington, and dictated our terms, or, at least, held Washington and marched over as much of Pennsylvania as we cared to, had we drawn the enemy into attack upon our carefully chosen position in his rear."[4]

The early postwar years witnessed a rapid escalation of the debate over Lee's generalship at Gettysburg. Longstreet served as a catalyst for an outpouring of writing, the opening salvo of which appeared the year after Appomattox in William Swinton's *Campaigns of the Army of the Potomac*. A Northern journalist, Swinton interviewed Longstreet and drew heavily on his opinions to portray Lee's tactics at Gettysburg as misguided and contrary to a precampaign pledge to "his corps-commanders that *he would not assume a tactical offensive, but force his antagonist to attack him.*" Lee's assaults on the second day were a "grave error" explained by overconfidence in the prowess of his soldiers, fear that withdrawal without battle would harm morale in the Army of Northern Virginia and among Southern civilians, and contempt for the Army of the Potomac. Having "gotten a taste of blood in the considerable success of the first day," suggested Swinton in language similar to that used elsewhere by Longstreet, "the Confederate commander seems to have lost that equipoise in which his faculties commonly moved, and he determined to give battle."[5]

Other early postwar accounts also highlighted questions about Lee's aggressive tactics. Edward A. Pollard, the staunchly pro-Southern editor of the *Richmond Examiner* during the war, alluded in 1866 to "a persistent popular opinion in the South that Gen. Lee, having failed to improve the advantage of the first day, did wrong thereafter to fight at Gettysburg." Granting the "extraordinary strength" of the Federal position, Pollard nonetheless asserted that the superlative morale of Lee's army might have justified the attempt to drive Meade's army from the field.[6] James D. McCabe, Jr.'s, generally appreciative *Life and Campaigns of General Robert E. Lee*, also published in 1866, argued that after July 1 the Confederate army "had before it the task of storming a rocky fortress stronger than that against which Burnside had dashed his army so madly at Fredericksburg, and every chance of success lay with the Federals." Citing Swinton's work as corroboration, McCabe endorsed Longstreet's proposal to shift around the Federal left and invite

Lee at Gettysburg, an early postwar engraving by Alfred A. Waud. From John Esten Cooke, *The Life of Gen. Robert E. Lee* (New York: D. Appleton, 1871), opposite 325.

attack from a position between the Union army and Washington. "There are those who assert that General Lee himself was not free from the contempt entertained by his men for the army they had so frequently vanquished, and that he was influenced by it in his decision upon this occasion," added McCabe in reference to Lee's resumption of assaults on July 2. "This may or may not be true. It is certain that the decision was an error."[7]

The interpretive tide turned in Lee's favor shortly after the general's death. Led by Jubal A. Early, a number of former Confederates eventually mounted a concerted effort in the Southern Historical Society's *Papers* and elsewhere to discredit Longstreet (whose Republicanism made him an especially inviting target) and prove Lee innocent of all responsibility for the debacle at Gettysburg. Speaking at Washington and Lee University on the anniversary of Lee's birth in 1872, Early disputed the notion that the Confederates should have refrained from attacking after July 1. "Some have thought that General Lee did wrong in fighting at Gettysburg," remarked Early in obvious reference to Longstreet's views, "and it has been said that he ought to have moved around Meade's left, so as to get between him and Washington. . . . I then thought, and still think, that it was right to fight the battle of Gettysburg, and I am firmly convinced that if General Lee's plans had been carried out in the spirit in which they were conceived, a decisive victory would have been obtained, which perhaps would have secured our independence."

As the most prominent member of the Lost Cause school of interpretation, Early won a deserved reputation as Lee's most indefatigable defender and Longstreet's harshest critic. He blamed defeat on Longstreet's sulking sloth in mounting the assaults on July 2. Lee expected the attacks to begin at dawn, insisted Early (a charge Longstreet easily proved to be literally untrue—though Lee certainly wanted the attacks to commence as early as possible); Longstreet began the offensive about 4:00 P.M., by which time Meade's entire army was in place. "The position which Longstreet attacked at four, was not occupied by the enemy until late in the afternoon," concluded Early, "and Round Top Hill, which commanded the enemy's position, could have been taken in the morning without a struggle."[8]

Although few veterans of the Army of Northern Virginia spoke publicly against Lee during the postwar years, many did not share Early's views. Benjamin G. Humphreys, who commanded the 21st Mississippi Infantry in William Barksdale's brigade on the second day at Gettysburg, revealed sharp disagreement with the Lost Cause writers in comments he scribbled in the margins of his copy of Walter Taylor's *Four Years with General Lee*. Humphreys deplored the "necessity of hunting out for a 'scapegoat'" to guarantee that the "'infallibility' of Lee must not be called into question." The commanding general "took upon himself all the blame for Gettysburg," observed Humphreys mockingly, "was that not an evidence of his infallibility?"[9]

Lee himself said little publicly beyond his official report. The fighting on July 1 had escalated from a meeting engagement to a bitter contest involving two corps on each side, during the course of which the serendipitous arrival of Ewell's leading divisions had compelled the Federals to withdraw through Gettysburg to high ground below the town. "It had not been intended to deliver a general battle so far from our base unless attacked," wrote Lee in apparent confirmation of Longstreet's assertion that he had envisioned acting on the tactical defensive in Pennsylvania, "but coming unexpectedly upon the whole Federal Army, to withdraw through the mountains with our extensive trains would have been difficult and dangerous." Nor could the Confederates wait for Meade to counterattack, "as the country was unfavorable for collecting supplies in the presence of the enemy, who could restrain our foraging parties by holding the mountain passes with local troops." "A battle had, therefore, become in a measure unavoidable," concluded Lee, "and the success already gained gave hope of a favorable issue."[10]

Lee offered the last hopeful statement despite a firm understanding of the terrain. "The enemy occupied a strong position," he conceded, "with his right upon two commanding elevations adjacent to each other, one southeast and the other, known as Cemetery Hill, immediately south of the town. . . . His line extended thence upon the high ground along the Emmitsburg Road, with a steep ridge in rear, which was also occupied. This ridge was difficult of ascent, particularly the two hills above mentioned as forming its northern extremity, and a third at the other end, on which the enemy's left rested." Stone and rail fences affording protection to defenders, together with generally open approaches three-quarters of a mile wide, complicated any plan of assault. Yet offensive thoughts dominated Lee's thinking. When Ewell declined to strike at Cemetery Hill late on the afternoon of July 1, the commanding general opted to await the arrival of Longstreet's two leading divisions: "It was determined to make the principal attack upon the enemy's left. . . . Longstreet was directed to place the divisions of McLaws and Hood on the right of Hill, partially enveloping the enemy's left, which he was to drive in." A. P. Hill would engage the Union center with a demonstration, while Ewell's troops would do the same on the enemy's right with an eye toward exploiting any opening.[11]

Almost matter-of-fact in its explication of the reasons for resuming attacks on July 2, Lee's report contains no hint that he considered the decision a bad one. Five years after the battle, he responded to a query about Gettysburg in a similar vein: "I must again refer you to the official accounts. Its loss was occasioned by a combination of circumstances. It was commenced in the absence of correct intelligence. It was continued in the effort to overcome the difficulties by which we were surrounded, and it would have been gained could one determined and united blow have been delivered by our whole line."[12]

Several secondhand accounts also suggest that Lee never deviated from the tenor of his report. Col. William Allan, former chief of ordnance in the Second Corps, made notes of a conversation with Lee on April 15, 1868, wherein Lee talked passionately about Gettysburg. Lee had hoped to avoid a general battle in Pennsylvania, recorded Allan, but "Jeb" Stuart's absence caused the opposing forces to stumble into one another on July 1. The commanding general "found himself engaged with the Federal army therefore, unexpectedly, and had to fight. This being determined on, victory w[oul]d have been won if he could have gotten one decided simultaneous attack on the whole line." Lee also observed that his critics "talked much of that they knew little about" and, in a likely reference to William Swinton's book, stated that he doubted Longstreet ever said Lee "was under a promise to the Leut. Generals not to fight a general battle in Pa. . . . He never made any such promise, and he never thought of doing any such thing."[13]

Nearly two years later, Lee again "spoke feelingly" about Gettysburg with Allan. "Much was said about risky movements," noted Allan. Lee believed that "everything was risky in our war. He knew oftentimes that he was playing a very bold game, but it was the only *possible* one." This justification of risk, though not specifically tied to any phase of the campaign, certainly could apply to Lee's pursuing assaults after the first day. As in his earlier pronouncements on the subject, Lee seemed content with his principal decisions. He still maintained that Stuart's failure had precipitated the fighting, and the fact that he "never c[oul]d get a simultaneous attack on the enemy's position" sealed the result.[14]

Accounts by Brig. Gen. John D. Imboden and Maj. John Seddon further buttress an image of Lee as comfortable with his tactical conduct at Gettysburg. Early on the morning of July 4, wrote Imboden in the 1880s, he met with Lee at army headquarters outside Gettysburg. The conversation turned to the failed assaults on July 3: "I never saw troops behave more magnificently than Pickett's division of Virginians did to-day in that grand charge upon the enemy," averred Lee. "And if they had been supported as they were to have been . . . we would have held the position and the day would have been ours." It is reasonable to infer from this passage that Lee also viewed the resumption of the offensive on July 2 as correct. Major Seddon, a brother of the Confederate secretary of war, met with Lee shortly after Gettysburg and subsequently related his conversation to Maj. Gen. Henry Heth. Heth quoted Seddon as stating that Lee acknowledged a heavy loss at Gettysburg but pronounced it "no greater than it would have been from the series of battles I would have been compelled to fight had I remained in Virginia." After making this observation, Lee rose from his seat and with an "emphatic gesture said, 'and sir, we did whip them at Gettysburg, and it will be seen for the next six months that *that army* will be as quiet as a sucking dove.'"[15]

A smaller body of evidence portrays Lee as subject to doubts about his tactical moves at Gettysburg. Perhaps best known is Fremantle's description of Lee's response to Brig. Gen. Cadmus M. Wilcox as the latter brought his brigade out of the fight on July 3: "Never mind, General, *all this has been MY fault*—it is I that have lost this fight, and you must help me out of it in the best way you can."[16] Whether or not Lee meant the entire battle when he spoke of "this fight," his comment can be extended to the decision to keep attacking after July 1. In early August 1863, Lee informed President Davis that he was aware of public criticisms of his generalship at

Gettysburg. "I do not know how far this feeling extends in the army," wrote Lee. "My brother officers have been too kind to report it, and so far the troops have been too generous to exhibit it. It is fair, however, to suppose that it does exist, and success is so necessary to us that nothing should be risked to secure it." Offering to step down as commander of the army, Lee implicitly recognized that he had erred in Pennsylvania: "I cannot even accomplish what I myself desire. How can I fulfill the expectations of others?"[17]

Two additional vignettes, though both hearsay, merit mention. Henry Heth remembered after the war that he and Lee discussed Gettysburg at Orange Court House during the winter of 1863–64. "After it is all over, as stupid a fellow as I am can see the mistakes that were made," said the commanding general somewhat defensively. "I notice, however, my mistakes are never told me until it is too late, and you, and all my officers, know that I am always ready and anxious to have their suggestions." Capt. Thomas J. Goree of Longstreet's staff recalled in an 1875 letter to his old chief a similar episode at Orange Court House in the winter of 1864. Summoned to Lee's tent, Goree found that the general had been looking through Northern newspapers. Lee "remarked that he had just been reading the Northern official reports of the Battle of Gettysburg, that he had become satisfied from reading those reports that if he had permitted you to carry out your plans on the 3d day, instead of making the attack on Cemetery Hill, we would have been successful."[18] Because Longstreet first argued for a movement around the Federal flank on July 2, it is possible that in retrospect Lee also considered the assaults of the second day to have been unwise.

Many later writings about Gettysburg by Confederate participants followed furrows first plowed by Jubal Early and his cohorts in their savaging of James Longstreet. They insisted that Longstreet disobeyed Lee's orders to attack early on July 2, dragged his feet throughout that crucial day, and was slow again on July 3. Had "Old Pete" moved with dispatch, the Confederates would have won the battle and perhaps the war. No questioning of Lee's commitment to bloody offensive action after July 1 clouded the simplistic reasoning of these authors, typical of whom was former Second Corps staff officer James Power Smith. In a paper read before the Military History Society of Massachusetts in 1905, Smith recounted the conference among Lee and his Second Corps subordinates on the evening of July 1. Events of that day dictated further attacks, stated Smith. "There was no retreat without an engagement," he affirmed. "Instead of the defensive, as he had planned, General Lee was compelled to take the offensive, and himself endeavor to force the enemy away. It was not by the choice of Lee nor by the foresight of Meade that the Federal army found itself placed on lines of magnificent defence." Persuaded that Ewell's corps lacked the power to capture high ground on the Union right, Lee concluded that Longstreet would spearhead an effort against the enemy's left on July 2. "Then with bowed head he added, 'Longstreet is a very good fighter when he gets in position, but he is *so slow*.'" This last comment, a staple of the Lost Cause canon with no direct supporting evidence from Lee's own hand, anticipated the further argument that Lee's sound planning ran aground on the rock of Longstreet's lethargic movements.[19]

Longstreet defended himself against his tormentors ineptly, launching indiscreet counterattacks that often strayed widely from the truth and provoked further onslaughts against his character and military ability. One notorious example of his poor judgment will suffice: "That [Lee] was excited and off his balance was evident on the afternoon of the 1st," claimed Longstreet in his memoirs, "and he labored under that oppression until enough blood was shed to appease him." Such statements provoked a massive response from Longstreet's critics, creating a body of evidence that would damn him in the eyes of many subsequent historians.[20]

The writings of Brig. Gen. Edward Porter Alexander stood in notable contrast to the emotional approach of many former Confederates. Easily the most astute military analyst among Lee's lieutenants, he sometimes is perceived as an apologist for Longstreet because he served for much of the war as chief of artillery in the First Corps. In fact, Alexander probed in brilliantly dispassionate fashion Lee's generalship at Gettysburg. He thought a casual reading of Lee's report "suggests that the aggressive on [the] second day seemed forced upon him, yet the statement is very much qualified by the expression 'in a measure,' & also by the reference to the hopes inspired by our partial success." Alexander bluntly declared that "no real difficulty" prevented Lee's shifting to the defensive on July 2 and maneuvering in such a manner as to force Meade to attack. Lee's reference to his trains failed to impress Alexander, who as the army's former chief of ordnance possessed an excellent grasp of the difficulties of moving large numbers of wagons.

With an engineer's love of precision, Alexander reckoned "it a reasonable estimate to say that 60 per cent of our chances for a great victory were lost by our continuing the aggressive. And we may easily imagine the boon it was to Gen. Meade . . . to be relieved from the burden of making any difficult decision, such as what he would have had to do if Lee had been satisfied with his victory of the first day; & then taken a strong position & stood on the defensive." Expressing astonishment that "the strength of the enemy's position seems to have cut no figure in the consideration [of] the question of the aggressive," Alexander labeled Meade's good fortune "more than impudence itself could have dared to pray for—a position unique among all the battlefields of the war, certainly adding fifty per cent to his already superior force, and an adversary stimulated by success to an utter disregard of all physical disadvantages. . . ."

These opinions aside, Alexander believed that victory eluded the Confederates on July 2 only because Longstreet's assaults began so late. Professing no doubt that the offensive could have started sooner, he expressed equal certainty that "Gen. Lee much desired it to be made very much earlier." Longstreet's preference to await the arrival of Evander M. Law's brigade, to which Lee acceded, and the delay occasioned by Southern infantry near Black Horse Tavern coming into view of Federal signalmen on Little Round Top slowed the flanking march. Present on the field the entire time and "apparently consenting to the situation from hour to hour," Lee bore a major portion of responsibility for the late opening of the attacks by Alexander's reading of the evidence.[21]

Modern writers have continued to explore Lee's choice to resume offensive operations on July 2. Easily the most influential of Lee's biographers is Douglas Southall Freeman. After discussing Lee's conferences with Ewell and Longstreet on the evening of July 1, Freeman asked, "But was it wise to attack at all? What alternatives were there?" Freeman listed four available courses of action: Lee could take up a defensive position on the field and invite attack from Meade; he could retreat to the western side of South Mountain; he could move around the Union left as Longstreet urged, placing the army between the Federals and Washington; or he could mount another series of attacks in the hope of achieving a complete victory. The first two alternatives Freeman dismissed quickly with a paraphrase of Lee's official report. The third he termed impractical, citing the opinions of "nearly all military critics"—the roster of whom included Jubal Early, William Allan, Armistead L. Long, and other stalwart members of the Lost Cause school of interpretation. With unintended irony, Freeman admitted in a footnote that George G. Meade "was the only critic who agreed with Longstreet. He said that Longstreet's proposal was . . . the step he feared Lee would take. . . ."[22]

Freeman thus brought himself to the fourth option. Once again paraphrasing Lee, he concluded: "Strategically, then, Lee saw no alternative to attacking the enemy before Meade concentrated, much as he disliked to force a general engagement so early in the campaign and at such a distance from Virginia." Tactically, Freeman approved of Lee's plan to use the divisions of McLaws and Hood to deliver the heaviest blow on the Union left, with Ewell's corps doing what it could against the enemy's far right. Little did Lee know, contended Freeman, that as he anticipated another day's combat his plans already were being undone. In a statement worthy of Jubal Early, Lee's great biographer closed his chapter on July 1: "The battle was being decided at that very hour in the mind of Longstreet, who at his camp, a few miles away, was eating his heart away in sullen resentment that Lee had rejected his long-cherished plan of a strategic offensive and a tactical defensive." That sullenness manifested itself in a performance on July 2 so sluggish "it has often been asked why Lee did not arrest him for insubordination or order him before a court-martial." Freeman answered that an absence of qualified officers forced Lee to make do with Longstreet, warts and all, even as he lamented the absence of "Stonewall" Jackson.[23]

Other historians offer a mixture of praise and censure for Lee's decision to attack on July 2. Clifford Dowdey, whom one reviewer aptly called "the last Confederate historian," endorsed Lee's offensive inclination, observing that Lee apparently never thought of shifting to the defensive. Dowdey emphasized the need for a quick Confederate triumph: "[Lee's] thinking was shaped by the background of the South's waning strength, by the present illustration of the attrition in high command, and by the need for a decisive victory away from home. . . . His men were driving the enemy, and, though Ewell had kept them from clinching the victory today, Lee thought only of how to complete it the next day." Poor execution robbed the army of success on July 2, but the decision to seek that success had been correct.[24] Frank E. Vandiver echoed Dowdey, with the twist that a spell of ill health in Pennsylvania rendered Lee edgy and more inclined to seek a quick resolution. His physical ailments and Longstreet's stubbornness left Lee "generally irritated and he's determined that he is going to attack." "He has every reason for wanting to do that," judged Vandiver, "he has his army in Pennsylvania, it's at its finest strength and gear and this is the time to cast the die. Across the field is a Union general, George G. Meade, who has been in command of the Army of the Potomac only two weeks [sic], doesn't know much about his army and might be unready to fight a major engagement."[25]

Even the British historian J. F. C. Fuller, widely known as a severe critic of Lee, essentially accepted the rationale in the general's official report of the campaign. The "defective supply arrangements and the absence of his cavalry (to disengage himself) compelled him to fight," wrote Fuller, "and to fight an offensive action in place of a defensive one; for, as he had to live on the country, it was impossible for him to stand still for any length of time." Fuller believed that an inability to move and forage simultaneously ruled out Longstreet's option. This approval of the decision to attack on July 2 contrasted sharply with Fuller's estimate of Lee's tactical blueprint, which he considered "a thoroughly bad plan" with little prospect of success.[26]

H. J. Eckenrode and Bryan Conrad generally treated Lee favorably in their harsh biography of Longstreet (their real hero was Stonewall Jackson), but at Gettysburg these authors deviated from their usual pattern. They found that the commanding general "blundered into battle" and once committed "showed no genius in the manner in which he conducted it, making no feints and relying on frontal attacks on a formidable position."[27]

Few historians probed the questions of Gettysburg more judiciously than Edwin B. Coddington, Harry W. Pfanz, and Alan T. Nolan—yet their careful examinations produced differing conclusions. Coddington weighed Lee's options for July 2, took into account the explanations in his official report, and resolved that although Lee's expressed concern about his trains and living off the countryside had some validity, the general perhaps overstated the dangers of withdrawal. The key to Lee's action was psychological—he and his army would not retreat unless pushed. "They had just achieved a smashing success against a part of the Union army," wrote Coddington, "and now was the time for them to finish the job. The stakes were high, and they might never again have as good an opportunity." Coddington viewed the decision as perfectly in keeping with the pattern of offensive combat forged by Lee and his army in previous campaigns.[28]

Pfanz agreed that Lee's decision to keep attacking was reasonable. Longstreet's proposed flanking movement posed logistical problems, Stuart was unavailable to screen the march, and the whereabouts of much of the Union army remained unknown; moreover, a "shift to the left and away from the valley that sheltered the Confederate line of communications was virtually out of the question." A defensive stand would transfer the initiative to Meade, who might circumscribe Southern foraging while calling up Union reinforcements, and thus "did not seem a practical course of action." "In General Lee's words," Pfanz stated in summary, "a battle had, therefore, become in a measure unavoidable." Nolan disagreed strongly, attributing rationales for Lee's aggressive behavior after July 1 to an unpersuasive school of apologists for the Southern chief. "When all is said and done, the commentators' rationalizations of Lee's most daring offensive thrusts seem contrived," insisted Nolan. "Although these commentators are aware that Lee's efforts were unsuccessful, costly, and destructive to the South's chances of victory in the war, they are committed to the Lee tradition and seem to strain to absolve him."[29]

Lee's decision to pursue the offensive on July 2 manifestly has produced such cacophonous opinions as to confuse the most earnest student. But despite the contradictory shadow cast by this imposing mass of material—and accepting the fact that definitive answers are impossible at a distance of more than a century and a quarter—it remains worthwhile to train a close lens on the crucial questions: Was it reasonable for Lee to renew assaults on July 2? On the basis of his knowledge at the time, did aggressive tactics offer the best chance for the type of sweeping success on Northern soil that might propel the Confederacy toward independence?

The situation at the end of the first day of fighting is well known. Lee had arrived on the field early in the afternoon and, in the words of Walter H. Taylor of his staff, "ascertained that the enemy's infantry and artillery were present in considerable force. Heth's division was already hotly engaged, and it was soon evident that a serious engagement could not be avoided."[30] Only two of Heth's brigades actually had experienced serious fighting at that point, however, and Lee found himself witness to a meeting engagement rather than a general battle. It soon became apparent that the positioning of units from Richard S. Ewell's Second Corps, which were arriving on the northern end of the field, afforded the Confederates a tactical edge that Lee promptly exploited to good advantage. By 4:30 P.M., Southern attackers had driven the Federals to defensive lines along the high ground south of Gettysburg. Lee watched the action from atop Seminary Ridge, sensed the makings of a striking victory, and shortly after 5:00 P.M. instructed Ewell to seize the heights below town if practicable. For a variety of reasons, Ewell decided not to do so. Why Lee refused to commit some of A. P. Hill's troops—especially the fresh division of Richard H. Anderson— to a final joint assault with Ewell's brigades remains a mystery; the upshot was that daylight expired with Union troops firmly entrenched on Cemetery Hill.[31]

About 5:00 P.M., James Longstreet found Lee on Seminary Ridge. Dismounting and taking out his field glasses, Longstreet scanned the high ground that eventually would constitute the famous Union fish hook. Impressed by the strength of the enemy's position, Longstreet soon engaged Lee in an increasingly tense conversation. The only eyewitness testimony about this exchange comes from Longstreet, who left three versions that agree in substance but differ in detail. Longstreet suggested to Lee that the Confederates move around the Federal left and take up a defensive position between the Army of the Potomac and Washington; once situated, they could force Meade to attack them and then seek an opening for a counterstroke. This proposed movement, claimed Longstreet in all of his later writings, conformed to an agreement between himself and Lee to pursue a strategic offensive but remain on the tactical defensive in Pennsylvania. He therefore was surprised at Lee's response: "If the enemy is there tomorrow, we must attack him." Loath to embrace aggressive tactics, Longstreet persisted in his arguments. But Lee did not "seem to abandon the idea of attack on the next day. He seemed under a subdued excitement, which occasionally took possession of him when 'the hunt was up'. . . . The sharp battle fought by Hill and Ewell on that day had given him a taste of victory."[32]

James Power Smith of Ewell's staff presently joined Lee and Longstreet with news that Jubal Early and Robert Rodes believed they could take the high ground south of Gettysburg if supported on their right. Thinking Hill's troops too exhausted for such duty, Lee asked Longstreet if the leading elements of the First Corps were near enough to assist. According to Smith, Longstreet "replied that his front division, McLaws, was about six miles away, and then was indefinite and noncommital."[33] Disappointed with Longstreet's response, Lee instructed Smith to tell Ewell "he regretted that his people were not up to support him on the right, but he wished him to take the Cemetery Hill if it were possible; and that he would ride over and see him very soon."[34]

Lest Smith's reading be deemed suspect because of his well-known antipathy toward "Old Pete," it is important to note that a trio of witnesses friendly to Longstreet also sketched a man deeply upset about the prospect of attacking on July 2. G. Moxley Sorrel of Longstreet's staff remembered that the lieutenant general "did not want to fight on the ground or on the plan adopted by the General-in-Chief. As Longstreet was not to be made willing and Lee refused to change or could not change, the former failed to conceal some anger." Raphael J. Moses, commissary officer of the First Corps, wrote in his unpublished autobiography that later in the evening Longstreet expounded at length to Fremantle about the enemy's position, insisting that "the Union army would have greater advantages at Gettysburg than we had at Fredericksburg." Fremantle himself noted that over supper on July 1, "General Longstreet spoke of the enemy's position as being 'very formidable.' He also said that they would doubtless intrench themselves strongly during the night."[35] Of Longstreet's deep misgivings there can be no doubt; nor is it likely that his words and gestures failed to convey his feelings to Lee.

Sometime after 5:30 P.M., Longstreet departed and Lee rode toward Ewell's end of the line. Lee must have worried about the attitude of his senior lieutenant, whose friendship he valued and upon whom he had relied heavily since calling him "the staff of my right hand" in the wake of the Seven Days.[36] Although he knew from a reconnaissance by Armistead L. Long of his staff that Federals held Cemetery Hill in strength, Lee also wondered why firing had slackened along the Second Corps front. He had instructed Ewell to take that high ground if possible, and his postwar conversations with William Allan clearly indicated deep dissatisfaction at Ewell's failure to press his assaults. Walter Taylor's memoirs

Maj. Gen. Jubal Anderson Early. From *Battles and Leaders of the Civil War* 4:529.

confirm that Lee was unhappy: "The prevailing idea with General Lee was, to press forward without delay; to follow up promptly and vigorously the advantage already gained. Having failed to reap the full fruit of the victory before night, his mind was evidently occupied with the idea of renewing the assaults upon the enemy's right with the dawn of day on the second."[37]

Lee thus reached Second Corps headquarters north of Gettysburg in a testy mood. He and the principal commanders of Stonewall Jackson's old corps gathered after dusk in the arbor of a small house near the Carlisle road. The ensuing conversation deepened Lee's frustration with his lieutenants. "It was evident from the first," recalled Jubal Early in the fullest eyewitness account of the meeting, "that it was his purpose to attack the enemy as early as possible the next day." Early maintained that "there was not the slightest . . . difference of opinion" about Lee's idea of continuing the offensive; however, all three Second Corps leaders argued against their troops spearheading the assaults. They had been impressed with the strength of Cemetery Hill, which Ewell's official report characterized as "a commanding position." Early took the lead in pointing to the Union left as the most vulnerable target.[38] Because Lee believed two of A. P. Hill's divisions had been fought out on July 1, the response of Ewell and his subordinates meant that the First Corps, headed by a suddenly peevish Longstreet, would perform the hardest work the following day.

Early averred in a controversial part of his account that Lee exhibited distress at the thought of relying on Longstreet: "When General Lee had heard our views . . . he said, in these very words, which are indelibly impressed on my memory: 'Well, if I attack from my right, Longstreet will have to make the attack;' and after a moment's pause, during which he held his head down in deep thought, he raised it and added: 'Longstreet is a very good fighter when he gets in position and gets everything ready, but he is *so slow.*'" This assertion, with its claim of precise accuracy nearly fifteen years after the alleged quotation was uttered, reeks of Lost Cause special pleading and lacks support from evidence closer to the event.[39] It is quite simply beyond belief that Lee would criticize his senior lieutenant in front of junior officers. Still, it is reasonable to assume that Lee did not relish the prospect of entrusting his assaults on July 2 to a man obviously opposed to resuming the offensive—and his facial expression may well have indicated as much to Early and the others.

Lee spent a long night working out details for the next day's fighting. Lack of enthusiasm among his subordinates for continuing the tactical offensive must have grated on him. The Army of Northern Virginia had built its formidable reputation on a series of impressive victories that with few exceptions included a large aggressive component. Had not the odds at the Seven Days or Second Manassas been less favorable for Southern success? And what of Chancellorsville? On all of those fields the army's offensive spirit had made the difference. Now Lee faced the prospect of planning a battle with substantive doubts regarding key Confederate commanders.

Although he strongly favored retaining the initiative, those doubts kept other options open. Longstreet's desire to flank the Federals remained on his mind. George Campbell Brown of Ewell's staff recalled in 1870 that Lee instructed him on the night of July 1 to tell Ewell "not to become so much involved as to be unable readily to extricate his troops." "I have not decided to fight here," stated Lee, "and may probably draw off by my right flank. . . . so as to get between the enemy & Washington & Baltimore, & force them to attack us in position."[40] During his meeting with the officers of the Second Corps, Lee had proposed moving their troops to the right but dropped the idea when Early argued, among other things, that it would hurt morale to give up ground won through hard combat. Lee returned to this idea later, however, sending Ewell orders "to draw [his] corps to the right." A second conference with Ewell, during which the corps chief expressed a willingness to attack Culp's Hill, persuaded Lee to leave the Second Corps in position on the left.[41] As stated before, the commanding general's final plan for July 2 called for Longstreet to make the principal attack against the Union left while Hill and Ewell supported him with secondary assaults against the enemy's center and right. Lee admonished Ewell to exploit any opportunity to convert his offensive into a full-blown attack.[42]

Few episodes in Lee's career reveal more starkly his natural aggressiveness. He had examined closely the imposing Federal position later described so graphically in his official report. Even the most optimistic scenario would project heavy casualties in an attempt to seize that ground. Jedediah Hotchkiss's journal records that on the morning of July 2, Lee discussed the upcoming assault at Second Corps headquarters and was not "very sanguine of its success. He feared . . . a great sacrifice of life." Lee knew from prisoners that two Union corps had been defeated on July 1, but he lacked information about the location of the bulk of the enemy's forces. In the absence of sound intelligence from his cavalry, he surmised only that the balance of Meade's army "was approaching Gettysburg."[43] His senior subordinate had disagreed sharply with the suggestion that offensive operations be resumed on July 2. Officers in the Second Corps were willing enough for Longstreet's soldiers to mount assaults but preferred a supporting role for their own men. In sum, powerful arguments could be raised against continuing the offensive.

Why did Lee choose to overlook all of them? His own explanations are unconvincing. Raphael Moses mentioned that Lee objected to Longstreet's flanking maneuver "on account of our long wagon and artillery trains"; as noted above, Lee also asserted in his official report that "to withdraw through the mountains with our extensive trains would have been difficult and dangerous." Lee further postulated a logistical crisis should he take a defensive position and await Meade's attack—his men had stripped the immediate region clean of supplies, and the enemy might use local troops to frustrate Southern efforts to forage on a large scale.[44]

Porter Alexander countered both of these points in one telling passage. "Now when it is remembered that we stayed for three days longer on that very ground, two of them days of desperate battle, ending in the discouragement of a bloody repulse," wrote the artillerist in the 1890s, "& then successfully withdrew all our trains & most of the wounded through the mountains; and finding the Potomac too high to ford, protected them all & foraged successfully for over a week in a very restricted territory along the river . . . it does not seem improbable that we could have faced Meade safely on the 2nd at Gettysburg without assaulting him in his wonderfully strong position." David Gregg McIntosh, like Alexander an artillerist who held Lee in the highest esteem, similarly dismissed the obstacles to Lee's pulling back on July 2: "The fact that he was able to do so after the battle, justifies the belief that Longstreet was right in his opinion that an attack in front was not advisable, and that General Lee committed an error in determining upon that course."[45]

Lee's notion that local units posed a serious threat to his army strains credulity. Jubal Early's memoirs captured the attitude of Confederates in the Army of Northern Virginia toward such troops. Describing a clash with soldiers of the 26th Pennsylvania Militia several days before the battle of Gettysburg, "Old Jube" identified them as "part of Governor Curtin's contingent for the defence of the State, . . . [who] seemed to belong to that class of men who regard 'discretion as the better part of valor.'" "It was a good thing the regiment fled quickly," added Early sarcastically, "or some of its members might have been hurt, and all would have been captured." Those who did fall into Southern hands received paroles the next day and were "sent about their business, rejoicing at this termination of their campaign." George Templeton Strong of the United States Sanitary Commission took an equally derisive view of the Pennsylvania militia. On learning that they were mustering in strength, Strong wrote an acidic entry in his diary on June 30: "Much good they would do, to be sure, in combat with Lee's desperadoes, cunning sharp-shooters, and stark, hard-riding moss troopers."[46] Furthermore, correspondence on July 2–3 among Secretary of War Stanton and various Union commanders involved with local troops leaves no doubt about the ineffectiveness of the latter.[47] Had Lee decided to forage on either side of the South Mountain range, it is almost certain that his soldiers could have handled local Federal troops with impunity.

Even offensive moves by a combination of local forces and units from the Army of the Potomac—a remote possibility due to problems of transportation and morale among the former—should not have given Lee undue pause. His decision to attack on July 2 betrayed confidence that his soldiers could take a strong position from the enemy. It makes no sense to assert that those men would fail to hold a position against attacks from the same foe. Porter Alexander turned to a quotation from Stonewall Jackson in emphasizing this point: "We did sometimes fail to drive them out of position, but they *always* failed to drive us."[48]

What of Lee's dismissal of Longstreet's proposed flanking movement? Possible weaknesses in the plan must be given consideration (though Lee did not mention any in his report). If Longstreet envisioned a strategic rather than a tactical shift around Meade's left, the Army of Northern Virginia might have opened its own left flank to the Federals. Moreover, lines of supply and communication west of South Mountain might have been somewhat vulnerable.

But no such dangers would have obtained had Lee remained on the victorious field of July 1. As Porter Alexander put it, "We had a fine defensive position on Seminary Ridge ready at our hand to occupy. It was not such a really *wonderful* position as the enemy happened to fall into, but it was no bad one, & it could never have been successfully assaulted." To the west lay even stronger ground in the passes of South Mountain. A fragment of Lee's army had been driven from such gaps on September 14, 1862; however, the Army of Northern Virginia in July 1863 possessed the numbers and morale to hold the eastern face of the mountain indefinitely, all the while foraging in the lush Cumberland Valley. Had Lee fallen back to South Mountain "with all the prestige of victory," thought Alexander, "popular sentiment would have forced Meade to take the aggressive."[49] The likely result of Northern assaults would have been a bloody repulse followed by some type of Confederate counterattack. Readily at hand was the example of Second Manassas, where Jackson had fixed the Federals with assaults on August 28, 1862, gone on the defensive the next day, and set the stage for Longstreet's smashing counterattack on the thirtieth.

The difficulty of Meade's situation after July 1 should be kept always in mind. Abraham Lincoln and the Republicans could not tolerate for long the presence of the most famous Rebel army on Northern soil. As early as June 14, a day before the first elements of the Army of Northern Virginia crossed the Potomac at Williamsport, Secretary of the Navy Gideon Welles sketched a very uneasy Union leadership. Noting "scary rumors abroad of army operations and a threatened movement of Lee upon Pennsylvania," Welles described Secretary of War Edwin M. Stanton as "uneasy" and Lincoln as fearful that thousands of Federal troops in the Shenandoah Valley would be lost—"Harper's Ferry over again." The next day Welles mentioned a "panic telegraph" from Pennsylvania's governor, Andrew G. Curtin, and rumors of Rebels in Chambersburg, Pennsylvania: "I can get nothing satisfactory from the War Department. . . . There is trouble, confusion, uncertainty, where there should be calm intelligence."[50]

The onus was on the Federals to force Lee away from Pennsylvania. Meade's initial orders underscored his responsibility as head of "the covering army of Washington as well as the army of operation against the invading forces of the rebels." Should Lee menace either Washington or Baltimore, stated General in Chief Henry W. Halleck in a telegram to Meade on June 28, "it is expected that you will either anticipate him or arrive with him so as to give him battle."[51] The crucial part of this order is that Meade was to *give* battle rather than simply await the enemy's moves. Lee's comment that a battle had become "in a measure unavoidable" after July 1 applied far more realistically to Meade than to himself.

Clearly a number of factors militated against Lee's attacking on July 2. Just as clearly, a defensive posture might have opened the way for a decisive counterattack. The prudent decision would have been to shift to the defensive following the tactical victory on July 1. From such a posture, Lee would retain great freedom of action following a likely Union attempt to defeat the Army of Northern Virginia through offensive tactics. The Confederates could have stayed north of the Potomac for a protracted period of time, thus adding logistical and political accomplishment to any military success. Finally, had Lee opted for the tactical defensive after the first day's battle, thousands of men shot down in assaults on July 2–3 would have been in the ranks for further service.

But acceptance of these statements does not prove that Lee made a foolish decision. A victory on Northern soil might aggravate internal dissension in the North and thus weaken Union resolve. Within the context of dwindling Confederate manpower (a state of affairs Lee's aggressive generalship had helped to produce), there was reason to believe the Army of Northern Virginia would never again face the Army of the Potomac on such relatively equal terms. Lee had seen his men perform prodigious feats on a number of battlefields—most recently against intimidating odds at Chancellorsville. The overriding influence in his choosing to resume the offensive on July 2 might have been a belief that the splendid Southern infantry could overcome the recalcitrance of his lieutenants, the difficulties of terrain, and everything else to achieve great results. Lee's subsequent comments that failures of coordination brought defeat suggest that he never doubted his soldiers might have won the fight. Fourteen years after the campaign, Henry Heth said simply, "The fact is, General Lee believed the Army of Northern Virginia, as it then existed, could accomplish anything."[52]

Ample testimony about soaring confidence in the Army of Northern Virginia lends credence to Lee's opinion, none more dramatically than Fremantle's description of morale on the night of July 1. Over supper that evening, recorded Fremantle, Longstreet discussed the reasons attacks might fail; however, in the ranks "the universal feeling in the army was one of profound contempt for an enemy whom they have beaten so constantly, and under so many disadvantages." Lee's great faith in his own men implied a degree of scorn for the Federals, an attitude noted by Fremantle's fellow foreign observer, Capt. Justus Scheibert of the Prussian army: "Excessive disdain for the enemy . . . caused the simplest plan of a direct attack upon the position at Gettysburg to prevail and deprived the army of victory."[53]

If Lee did experience any regret about his decision to remain on the offensive after the first day's victory, perhaps it stemmed from a sense that he had asked the men to do so much despite obvious signs of trouble among his top lieutenants. Two of Lee's statements at the time illustrate this point. He wrote Mrs. Lee on July 26, 1863, that the army had "accomplished all that could reasonably be expected." "It ought not to have been expected to perform impossibilities, or to have fulfilled the anticipations of the thoughtless and unreasonable," admitted the general in a sentence that could well be taken as self-criticism. Five days later Lee wrote a preliminary report for Adjutant General Samuel Cooper in which he praised the "heroic valor and fortitude" of his troops. "More may have been required of them than they were able to perform," he acknowledged, "but my admiration of their noble qualities and confidence in their ability . . . has suffered no abatement. . . ."[54]

R. E. Lee confronted a crucial choice on the evening of July 1, 1863. His selection of the tactical offensive for July 2 reflected his predilection for aggressive action. Porter Alexander thought even Napoleon failed to surpass "some of the deeds of audacity to which Gen. Lee committed himself" and saw Gettysburg as an example of Lee's unnecessarily taking "the most desperate chances & the bloodiest road."[55] Without question Lee did gamble a very great deal on the throw of his offensive dice after July 1. He ruled out defensive maneuvers that might have opened breathtaking possibilities, and in the process he bled the future offensive edge from his magnificent army. It is not unfair to state from the safe confines of historical perspective that Lee erred in his decision. Many of his own contemporaries realized as much at the time. But it is unfair to look at the grisly result and argue that his actions were entirely unreasonable. Momentum and morale count heavily in warfare, and it was probably those two factors that motivated Lee to a significant degree. Had Southern infantry solidified the first day's victory through successful assaults on July 2, as they almost did, many of Lee's critics would have been silenced.

The Peach Orchard Revisited

Daniel E. Sickles and the Third Corps on July 2, 1863

William Glenn Robertson

WARFARE RANKS AMONG THE MOST COMPLEX OF HUMAN endeavors. Participants must take into account a wide variety of variables, including terrain, weather, technology, and human frailties, all of which combine to produce a particular outcome. Not the least of warfare's complexities stems from the interaction of personalities among senior commanders. In any army in any century leaders have had their friends and their enemies, equals and subordinates they could trust and those they could not. Strong personalities breed strong reactions, both positive and negative. Such interpersonal relationships always affect the outcome of great events, far more in fact than participants usually admit. So it always has been, and so it always will be, as long as humans make war on each other in an organized manner. Obvious to contemporaries, this important web of interpersonal relationships often disappears from view after a conflict unless individuals choose to illuminate the relationships in their writings. Even when described in memoirs and other postwar accounts, these relationships often become distorted, generating claims and counterclaims that increasingly obscure the original issues and circumstances.

In seeking to reconstruct and analyze past events, historians must be aware of the relationships among senior officers and the frequent distortions of those relationships in postwar writings. Some historians unfortunately become parties in the debate rather than honest brokers, doing little more than perpetuating the arguments of principals with whom they have come to identify. Objective truth is thus obscured rather than illuminated.

Was Maj. Gen. Ambrose E. Burnside as incompetent as conventional wisdom would have it? Probably not, as a recent biography argues. Was Maj. Gen. Benjamin F. Butler as lacking in morality and military skills as his detractors, contemporary and otherwise, have so loudly proclaimed? Again, probably not. Historians should strive to meet the admittedly difficult test of viewing senior commanders with strong personalities and controversial records as impartially as possible. These officers should not be caricatured as either heroes or villains but should be seen as complex personalities interacting with others of a like nature in extremely stressful situations. Only in this manner can their decisions be analyzed dispassionately and understood.

Among senior commanders on both sides in the American Civil War, Maj. Gen. Daniel Edgar Sickles enjoyed one of the most colorful careers. Sickles gained notoriety years before he donned a Federal general's uniform. His spirited personality and mixed reputation generated friends and enemies alike. He brought this baggage with him to Gettysburg, where his bold decision on the battle's second day added to the controversy already swirling about him. For various reasons that decision continued to generate debate long after the battle. Partisans gathered on both sides of the issue and quickly skewed the arguments of the principals. Even today Dan Sickles and his Gettysburg decision have the power to excite passions, as the most judicious student of the subject, Richard Sauers, has admitted. It is time to look again at Sickles's actions on July 2, 1863, with as much objectivity as possible. What was the context within which Sickles operated? What actions did he take? What were the results of those actions? What result might a different decision have generated?[1]

Born on October 20, 1819, in New York City, Daniel Edgar Sickles was the son of prominent patent lawyer George Garrett Sickles and his wife Susan Marsh. Blessed with a nimble intelligence and boundless self-confidence, young Sickles vexed his parents by running away from home several times. An effort to instill discipline by sending him to boarding school in Glens Falls, New York, at the age of fifteen failed. Leaving school after an altercation with a teacher, Sickles worked as a printer's helper for more than a year before returning to New York City. There he soon began to associate with an unsavory crowd and to indulge in what would become a lifelong proclivity to dally with women of ill repute. His parents sought to separate him from his friends by moving the family to New Jersey, but Sickles again left home. Realizing that he could not bring his wayward son back to the family fold by force, George Sickles offered forgiveness and the promise of a free education. For two years Dan lived in the household of Lorenzo Da Ponte, a family friend who endeavored to prepare him for

Maj. Gen. Daniel Edgar Sickles. Courtesy of the Library of Congress.

college. In the same household were the Antonio Bagiolis and their infant daughter Teresa, who eventually would become Sickles's wife. Sickles entered New York University during his second year with the Da Pontes.

When Da Ponte died suddenly, Sickles lost interest in college and pursued an entirely new path. He left school and studied law in the office of Benjamin F. Butler, President Martin Van Buren's attorney general, while beginning a long association with Democratic party politics at Tammany Hall. Admitted to the bar in 1843 at the age of twenty-four, Sickles soon gained a reputation as a rake, a spendthrift, and a partisan politician of high visibility. Election to the New York state assembly in 1847 offered a new arena to Sickles, who scandalized polite society by escorting a known prostitute into the legislative chambers. Sickles ignored censure by his peers, and both his political and legal careers prospered. On September 27, 1852, Sickles and Teresa Bagioli were married against the wishes of both families. She was sixteen and he almost thirty-three. Anyone who believed that marriage would transform Sickles's life-style experienced swift disappointment. In the words of one biographer, Sickles was a man of such "violent, undisciplined impulses" that he could hardly be expected to alter his behavior overnight, and indeed he did not.[2]

In 1853 Sickles took the position of confidential secretary to James Buchanan, newly appointed minister to Great Britain. Viewing Buchanan as a rising political figure, Sickles determined to advance along with his new superior even if it cost him money and entailed an absence from his pregnant wife. He cut quite a swath in England until July 1854, when he publicly refused to toast the health of Queen Victoria at an Independence Day banquet. This diplomatic faux pas, a backstage role in the abortive and infamous Ostend Manifesto, and an increasing need for more income led to Sickles's return to the United States late in 1854. Resuming his law practice, his political career, and his philandering where he had left them in 1853, he was elected to the New York state senate in 1855. Buchanan returned from abroad to run for president in 1856, while Sickles ran for Congress. Both were elected, but for different reasons neither would find the prize worth having. Buchanan soon began to struggle with the Union's greatest crisis; Sickles fell into a domestic squabble.[3]

Sickles's life-style in the nation's capital followed a predictable pattern. He lived far beyond his apparent means, continued his rakish indiscretions, and generally made himself notorious in Washington society. Re-elected in 1858, he immersed himself even more fully in political intrigue while Teresa languished at home. Some time in the spring of 1858 she began an affair with Philip Barton Key, the handsome U.S. attorney for the District of Columbia and son of Francis Scott Key. Eventually much of Washington came to know of their trysts, though Sickles did not learn of the affair until February 26, 1859. He confronted Teresa on that date, and she signed what amounted to a full confession. On seeing the unsuspecting Key signaling to Teresa the next day, Sickles rushed out of his house and shot him to death. Arrested and tried for murder, Sickles was acquitted in April. His successful defense rested on a plea of temporary insanity (by some accounts the first use of this defense), strong circumstantial evidence to the contrary nonwithstanding. Sickles created even greater comment when he accepted Teresa back into his household in July 1859. Surprisingly, few blamed Sickles for Key's demise, but fewer still could accept his decision to forgive Teresa.[4]

Most of Washington society ostracized Sickles, who completed his term in Congress under a cloud. Too realistic to make another race for office, Sickles returned to New York City in early 1861 to resume the practice of law. Thus he was relatively unencumbered when the secession crisis turned from words to acts of violence in April 1861. At the suggestion of a political friend, Sickles decided to raise a regiment. Authority from the governor of New York to raise one regiment soon mushroomed into authority to raise a brigade of five regiments. Sickles and his friends quickly recruited the brigade, calling it the Excelsior Brigade, and after considerable political and financial difficulty saw it accepted into Federal service in late July 1861. Assigned to a division commanded by Brig. Gen. Joseph Hooker, Sickles quickly fell into disfavor with his superior (they would later become friends). Further problems arose when the Senate refused to confirm his appointment as brigadier general. Fast political footwork and astute lobbying finally brought Sickles the coveted star on May 13, 1862, but his beloved Excelsior Brigade already had sailed to the Virginia Peninsula.[5]

Sickles's late arrival in the theater of war caused him to miss the battle of Williamsburg, the only significant action for the Excelsior Brigade during the Peninsula campaign. Present but only lightly engaged at Seven Pines, Oak Grove, Glendale, and Malvern Hill, the brigade nevertheless shared the accolades bestowed on Hooker's division by friendly newspapermen. Hooker himself praised Sickles's performance in combat. The brigade acquitted itself well at Second Bull Run in August 1862 while Sickles was absent in New York on recruiting duty. In the reorganization following that battle, Hooker rose to command the First Corps and Sickles took charge of Hooker's old division in the Third Corps. Although the division spent the Antietam campaign in reserve at Alexandria, Sickles's star continued to ascend with Hooker's. On November 29, 1862, Sickles was promoted to the rank of major general. His division again remained in reserve and saw little action at the Battle of Fredericksburg in December. More significant for

Dan Sickles, the disaster at Fredericksburg prompted the Lincoln administration to select a new commander for the Army of the Potomac. Maj. Gen. Joseph Hooker, Sickles's old superior and now his patron, replaced Burnside in late January 1863.[6]

Known for his aggressive fighting qualities as well as for an arrogant and dissolute life-style, Hooker skillfully reorganized the army. Sickles received command of the Third Corps on February 5, 1863, becoming the only non-West Pointer among the seven corps chiefs and the only one lacking experience at that level of responsibility. Hooker had seen Sickles in action on the Peninsula and remained confident that the New Yorker would acquit himself well. Others in the Army of the Potomac expressed doubts about Sickles's promotion. Indeed, many regular army officers objected to Hooker's appointment. Riddled with, and often hampered by, internal politics, the officer corps of the Army of the Potomac prepared for the next campaign in a sour mood.

More judicious than most of his peers, Maj. Gen. George G. Meade of the Fifth Corps spoke of the situation to his wife in late January: "As to Hooker, you know my opinion of him, frequently expressed. I believe my opinion is more favorable than any other of the old regular officers, most of whom are decided in their hostility to him." "I believe Hooker is a good soldier;" continued Meade, "the danger he runs is of subjecting himself to bad influences, such as Dan Butterfield and Dan Sickles, who, being intellectually more clever than Hooker, and leading him to believe they are very influential, will obtain an injurious ascendancy over him and insensibly affect his conduct." Meade further underscored his opinion of Butterfield and Sickles in February, when he wrote that "such gentlemen as Dan Sickles and Dan Butterfield are not the persons I should select as my intimates, however worthy and superior they may be." The cause of Meade's distaste for Sickles is unknown, but the latter's life-style and lack of professional military education must have played a large role.[7]

The Army of the Potomac embarked on the Chancellorsville campaign in late April 1863 burdened with a divided officer corps. For once Sickles's command found itself heavily engaged. Occupying the right center of Hooker's perimeter around the Chancellorsville crossroads on May 2, Sickles's troops discovered what ultimately proved to be the march of Stonewall Jackson's corps around the Union flank. Sickles advanced aggressively to deal with the Confederates, only to be recalled by Hooker. That evening the massive Confederate column rolled up the Federal right. Strongly positioned on dominant terrain at Hazel Grove, Sickles's Third Corps held its ground but became increasingly exposed by the morning of May 3. Although Sickles wanted to remain at Hazel Grove, Hooker ordered the

Third Corps to withdraw to Fairview. In military terms Hazel Grove was an excellent place from which to dominate Fairview with artillery, a fact soon discovered by Confederates. Blasted by Southern guns at Hazel Grove, the Third Corps and the Army of the Potomac withdrew even farther, eventually leaving the field altogether. The Army of the Potomac had suffered another crushing defeat, but this time Dan Sickles's men had fought as long and as hard as any of the army's units. Losses in the Third Corps amounted to 4,119 killed, wounded, or missing, the largest total for any corps on the Chancellorsville field itself, as even Meade grudgingly admitted.[8]

The debacle of Chancellorsville exacerbated existing fractures in the command structure of the Army of the Potomac. Hooker had called a conference of his corps commanders late in the battle to seek their advice. Although a majority recommended an advance instead of a retreat, Hooker had withdrawn the army to its camps. Meade was among those favoring an advance. When he learned after the battle that Hooker was misrepresenting his position, Meade confronted his superior and asked for corroboration from his fellow corps leaders. He received satisfaction from all but Sickles, who, ever the Hooker partisan, reported that by the end of the conference Meade had waffled on the question. Meade's reaction to Sickles's response is unknown but can easily be surmised. As the Army of the Potomac moved northward in the early stages of what would become the Gettysburg campaign, most of its senior leaders had taken sides on the larger question of Hooker's leadership. Chief of Staff Daniel Butterfield and Sickles stood as Hooker's principal defenders. Notable among Hooker's detractors were Maj. Gen. John F. Reynolds of the First Corps and George Meade. When a minor dispute over the Federal garrison at Harpers Ferry supplied a pretext, the Lincoln administration removed Hooker on June 28, 1863, and replaced him with Meade.[9]

Meade's rise to supreme command brought not only a fresh face to army headquarters but also an entirely new faction to control of the Army of the Potomac. Although he kept Dan Butterfield as chief of staff for a time, Meade soon dispensed favors to his friends at the expense of those considered to be Hooker's sycophants. Prominent among Meade's friends were John Reynolds and Second Corps chief Winfield S. Hancock. Sickles headed the list of Meade's enemies. Perhaps Sickles's lack of professional military education or his close association with the discredited Hooker explained Meade's attitude. Given Meade's strict personal rectitude, the root cause of his distaste more likely could be traced to Sickles's unsavory private reputation. Whatever the underlying reasons, Sickles found himself subordinate to a man whose behavior toward him would be coldly correct at best and actively hostile at worst. Sickles would have to be careful—behavior foreign to the New Yorker—with Meade in charge of the army. Meade himself took charge in the midst of a dangerously fluid situation. All eyes would be on him, especially those of the Hooker faction represented by Sickles. Burdened by this personal baggage, the two men soon found themselves engaged in the greatest military campaign of their lives and about to commence a personal conflict that would end only with their deaths.[10]

As might be expected, Meade and Sickles began their relationship inauspiciously. Bad weather, poor maps, lack of knowledge about the enemy, and a general malaise among the Federal troops hampered Meade's efforts to move the army northward. June 29 proved especially frustrating because most of the corps fell short of their assigned objectives. Only Reynolds's First Corps met its target. Not only was Hancock's Second Corps delayed three hours but its failure to march on time caused the Fifth Corps to lag even farther behind. In response, Meade wrote understandingly to Hancock with no hint of a rebuke. When the commander of the Twelfth Corps reported that he was being delayed by the trains of the Third Corps, however, Meade instructed his assistant adjutant general to inform Sickles that "the train of your corps is at a stand-still at Middleburg, and delaying, of course, all movements in the rear. [General Meade] wishes you to give your immediate attention to keeping your train in motion."[11]

Apparently the more Meade thought about Sickles's lack of success on June 29, the more he believed this relatively gentle rebuke was not sufficient. On June 30, Sickles received the following more pointed note from army headquarters:

The commanding general noticed with regret the very slow movement of your corps yesterday. It is presumed you marched at an early hour, and up to 6 P.M. the rear of your column had not passed Middleburg, distant from your camp of the night before some 12 miles only. This, considering the good condition of the road and the favorable state of the weather, was far from meeting the expectation of the commanding general, and delayed to a very late hour the arrival of troops and trains in your rear. The Second Corps in the same space of time made a march nearly double your own. Situated as this army now is, the commanding general looks for rapid movements of the troops.

Sickles's reaction to this note is unrecorded, but he scarcely could have mistaken the tone and its import. His friend Joe Hooker no longer commanded the Army of the Potomac. In addition, the reference to Hancock, who stood high in Meade's estimation, must have been especially galling in light of the problems caused by Hancock's failure to meet his marching goal on June 29.[12]

Sickles received a series of confusing and contradictory orders from either Meade or his designated representatives over the next two days. On June 30, Meade empowered his friend Reynolds to coordinate the movements of three corps, including that of Sickles. Sickles received several conflicting orders that day from both Reynolds and Meade. Rather than fall further into Meade's bad graces, Sickles reported the contradictions to army headquarters and waited for Meade to indicate his preferred course of action. A similar situation prevailed on July 1—Meade's Pipe Creek Circular mandated that the Third Corps remain at Emmitsburg, whereas a message from Reynolds summoned the corps northward to Gettysburg, leaving Sickles again undecided as to his proper course of action. Sickles acted promptly when additional messages from Gettysburg on July 1 announced that Reynolds was dead, that Maj. Gen. Oliver O. Howard was in charge, and that Howard wanted the Third Corps to march north. Leaving one brigade from each of his two divisions at Emmitsburg, he moved toward Gettysburg with the remainder of his corps and notified Meade of his actions. En route to Gettysburg, Sickles received another message from Meade confirming the original order to remain at Emmitsburg. Sickles disregarded this message, continuing his march on the grounds that events had changed the context within which Meade had issued the instructions.[13]

Sickles arrived at Gettysburg via the Emmitsburg Road with two brigades of Maj. Gen. David B. Birney's First Division at about 6:00 P.M. on July 1. Moving on a parallel track west of the Emmitsburg Road, Brig. Gen. Andrew A. Humphreys's Second Division stumbled into Confederates near Black Horse Tavern and did not join the corps bivouac on Cemetery Ridge until approximately 2:00 A.M. on July 2. Meade reached the Federal positions on the hills just south of Gettysburg a little after midnight. His actions on that trying day were not those of a man completely sure of himself or his situation. The enemy had been discovered and momentarily checked, the army was concentrating on Gettysburg, and the situation was quite stable by the end of the day on July 1. But Meade had not been solely responsible for this outcome. However necessary, his delegation of responsibility to Reynolds had introduced a level of confusion into the command structure that could have had serious consequences. From any point of view other than that of a Meade partisan, the new army commander's performance over the preceding forty-eight hours had been less than inspirational. Certainly from the perspective of Dan Sickles, Meade's actions thus far had encouraged little confidence in his leadership.[14]

Some time before sunrise, Meade rode along his line to get some idea of its contours. His route first took him southward from Cemetery Hill along Cemetery Ridge toward Little Round Top. Turning northward before he reached the Round Tops, Meade surveyed the area of Culp's Hill on his right. His ride complete, he used a hastily drawn map to indicate positions for the infantry corps then on the field or soon to arrive. The Twelfth, Eleventh, and First Corps would hold the Federal right on the hills nearest Gettysburg. Hancock's Second Corps came next, occupying the northern end of Cemetery Ridge, and Sickles's corps extended Hancock's line southward. In taking the specified position, Sickles was to relieve Brig. Gen. John W. Geary's Second Division of the Twelfth Corps, which would then march to Culp's Hill to rejoin its parent unit. The Fifth Corps would remain behind the front line as the army's reserve pending arrival of Maj. Gen. John Sedgwick's large Sixth Corps. Having thus designed a satisfactory line, Meade ordered his chief of staff to draft a contingency plan should the army have to retreat. Meade could see Confederates only opposite his right and center and understandably concentrated his attention on those sectors. Nevertheless, between 6:00 and 7:00 A.M., he sent his son and aide, Capt. George Meade, to check the position of the Third Corps on the army's left.[15]

Riding southward from army headquarters, young Meade found Sickles's command post just west of the Taneytown Road. The captain failed to see Sickles, who was inside his tent, but heard from a staff officer that the Third Corps remained out of position because Sickles was unsure of the ground the army commander wished him to occupy. Captain Meade hastened back to his father with this disturbing information. General Meade then forcefully reiterated his earlier directions to Sickles: move the Third Corps to the left of Hancock's Second Corps and occupy the position formerly held by Geary's division of the Twelfth Corps. Upon returning to the Third Corps, Captain Meade delivered his father's message to Sickles himself. Sickles retorted that his men were already in motion, but that Geary's supposed position had been a simple bivouac area with no clearly defined front line. Capt. George E. Randolph, Sickles's chief of artillery, then asked Captain Meade to convey a request to army headquarters for Brig. Gen. Henry J. Hunt, the army's chief of artillery, to survey the new location for gun positions. As Sickles left to join his four brigades, Captain Meade rode back to his father's headquarters. Approximately two hours later, about 9:00 A.M., Sickles's last two brigades arrived from Emmitsburg to bring the corps to full strength.[16]

General Meade became increasingly preoccupied with the army's right as the morning progressed. Confederate units continued to mass openly on that end of the line. Rather than await an assault, Meade briefly contemplated launching a spoiling attack but abandoned the idea because of the broken nature of the terrain around Culp's Hill. His focus nonetheless remained on his right flank until Sickles arrived at army headquarters at about 11:00 A.M. Sickles reported his continuing uncertainty about the position assigned his corps. Meade repeated that the Third Corps should extend its line southward on Cemetery Ridge from the left of the Second Corps through Geary's old position toward the Round Tops. Apparently satisfied, Sickles asked Meade if he might post his two divisions according to his own discretion. Meade responded affirmatively, with the caveat that his lieutenant observe the general defensive scheme already outlined. In parting, Sickles reiterated the earlier request that General Hunt visit the new position to assess its suitability for artillery. Meade agreed, and Hunt left army headquarters with Sickles.[17]

Instead of taking Hunt directly south along Cemetery Ridge, Sickles guided him in a southwesterly direction along the Emmitsburg Road. They rode to a peach orchard that stood on rising ground approximately fifteen hundred yards west of Geary's old position, where Sickles stated that he much preferred to deploy his corps so as to encompass the high ground around the orchard. Standing some forty feet higher than the position Meade identified, the orchard, argued Sickles, clearly dominated the line then held by the Third Corps. Hunt generally agreed that the Peach Orchard ridge offered potential, especially if the Federals mounted an offensive from their left. He also pointed out deficiencies in the proposed position: the line was too long, the resulting salient could be attacked simultaneously from two directions, and both flanks of the Third Corps would be in the air. Pressed by Sickles for authorization to move the Third Corps forward to the new line, Hunt refused to assume authority rightfully belonging to Meade. He did, however, agree to inform Meade of the situation. Before departing, Hunt also suggested to Sickles that a reconnaissance of the woods west of the Emmitsburg Road might be both prudent and fruitful. The artillery chief then headed toward Cemetery Hill via Devil's Den.[18]

Acting on Hunt's suggestion, Sickles ordered General Birney to dispatch a scouting party into the woods beyond the Emmitsburg Road. Birney detailed four companies of Col. Hiram Berdan's First U.S. Sharpshooters, supported by a small infantry regiment, to undertake the mission. Upon entering Pitzer's Woods, the sharpshooters encountered Confederate pickets and drove them northward until a Confederate battle line appeared. Forced into a hasty retreat, the sharpshooters returned across the Emmitsburg Road with startling news of Confederates swarming into the woods to

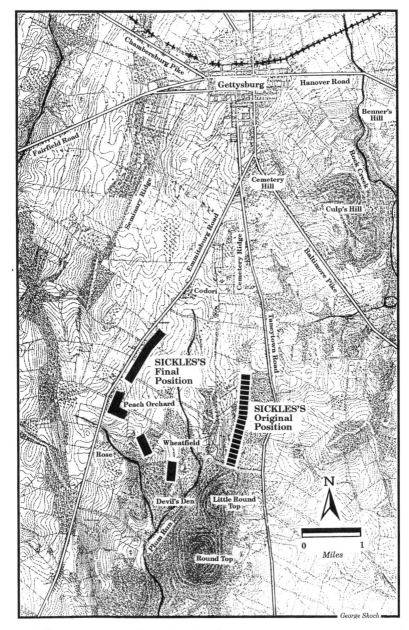

Chambersburg Pike

Gettysburg

Hanover Road

Benner's
Hill

Fairfield Road

Rock Creek

Seminary Ridge

Emmitsburg Road

Cemetery
Hill

Culp's Hill

Cemetery Ridge

Baltimore Pike

Codori

Taneytown Road

**SICKLES'S
Final
Position**

Peach Orchard

**SICKLES'S
Original
Position**

Wheatfield

Rose

N

Devil's Den

Little Round
Top

0   1
Miles

Plum Run

Round Top

George Skoch

Sickles's Movement to the Peach Orchard

the west. Berdan's report convinced Sickles that strong Confederate forces were moving to his left. Should he fail to act quickly, enemy guns might deploy on the coveted Peach Orchard ridge and place the Third Corps in another Hazel Grove–Fairview situation. Believing that the merits of the Peach Orchard salient outweighed its disadvantages, and concluding that there was no time to lose, Sickles decided to occupy the high ground without waiting for Meade's permission. Even before Berdan reported the results of his reconnaissance, Sickles had begun to advance units of the corps piecemeal. Now, about 2:00 P.M., he ordered the remainder of the corps forward. Humphreys's division occupied the right of the salient along the Emmitsburg Road with one brigade in line, one in support, and one in reserve. On Humphreys's left, Birney placed all three of his brigades in line— a futile attempt to stretch his division from the Peach Orchard to Little Round Top.[19]

Meade dispatched a message at 3:00 P.M. summoning all of his corps commanders to a conference at army headquarters. Before Sickles arrived, Meade learned from Brig. Gen. G. K. Warren, his chief engineer, that the Third Corps was not in its assigned position. Sickles appeared at the conference just as Meade prepared to ride to the Third Corps sector. Instructed to return to his command immediately, Sickles preceded Meade back to the vicinity of the Peach Orchard. Meade and part of his staff arrived shortly to see that only rapid remedial action would prevent the isolation of the Third Corps from the remainder of the army. When Sickles offered to return his divisions to their old position, Meade initially ordered him to do so but changed his mind when Confederate artillery opened fire on the Third Corps. Telling Sickles to remain where he was, Meade directed the Fifth Corps and a division of the Second Corps to come to the aid of the Third Corps. He also arranged for more artillery to support Sickles, then rode to the rear to expedite the movement of reinforcements. Before any of the reinforcing units could arrive, a heavy attack by two divisions of Lt. Gen. James Longstreet's Confederate corps smashed into the Federal troops in the Peach Orchard salient and drove them back in confusion. During the attack Sickles was gravely wounded in the leg and taken from the field. Ultimately the damaged limb required amputation, ending Sickles's field career.[20]

As he recovered gradually, Sickles harbored the idea that he could return to his beloved command. That hope ended on October 18, 1863, when Sickles visited Meade and asked to resume leadership of the Third Corps. Pointedly referring to Sickles's physical incapacity, Meade declined to reinstate the New Yorker. With his path blocked by a man he had long disliked, Sickles returned to Washington to ponder his next move. Maj. Gen.

Henry W. Halleck completed his report of events at Gettysburg in November 1863. No friend of Sickles, Halleck demonstrated open sympathy for Meade: "General Sickles, misinterpreting his orders, instead of placing the Third Corps on the prolongation of the Second, had moved it nearly three-quarters of a mile in advance—an error which nearly proved fatal in the battle." Soon made public, these words struck a blow at Sickles's vulnerable pride. He resolved to even the score against his enemies, casting about for a forum in which to air his own version of events on July 2.[21]

Sickles chose to make his primary case in a series of hearings held by the Joint Committee on the Conduct of the War. Chaired by Senator Benjamin Wade, the seven-member committee had the reputation of bias against most West Pointers. Neither Halleck nor Meade was a favorite of the committee, so Sickles's testimony against Meade in early 1864 fell on friendly ears. The general's statements before the committee masterfully presented his interpretation of events at Gettysburg through a complex blend of truth, half-truth, and occasional falsehood. Subsequent testimony from Generals Abner Doubleday and Daniel Butterfield generally reinforced Sickles's case against Meade. Meanwhile, an author cloaked by the pseudonym "Historicus" vigorously argued Sickles's side of the story in several widely read articles in the New York Herald. Meade responded by twice giving testimony before the committee utterly at variance with that of Sickles; however, he followed advice to remain silent in the face of the barrage from "Historicus." About the same time, on March 24, 1864, the Third Corps was abolished and its units transferred into other corps. This consolidation, carried out for reasons totally separate from the Meade-Sickles controversy, ensured that Sickles would never again stand at the head of his old unit. With the Third Corps gone, Sickles increased his determined effort to keep fresh the memory of its greatest day.[22]

Several factors thus combined to keep the controversy over Sickles's conduct at Gettysburg before the public and eventually the historical community. They included the bitter animosity between partisans of Meade and Hooker in the Army of the Potomac, the political agenda of the Joint Committee on the Conduct of the War, the abolition of the Third Corps, and, by no means least, Dan Sickles's desire for self-justification and self-promotion. Meade died in 1872; Sickles lived until 1914 and vigorously defended his actions at Gettysburg until the end. Although the thrust of his defense changed at various times, Sickles's arguments usually boiled down to four contentions. First, major elements of the Army of Northern Virginia were clearly shifting to his left. This statement was true but not for the reasons Sickles alleged, because the forces his reconnaissance encountered were not part of Longstreet's later movement. Second, Meade's orders to

Sickles were either nonexistent or vague. In fact, Meade had given Sickles verbal orders that, although general, were specific enough for the Third Corps eventually to reach Geary's sector. Third, Meade desired Sickles to occupy an exceedingly poor position. Here Sickles scored his strongest point, because the ground was lower than terrain to both the west and south and was too extensive for the Third Corps to hold in strength. Finally, Sickles portrayed Meade as a weak commander planning a retreat from the field at Gettysburg. In this, too, Sickles was wrong. Nevertheless, throughout the remainder of his life, Dan Sickles served to all who would listen this mixture of fact, partial truth, and error.[23]

Time and historical fashion have not served Sickles well since his death. For all his flaws, Meade has become the victor of Gettysburg, the man who defeated Robert E. Lee. Meade enjoys an image as the Army of the Potomac's most successful battle commander, if only because he led it for the remainder of the war. In contrast, Sickles is remembered more for his flamboyant personality and his peccadillos than for any positive characteristics as a soldier. His performance at Chancellorsville rarely emerges from the shadow of the far greater debacle suffered by his patron Hooker. Indeed, the movement of the Third Corps to the Peach Orchard salient on July 2, 1863, and its subsequent retreat from that position define Sickles's military career in the public mind. Sickles may have vanquished Meade in the former's lifetime, but Meade's partisans have won in the end. Their victory has been so complete that a modern defense of Sickles's actions may be likened to the proverbial tilting at windmills. But a case can be made for Dan Sickles without resorting to his characteristic bombast. The assessment that follows constitutes just such a case.

Both George Meade and Dan Sickles carried mental baggage to Gettysburg that hampered their smooth cooperation in the crisis. Enmity between them reached far back and was exacerbated by Meade's elevation to succeed Hooker. Meade's plans and actions proved tentative during his first few days in command of the army. Although it may have been necessary under the circumstances, his reliance on favorites such as Reynolds and Hancock led to the issuance of conflicting orders from multiple sources. The image Meade projected, especially to those predisposed to dislike him, was thus scarcely authoritative. He had yet to solidify his hold on either the Army of the Potomac or its quarrelsome command structure. It would not be surprising, therefore, for Sickles to question Meade's judgment and rely on his own if circumstances seemed to warrant such a course of action. Moreover, only two months earlier Sickles had been ordered to relinquish a strong position at Hazel Grove and forced to occupy an inferior one at Fairview with unfortunate results. With his own judgment seemingly vindicated so recently, he could be expected to assert it again in similar circumstances—especially in opposition to orders from a new commander he hardly respected.[24]

When Sickles received Meade's instructions to occupy Geary's old position on the southern extension of Cemetery Ridge early on July 2, he apparently understood what Meade intended but found the prospect unpleasant. Geary's men had held low ground in relation to the surrounding terrain, especially that to the west where the Peach Orchard ridge rose at least forty feet higher. Fields of fire to the west of Geary's position also were seriously limited. Clearly preoccupied with his right, Meade had made only a cursory investigation of the terrain to his left. Little Round Top dominated the ground southward beyond Cemetery Ridge, but Sickles believed he lacked enough troops to reach that eminence and occupy it in force. Berdan's reconnaissance to the west of the Peach Orchard ridge yielded information that added to Sickles's concern. With the enemy apparently moving around his left flank, dominant terrain reminiscent of Hazel Grove in his front, and his own confidence in Meade's judgment minimal, Sickles eventually concluded that he must take the situation into his own hands. Once he selected a course of action, he implemented it without much reference to the remainder of the Army of the Potomac.[25]

From the perspective of the Third Corps, Sickles's advance to the Peach Orchard ridge made sense. It could have been the right move from the Army of the Potomac's perspective, too, if coordinated with Meade and adjacent units in time to adjust the overall Federal defensive alignment. Executed unilaterally, however, Sickles's movement was decidedly improper. Unfortunately, the personalities of Sickles and Meade, and the peculiar chemistry between them, ensured that Sickles would act unilaterally. Sickles clearly should have made a greater attempt to coordinate his advance with army headquarters. Equally clearly, Meade should have paid more attention to his left. Neither commander took these actions, which in hindsight appear so reasonable, and thus the two divisions of the Third Corps broke their connection with the Second Corps on their right and occupied the Peach Orchard ridge. There Longstreet's late afternoon assaults found them; there the Third Corps suffered severely; there Dan Sickles lost both his leg and his field command forever.[26]

What if Sickles had obeyed Meade's orders and simply prolonged the Federal line southward along Cemetery Ridge? Any answer to this hypothetical question must be purely speculative, but some results seem probable. First, Sickles's corps likely would not have occupied Little Round Top in strength. Just north of Sickles, Hancock's Second Corps, with 11,347 men, held a front of approximately 1,300 yards. With only 10,675 soldiers,

Sickles almost certainly would not have covered a front of 1,500 yards—the distance necessary to hold the crest of Little Round Top in force. Second, the flaws on the left of Meade's line probably would not have been addressed in a timely fashion. Thus Warren might not have visited Little Round Top and brought forward the reinforcements that saved the position. Third, much of the ground on the Federal left for which Longstreet's men fought fiercely would have fallen to the Confederates with only the slightest resistance. Given these hypothetical changes to actual events, it is quite possible that the Army of the Potomac might have lost the Round Tops and the southern end of Cemetery Ridge. Such a disaster might in turn have triggered the loss of Meade's entire fish-hook position.[27]

The foregoing possibilities suggest that Sickles's movement to the Peach Orchard ridge can be interpreted as fortuitous. His seemingly outrageous action forced Meade to address the situation on his left at a crucial time. The advance also threw Confederate attackers off stride. Further, the defense of a critical point always should begin forward of its final protective line, and Sickles's new position was forward of Little Round Top. The cost of Sickles's action was great, but quite possibly, even probably, the movement accomplished more than if the Third Corps had defended the line originally envisioned by Meade. It must be stated, however, that Sickles erred in the way he executed his decision. An advance coordinated with the remainder of the Army of the Potomac would have brought the advantages of the Peach Orchard position without the detrimental effects of an unsupported move by a single corps. Unfortunately, the absence of trust and respect between Meade and Sickles precluded such a rational solution to the problem.

The entire episode has been clouded since 1863 by issues of politics and personality that hinder unbiased analysis. It is time to put aside such extraneous issues. When Sickles's scandalous prewar behavior, postwar bombast, and special pleading are discounted and the case is considered solely on its merits, the results of the Third Corps advance to the Peach Orchard salient speak for themselves. Dan Sickles was not perfect on July 2, 1863, but neither was he the military buffoon so often portrayed.

"If Longstreet . . . Says So, It Is Most Likely Not True"

James Longstreet and the Second Day at Gettysburg

Robert K. Krick

WHEN GENERAL JAMES LONGSTREET DIED IN 1904, HE HAD long since passed his optimum life span for Confederate image building. Had the bullet that maimed the general in the Wilderness on May 6, 1864, killed him instead, there can be little doubt that a bronze equestrian Longstreet would stand on Richmond's Monument Avenue today. Through four postwar decades, however, the contentious Longstreet launched a steady flood of attacks against his former Confederate colleagues, often straying from the demonstrable truth and regularly contradicting his own accounts from one article to the next. When a Petersburg newspaper called Longstreet's poison-pen ventures the "vaporings of senility and pique,"[1] it echoed the views of millions of Southerners. The general's modern supporters insist that in analyzing his war record, we must ignore his late-life posturing, and in fact that is both appropriate and readily achievable in weighing his style during the 1860s. On the other hand, although the senility doubtless was something new, the pique was not a sudden anomaly, sprung whole from the postwar ground. The change in Southern attitudes toward James Longstreet after the war came in large part because he survived to reveal glimpses of his soul that left observers repulsed, rather than simply in response to his postwar political maneuvering. The record shows that Longstreet operated at times during the war with an unwholesome and unlovely attitude. He had a tendency to be small minded and mean spirited, and he behaved in that fashion to the detriment of his army on a number of occasions, including during the second day at Gettysburg.

By December 1861, James Longstreet had experienced a meteoric rise in rank. A few months earlier he had been a major and paymaster in the U.S. Army; now he was a major general of infantry. No one in the army had fared better and most had done far less well. No observers had thought of heaping calumny on Longstreet's head for any reason—justified or not. He was in no way controversial. He was, nevertheless, a confirmed sulker—apparently entirely of his own volition, without having been forced to it by a hostile public opinion, because none such existed. A young Texan on his staff, who was friendly with Longstreet and remained so into old age early in the twentieth century, described Longstreet's tendency to pout in a letter written to his mother that month: "On some days [Longstreet is] very sociable and agreeable, then again for a few days he will confine himself mostly to his room, or tent, without having much to say to anyone, and is as grim as you please." The general behaved that way when he was unwell, as might be expected, but he also acted in that fashion when "something has not gone to suit him. When anything has gone wrong, he does not say much, but merely looks grim." The staff had learned to expect this behavior and did not "talk much to him" before finding out if he was in "a talkative mood."[2] It would be hard for a Longstreet detractor, convinced of his tendency to sulk, to fabricate a more telling description of the general's demeanor when "something [had] not gone to suit him."

A member of J. E. B. Stuart's staff described Longstreet's personal style at about the same time. W. W. Blackford and Stuart boarded for a time at the same house in Fairfax Court House with Longstreet. Blackford wrote: "Longstreet . . . impressed me then as a man of limited capacity who acquired reputation for wisdom by never saying anything—the old story of the owl. I do not remember ever hearing him say half a dozen words, beyond 'yes' and 'no,' in a consecutive sentence, though often in company with his old companions of the old army." A civilian woman who had dinner with Longstreet the following year described his gruff performance as being "shy and embarrassed in manner."[3]

Longstreet's stolid persona often produced in observers the certainty that he must surely be a bulwark in a storm. The general did perform in just that manner for the Army of Northern Virginia on a number of crucial occasions. His style, however, may also have been mixed with more than a tincture of the dullard. Was Longstreet a quiet genius or just quietly slow? A bulwark or a dullard? He probably combined elements of both. At West Point, where one of his roommates was the notorious John Pope,

Lt. Gen. James Longstreet, a wartime engraving from early 1863. From *The Southern Illustrated News*, February 21, 1863.

Longstreet displayed no hint of mental agility. He finished fifty-fourth among fifty-six graduates in the class of 1842. His worst mark was fifty-fifth in Ethics, behind even the spectacularly unethical Earl Van Dorn.[4]

The phenomenon of dullard as bulwark is a familiar one in military history. In a wonderfully droll eighteenth-century book of satirical advice to army officers, a British veteran commented on the syndrome: "Ignorance of your profession is . . . best concealed by solemnity and silence, which pass for profound knowledge upon the generality of mankind." Longstreet's own dear friend both before and after the war, Ulysses S. Grant, is among the prominent Americans most often discussed in that vein. An English diplomat commented that Grant, during his attempts to cope with the duties of president, could not "deliver himself of even the simplest sentence." During the midst of the Belknap scandal, Grant appeared to James A. Garfield so indifferent to the mess and its resultant turmoil that Garfield wrote in his diary: "His imperturbability is amazing. I am in doubt whether to call it greatness or stupidity."[5] Opinions vary, and always will, about the characteristics of long-dead historical figures. If there was something of the dullard in James Longstreet's mix, it probably served him well on some occasions, just as the misanthropic tunnel vision of Longstreet's bête noire, "Stonewall" Jackson, proved to be an asset in that officer's aggressive military behavior. The sullen side of Longstreet's dull personality, however, contributed to his military failures.

A popular and appropriate query posed by Longstreet supporters runs something like this: If the general was given to sulking, and was otherwise deficient in dedication and deportment, why were he and Lee on such good terms? To quote Gary W. Gallagher, from his essay in this book, Longstreet was a man "whose friendship he [Lee] valued." Lee's calm, poised style included an ingenuous element that accepted individuals at face value. He also recognized that the raw material at hand was the best to be had in his country. Lee concluded a May 1864 review of the performance of a brigadier general by posing the query, "Besides, whom would you put in his place?"[6] In any event, there is ample evidence that Lee was genuinely fond of Longstreet, and of course he valued his subordinate's high services to the army. It is interesting to speculate how Lee would have reacted had he known the extent of Longstreet's disloyalty, or whether he in fact was aware of the situation. Because Lee declared that he did not believe Longstreet would say such things—precisely the things Longstreet said repeatedly for thirty years after Lee's death—when he heard rumors of them, he probably remained unaware of Longstreet's distaste for him.

The true nature of the corps commander's feelings for Lee stands out beyond any shadow of doubt in a letter written by Longstreet to Joseph E. Johnston on October 5, 1862. Just four months earlier, Lee had taken over Johnston's army as it crouched beneath the gates of Richmond, having just been beaten at Seven Pines—a battle in which, not coincidentally, Longstreet had conspired with Johnston to transfer blame dishonestly to an innocent colleague. Now Lee had completely remade the face of the war, having driven the enemy army from the verge of his own capital and pursued it across the Potomac. Longstreet clearly wanted his pliant collaborator back, and professed to know that the army preferred to be rid of Lee (an idea either patently dishonest or else breathtakingly out of touch with the ranks): "I feel that you have their hearts more decidedly than any other leader can ever have. The men would now go wild at the sight of their old favorite." Speaking for himself, Longstreet quailed at the prospect of being stuck longer with Lee: "I cant become reconciled at the idea of your going west." Could Johnston find some means to return to the army even in a subordinate role, Longstreet had "no doubt but the command of the entire Army" would fall to him "before Spring." Having been thus blunt, the disgruntled general implied that he would love to say more: "Cant always write what we would like to say." While laboring under Lee's misrule, Longstreet and his staff had used captured champagne to drink to Johnston "whenever we opened a bottle" but thought of Johnston "more seriously at other times."[7] Had Lee seen this missive, or learned of its contents indirectly (as he may have done), it probably would have made not one whit of difference in his dealings with Longstreet.

There can of course be no grounds for denying Longstreet the right to dislike Lee or to prefer Joseph E. Johnston. His distaste for Lee does put him in the rather select, if not exclusive, company of Roswell S. Ripley, apparently the only other general officer who actively disliked the army commander after he began active operations in June 1862. Longstreet's anti-Lee posture wins for him the approval of his modern soul mates, historians eager to debunk Lee's wartime status in the South. More important for present purposes is the degree to which the subordinate disdained the superior, as an element in considering Longstreet's response to those instances when he did not get his way.

A traditional folk saying summarizes how alarmingly easy it is to fool yourself, how readily you may fool a superior, but how impossible it is to fool subordinates over the long term. Stonewall Jackson's world view left him unpopular with virtually every immediate subordinate; basking in his reflected glory was far more comfortable among officers and men a layer or more away from his difficult presence. None of Jackson's bruised officers ever expressed much doubt, however, about their general's whole-hearted commitment to the tasks at hand—which was, in fact, the cause of much of the abrasion in the first place.

A great many of James Longstreet's subordinates liked and admired him, including such clever and thoughtful fellows as E. P. Alexander and G. Moxley Sorrel. Those two men also provide some pointed critique of his attitude at Gettysburg. Longstreet's own favorites included generals such as Robert Toombs, who deserves consideration as at least a finalist for designation as worst general officer in the Army of Northern Virginia. According to one of his staff, Longstreet "had a high opinion of Toombs, and I heard him say that if Toombs had been educated at West Point . . . he would have been as distinguished as a soldier as he was as a civilian." Longstreet also "was exceedingly fond" of George E. Pickett, perhaps because the younger man was one of the few antebellum graduates of West Point with a worse scholastic record than his own. Sorrel recalled how "taking Longstreet's orders in emergencies, I could always see how he looked after Pickett, and made us give him things very fully; indeed, sometimes stay with him to make sure he did not get astray." A third favorite was Gen. Louis T. Wigfall (to whom Longstreet was, in his own words, "strongly attached"), a military failure as pronounced as any in the army, excepting, always, Toombs.[8]

Others of Longstreet's subordinates displayed considerable discomfort with the corps commander's attitude. Cadmus Marcellus Wilcox served long and faithfully as a brigade commander for the first half of the war, and then as a major general at the head of a division during the rest of the conflict. In November 1862 he was anxiously seeking a means to leave Longstreet's corps, presumably because of discontent with its commander. The details are not clear because Lee typically destroyed his half of the correspondence with Wilcox and then gently persuaded the disgruntled general to look beyond local issues to the good of the army and the country. Wilcox's attitude toward Longstreet is anything but indistinct in two letters he wrote soon after the war, which apparently never have been published. Writing to a fellow First Corps general, the usually reticent Wilcox declared emphatically, "I never had any respect for Longstreet's ability for I always knew he had but a small amount." Furthermore, Wilcox had "always regarded him as selfish & cold harted [sic], caring for but little save his own self." General Wilcox insisted that at Frayser's Farm and Williamsburg, the brigade commanders suffered under Longstreet's absence from the front "& we brigadiers talked of it." To Wilcox's chagrin, Longstreet "is spoken of as the hard & stubborn fighter, his troops did fight well, but not from any inspiration drawn from him & he of course gets the credit of it."[9]

As Longstreet fell into steadily greater disfavor after the war, he adopted the expedient of blaming his difficulties on individuals hostile to him because of political considerations and his other unpopular postwar traits. His modern supporters believe that whole-souled admiration for the general only faded after the war for irrelevant reasons, and under the prompting of consciously dishonest Lost Cause myth makers. Longstreet might be viewed as a man far ahead of his times, with his very 1990s-like stance of insisting that having outraged much of the community by one set of actions, he was immune to criticism for anything else: obviously everyone hated him and therefore must be ignored as prejudiced; citing a recidivist's chronic misdeeds is unfair, we are told. The innocence-through-unpopularity motif might in fact obtain in some instances. Longstreet really did a thorough job of making himself unlovable, and prompted some outraged hyperbole in the process. Cadmus Wilcox, however, was anything but a controversialist. He was about the quietest man of his rank in the matter of postwar speaking and writing and quarreling. Wilcox's private letters to a friend of Longstreet's—not to some fiendish Lost Cause journal—scarcely can be impeached as polemics. Right or wrong, General Wilcox simply and privately thought little of Longstreet's ability and appreciated even less his "selfish & cold harted" attitude.

Maj. Gen. Lafayette McLaws of Georgia was among the most pointed detractors Longstreet ever earned. His position is the more remarkable because for a long time the corps commander viewed McLaws as a special protégé. McLaws provides key testimony about his chief at Gettysburg and Knoxville below, but this generic commentary on Longstreet's "contemptible mode of procedure" summarizes his notions: "You can follow Longstreet's career, from the First battle of Manassas to the close of the war, and you will see that the first act, in any engagement, was to call for reinforcements; not that any reinforcements were needed, but that was his policy." McLaws knew from close experience that Longstreet's reports "will lay the blame of failure . . . upon some one else, and in case of real fiasco he will undertake to do something where success is impossible and find faults and lay the blame of the failure in his last venture upon some one else he has a spite against. All this is to draw attention away from his own mismanagement of the real issue."[10]

The best example of the blame-shifting technique cited by McLaws was Seven Pines. In a fantastic display of poor planning, miscommunication, and arrant ineptitude, James Longstreet left the presence of Joseph E. Johnston with instructions to march northeastward up the Nine Mile Road to implement the army commander's sloppy and casual battle plan but somehow contrived in befuddlement to head more than ninety degrees away from his intended goal. No major battle in Virginia includes any more bizarre confusion. In the process Longstreet blocked for long hours the route of troops under General Benjamin Huger who were earmarked for triggering the attack. Some have suggested that Longstreet consciously scrambled the plan in order to reach an area where distinction might be found, but that seems highly unlikely. McLaws noted that Longstreet "disobeyed his orders (supposed to be from stupidity)." Far more significant than the peculiar events was Longstreet's apparently instinctive reaction to blame it all on a convenient bystander. With Johnston's connivance, he succeeded in blaming Huger—who had been most directly wronged—as the author of the confusion! As Douglas Southall Freeman has noted, "Longstreet, whose conduct at Seven Pines was most subject to question, emerged not only without blame but also with prestige increased."[11] Huger proved to be a fortuitous choice as scapegoat, as he soon demonstrated a genuine tendency toward sluggishness.

Later that summer Longstreet had occasion to refine his technique. When his friend and subordinate Robert Toombs disobeyed orders and left a ford on the Rapidan unguarded, a Federal cavalry column slipped through unnoticed. The Yankees very nearly captured J. E. B. Stuart at Verdiersville. Stuart thought that the cavalrymen were Fitzhugh Lee's troopers, whom he expected to arrive soon. Although this relatively minor incident caused some inconvenience to the army, it hardly warranted the historiographical counteroffensive launched by Longstreet. He spread the word that

Maj. Gen. Lafayette McLaws. From *Battles and Leaders of the Civil War* 3:333.

Lee, who was among the victims of the malfeasance by Longstreet's friend Toombs, was really the culprit, and escalated the result so egregiously that he later subscribed to the amusing premise that Lee "lost the Southern cause" on that largely forgotten morning. Longstreet later explained that all of the Virginia cavalrymen required guidance. Stuart in particular needed "an older head"—no doubt Longstreet had himself in mind—"to instruct and regulate him."[12]

Debate raged postwar about whether Longstreet disobeyed Lee in delaying his offensive at Second Manassas, where the armies met ten days after Fitz Lee lost the war at Verdiersville. Supporters of the First Corps commander continue to insist that his delay in executing Lee's wishes at Second Manassas was the right thing to do. But they can hardly cling to the notion that Longstreet was not dragging his feet, since he calmly admitted to doing so. "I failed to obey the orders of the 29th," he boasted, "and on the 30th, in direct opposition to my orders, made the battle from my position and won it." In describing tactical developments on the field, Longstreet gerrymandered them through an arc of nearly 180 degrees in a display of either extraordinary sloppiness or blatant dishonesty.[13]

Judging from his letter to Joe Johnston quoted above, Longstreet obviously believed from the early days of his association with Lee that he knew better how to run the army. That belief apparently had grown by the summer of 1863 to include warwide strategic concepts, according to Longstreet's postwar declarations. The corps commander claimed to have been brimming with unbeatable options for forays into Tennessee, Ohio, and other such exotic latitudes, but Lee was immune to reason. A contemporary letter from Longstreet to McLaws hints that the lieutenant general's hindsight was much crisper than his foresight. McLaws hoped to get back to the vicinity of Georgia and his family—the direction in which Longstreet's strategic vision was supposed to be gamboling. Longstreet thought he might be able to work it out, but if McLaws went south and west, he must remember that "we want every body here that we can get and . . . you must agree to send us every man that you can dispense with during the summer particularly."[14] That would seem to indicate that Longstreet's strategic vision about the poor chances in Lee's theater were somewhat more autobiographical than contemporary.

Longstreet's version of his dismayed abandonment of the various better ideas includes two remarkable words. After badgering Lee about Cincinnati, Vicksburg, and other such chimeras, Longstreet "found his [Lee's] mind made up not to allow any of his troops to go west. I then *accepted* his proposition to make a campaign into Pennsylvania, *provided* it should be offensive in strategy but defensive in tactics" (emphases added). That a corps commander would use words of that sort in describing the decisions of his army's head reveals a phenomenal degree of cocky disrespect. Lee of course had not struck such a "bargain," and in the event behaved without respect to the nonexistent pact. Longstreet later professed to know somehow that Lee had missed his only real chance to breach successfully this pseudocartel when he overlooked a great opportunity at Brandy Station, "when he could have caught Hooker in detail, and, probably, have crushed his army."[15]

General Longstreet's corps fought one of the war's most desperate engagements on July 2, 1863, on the Confederate right at Gettysburg. Despite the corps's brave and stubborn performance, its commander came in for bitter criticism for his attitude and behavior on that crucial day. There was generously ample basis for such criticism, but as controversy swirled around the subject some of the general's detractors—most notably the Reverend William Nelson Pendleton—produced inaccurate and misleading testimony. The nature and processes of the controversy itself have become controversial, but this essay inquiring particularly into the nature of Longstreet's attitude must focus on primary evidence.

Longstreet did not want Lee to take the initiative on July 2. He made that unmistakably clear to his superior, but Lee determined that the army must find the best possible spot at which to seek a continuation of the striking success it had won the previous day. After an often-discussed series of conferences with Lee, some of them turbulent, Longstreet faced the simple fact that he must move to the right and attack. He accepted that responsibility in the poorest possible grace. Had Tom Goree been writing to his mother on this day he most certainly could have duplicated his December 1861 letter: when "something has not gone to suit him. . . . [he] merely looks grim." James Longstreet spent most of July 2 "without having much to say to anyone, and . . . as grim as you please," in accordance with Goree's earlier description.

One early and striking manifestation of Longstreet's sullen execution of his orders has not received much attention in the voluminous literature on Gettysburg. His two divisions faced a long and uncertain march to their intended destination. The march surely would take considerable time under the best of circumstances. Inevitably such moves involved delays. Given the urgency of the situation, celerity (to use one of the favorite words of the sorely missed T. J. Jackson) clearly was in requisition. Longstreet ignored that patently obvious imperative from the outset. Evander M. Law's brigade of Alabama troops, one of eight brigades scheduled for the march, was not yet up. Longstreet insisted on waiting for its arrival. As he reported officially to Lee, "I delayed until General Law's brigade joined its division."

Even then he was not ready, having "*after* his arrival" (emphasis added) to "make our preparations." While the clock inexorably ticked off moments potentially golden for the South, Longstreet lounged with division commander John B. Hood "near the trunk of a tree" and explained to Hood that General Lee "is a little nervous this morning; he wishes me to attack." Hood's description of this relaxed encounter, written after the war to Longstreet himself, concluded ominously: "Thus passed the forenoon of that eventful day. . . ."[16]

Had Longstreet insisted on awaiting Law's arrival at the line of departure before launching his attack, he might have been able to make a weak case; though under the circumstances that afternoon, a delay in attacking to augment the force by one-eighth would not have made good sense, especially given the en echelon arrangement that was used. He was not waiting to attack, however, but merely to *begin* a complicated march. Law of course would have arrived at the jump-off point for the march long before his turn came to fall in at the end of the column. Longstreet simply was dragging his feet.

Once the march finally began, on a dismally tardy schedule, the sulking corps commander put on a display of pettiness of heroic proportions by pretending to think that he could not direct his own troops. Capt. Samuel Richards Johnston, engineer officer on Lee's staff, had reconnoitered early that morning in the area toward which Longstreet was grudgingly headed. Beginning at about 4 A.M., Johnston rode over the ground between Willoughby Run and Marsh Creek leading east toward the Emmitsburg Pike. He examined the terrain between the pike and the Round Tops, rode over the slopes and to the crests of those soon-to-be-famous knobs, crossed the Slyder farm, and returned. When the scouting captain reached headquarters, General Lee "was surprised at my getting so far, but showed clearly that I had given him valuable information." Lee suggested that Captain Johnston join Longstreet's column on its march; any other use of the man best informed about the ground would have been criminally negligent. The army commander of course gave his staff captain no special authority. In fact, he gave him "no other instructions" at all beyond joining Longstreet. Johnston thought it was about 9 A.M. when he joined Longstreet, and added what everyone else well knew: "He did not move off very promptly—nor was our march at all rapid. It did not strike me that Genl Longstreet was in a hurry to get into position. It might have been that he thought hurry was unnecessary."[17]

Longstreet decided to play an ugly game with the misguided Lee—and with thousands of unfortunate soldiers and the destiny of a mighty battle— by taking the ludicrous position that Sam Johnston really commanded the march. He was Lee's man on the spot, and this wholly silly march and attack were Lee's idiotic idea, so let him have his way and then we'll just see who really knows best! No episode in the army's long history, which included more than a few displays of temper and spite and small-mindedness, can measure up to this exhibition by Lieutenant General Longstreet. More than two hundred officers in the marching column out-ranked Sam Johnston, if in fact his staff rank could be counted at all in the face of line commanders. To make matters even worse, this tragicomic affair unfolded without Johnston knowing that he was the stalking horse for the pouting corps commander.

When the head of the marching column passed Black Horse Tavern it quickly came to a point where the narrow road crawled over a high knoll. At its top, the Confederates would come in clear view of Federals on Little Round Top. Sam Johnston innocently told Longstreet that this would "discover your movements to the enemy," but Longstreet had no comment. He watched as the column went over the crest into view of the Federals and halted. The knoll with the naked crest actually extended only a short distance in either direction. Porter Alexander moved his large artillery battalion around the far edge of the knoll without a second thought. When he noticed the infantry not only failing to follow his example but also halted in clear view of Little Round Top—thus canceling both secrecy and speed—he was astonished. The infantry never did follow Alexander's simple and convenient route. Instead they retraced their steps and went on a great looping detour that covered, Alexander noted disgustedly, "four miles to get less than one."[18] The spectacle of a corps under arms, groping its way without a commander at a crucial moment, makes one of the most pathetic vignettes in the army's annals.

Longstreet's little game, with his own rules developed as he went, eventually allowed him to assume command of Hood's division but not that of McLaws. Under this system, Longstreet could declare that he "did not order General McLaws forward, because, as the head of the column, he had direct orders from General Lee to follow the conduct of Colonel [sic] Johnston. Therefore, I sent orders to Hood, who was in the rear and not encumbered by these instructions." All of this petty and dishonest posturing dramatically exacerbated the tendency of Longstreet's command to move with what some observers thought was unwonted sluggishness even under ordinary circumstances. A member of General Ewell's staff remarked of operations during July that "Longstreet was . . . himself notorious for moving slowly, & McLaws' Divn of his Corps was . . . the slowest of Longstreet's troops & a clog on the whole Army." An engineer officer who had nothing to do with Longstreet and expressed no opinion of any sort about him referred to him as "Old Snail" in a routine diary entry during July, as though that were his common nickname.[19] Troops with that marching tendency were particularly vulnerable to the sort of sulky delaying action that Longstreet employed on July 2.

Why did Lee not accompany his grumpy subordinate, insist on greater organization and speed of movement, and make his presence felt at the point of decision? Because he came to Gettysburg with two brand-new corps commanders and neither of them was James Longstreet. He had already had cause to be deeply concerned about Ewell, and Hill's inaugural attempt at corps command at Gettysburg had very little impact on the battle. It must have been easy for Lee to decide to stay near the sectors of his two tyros while leaving his one veteran to operate with greater independence, as was Lee's preferred system. Longstreet's admirer Porter Alexander concluded categorically: "There seems no doubt that had Longstreet's attack. . . . been made materially sooner, we would have gained a decided victory"; but Alexander says Lee somehow should have done a better job of forcing Longstreet to conform to his will. We can of course recognize that Lee's presence with Longstreet was desperately needed, using hindsight, but that incomparable tool by definition was not in the army commander's arsenal. Lee was left to ask, according to one of his staff, "in a tone of uneasiness, 'what can detain Longstreet? He ought to be in position now.'" When Lee learned of the advance of Federal general Daniel E. Sickles to the Emmitsburg Pike he "again expressed his impatience."[20]

When at last the marching comedy of errors reached the vicinity of the Emmitsburg Pike opposite the Peach Orchard and the Round Tops, Longstreet for the first time could see the ground over which he was to attack. It obviously offered strong advantages to the defenders, if they were present in strength, but by the same token it offered equally alluring opportunity to the Confederates if they could occupy the high ground by some means. Longstreet had been stubbornly opposed to fighting on the offensive under any circumstances. His churlish behavior all day had resulted from that general conviction, not from any idea of the terrain, which he only now could see. As Porter Alexander aptly commented: "The long & the short of the matter seems to me as follows. Longstreet did not wish to take the offensive. His objection to it was not based at all upon the peculiar strength of the enemy's position for that was not yet recognized, but solely on general principles."[21]

As Longstreet's two strong and tested divisions neared action, the corps commander adjusted his horizon to the point that he was willing to resume his abdicated command of McLaws. Capt. Sam Johnston would have been relieved to relinquish the command, we can suppose, had he ever known that he had it in the first place. It might have appeared that the lieutenant general was prepared to go back to work in the interests of his faithful and trusting riflemen who were about to head into mortal combat, but in fact his taste for charade and for self-fulfilling prophecy had only been whetted. The most pressing question facing the corps, which should have occupied the energies of its commander, was how to align the troops and commit them to battle. Longstreet abdicated that responsibility and insisted that Lee's plan, now long stale and necessarily only a general guide in any event, be rigidly honored. It had become apparent that Lee knew far less well than Longstreet how to win a battle, and here was an irresistible opportunity to prove it to him.

The division and brigade commanders, together with some aggressive regimental officers, had looked at the zone of attack eagerly and with pragmatic eyes. Some of them quickly discerned that the Federal left dangled amorphously in a large and vaguely defined region north of Round Top. John B. Hood, whose division stood on the far right, at once requested permission to turn that flank. Longstreet refused to entertain any such deviations from Lee's plan, which he now suddenly endowed with a categorical aura. To alter it would be to impair the lesson Lee needed to learn. Hood later reminded Longstreet how he had urged "that you allow me to turn Round Top and attack the enemy in flank and rear." Longstreet replied curtly, "Gen'l Lee's orders are to attack up the Emmettsburg [sic] road." A second heartfelt plea met a similar response. "A third time I dispatched one of my staff to explain fully," Hood recalled, "and to suggest that you had better come."[22] Longstreet refused to go look for himself or to consider any alternatives. To do so would have been to exercise corps command, and he was not yet ready to climb off his high horse.

Moxley Sorrel confirmed Hood's account of his desperate attempts to operate intelligently. Hood "begged me to look at" his division's plight, Sorrel remembered, "report its extreme difficulty, and implore Longstreet to make the attack another way." The staffer complied, but elicited the same answer from Longstreet. McLaws was not involved in the vain attempt to move around the right, but his superior found opportunity nastily to force him too into misguided positions as a means of venting his spleen. Longstreet in fact never denied having refused to consider alternatives. He actually reiterated his position as a means of clarifying Lee's bad plan; that was the point of the whole business. "General Hood appealed again and again for the move to the right," Longstreet confirmed.[23]

What Hood wanted to do, Longstreet insisted, "had been carefully considered by our chief and rejected in favor of his present orders."[24] Longstreet had the genetic equipment to be naturally, as well as intentionally, obtuse. In this instance he certainly was employing a calculated density rather than his ample native supply. He and Lee had disagreed over whether it was desirable—to say nothing of practicable—to relocate the army in some miraculous fashion to a point between Gettysburg and Washington. That would have been more or less to the Federal strategic left (if not right in the midst of their approaching columns). In rejecting that visionary notion, Lee of course was offering no comment of any sort about moving against the Federals' tactical left on the battlefield. The whole movement of July 2 was aimed toward just that target. Lee always left the means of committing a corps to action up to its commander, certainly when out of his presence and almost invariably even when he was nearby. He had refused to attempt to relocate his army southeastward into a different county; that had nothing at all to do with relocating its tactical arrangements in the same direction—or in any other—by the width of a pasture or two or a few hundred yards of woods.

Among the most telling indictments of Longstreet's behavior are the words of two of his intimates, one who remained so for life and one who broke with him on the spot. Both Moxley Sorrel and Lafayette McLaws commented pointedly on their superior's attitude on this dark and bloody day. Sorrel stayed on close terms with his chief to the end of his life but could not conceal some surprise about how Longstreet acted on July 2. The lieutenant general "failed to conceal some anger. There was apparent apathy in his movements. They lacked the fire and point of his usual bearing on the battlefield." Sorrel admitted to imagining Lee's horror about "what was going on to the disadvantage of the army," then reined himself in with a visible jolt. "This is all I shall permit myself to express on this well-worn . . . subject."[25]

Lafayette McLaws stood high among James Longstreet's favorites on July 1. Just a few weeks before, he had been Longstreet's candidate for a lieutenant generalcy and command of one of the new corps. To the end of his life Longstreet grumbled about the dark Virginian plot that gave those billets to Ewell and A. P. Hill instead of to McLaws. By the end of July 2, however, the veteran division commander had been so revolted by his chief's behavior that he was unable to abide his further patronage. The two generals remained at loggerheads and wound up in open conflict later in the war. Their hostility extended unabated through McLaws's life, despite some periods of superficial postwar rapprochement. After the feud erupted, McLaws's testimony must be viewed in that context, though it remains more important than would be admitted by the school of thought that suggests that no one could effectively criticize Longstreet because so many hated him.

The misbegotten tendency to flick away attacks on Longstreet's behavior as the work of a dishonest postwar cabal just will not stand up in considering McLaws's most pointed description of July 2. It came in the intimate forum of a letter to his wife, and was written not in the grip of some 1880s political frenzy but on July 7, 1863. "General Longstreet is to blame for not reconnoitering the ground and for persisting in ordering the assault when his errors were discovered," he told Mrs. McLaws. "During the engagement he was very excited, giving contrary orders to every one, and was exceedingly overbearing." In consequence, McLaws said, "I consider him a humbug, a man of small capacity, very obstinate, not at all chivalrous, exceedingly conceited, and totally selfish."[26] A stronger bill of particulars would be difficult to contrive. If McLaws's description is in any wise accurate, and it seems to be substantially correct, James Longstreet's deportment stands in stark and ugly contrast next to the selfless devotion shown by the thousands of men who were bleeding and dying that afternoon under his direction—or, more accurately, his lack of direction.

A striking and fascinating comparison can be made between the actions of James Longstreet on July 2 and those of Stonewall Jackson on May 2 at Chancellorsville. On May 2, 1863, Lee chose to send his ranking subordinate on an extended march toward his enemy's most exposed flank on the second day of battle. Lee remained with the fixing element of his army to supervise its less experienced leaders, assigned to the maneuver element the key tactical responsibility, and instructed the commander of the maneuver element to attack the enemy flank at a specific point at which it apparently rested. In the event, Jackson managed his march with his accustomed energy and skill; Lee remained with the static element of the army and succeeded in bemusing the Federals opposite him; Jackson accepted the tactical responsibility eagerly; and, most significantly, when Jackson reached the enemy flank and found the situation somewhat different than what had been expected, he altered the tactical plans without a moment's hesitation and realized in consequence a staggering victory.

The situation facing Lee at Gettysburg two months later to the day was not identical, but it was analogous to an interesting degree. He again chose on the second day of battle to send his ranking subordinate toward what he believed to be the most vulnerable enemy flank. He remained with the static element of his army to supervise its inexperienced leaders, expected the point of decision to be where his maneuver element struck, and surely expected the lieutenant general on the scene to seek the best possible terms when he attacked at the end of a careful and rather risky march. Longstreet, of course, prosecuted the march execrably (or Captain Johnston unwittingly did, if you will). The most arresting parallel between the two days is the way in which Jackson, as was his custom, sought—and found—the best way to accomplish the purpose for which so much effort and risk had been incurred. In doing so Jackson received timely advice from a number of subordinates, most notably Fitzhugh Lee. Longstreet not only sulkily failed to seek out the best means of accomplishing his assigned task but also refused to countenance intelligence toward that end voluntarily supplied by subordinates. When he ostentatiously announced to all listeners, then and later, that Lee's bad plan must be followed, Longstreet was delineating as starkly as any critic ever could the chasm that separated his attitude from that of Stonewall Jackson. The contrast is an unpleasant one not only in theoretical fashion but particularly because it was drawn in the blood and suffering of thousands of his own men, and at a time that caused immense damage to his country.

Longstreet's demeanor on July 3 affecting the major assault on that day is another subject and beyond the scope of this essay. Later on the third, as the army contemplated disengagement, the general displayed further confusion and pique affecting McLaws. In an episode that has not received much attention, Longstreet again thrashed angrily about, giving more of what McLaws had called "contrary orders to everyone." McLaws promptly obeyed the first set of new orders, although he remonstrated against their pertinence with Moxley Sorrel; this obviously was not the week to seek sweet reason from Longstreet. After a time Sorrel came back and asked whether McLaws could resume his original position. McLaws of course reminded the staff officer of their earlier discussion. Sorrel responded, "Yes, I gave you the order to retire and it was given to me by Genl. Longstreet himself, but he now denied having given it!" Generals Law and Benning were also victims of this unusual proceeding and compared disgruntled notes with McLaws. A few weeks later, McLaws recalled, he wrote to Longstreet seeking an explanation and received the response that the corps commander "had no recollection concerning the orders."[27]

No better credo could be imagined for a subordinate in disagreement with his superior than one Longstreet himself wrote, or claimed to have written, on July 24, 1863. In a letter that Longstreet published as written to his uncle, he declared: "I consider it a part of my duty to express my views to the commanding general. If he approves and adopts them, it is well; if he does not, it is my duty to adopt his views, and to execute his orders as faithfully as if they were my own."[28] It is difficult to imagine a more prudent guideline for application to circumstances such as Longstreet faced at Gettysburg. Only the most intransigent of the general's supporters can cling to the notion, however, that he executed Lee's orders in Pennsylvania "as faithfully as if they were my own." Was his July 24 letter the special pleadings of a guilty conscience?

In terms of strategy and tactics, Lee's army suffered most at Gettysburg because of the unwonted absence of J. E. B. Stuart and his skilled mounted men. It suffered next, both chronologically and with regard to impact, from the sloth and equivocation of Richard S. Ewell on July 1. Longstreet's uncertain opportunities lost in the midst of an unseemly sulk on July 2 can only be reckoned as third behind those more crisply defined shortcomings. The salient difference is that evidently Stuart and Ewell were not displaying petty personality traits as they strove in vain.

A peculiar footnote to the Gettysburg controversies cropped up late in the nineteenth century when Gen. Cullen A. Battle publicly reported that a formal court of inquiry actually convened to examine the campaign. Gen. William Mahone presided, according to Battle, who claimed to have been appointed recorder for the court. In its verdict the court "censured both Stuart and Longstreet, but General Lee suppressed the report, and took the blame upon himself."[29] General Battle's account must be classified as falling among the bizarre satellite claims that cluster tenaciously around the larger Gettysburg controversies.

Longstreet's career after Gettysburg included further refinement of his blame-shifting techniques. It also included what must have been for him the startling lesson that fondness for the tactical defensive cannot be readily translated into battlefield results. Twice during the war, Longstreet had the chance to operate on a large scale independent of Lee's oppressive damper on his creative skills. Not long before Gettysburg the ambitious corps commander had led a strong force in a campaign around Suffolk. Such initiatives as Longstreet found occasion to use included no tactical defensive; cooperative Federals proved to be in short supply. Federal general John G. Foster, who faced Longstreet, was hardly a commander of legendary proportions, but he was able to restrain any impulses he might have had to cooperate with Longstreet. The Suffolk command produced no striking results for Longstreet and might be classified as an embarrassment rather than a humiliation. Longstreet earned humiliation in ample doses in Tennessee later in the year.

During the last week of November 1863, Longstreet tasted the bitter dregs of total defeat around Knoxville. His attack on Fort Sanders—not only a tactical offensive but a brutal frontal assault—cannot be adjudged anything other than a pathetic exhibition of ineptitude. No large veteran contingent of Army of Northern Virginia troops experienced anything so grotesque during the war, even during its closing hours. The few dozen

Federals in the fort routed the thousands of attackers with great slaughter. The Northern assaults on Marye's Heights on December 13, 1862 (probably the only battle that really suited Longstreet, first and last), look like classic practice of military science compared to Fort Sanders. It is impossible to imagine R. E. Lee or T. J. Jackson—or Robert E. Rodes, William Dorsey Pender, S. Dodson Ramseur, John B. Gordon, or William Mahone, for that matter—caught up in so dreadful a situation.

After Knoxville even Longstreet must have admitted to himself that his cherished dreams of independent success were only cloud castles. He had been rebuffed by one John G. Foster at Suffolk, and then humiliated by Ambrose E. Burnside, of all people, for it was the inept Burnside who tormented Longstreet at Knoxville. The solution, once again, was to distribute blame amongst whatever targets came to mind. It seemed obvious to blame them for lack of enthusiastic support of their commander; after all, Longstreet knew with conviction that subordinates who lacked enthusiasm could foul up operations pretty thoroughly. The general put in arrest Generals McLaws, Evander M. Law, and Jerome B. Robertson. These sweeping arrests outstripped the record of the notoriously litigious Stonewall Jackson, who, though harsh and fond of courts, had no need of scapegoats.

Writing at the time, McLaws declared, "The charges were forced on him by public opinion & he attempts to make me a blind to draw public inquiry from his complete failure in the whole Tennessee campaign. . . . When it is considered that Gen. L . . . has nothing to recommend him as a commander, but the possession of a certain Bullheadedness, it is mortifying when one feels that he is allowed to tyranise, as he is doing." After the war McLaws summarized Longstreet's conduct of the campaign harshly but essentially accurately: "He was so out-witted and his movements so timid and managed as to conform exactly to those of the enemy, and as the enemy must have wished him to order, so as to give them every success and bring disaster and shame upon us."[30]

Longstreet sought to avoid charging McLaws formally, which he must have known would lead to embarrassment. He attempted merely to arrest his subordinate without either charges or a trial. McLaws insisted on being charged and tried, and Longstreet was indeed embarrassed by the results. Confederate court-martial transcripts survive only in collections of personal papers, but fortunately most of the documents from this court have been preserved. Longstreet charged McLaws with six specific misdeeds. Five of them misrepresented objective facts—facts that many thousands of veterans of the attack knew to be entirely contrary to Longstreet's claims. One specification damned McLaws, for instance, because he "failed to attack at NW corner [of Fort Sanders] where there was no ditch." More than fifty men who took part in Longstreet's absurd attack testified unanimously that McLaws did precisely what Longstreet claimed that he did not do. The sixth charge was subjective enough to be beyond substantive proof either way. The court ruled against McLaws on that single issue and in his favor on the other five, but the War Department overturned even that vague stricture, and censured Longstreet for his fiddling with the proceedings of the court.[31]

Tactical offensives in the Civil War, and perhaps in most military epochs, required a good deal more from their commanders than did defensive arrangements—more coordination, diligence, moral force, breadth, grasp, and strength of purpose and mind. This is not to postulate that they were the preferable alternative, because they surely were not. A cooperative foe such as Burnside at Fredericksburg only turned up intermittently. Meanwhile the initiative regularly required taking the offensive; witness even the defensive oracle Longstreet staggering helplessly into an offensive mode at Knoxville. Neither Longstreet nor his special hero Joe Johnston ever managed an offensive well in independent campaigning. When the two kindred spirits collaborated at Seven Pines, "no action in the war was planned with such slovenly thinking or prepared so carelessly," in the apt words of Clifford Dowdey (who may have overlooked Knoxville in choosing his superlative). "Johnston's aversion to details . . . was typical of him," and of Longstreet's feeble offensive gesture too.[32] Lassitude and whatever else went into the formula left Longstreet incapable of managing an offensive campaign when he—even he—recognized no alternative. That may well have affected his attitude throughout the war.

On the eve of the 1864 Wilderness campaign, Longstreet rejoined Lee's army with far more relief and gratitude than he could have imagined when he left to do great things on his own. The McLaws results, which must have embarrassed Longstreet, were published in Richmond the day Grant crossed the Rapidan. At the same time, General Law, one of McLaws's fellow sufferers, was preparing to file formal charges against Longstreet on several counts, including "conduct unworthy of an officer and gentleman in making a false report of the fight" at Wauhatchie. Law had caught Longstreet in another "*infamous lie*," and he told McLaws, "If you will cover the Knoxville Campaign in your charges, I believe we can oust him." "Longstreet," Law insisted, "is most certainly on the wane both in, and out of the army."[33] In fact the general was on his way out of the army by means of convalescent leave.

Longstreet arrived in the Wilderness on the second day of battle, May 6, 1864, from a bivouac far to the southwest. Some sources suggest that

Lee was dismayed over the tardiness of that arrival, including G. W. C. Lee quoting his father, C. S. Venable to Longstreet himself, and H. B. McClellan of Stuart's staff. The morning of the sixth proved to be Longstreet's last with the army for many months, as he fell dangerously wounded, the victim of a mistaken volley fired by Confederates in the tangled thickets of the Wilderness.

When Longstreet returned to duty during the autumn of 1864, Lee must have eagerly welcomed the return of his seasoned lieutenant and best corps commander. Whether Longstreet ever recovered his full ability to control his corps remains uncertain. Early in 1865 (on Lee's fifty-eighth birthday, in fact), the commanding general sent an inspection summary to Longstreet that expended nearly one thousand words in criticism of the condition of the First Corps. Although it no doubt was primarily a staff-to-staff communiqué, the document bore Lee's signature and was addressed to the corps commander. It cited "unsatisfactory" reports, officers who "have failed to do their duty," and units "lax in discipline" and "unsoldierly & unmilitary." The letter exhorted Longstreet in stern phrases: "Prompt measures must be taken"; "I desire that you will give particular attention . . . and exact unceasing effort"; "I desire you to correct the evils . . . by every means in your power"; "I beg that you will insist upon these points"; and, "this should be at once corrected."[34]

As Lee's senior subordinate, Longstreet enjoyed the applause of most officers and enlisted men, but at least a few of them felt that his late-war performance let them down. A novice artillerist declared on March 19, 1865, that he considered Longstreet "the poorest general we have." Another man in the same eighty-man battery wrote later, "For a few months near the close of the war . . . to our great regret we had to serve under Longstreet."[35] Neither artillerist ever earned an epaulet as military critic, but their unease suggests that Longstreet's 1865 aura as seen from the ranks was not quite what it once had been.

James Longstreet spent nearly four decades after the war assailing his former comrades in arms, beginning just slowly enough to avoid open assaults on Lee until after the death of the former army commander in 1870. When Lee heard the first mutterings about Longstreet's fabulous assertions and criticisms, he simply refused to believe that his former subordinate had said such "absurd" things.[36] Longstreet reached vitriolic high gear soon after Lee's death and maintained his momentum ever after. When the aging general's first wife died (she had been a Virginian, remarkably enough), he married a young woman—born the year of Gettysburg—who was herself a born controversialist and who acted on the general as kerosene would on a raging blaze.

At his death in 1904, Longstreet was one of the most thoroughly loathed men in the South. Many who found Longstreet's behavior distasteful would have echoed the mature judgment of Dr. Hunter Holmes McGuire, who read the general's mean-spirited memoir "more in sorrow for the man than indignation at his bad taste and temper." A substantial body of observers also shared McGuire's empirical conclusion: "If Longstreet . . . says so, it is most likely not true."[37]

Had General Longstreet died at the head of his corps on May 6, 1864, he surely would stand tall in the pantheon of Confederate heroes. We would see him in bronze on more than one battlefield, and probably in Richmond as well. The mortal wounds inflicted on Longstreet's reputation therefore seem to some observers to be the result of what he did after the war. The hurtful impact, however, came not from postwar deeds but from the vistas Longstreet unveiled in the long life left to him. His longevity gave him numerous opportunities to bare his soul—the same one with which he had been saddled during the war—and the view was not a savory one.

Lt. Gen. Richard Taylor surveyed the Gettysburg controversy a few years after the war with interest and some detachment. As a son of a president of the United States, a brother-in-law of the president of the Confederate States, and a general officer who served in the Virginia theater, Taylor was blessed with exemplary connections in high circles. He had gone west well before Gettysburg, so had no vested interest in the specific details under debate. He did know the principle figures well enough, however, to offer a lively and apposite comment:

A recent article in the public press, signed by General Longstreet, ascribes the failure at Gettysburg to Lee's mistakes, which he [Longstreet] in vain pointed out and remonstrated against. That any subject involving the possession and exercise of intellect should be clear to Longstreet and concealed from Lee, is a startling proposition to those having knowledge of the two men.[38]

"A Step All-Important and Essential to Victory"

Henry W. Slocum and the Twelfth Corps on July 1–2, 1863

A. Wilson Greene

EVERY CIVIL WAR BATTLE PRODUCED A GALLERY OF HEROES and rogues—commanders whose conspicuous valor, bold gambles, or fatal errors pursue them through history to their everlasting glory or shame. At the Battle of Gettysburg, the Army of the Potomac certainly conformed to this pattern. On one side proudly stand the likes of Brig. Gen. John Buford, Maj. Gen. Winfield Scott Hancock, and Col. Joshua L. Chamberlain, whereas on the other lurk the blemished visages of Maj. Gen. Oliver Otis Howard, Maj. Gen. Daniel E. Sickles, and Brig. Gen. Alexander Schimmelfennig.[1]

Usually absent from either list are the ranking officers of the Twelfth Corps. Maj. Gen. Henry W. Slocum and his eight subordinate commanders have attracted less attention from Gettysburg scholars than the leaders of any other Union corps. Despite this neglect, some observers have credited Slocum's corps with crafting the Union victory, none more eloquently than Oliver Otis Howard: "The most impressive incident of the great battle of Gettysburg," wrote the Eleventh Corps commander in 1894, "was Slocum's own battle. . . . Slocum's resolute insistence the afternoon of July 2nd and his organized work and battle the ensuing morning, in my judgment prevented Meade's losing the battle of Gettysburg. It was a grand judgment and action; a step all-important and essential to victory."[2]

Maj. Gen. Henry Warner Slocum. From Miller's *Photographic History* 10:177.

Was Howard correct in ascribing a critical role to the Twelfth Corps at Gettysburg? If so, what part did Slocum and the rest of the relatively anonymous hierarchy of his corps play on July 1–2? Did they render service that altered the outcome of North America's most famous battle?

The Twelfth Corps embarked on the Gettysburg campaign after suffering nearly three thousand casualties in the Battle of Chancellorsville.[3] Henry Warner Slocum, thirty-five years old and from Onondaga County, New York, led the corps at Chancellorsville as he had since October of the previous year. Slocum graduated seventh in the class of 1852 at West Point, having roomed part of the time with Philip H. Sheridan. After a brief career

Brig. Gen. Alpheus Starkey Williams. From Miller's *Photographic History* 10:85.

in the Old Army, Slocum resigned to practice law but maintained connections with the New York state militia. Shortly after the fall of Fort Sumter, he offered his sword to the Union, reentering the service as colonel of the 27th New York Infantry.[4]

Admirers praised Slocum's manner, which "inspire[d] faith and confidence," and noted that his sparkling brown eyes contributed to a "magnetic power over his troops."[5] A less impassioned assessment might mention that the beardless Slocum lacked dash, loved discipline and order, and gained the respect, if not the devotion, of his men. Nothing in Slocum's record prior to the Gettysburg campaign either cast doubt on his military skills or marked him for higher responsibility.

Slocum's command consisted of only two divisions. The First Division belonged to Brig. Gen. Alpheus S. Williams, whose published letters make him familiar to modern students. "Old Pap" hailed from Connecticut and earned a degree from Yale, but after extensive travel abroad he settled in Michigan and established a Detroit law practice. Williams served in the Mexican War and presided over the state military board in the spring of 1861. A temporary replacement for the mortally wounded Maj. Gen. J. K. F. Mansfield as Twelfth Corps commander at Antietam, he returned to his division after the battle. Fifty-two years old in early summer 1863, Williams sported a luxuriant beard embellished by extravagant mustachios rivalling the hirsute splendor of fellow brigadier John C. Robinson.[6]

The three brigades of Williams's division experienced considerable reorganization following Chancellorsville. The 28th New York and 128th Pennsylvania mustered out of the First Brigade in May, and the brigade commander, Brig. Gen. Joseph F. Knipe, temporarily left the field nursing a bothersome wound sustained the previous August at Cedar Mountain. The army consolidated the Second Brigade with the First's remaining two regiments and named Col. Archibald L. McDougall of the 123d New York as commander of this new First Brigade. Gettysburg would be the only battle at which McDougall exercised so high an authority.[7] The Third Brigade remained intact under the able direction of Brig. Gen. Thomas H. Ruger of New York. Like Slocum, the thirty-year-old Ruger was a high-ranking graduate of West Point who resigned his commission to practice law. Ruger settled in Janesville, Wisconsin, and reentered the army as lieutenant colonel of the 3d Wisconsin, one of six western regiments in the corps at Gettysburg.[8]

The other division of the Twelfth Corps, known as the White Stars, served under Brig. Gen. John White Geary. This Pennsylvanian, in keeping with the coincidental character of the corps, also possessed a legal background. His law career, however, would be eclipsed by politics. After volunteer duty with Winfield Scott in Mexico, Geary moved to California where he became the first mayor of San Francisco. In 1856, at age thirty-seven, he received an unenviable appointment as territorial governor of turbulent Kansas; the strains of this office led him to an early retirement at his Pennsylvania farm. Geary raised a regiment in 1861 and advanced steadily through the ranks to division command.[9]

The Second Division experienced little organizational change between Chancellorsville and Gettysburg. Col. Charles Candy led the First Brigade, a unit comprised entirely of Ohioans and Pennsylvanians. Twenty-nine years old and a native of Lexington, Kentucky, Candy had served a decade as an enlisted man in the regular army when the war commenced. Commissioned an officer in the volunteers, he would eventually receive a brevet promotion to brigadier general, making him one of the few soldiers to rise from private to general during the course of the war.[10]

Colorful Thomas L. Kane held the official command of the Second Brigade. Yet another lawyer, Kane had earned a reputation before the war as an ardent abolitionist and principal in the Underground Railroad. Following an eventful period with the Mormons in Utah, Kane returned to his native Pennsylvania, founded a village he named after himself, and recruited

Brig. Gen. John White Geary. Courtesy of the National Archives.

the famous Pennsylvania Bucktails. A bout with pneumonia after Chancellorsville forced Kane to leave the field temporarily and entrust his brigade to Colonel George A. Cobham of the 111th Pennsylvania. The thirty-seven-year-old Cobham, perhaps because he was an Englishman, did not practice law but earned his living as a bridge builder and contractor.[11]

The Third Brigade consisted of five New York regiments led by Brig. Gen. George Sears Greene of Rhode Island. One observer described this unit as "the best brigade of the biggest state led by the best general of the smallest state." Sixty-two years old, Greene had graduated second in the West Point class of 1823 and lost his wife and three children during one seven-month period at Fort Sullivan, South Carolina. He resigned his commission in 1836 to pursue civil engineering in New York. Greene's troops called their commander "Pop" and deeply respected him as a stern authority figure.[12]

The Twelfth Corps, smallest in the army at only nine thousand soldiers and officers present for duty,[13] marched north on June 29 from Frederick, Maryland. Entering Pennsylvania the next day, the troops arrived hot and dusty at Littlestown about 2:00 P.M. Although Pennsylvanians generously dispensed refreshments and encouraging words to the tired troops, General Williams most vividly remembered the provincialism of the locals: "The inhabitants are Dutch descendants and quite Dutch in language. . . . The people are rich, but ignorant of everybody and [every] thing beyond their small spheres. They have immense barns, looking like great arsenals or public institutions, full of small windows and painted showily. Altogether, they are a people of barns, not brains."[14]

As some soldiers mustered for pay, word came that Rebel cavalry had attacked Union horsemen to the north. The Twelfth Corps quickly prepared to go to their cavalry's assistance, but by the time the men hurried through Littlestown the alarm had been cancelled. The corps made a comfortable camp about one mile northeast of town on the road to Hanover. From army headquarters, Maj. Gen. George G. Meade then instructed Slocum to become familiar with the roads between Littlestown, Gettysburg, and Maj. Gen. John F. Reynolds's position farther west, and informed Slocum of Confederate movements toward Gettysburg.[15]

July 1 dawned, according to one soldier, "wet and lowery." Following "a hasty breakfast of coffee, crackers and pork," elements of Williams's division left their bivouacs about 5:00 A.M. The corps retraced its route to Littlestown then gained the Baltimore Pike leading northwest toward Gettysburg about ten miles distant. By 9:00 A.M. the last units of Geary's division had commenced what everyone described as a leisurely march.[16]

The pace proved so casual, in fact, that members of the 66th Ohio of Candy's brigade found an opportunity for a little spontaneous recreation. William Henry Harrison Tallman remembered stopping at a farm house along the road where he and his comrades "squandered our shin plasters for soft bread, butter, apple butter, and a cheese the like of which I never smelled before. This cheese was made up in round balls about the size of a regulation baseball and [when] broken open perfumed the air for rods around us. Then commenced a lively pelting of each other with the cheese balls and the odor in and around our company was dense enough to cut with a knife."[17]

Slocum's immediate goal, as specified in orders communicated by Meade the previous day, was the hamlet of Two Taverns, a six-mile march and more than halfway to Gettysburg. The only event that disturbed the tranquility of this movement, cheese-ball battles notwithstanding, came from the north in the form of "the dull booming of cannon" heard by some of the troops. Slocum later described the sounds as cavalry carbines occasionally accompanied by artillery rather than the racket caused by a general engagement.[18] Williams's vanguard reached Two Taverns in midmorning and Geary's leading units arrived about 11:00 A.M., filing to the west of the road and encamping on a small hill.[19]

The day had grown uncomfortably muggy, and some of the pickets posted around the camp collapsed from heatstroke. The men sought solace from the weather in their rations and by gossiping, "the air . . . full of the rumors which circulate so freely when a battle becomes imminent." The air also resounded with the unmistakable echo of combat. "Heavy and continuous firing in the direction of Gettysburg" gradually grew more rapid. "The cannonading became more and more furious as the minutes passed," according to a Wisconsin soldier, "until in the distance it sounded like one continual roll of thunder."[20] Some listeners climbed to the tops of nearby barns where the bursting of shells could be plainly detected; others witnessed "smoke from the cannon and the little puffs in the air" from high points at the bivouac itself.[21]

The men completed their meal and some had begun the regular monthly inspection when a civilian dashed up to Slocum's headquarters with word of "a great battle" in progress at Gettysburg. The general dispatched Maj. Eugene W. Guindon of his staff to ride north and investigate this report. Guindon soon observed what other witnesses had seen from their lofty vantage points at Two Taverns, returning to Slocum with confirmation of the citizen's veracity.[22]

Meanwhile, Edmund R. Brown of the 27th Indiana saw no fewer than three couriers arrive at Two Taverns, "their horses in a lather and jaded, prov[ing] that they had come a distance and ridden fast." Brown identified them as emissaries from Maj. Gen. Oliver O. Howard, in command of Union forces at Gettysburg. In fact, Howard had sent a message to Slocum at 1:00 P.M.: "Ewell's corps is advancing from York. The left wing of the Army of the Potomac is engaged with A. P. Hill's corps."[23]

In response to this corroborated intelligence, the Twelfth Corps resumed its northward march on the Baltimore Pike but arrived too late to participate in the desperate defense mounted by Howard north and west of Gettysburg. Howard's strategy on the afternoon of July 1 depended in large part on the timely arrival of the Twelfth Corps, which he knew to be located only five miles to the southeast. Did Howard have reason to expect help from Slocum, and if so, why did it not materialize?

The most apposite document in this inquiry is Meade's famous Pipe Creek Circular, which was sent to Slocum on July 1.[24] The circular clearly stated Meade's intention to assume a defensive position along northern Maryland's Pipe Creek in the event of certain contingencies. First, the enemy would have to attack. Thanks to the civilian's report and Howard's messengers, Slocum knew early in the afternoon that a battle had been joined near Gettysburg. He did not know until later that the Confederates had initiated the action. Second, and more important, Meade wrote that the time for the withdrawal could "only be developed by circumstances" and that those circumstances would be "at once communicated to these headquarters and to all adjoining corps commanders." In other words, in the event of a Confederate assault, Reynolds would make the determination whether or not to retreat. Moreover, Meade specifically allowed for a Union advance by concluding his circular with the admonition that "developments may cause the commanding general to assume the offensive from his present positions."[25]

To be sure, Slocum's position at Two Taverns was consistent with Meade's instructions. Although it is clear that many Twelfth Corps soldiers heard the sounds of battle even before they reached the village, it is possible that the rolling terrain caused Slocum to misidentify the distant noise as cavalry skirmishing. When specific word of the engagement arrived from Howard and the civilian, however, Slocum apparently hesitated to either order his troops forward or, more negligently, take a short ride to find Howard and ascertain the facts for himself.[26]

In referring to Howard's messengers, one of Slocum's biographers observed that this "call did not give sufficient reason for Slocum to answer it immediately as desired inasmuch as Howard, as well as Slocum, had received a copy of the circular directing retreat on Pipe Creek." Under orders not to precipitate a general engagement elsewhere, Slocum occupied the place designated by his commanding officer, and "like the faithful, obedient commander that he was, he remained at his post of duty." This explanation simply misreads the intent of the Pipe Creek Circular. Moreover, Slocum's defenders then turn their argument on its head by praising the general's flexibility when he finally did direct his corps forward once convinced that its presence was necessary at Gettysburg.[27] A more critical historian, Samuel Bates, concluded that "General Meade anticipated, that if the forces in advance were attacked, any corps within supporting distance would go to their assistance; that it would act upon the Napoleonic principle, 'March to the sound of the enemy's guns.'" This Slocum did not instantly do and thus Bates held Slocum accountable for a measure of Howard's discomfiture.[28]

Slocum defended himself against this accusation by mentioning that none of his subordinates criticized his actions on July 1. "If all, or even any of these officers . . . had known at the time that the 12th Corps was kept idle, while two other corps were engaged with the enemy at a point only five miles distant, would not some of them, Yea! would every one of them have denounced the commander of the idle corps?" In fact, no one in Slocum's corps questioned his generalship on July 1—his loyal subordinates, it should be added, lacked crucial information that would warrant second guessing their chief's actions that day. In contrast, Howard's brother Charles penned a letter a week after the battle decrying Slocum's willingness "to demonstrate the fitness of his name Slow Come."

Generals Howard, Meade, and Abner Doubleday would fault Slocum in later years, but without acrimony.[29]

Howard's couriers probably reached Two Taverns shortly after 1:30 P.M. Although Geary claimed his division resumed the march at 2:00, reliable accounts from officers on Williams's and Geary's staffs, among others, state that the corps left Two Taverns between 3:00 and 4:00.[30] Once Slocum issued the order to advance, the movement commenced rapidly. "Between three and four P.M.," remembered William Tallman, "the order was given to fall in. From the sound of the bugle at the head of the division we knew it meant hurry up."[31]

The northbound troops encountered wounded soldiers and Confederate prisoners as well as residents of varying loyalties. One "hard-featured woman" rushed toward the passing column with evident delight. In the midst of enthusiastic hand shaking and expressions of welcome, a United States flag passed by, causing, as a Massachusetts soldier remembered, "a new idea to dawn upon [the woman]. In a tone of great disgust she said, 'I thought you were Rebs' and without another word turned her back on us. . . . It is fair to presume, that . . . she immediately proceeded to bake bread and sell to the soldiers at one dollar per loaf."[32]

Personally exhorting his men to march as rapidly as possible, Slocum learned en route of Reynolds's death.[33] He turned command of the corps over to "Pap" Williams and rode on ahead of his troops. The soldiers pressed forward in the afternoon heat, some collapsing along the roadside and many divesting themselves of playing cards and other nonessential items.[34]

About 5:00 P.M., a time when Howard had restored a viable defense line on Cemetery Hill, the head of Williams's division approached a crossroads one mile south of Rock Creek and two miles from the cemetery. Ordered by Slocum's couriers to move to the right of Gettysburg and informed by his own staff officers of a "high bare hill" to the east, Williams determined to occupy the eminence. Moving on a "narrow winding path" toward this elevation, called Benner's Hill, Williams soon reached the Hanover Road. He saw Benner's Hill looming before him but learned that Confederates had beaten him to it. The Michigander countermarched a short distance then deployed his men to assault the hill. Ruger's brigade had begun its advance, meeting no opposition, when orders came from Slocum to return to the Baltimore Pike. Williams obeyed and quietly withdrew his division.[35]

Meanwhile, Geary pushed ahead, intending to report to General Howard for duty on Cemetery Hill. The Pennsylvanian failed to locate Howard but found Winfield Scott Hancock, now in temporary command of the army until Slocum appeared, who told him to occupy a range of hills south of town on the Union left. Geary detached Kane's brigade as a reserve at the base of Cemetery Hill and marched with Candy's and Greene's troops toward Little Round Top.[36] The 5th Ohio and 147th Pennsylvania of the First Brigade took position on or near the rocky crest that would prove so critical the following day. Geary's skirmishers ranged as far west as the Emmitsburg Road, and the division commander extended his right northward to connect with the left of the First Corps.[37]

Combat on the first day had ended by then. Williams deployed his men along the Baltimore Pike northeast of where they had turned off on their aborted adventure toward Benner's Hill. Geary's men remained on the Union left from Little Round Top north along Cemetery Ridge. Except for the bloodless charge at the base of Benner's Hill, the Twelfth Corps saw no action on July 1.[38]

This might not have been the case had Slocum reacted more quickly to the fighting at Gettysburg. Based on actual distances and the rate of march achieved by the corps, it is reasonable to believe that portions of Slocum's command could have reached Cemetery Hill about the time Howard's battle lines evaporated north and west of town. It is unlikely that Slocum's men could have prevented the Union retreat, although historian Edwin B. Coddington believes that Williams might have deployed at Gettysburg in time to protect the First and Eleventh corps in their final, costly withdrawal.[39] Because Lt. Gen. Richard S. Ewell declined to test Union defenses on Cemetery Hill in the late afternoon of July 1, the potential value of the Twelfth Corps becomes moot. Had Slocum's forces arrived earlier, however, Ewell's oft-criticized decision would be significantly less controversial.

General Slocum's personal behavior compounds the indictment against his generalship. Howard's calls for help contained implicit and explicit requests for Slocum to ride forward and consult with him. Slocum ignored these entreaties, although he did canter ahead of his men when he met Capt. Addison G. Mason of Meade's staff. Mason informed Slocum of Reynolds's death (if someone else already had not) and passed on Meade's desire that he "push forward with all dispatch."[40] Slocum still refused to press on. He next met Maj. Charles Howard, the general's aide-de-camp, on the Baltimore Pike about a mile from Cemetery Hill. The younger Howard implored Slocum to repair to his brother's command post and take responsibility for the fight. Slocum declined, lamely citing his belief that Meade wished not to bring on a general engagement.[41]

Lt. Col. Charles H. Morgan, Hancock's chief of staff, then rode south from Cemetery Hill to oversee the arrival of the Twelfth Corps. Morgan met Slocum en route, and the general heard again, this time on Hancock's authority, that his presence was desired at the front. Slocum "objected to taking command on the ground that General Hancock had been specially selected over his head to do so, and had become familiar with the position and the location of the troops," remembered Morgan. Slocum explained further that he "did not care under the circumstances to assume the command which might make him responsible for a condition of affairs over which he had no control."[42]

Some historians explain Slocum's behavior as a reflection of his understanding of Meade's defensive and geographic preferences or point to Meade's failure to order his subordinate to assume command on the field by virtue of seniority.[43] Such arguments are unconvincing. If Slocum felt justified, albeit tardily, to commit his regiments to combat, he surely should have met his obligation to exert personal leadership. He never had displayed this type of hesitation, if not outright cowardice, during the Civil War and never would again, but his performance on July 1 certainly tarnishes his record.

Morgan finally persuaded Slocum to discharge his duty by informing the general that Meade's order naming Hancock as temporary field commander included instructions for Hancock to surrender his authority the moment Slocum appeared. The Twelfth Corps commander arrived on Cemetery Hill after 6:00 P.M. and finally relieved Hancock. Howard officially recognized Slocum's primacy when the two met some minutes later.[44] Meade arrived from Taneytown after midnight and assumed control from Slocum. At this juncture, Slocum returned to command of his corps, a responsibility technically discharged since late in the afternoon by Williams.[45] About midnight, General Kane rolled up in an ambulance after a harrowing trip from Baltimore. He reported to his brigade early the next morning but in a few minutes ordered Colonel Cobham to resume command. Kane remained "gallantly but unofficially" with his troops for the rest of the battle, "too feeble to resume the arduous duties of his post."[46]

As the first rays of light brightened the eastern sky on July 2, Geary received orders to move to the right from Little Round Top and southern Cemetery Ridge, leaving the defense of the Union left to the Third Corps.[47] His goal was Culp's Hill, a prominent eminence rising 180 feet above the surrounding terrain eight hundred yards southeast of Cemetery Hill. A thick blanket of second-growth hardwoods covered this rocky knob (which certainly was not the "mountain" described euphemistically by some Confederates), and huge boulders littered its slopes and crest.[48]

Geary's men arose at daybreak and noticed the "hazy and mysterious appearance" of Third Corps troops who had arrived during the night and were now "sleeping on the ground or groping about preparing food to eat." After pausing to consume a little breakfast of their own, Greene's Empire Staters countermarched through the fields they had tramped the day before, crossed the Baltimore Pike, and arrived on Culp's Hill about 6:00 A.M.[49] Greene's fourteen hundred men formed at right angles to Brig. Gen. James S. Wadsworth's division of the First Corps, extending Wadsworth's line from the crest down the south slope of Culp's Hill. A heavy growth of timber, relatively free from brush, covered their position, and the granite ledges and boulders provided good cover for riflemen. Greene's line extended about fifteen hundred feet, with the 78th on the left, followed in order by the 60th, 102d, 149th, and 137th. His right rested above a pronounced ravine that bisected the hill four hundred yards from its summit.[50]

Kane's brigade, nine hundred strong under the de facto command of Colonel Cobham, moved somewhat later from its reserve position near Powers Hill and formed on Greene's right. Cobham deployed his regiments to conform to the descending military crest of the ridge south of the ravine, causing his left to project at a forty-five-degree angle from Greene's right. The 109th and 111th Pennsylvania regiments, in that order, extended Geary's line from the ravine to a modest knob six hundred feet south. The 29th Pennsylvania formed as a brigade reserve in the rear.[51] Candy's was the last of the Second Division's brigades to shift to the right. The Ohioans and Pennsylvanians left their positions at the north of Little Round Top about 8:00 A.M. and formed behind Greene. The 28th Pennsylvania advanced along with detachments from the Third Brigade to serve as skirmishers on the west bank of Rock Creek."[52]

While Geary's White Stars moved to the right, Williams and Slocum met briefly at Williams's bivouac. The corps commander instructed his subordinate to advance again toward the Hanover Road to make contact with the Fifth Corps, then arriving from the east. Williams promptly obeyed, and Ruger's brigade deployed in line of battle facing north. A Fifth Corps division soon appeared to join Williams's men in a relatively harmless exchange of fire with Confederate infantry. At 8:00 A.M., Slocum ordered Williams to withdraw the First Division and place it on Geary's right. Williams rode ahead of his troops to reconnoiter the ground he would occupy and met Geary at Culp's Hill. The two officers then examined the terrain and Geary's recently established line.[53]

Ruger and McDougall, meanwhile, marched their brigades back to the Baltimore Pike, crossed Rock Creek, and before 11:00 A.M. moved into the woods between the south slope of Culp's Hill and the creek. McDougall and his brigade led the way across a three hundred-foot-wide marshy swale watered by Spangler's Spring and clambered up the gentle southern slope of Culp's Hill. The New Yorker deployed his six regiments in two

lines. The 123d New York, 20th Connecticut, and 46th Pennsylvania occupied the front from left to right, the 123d linking up with Cobham's
Pennsylvanians. The 3d Maryland, 145th New York, and 5th Connecticut
took cover behind a stone wall some forty paces behind their comrades. The
right of the 46th Pennsylvania and 5th Connecticut did not quite reach
the swale.[54]

'Ruger's brigade moved to the Baltimore Pike in the wake of McDougall's
men. An old woman stood along the road offering words of support to the
soldiers in what a Wisconsin man remembered as a strong Pennsylvania
Dutch accent: "Dot ish right, poys, go and drive dose fellows off. Dey has
shtole enough around here." Her comments "amused and encouraged the
men in that hour of high excitement," wrote the veteran. Col. Nirom M.
Crane, a New York banker, led the 107th New York across the headwaters
of Spangler's Spring and onto the low base of Culp's Hill. The future
Antietam cartographer Ezra A. Carman followed with the 13th New Jersey,
forming on the right of the 5th Connecticut behind the stone wall.[55]
The 2d Massachusetts also may have crossed the swale initially but eventually deployed in a moderately thick elevated forest, known as McAllister's Woods, between the swale and Rock Creek. The 3d Wisconsin
filed in on the right of the Bay Staters, and the 27th Indiana completed
the line. Ruger's brigade formed a rough arc on the morning of July 2—
the 107th New York, 13th New Jersey, and 2d Massachusetts protected the
swale from opposite sides, with the Badgers and Hoosiers facing east and
south toward Rock Creek, guarding the right flank of the corps.[56]

By the time Ruger completed these dispositions, Brig. Gen. Henry Hayes
Lockwood's brigade, freshly arrived from Baltimore and assigned for duty
with the Twelfth Corps, had arrived on the field and extended Ruger's
line toward the Baltimore Pike. A native of Delaware who graduated from
West Point in 1836, Lockwood had left the army after one year to accept a
teaching position at the Naval Academy. Only a stint of active duty aboard
a vessel off the California coast during the Mexican War interrupted Lockwood's antebellum academic pursuits in Annapolis. In 1861 he became
colonel of the 1st Delaware and subsequently commanded the Eastern
Shore District of the Middle Department, a military backwater if ever one
existed.[57]

In mid-June, Lockwood's brigade consisted of three regiments charged
with defending Baltimore from Lee's rampaging legions. The 1st Maryland
Eastern Shore Regiment, a three-year unit raised expressly to protect Federal interests in that part of the state, would not arrive at Gettysburg until
July 3. The 1st Maryland (Regiment) Potomac Home Brigade numbered
739 men on the eve of battle and was one of four such outfits originally

formed to guard the Potomac Valley, the B&O Railroad, and other Union resources in the Free State. Col. William Pinckney Maulsby, a forty-seven-year-old lawyer from Frederick, led this oversized but inexperienced unit. The 150th New York, known as the Dutchess County Regiment, completed Lockwood's brigade. It recruited in late 1862 under the slogan "come in out of the draft," and its six hundred troops looked to thirty-year-old farmer John Henry Ketcham for leadership. Like their comrades in the brigade, soldiers of the 150th had seen no serious combat.[58]

The 1st Maryland and 150th New York left Belger Barracks in Baltimore on June 25 (the 1st Maryland Eastern Shore would not leave until the 27th) and marched toward Frederick. They reached Monocacy Bridge in two days and encamped, watching awestruck as the Army of the Potomac, a "vast enginery of war," filed into and through the area. Like many green troops, Lockwood's men had overpacked their knapsacks. Veterans in Meade's army "guyed and blackguarded" the novices unmercifully for being so encumbered, and the newcomers quickly shed their excess baggage before heading north toward Pennsylvania.[59]

Lockwood's brigade arrived at Littlestown on July 1 in the wake of the Twelfth Corps. Its thirteen hundred rookies formed in line on the road to Gettysburg at 3:00 A.M. the next morning, were on the move by dawn, and reached the battlefield after a forced march. General Williams recently had completed his consultation with Geary about deploying the corps when Lockwood reported. The division commander, who never had met Lockwood and knew little about his abilities, found his new subordinate "a very pleasant gentleman" and ordered the brigade to take position along Rock Creek extending the right of Ruger's brigade. This allowed Williams to anchor his right flank on the Baltimore Pike.[60]

By late in the morning, the six brigades of the Twelfth Corps covered nearly a mile of front from the crest of Culp's Hill to (but not across) the swale at Spangler's Spring, through McAllister's Woods, and along the west bank of Rock Creek to the Baltimore Pike. Corps artillery could not drop trail directly along the line of battle because "the density of the growth of timber, [and] the irregularity and extremely broken character of the ground" prevented it from doing so with any advantage. Some guns were placed on Power's Hill west of the Baltimore Pike to offer long-range support. Although Meade defined the general position for the corps, credit for selecting this well-conceived emplacement belongs to Geary and Williams.[61]

Meade initially considered taking the offensive on his right. At 9:30 A.M., he ordered Slocum to examine the ground in front of Culp's Hill to determine if circumstances warranted an attack. Brig. Gen. Gouverneur K.

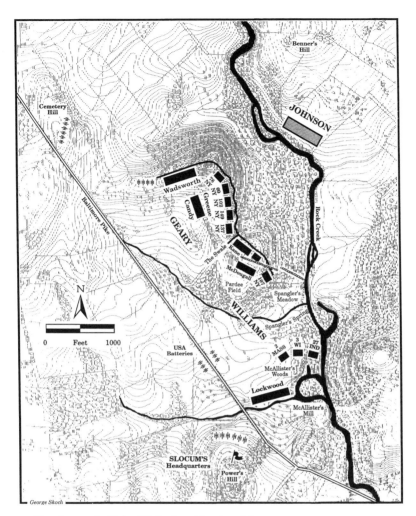

Situation on the Union Right, Late Morning, July 2

Warren, the army's chief engineer, received a similar directive from Meade. Should prospects seem propitious, Meade intended to launch a powerful assault led by the Twelfth and Fifth corps, supplemented by the Sixth Corps once it arrived. Slocum replied that he already had conducted a reconnaissance (apparently when he visited Williams early in the morning) and recommended against an assault. He worried about Confederate formations on his right despite believing that the enemy's position possessed no particular advantages. Warren concurred with this judicious assessment.[62]

Although never acted upon, the concept of an offensive from the right prompted changes in the Twelfth Corps command structure during the remainder of the battle and created controversy that festered for months. Meade had suggested a combined attack of several corps, which meant that Slocum's seniority entitled him to direct the assault.[63] Williams once again assumed control of the Twelfth Corps and ordered Ruger to lead the First Division. Col. Silas Colgrove of the 27th Indiana, a forty-seven-year-old lawyer and state legislator, inherited command of the Third Brigade; responsibility for the 27th passed to Lt. Col. John R. Felser, a Hoosier merchant and last of the human dominoes in this chain.[64]

The Fifth and Sixth corps would deploy on the opposite end of Meade's line in the afternoon, emasculating Slocum's phantom wing. This irrelevant command arrangement continued to live in Slocum's mind, however, and he illogically considered himself a wing commander for the rest of the battle. Slocum thus proved as unwilling to shed authority on July 2 as he had been to accept it the day before.

This makeshift situation also posed problems for Williams. Lockwood ranked Ruger and by rights should have served as acting division commander. But Williams balked at assigning responsibility for half the corps to an inexperienced stranger unfamiliar with the other brigades of the First Division. Displaying a good attorney's imagination and mental flexibility, Williams told Lockwood to "regard his command as an unattached brigade pending present operations" and to report directly to the acting corps commander.[65]

While the high command pondered an offensive and shuffled authority to accommodate Slocum's ephemeral wing, the men of Greene's brigade labored on a more tangible task. Shortly after the Second Division began occupying its new positions on Culp's Hill, General Geary met with Greene and perhaps his other brigade leaders to discuss the advisability of constructing earthworks along their line. Geary expressed doubts about the utility of building works. Perhaps because the division's entrenchments at Chancellorsville had proved of little use, many of the troops also viewed such field engineering as a waste of time and energy. Apart from the question of utility, Geary fretted about the loss of morale consequent on fighting behind barricades. Pop Greene respectfully disagreed, believing that saving lives superseded all other considerations. Geary acquiesced to Greene's appeal and granted permission to go ahead with the digging.[66]

Greene began immediately to fortify his line. The men grumbled a little at this early morning exercise, but soon everyone pitched in with adequate enthusiasm. Many of the soldiers hailed from western New York and possessed skills as woodsmen. Well supplied with axes, picks, and shovels, they soon sent the sounds of falling timber and the stacking of rocks and trees echoing along the slopes of Culp's Hill. By 9:00 A.M., a substantial line of logs and stones, shored up on the outer face with cordwood and earth, appeared along the entire Third Brigade front. The New Yorkers then placed a heavy abatis in advance of the line, so concealing it in the woods that it could not be seen at a distance of more than fifty yards.[67]

The troops continued to improve their defenses throughout the morning, including the construction of a traverse trench running at a ninety-degree angle east to west along the brigade's right flank. Greene ordered this innovation as a matter of local protection. The troublesome ravine ran below and parallel to his traverse and created a natural weak point where his right connected with Cobham's left. By the time Greene's New Yorkers laid down their tools at noon, defenses nearly five feet thick and substantial enough to stop a shell frowned from the upper and middle reaches of Culp's Hill.[68]

Much of the rest of the Twelfth Corps engaged in similar activity. The Pennsylvanians of Cobham's brigade arrived while Greene's New Yorkers pursued their labors. General Kane claimed that he left his ambulance long enough to indicate where the Second Brigade should build its earthworks. Taking their cue from Greene's troops, the three Keystone State regiments completed their own line in about three hours.[69] McDougall's brigade appeared next. Motivated by the desire to create a more formidable defense than at Chancellorsville, the troops of the 123d New York, 20th Connecticut, and 46th Pennsylvania extended Cobham's line to near the base of the hill. By midafternoon they completed this work. The brigade's other three regiments took cover behind the existing stone wall.[70] Williams, Ruger, and Colgrove all ordered the Third Brigade of the First Division to build works of logs, rails, and stones on both sides of the swale, although the fortifications in McAllister's Woods were substantially less elaborate than those on Culp's Hill.[71]

The Twelfth Corps thus entrenched from the top of Culp's Hill to Rock Creek and the Baltimore Pike. Just as with initial deployment of the corps, Slocum bore little responsibility for construction of these defenses. Greene overcame whatever initial objections Geary may have harbored, and the rest of the corps followed the aged New Yorker's example without debate.

Once ensconced behind their works, the men of the Twelfth Corps felt a sense of security. The Spangler's Meadow–McAllister's Woods area had been popular with local residents as a picnic grounds, and, as one poetic soldier recalled, "the oaks [formed] a grateful tent above our heads, as they had . . . over generations of pleasure groups; the pellucid waters of the spring [were] refreshingly cool." Some troops lounged quietly behind the breastworks, while others visited on the picket line or observed Confederates near Gettysburg from Wadsworth's vantage point on the crest of Culp's Hill.[72]

Unknown to these casual spectators, the four brigades of Edward "Allegheny" Johnson's Confederate division were preparing to end their pacific interlude. Instructed after midnight to occupy Culp's Hill by General Ewell, Johnson had begun to execute his orders when he learned that Williams's division inhabited the area and that the Fifth Corps was approaching from the east. Johnson correctly decided to consult with Ewell before moving forward. By the time Ewell heard about Johnson's concerns, General Lee already had postponed the advance. Ewell's offensive now would be triggered by an attack against the Union left led by Lt. Gen. James Longstreet. Once Longstreet's guns opened fire, Ewell would conduct a demonstration against Culp's Hill that he could convert into a real attack if a favorable opportunity appeared.[73]

Johnson's division numbered more than six thousand troops on July 2. Its units included the famous Stonewall Brigade of Brig. Gen. James A. Walker, another brigade of Virginians under Brig. Gen. John M. Jones, the five Louisiana regiments of Francis T. Nicholls's brigade led at Gettysburg by Col. Jesse M. Williams of the 2d Louisiana, and a mixed unit of North Carolinians, Marylanders, and Virginians commanded by Brig. Gen. George H. Steuart. Many of these regiments had fought in "Stonewall" Jackson's original division, and the troops enjoyed an esprit as exalted as their combat record.[74]

Maj. Joseph W. Latimer, a youngster of not quite twenty years, known as "the boy major," commanded the artillery battalion attached to Johnson's division. Early in the morning, Latimer reluctantly had occupied Benner's Hill, across Rock Creek and one-half mile to the northeast of Culp's Hill, as the only practical position for his guns. The open height offered little shelter for his horses and caissons and provided inadequate room for proper deployment of all his pieces. Latimer crowded fourteen guns onto Benner's Hill and placed two 20-pounder Parrotts across the Hanover Road to the north.[75]

The afternoon passed quietly, interrupted only by occasional skirmish fire along Rock Creek. Then at 4:00 P.M., Ewell ordered Johnson to commence his artillery bombardment against Culp's and Cemetery hills. Timed to coincide with the expected start of Longstreet's offensive on the opposite end of the battlefield, Latimer's barrage exploded with a metallic roar, sending shot and shell hurtling toward the Twelfth Corps infantry now huddled behind their entrenchments.[76]

Maj. Gen. Edward Johnson.
Miller's *Photographic History*
10:107.

Union artillery immediately engaged Latimer's battalion in a fierce duel. Col. Charles S. Wainwright, in charge of the guns east of the Baltimore Pike, turned his batteries on Cemetery Hill against Southern cannon on Benner's Hill. One piece of Knap's Pennsylvania Battery had moved to the crest of Culp's Hill shortly before the bombardment began. Soon thereafter, two more 10-pounder Parrotts appeared under the command of Lt. John Geary, the general's son. Two 12-pounders from Battery K, 5th U.S. Artillery, joined these three rifles, and some of the Twelfth Corps ordnance on Power's Hill also focused on Latimer's exposed batteries.[77]

Confederate projectiles found their marks on Culp's Hill, forcing volunteers from the 60th and 78th New York to stand in for Geary's fallen gunners. But Latimer's cannoneers faced converging fire in an exposed area and suffered more severely than did the Federals. When a Rebel ammunition wagon exploded spectacularly thirty minutes into the fight, fire from Benner's Hill slackened perceptibly. The artillery continued to exchange shots, albeit at a slower pace, until Latimer sustained a mortal wound late in the action. By 6:30 P.M., Latimer's successor withdrew his batteries to the rear, and once again quiet, along with the fading sun, descended on Slocum's front.[78]

It had been anything but quiet on the Union left since 4:00 P.M. Longstreet's attack finally commenced at that hour and succeeded in driving

Daniel E. Sickles's Third Corps from its advanced positions west of Cemetery Ridge and Little Round Top. Meade responded by ordering reinforcements from other sectors of the battlefield, including the Twelfth Corps, to respond to the crisis on his left.[79]

The precise sequence of events by which the Twelfth Corps shifted to the southwest on the evening of July 2 remains one of the minor mysteries of the Gettysburg campaign. Countless writers have addressed the subject (most of them only fleetingly), drawing on a corpus of contradictory primary sources that seemingly support a variety of potential scenarios.

It is known that at 5:30 P.M., a time at which the duel between Latimer and Union cannoneers was winding down and the chaos of an uncertain outcome raged in the Wheatfield and the Peach Orchard, Meade's signal officers informed Slocum that they had seen "a heavy column of [Confederate] infantry" moving toward the Twelfth Corps. Shortly thereafter, Meade sent orders to Slocum, the text of which regrettably has been lost. Secondary testimony provides the best evidence about the contents of these orders, and the two most important witnesses are Generals Williams and Slocum. In an 1875 letter defending himself against criticisms lodged in a recently published history of the battle, Slocum unequivocally stated that "Gen. Meade sent me an order to remove the entire 12th Corps from its position on the right, to one on the left." Because, as described below, Slocum retained a part of his corps on the right and engaged in a fierce battle that evening with attacking Confederates on Culp's Hill, many writers have applauded his "resolute insistence" that paid dividends for the Union army.[80]

Williams's version of events, however, casts doubt on the degree of Slocum's resolution, if not the happy outcome of his indecision. Nine months after the battle and again a year later, Williams recalled that at 5:30 or 6:00 P.M. Slocum sent him an order "to detach all I could spare, at least one Div. to support our left." Williams responded by ordering Ruger's First Division, situated closest to the southern end of the battlefield, to move out. Accompanying Ruger's troops, Williams met Slocum near "wing" headquarters at Power's Hill, explaining that he feared for the security of the Union right and had ordered Geary to extend the Second Division to cover Ruger's vacant works. Williams also ventured the opinion that it would be unwise to detach any more troops from the Twelfth Corps front. According to Williams, Slocum replied that Meade's orders were "urgent" and instructed him to send "all the troops [I] could spare" to the south, a clear indication of both Meade's acute sense of emergency and a degree of discretion Slocum neglected to mention in 1875. Slocum concurred with Williams's appraisal of the situation on the Union right, and Pap marched off to the left believing that Geary would remain on Culp's Hill. In fact, only after fighting ended on the second day would Williams discover that any of Geary's troops had decamped.[81]

Slocum's postwar account continues at variance with Williams's more contemporary story. The New Yorker stated that on receiving Meade's categorical directive to move the entire corps, he instantly set each brigade in motion. At the same time, he dispatched his adjutant general, Col. Hiram C. Rodgers, to Meade's headquarters with a request that he be allowed to retain "at least a division" on the Culp's Hill front. According to Slocum, Rodgers returned shortly with Meade's permission to keep one brigade rather than a division on the right. Slocum selected Greene's brigade, last in line and yet to begin its march to the left, to remain on Culp's Hill with instructions to stretch as far as possible to protect the abandoned trenches.[82]

At this point it is useful to consult General Geary's recollection of events. His official report stated: "By a staff officer of Major-General Slocum, at 7 P.M. I received orders to move the division by the right flank, and follow the First Division, leaving one brigade to occupy the line of works of the entire corps. The First Division had gone nearly half an hour previously."[83] Geary's testimony contains two salient points. First, he mentioned no preliminary order from Slocum to move his entire division, later modified to omit Greene's brigade (neither did he say anything about orders from Williams to extend his front to McAllister's Woods). Second, Geary confirmed that thirty minutes transpired between Ruger's departure and his receipt of orders to shift two brigades to the south, time enough for Rodgers to have ridden from Power's Hill to Meade's headquarters at the Widow Leister's house, receive clarification from Meade, and report back to Slocum.

The final source on this subject is the most confusing and perhaps the least credible. Capt. Charles P. Horton, General Greene's assistant adjutant general, remembered that at 6:00 P.M. the brigade received orders to move out and was in the act of doing so when engaged by Confederate skirmishers along Rock Creek. According to Horton, Greene halted his men, reinforced his skirmishers, and sent word of the situation to Geary. Geary allegedly ignored Greene's dilemma and simply reiterated his order for the Third Brigade to vacate Culp's Hill. As the courier bearing Geary's ill-advised instructions returned to Greene's position, he met Colonel Rodgers, who invoked Slocum's authority to countermand Geary's directive, told Greene to remain where he was, and promised to return the rest of Geary's division to Greene's support.[84]

What is to be made of this welter of conflicting accounts? If Meade's original orders to Slocum survived, decisions by the principal general officers of the Twelfth Corps could be readily reconstructed. In the absence of that evidence, however, certain speculative conclusions may be drawn. First, Meade unquestionably viewed the situation on his left with alarm and gave what in hindsight seems to be undue precedence to that flank over the security of the rest of his line. Although aware of potential danger on Slocum's front, the army commander indisputably wanted the Twelfth Corps to help defend the southern portion of the field. It is probable that Meade's orders conveyed a strong desire that Slocum detach as much of his corps as possible and preferably all of it.

Slocum must have read these orders with deep misgivings. He knew that unseen Confederate forces opposed him across Rock Creek, and he had the benefit of Williams's recommendation that at least one entire division be retained along his line. Facing uncertain conditions on the previous day, Slocum had reacted timidly and irresponsibly to discretionary orders; he faced the same quandary on the late afternoon of July 2. He sent Rodgers to Meade ostensibly to secure permission for Geary's division to remain in its fortifications on Culp's Hill, but he also wished to quantify Meade's orders—in other words, to eliminate any discretion contained in the original directive.

Slocum avers that he instantly placed his whole corps in motion, a contention that Horton indirectly confirms.[85] But both Geary and Williams state that the First Division departed before the Second Division received any instructions to move. Considering the self-justifying nature of Slocum's account and Horton's chronologically confused recitation of events, the weight of evidence indicates that Slocum, wisely enough, hedged his bet.

If Meade's order to Slocum encouraged but did not explicitly require shifting the entire Twelfth Corps to the left, Slocum could have retained all of Geary's division on the right without exceeding the scope of his authority. Such a decision probably would have avoided the near disaster Greene's brigade experienced later that evening. Slocum's refusal after the war to acknowledge the probable latitude contained in Meade's orders perhaps reflected sensitivity about what many considered a mistake at Culp's Hill. Meade bears principal responsibility for the fact that only Greene's brigade, surely an inadequate force, remained to defend the position. But Slocum had the chance to avert the error.

Meade, Slocum, and Geary played out this drama while the First Division hastened toward the Union left. Under the watchful eye of General Williams, who was unwilling to entrust command of the movement to any of his subordinates, Lockwood's brigade led the march followed by Colgrove and McDougall. The soldiers progressed at a brisk pace, at times practically running, motivated by the sound of rapid musketry that reminded L. R. Coy of the 123d New York of "a bunch of China crackers connected and fired at once." The troops turned south on the Baltimore Pike until they reached the Granite Schoolhouse Lane, a dirt road that skirted the southern base of Power's Hill. Following this track, the men eventually emerged onto the Taneytown Road. "Hurrying to the right up this road," wrote Williams, "I soon began to pass masses of disorganized portions of the 3d Corps."[86] Williams's sound instincts and the roar of battle explain the division's appearance near the scene of combat. Neither Meade nor Slocum had provided Williams with precise instructions about his destination, and the staff officer detailed by Slocum had no idea where to direct the reinforcements.[87]

Confederate artillery shells fell among the approaching troops, who at one point became alarmed at what seemed to be a battery of guns tearing down the road in panic. A German ordnance sergeant astride an empty caisson and in search of ammunition assured the Red Stars as he galloped by that "dis ish nod a retread!" The Twelfth Corps men were glad to hear it. They received additional comfort from an old woman who, as the shriek of the Rebel yell became audible on the distant winds, stood by the roadside and told the passing bluecoats, "Never mind, boys, they're nothing but men."[88]

Williams searched amidst throngs of stragglers and the slightly wounded along the east slope of Cemetery Ridge for someone in authority to advise him about the situation ahead. Although these fugitives offered enthusiastic encouragement, no one had knowledge about current tactical conditions. Williams's best geographical information came from Colonel Maulsby of the First Maryland Home Brigade, who had lived in nearby Westminster, Maryland, and knew the countryside around Gettysburg fairly well. With Maulsby's neophytes in the forefront, Williams pointed toward the first opening at the summit of the ridge.[89]

As Lockwood's brigade pressed forward near the crest, Lt. Col. Freeman McGilvery rushed toward Williams expressing great delight at the appearance of the Twelfth Corps. McGilvery commanded the First Volunteer Brigade of the Artillery Reserve at Gettysburg and knew Williams from their service together earlier in the war. The cannoneer explained, "with the rapidity that such occasions require[d]," that his beleaguered artillery lacked infantry supports and that the Confederates already had captured some of his pieces. Williams ordered Lockwood to charge the woods in his front, specifying that Maulsby's Marylanders fix bayonets and move at the double quick.[90]

Colonel Maulsby promptly obeyed this directive—so promptly, in fact, that his men advanced without properly deploying from marching column into battle line. With Lockwood at the head of the formation and the 150th New York in close support, the 1st Maryland dashed west toward the Trostle Farm in the gathering twilight. Both Lockwood and Colonel Ketcham reported facing "the most terrific firing of shells and musketry" during the onslaught, an exaggerated impression that may have reflected their lack of combat experience. The Confederates already had fallen back by the time Lockwood's troops moved off Cemetery Ridge, and as Maulsby said, "our friends on the other side did not stand long enough to give [our] bayonets a chance to show what metal they were made of." Considering the reckless tactics employed by the gallant, impetuous Marylanders, they were fortunate that no Confederate brigade challenged their attack.[91]

Maulsby's momentum carried his regiment into the fields east of the Peach Orchard. The 150th New York swept through the Trostle farmyard after the Marylanders, taking possession of three guns from Capt. John Bigelow's Massachusetts battery captured earlier by the 21st Mississippi. Companies B and G of the Dutchess County men removed their prizes by hand while the rest of the regiment dutifully attended to the myriad wounded who littered the ground in the nearby orchard, fields, and woods.[92]

Meanwhile, Williams had ordered Ruger's division to take position on Cemetery Ridge south of where Lockwood began his attack. Ruger formed his brigades in two lines and pushed westward a short distance into Weikert's Woods, encountering no Confederate resistance. By now the sun's remaining influence had all but vanished. Williams instructed Ruger to halt and rode forward to retrieve Lockwood from his isolation near the Peach Orchard.[93] Thus ended the First Division's brief bravura on the Federal left that evening.

The Twelfth Corps had not played a crucial role in repulsing the Confederates. By the time Lockwood and the Red Stars arrived, the Southern tide had crested and begun to recede. Still, the First Division accomplished all that was asked of it, and Pap Williams discharged his responsibilities competently. Although some accounts suggest that General Meade personally led Lockwood's brigade forward, the commanding general in fact took no direct hand in guiding the First Division.[94]

However small Williams's part in rebuffing Lee's offensive on July 2, Geary contributed even less. What happened to the First and Second brigades of Geary's division that evening is foggy enough, but why it happened defies explanation.

Ordered to leave Greene's brigade on Culp's Hill and march with Candy and Cobham to Williams's assistance on the army's left, Geary placed his troops in motion and eventually reached the Baltimore Pike. Turning south with Candy's brigade in the lead, the White Stars marched past corps headquarters at Power's Hill and beyond the country road used by Williams to reach Cemetery Ridge. They continued southward, crossed Rock Creek, and halted on a hill south of the stream. As far as the Battle of Gettysburg was concerned, Geary's two brigades had stepped off the map.[95] Slocum referred to Geary's march as "an unfortunate and unaccountable mistake." A Wisconsin soldier termed Geary's performance "a singular blunder," and the historian of the 2d Massachusetts concluded that "it did not show much of a soldier's instinct to take a road leading to the rear and follow it for about two miles before halting."[96]

Geary's own testimony sheds little light on the puzzling episode. Clearly he suffered from the same lack of information that plagued Williams. "I received no specific instructions as to the object of the move, the direction to be taken, or the point to be reached, beyond the order to move by the right flank and to follow the First Division," he wrote in his report. Because Williams had a half-hour head start, Geary lost track of his colleague's whereabouts and followed some stragglers he assumed were trailing the Red Stars. Once across Rock Creek, Geary claimed to have received an order at 7:30 P.M. to hold the position "down to the creek at all hazards," at which point he formed a line with his right on the pike near the Rock Creek bridge and his left on the creek itself.[97] This order has no relevance unless it actually applied to Geary's former position on Culp's Hill. If so, this could have been the directive Williams said he issued when Slocum first told him to move to the left.

Geary's initial confusion is understandable, if not justifiable. His inability to find the rest of the corps on Cemetery Ridge and willingness to keep his men uselessly idle cannot be excused. Why did Geary fail to send couriers to Slocum's headquarters or westward until they found the Union left? How could an experienced and brave man not deduce that his position south of Rock Creek contributed nothing toward mitigating the emergency that had summoned him from Culp's Hill? How could Slocum lose track of half his corps for hours and not send an adequate number of orderlies to locate it?[98] Had Geary's troops been needed on the Union left that evening, and Geary had no inkling that they were not, history would have remembered the general unkindly indeed. As matters developed, his folly cost the Federals nothing in a strategic or tactical sense. But his absence from Culp's Hill was not inconsequential. Five of the six Twelfth Corps brigades had decamped from the Union right, leaving only Greene's New York regiments to defend their positions. In a short time, Pop Greene would face one of the critical challenges of his long life.

Greene's imminent adversary, "Old Clubfoot" Johnson, had hidden his four Confederate brigades on low ground north of the Hanover Road that

Brig. Gen. George Sears Greene. From Miller's *Photographic History* 10:305.

morning. There he awaited Ewell's signal to assail his designated target one mile away. Except for employing a few skirmishers east of Rock Creek, Johnson kept his infantry concealed and quiet throughout the day. He did direct Jones's Virginians to support Latimer near Benner's Hill during the afternoon artillery duel. When the Southern gunners retired from their unequal contest, Ewell sent Johnson the long-anticipated directive to attack. Ewell's other two divisions waited farther west, poised to move forward once Johnson successfully engaged the Yankees in his front.[99]

Happily for Ewell, he chose to attack at the very moment in which 83 percent of the Twelfth Corps was vacating its prepared positions. This spectacular timing appears to have been entirely serendipitous. Although some Union pickets did withdraw from their posts near Rock Creek, no evidence indicates that Ewell reacted to any specific information about Slocum's dispositions. Instead, he merely adhered to Lee's timetable for engagement of the Second Corps.[100] In any case, Lee intended Ewell's offensive either to prevent Union reinforcements from reaching Longstreet's sector or to exploit the absence of those forces in his own front. The exploitation was about to begin.

Johnson's advance encountered three immediate obstacles. First, the appearance of Union cavalry to the east prompted Old Clubfoot to detach the Stonewall Brigade to guard the division's left and rear. This deprived the Confederates of one-fourth of their strength.[101] Second, as the brigades of Jones, Williams, and Steuart, in that order, reached Rock Creek, they discovered waist-deep water that would take time to negotiate.[102] The crossing became even more difficult when Union skirmishers scattered about one hundred yards west of the creek and peppered the graycoats with a persistent and surprisingly effective fire.

Lt. Col. John O. Redington of the 60th New York commanded the advanced Federal line. When he saw Johnson's troops forming for their strike across Rock Creek, he sounded a bugle summoning the 78th New York, known as the Cameron Highlanders and led by Lt. Col. Herbert von Hammerstein, to come to his assistance. Redington maintained a brisk fire that compelled the Confederates to lie down in the grass on the creek's far bank. The Federals exchanged musketry for thirty minutes, slowly withdrawing up the slope of Culp's Hill as Jones and Williams crossed the stream and pursued in the gathering gloom. Fifty yards from the main Union line, the plucky marksmen dashed for the works and joined their comrades behind the entrenchments.[103]

While the skirmishers delayed Johnson's approach, Greene ordered his remaining regiments to fan out and extend their front to cover as much of the forsaken line as possible. The 60th stretched to the top of the hill on the left to occupy ground vacated by the 78th. The 102d expanded to its right the length of a regiment, a maneuver repeated by the 149th and 137th, which now held the portion of the line previously controlled by Cobham's men. The trenches McDougall's soldiers had built near the base of Culp's Hill remained empty. Greene's men stood in one rank a foot or more apart and had no local reserve.[104] Realizing that his brigade would need help to resist a major Confederate assault, Greene notified Wadsworth and Howard, who promptly dispatched a total of seven regiments numbering 755 men.[105] Until these reinforcements arrived, only the New Yorkers would confront Johnson's three brigades.

The Confederates formed with Jones on their right opposing the 60th New York on the hill's steepest grade, Williams next in line opposite the 78th, 102d, and 149th, and Steuart trailing on the left aimed at the 137th New York farthest from the crest. Johnson mustered seventeen regiments three lines deep and outnumbered Greene more than three to one.[106]

Those odds were not as overwhelming as they might appear. Twilight obscured the Federal line until the Confederates reached pistol range. There Greene's concealed bluecoats staggered the brigades of Jones and Williams with a deadly volley. The terrain also favored the defenders. Jones's men had to scale the precipitous northern end of Culp's Hill in the

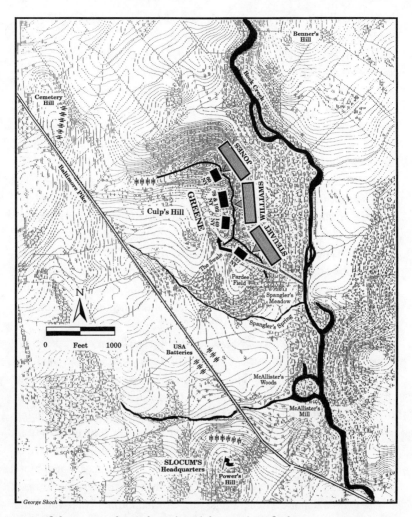

Confederate Assaults on the Union Right, Evening of July 2

face of rapid fire. Johnson's first attack failed, and the Virginians and Louisianians dropped back among the rocks to regroup.[107]

The initial Union reinforcements now began to arrive from Cemetery Hill, including the 61st Ohio, which took position alongside the determined New Yorkers. These troops appeared not a moment too soon because the Confederate line, "yelping and howling in its peculiar manner," emerged again from the smoke and darkness to renew the assault. "Out into the murky night like chain lightning [leapt] the zigzag line of fire" from the Union rifles. "A thousand tongues of flame thrust themselves into the darkness toward the foe, and winged death hisse[d] through the rebel ranks." This time the two Confederate brigades actually reached the works, but they could not hold them. In short order, Federals drove them back into the night.[108] More fresh regiments began to appear. Some relieved the New Yorkers, who withdrew temporarily to replenish ammunition and clean fouled muskets. Other units headed straight for the Federal right, where Col. David Ireland's 137th New York had been conducting a private war with "Maryland" Steuart's command.[109]

A Scottish tailor from New York City, Ireland had posted his men in the most vulnerable portion of Greene's attenuated line. Not only was his right flank completely in the air, but the ground in his front also ascended more gently toward the Federal works, making the Confederate approach relatively easy. Ireland was in the process of sliding his regiment southward when Confederates exploded from the woods to his front and right. The attackers progressed by the guiding light of muzzle flashes from Ireland's line. Discovering that the works on Ireland's right lay unprotected, Steuart sent his men surging toward the pregnable area. Ireland ordered his rightmost company to pivot west and block the incipient flank attack. These few troops obeyed, but after a short while fell back to establish another position at right angles to their breastworks.[110]

At this point the unfortunate 71st Pennsylvania (known as the "California Regiment") made its brief and undistinguished entrance onto the stage. General Hancock had heard the racket on Culp's Hill and deduced that the Union troops there needed assistance. He instructed a division commander to rush two regiments to the threatened sector, and the 106th and 71st Pennsylvania regiments moved rapidly to the right. The 106th misunderstood its mission, halting on Cemetery Hill. The 71st arrived at Culp's Hill, reporting to Ireland as the Confederate attack erupted in its presence.[111]

Considerable confusion exists today, as it did in 1863, about the actions of the California Regiment at Culp's Hill on July 2. Greene referred to it as an Eleventh Corps unit in an article written nearly a generation after the battle. Geary assigned it to the First Corps in his account of the fight. Ireland and Lieutenant Colonel Horton described its arrival in substantially different ways. In the absence of a definitive narrative, it appears that a staff officer led the Pennsylvanians to Ireland's end of the Union position just as Ireland had ordered his right flank to face south. The 71st briefly extended this line but soon departed—not in response to Confederate pressure but under orders from its commanding officer, Col. Richard P. Smith. This withdrawal heightened the crisis faced by the 137th, but there is no evidence that the unseemly maneuver besmirched Colonel Smith's reputation.[112]

Ireland next played his last remaining card. Falling back again, this time with his entire regiment, he took position behind the traverse constructed earlier on Greene's orders. This deployment strengthened the 137th in relation to any threat from the south. Steuart's troops witnessed this realignment, which one of them termed a Yankee "skeedadle," and took possession of all the works built by Cobham and McDougall. Three companies of the 149th New York formed on Ireland's right, a maneuver momentarily misinterpreted as a retreat by the rest of the regiment until their colonel, Henry A. Barnum, stabilized the line. The New Yorkers defended their new front, which was also exposed in the tangled, rocky woods to its right, until the 14th Brooklyn arrived to assist them.[113]

Conventional Confederate wisdom asserted that Federals had occupied the works captured by Steuart's brigade. Union accounts disagreed, ascribing their foe's confusion to fierce flanking fire delivered by Ireland and his supports and to a mistaken interpretation of the 71st Pennsylvania's precipitate retreat as a forced withdrawal. Whatever the case, no regiment in Greene's brigade suffered more casualties or acquitted itself more honorably than did the 137th.[114]

The other New York regiments distinguished themselves as well. Greene's command turned away two more attacks on its right before Johnson relinquished the offensive between 10:00 and 11:00 P.M. In the process, the 149th's regimental flag sustained eighty-one shots through its silk and seven through its staff. The 60th captured Jones's brigade flag and one of the Virginia regimentals along with some five dozen prisoners snatched from across the works in their front. "The appearance of the men in the trenches," observed one New Yorker, "with their clothes ragged and dirty, their faces black from smoke, sweat and burnt powder, [and] their lips cracked and bleeding from salt-petre in the cartridges bitten by them . . . resembled more the inhabitants of the bottomless pit than quiet peaceful citizens of the United States of America." An admiring Henry W. Slocum attributed "the failure of the enemy to gain possession of our works . . . entirely to the skill of General Greene and the heroic valor of his troops."[115]

Slocum's praise rang true, but did Greene's stouthearted victory hold significance beyond the mere maintenance of his position? Many writers have thought so, claiming that Greene's triumph marked the turning point in the entire Battle of Gettysburg. "The battle was at no other time so nearly lost as it was in the emergency when old George Greene and his men did the impossible and saved the day that won the war," enthused one observer. "Had Greene and his gallant little band been defeated in this action," echoed a Pennsylvania veteran, "the battle of Gettysburg might not have been the glorious victory it was for our arms."[116]

Such analysts based their claims on the proximity of Johnson's division to the all-important Baltimore Pike on the evening of July 2. Once Geary and Williams abandoned their positions on the Union right, no Federal troops barred the way to that vital road. A four hundred-yard march would have brought the Confederates to the pike and a nearby supply and ammunition train. Meade's headquarters lay a short distance beyond. Southern control of the pike would threaten the rear of the Northern army on Cemetery Ridge and sever one of two potential Federal routes of retreat. In short, goes the argument, "Ewell then held for a time in his hands the most golden opportunity that ever fell to a subordinate commander during a battle that was to decide the destinies of a Nation." But instead of exploiting this decisive advantage, Johnson hunkered down behind his captured earthworks, and, fearing a trap, refused to venture forward and seize the day.[117]

In fact, Johnson enjoyed a very brief window of opportunity to reach the Baltimore Pike unopposed. If Ewell had started the offensive earlier to take advantage of waning sunlight, his troops would have encountered the entire Twelfth Corps, the departure of which coincidentally mirrored the Confederate advance. By the time Johnson suspended further efforts to capture Culp's Hill, Williams and Geary were already en route to their old lines. Furthermore, Union troops on Cemetery Hill and a brigade of reinforcements from the Sixth Corps under Brig. Gen. Thomas H. Neill could have opposed the Confederates. The only fresh unit available to Johnson was Walker's brigade, still posted to block Federal cavalry along the Hanover Road. As Edwin B. Coddington wrote, "The lost opportunity of the Confederates, which had been fleeting at best, to envelop the right of the Union army existed less in actuality than in the minds of broken-hearted veterans seeking the reason why." Ewell missed no chance to wreck the Army of the Potomac on July 2.[118]

Slocum ensured this by ordering the Twelfth Corps to return to its former position "immediately after the repulse of the enemy on the left." Williams had no idea that any of Geary's division had moved from Culp's Hill, but he quickly directed Ruger to shift the First Division back to its entrenchments. On the way, the acting corps commander spotted "a large collection of General and other officers," including Meade, in an open field near the Taneytown Road. Williams paused at this "pleasant gathering" to exchange congratulations on the day's results, while Ruger continued forward toward the Union right.[119]

The Third Brigade led the march under a full moon. Between the Taneytown Road and the Baltimore Pike, a staff officer from Slocum's headquarters informed Ruger that not only had most of the Second Division temporarily vacated Culp's Hill but also the remaining Federals had recently concluded a desperate struggle. Although this messenger erroneously reported that Geary's men had reoccupied their old lines, Ruger prudently ordered skirmishers from both Colgrove's and McDougall's brigades to ascertain the situation. Colgrove told Lt. Col. Charles R. Mudge of the 2d Massachusetts to have scouts determine if Confederates occupied McAllister's Woods or ground across the swale at the base of Culp's Hill. When the works nearest Rock Creek proved to be empty, the 13th New Jersey, 27th Indiana, and 3d Wisconsin filled in from right to left securing the ground south of the swale.[120]

Company F of the 2d Massachusetts then cautiously probed across the open meadow and into the edge of the woods just beyond Spangler's Spring. The New Englanders heard voices in the darkness, and closer investigation revealed that Virginians from Steuart's brigade were filling their canteens at the spring. The Unionists captured nearly two dozen thirsty Confederates before returning to McAllister's Woods, where the entire regiment deployed facing north at right angles to their old lines. The 107th New York later formed on the left and rear of the 2d Massachusetts facing more easterly than to the north.[121]

Other Federals also groped their way toward old positions. Colonel McDougall dispatched Company I of the 123d New York and a portion of Company E of the 5th Connecticut to reconnoiter the First Brigade's former line. Finding Southerners along their entire portion of Culp's Hill, they avoided capture when a New York lieutenant shouted a warning. Apparently troops from the 20th Connecticut and 46th Pennsylvania also ventured forward in the shadows and encountered parched graycoats at Spangler's Spring. Everyone happily gathered water until an unwary Federal casually announced that "the rebels had caught 'hail columbia' over on the left." The Confederates took exception to this remark, a short mêlée ensued, and both sides took a few prisoners.[122]

McDougall withdrew his vanguard and deployed the brigade to extend Colgrove's left toward the Baltimore Pike. The 123d New York occupied a somewhat advanced position with the 3d Maryland, 145th New York, 20th Connecticut, 5th Connecticut, and 46th Pennsylvania forming ranks from right to left. Ruger's line now faced east toward the swale and Rock Creek, and north to cover the gap between the base of Culp's Hill and the Baltimore Pike one-quarter mile away.[123]

Lockwood's two regiments were the last of Ruger's troops to return to the right. They withdrew from their advanced positions at the west of the Trostle Farm, unsettled by the cries of the wounded they heard along the way. Arriving at the Baltimore Pike about midnight, they secured McDougall's left and provided support for newly posted Union artillery.[124]

In the meantime, Slocum's couriers finally located Geary and told him to return to Culp's Hill. Geary issued marching orders to the Second Division about 9:00 P.M.[125] Cobham's brigade countermarched on the Baltimore Pike with the 29th Pennsylvania in the lead and pivoted into the woods toward its old breastworks. Two hundred yards from the destination, a volley from the forest in Cobham's front claimed fourteen casualties. Cobham, assisted by General Kane, extracted his brigade and marched it farther north to a position behind Greene's survivors. The Pennsylvanians relieved the 137th New York, forming a longer line running west and oriented south toward McDougall's position one thousand feet away. Any Confederate troops now attempting to reach the Baltimore Pike would face a potentially blistering crossfire. Candy's brigade arrived last, probably about 1:00 A.M., and deployed in two lines. One rank supported the right of Greene's brigade and the other debouched behind and to the right of Cobham. Their presence allowed the 149th New York and Greene's other weary regiments to leave the trenches, refit, and steal some sleep on the hill's rocky slopes.[126]

The realignment of the Twelfth Corps between 10:00 P.M. and 1:00 A.M. occurred while both Slocum and Williams attended a council of war convened at Meade's headquarters shortly after 9:00 P.M. One of Meade's staff officers had found Williams near the Baltimore Pike and summoned him to the conference in his capacity as acting corps commander.[127] Slocum participated as Meade's senior lieutenant. When Meade polled his subordinates regarding the army's next move, Slocum offered his oft-quoted advice to "stay and fight it out." That is precisely the policy the generals adopted before the meeting adjourned shortly before midnight.[128]

Williams finally rejoined his division, only to receive "the astounding intelligence" that Confederates manned a large section of his works. Apparently Slocum had not been informed about Greene's battle either and learned of the situation from Williams. Williams placed two additional batteries on the rise of ground west of the Baltimore Pike and opposite the lower reaches of Culp's Hill. These guns joined ordnance already in position on Power's and McAllister's hills to provide the infantry with substantial artillery support. Slocum instructed Williams to "Drive [the Confederates] out at daylight," and Williams spent the next several hours preparing to do so.[129]

Thus ends the story of the Twelfth Corps on the first two days at Gettysburg, except for an unpleasant postscript. Meade penned his report of the campaign in the fall of 1863; Slocum and Williams, then serving in the western theater, had the opportunity to read it in late November.[130] The narrative slighted the contribution of the Twelfth Corps in several respects, particularly in relation to Williams and the First Division, and contained a number of factual errors. Williams confessed to being "pretty mad" about this public injustice, observing that "Gen. Slocum is a mile or so ahead of me in indignation." Both Slocum and Williams had thought highly of Meade in July; however, Slocum's attitude toward army authority had soured by November. Unhappy with his transfer from the Army of the Potomac to the West, Slocum had suffered the further affront of assignment under Maj. Gen. Joseph Hooker, an officer he considered scarcely worthy of respect. Meade's inaccurate report provided the last straw for the New Yorker's prickly sensibilities.[131]

Slocum drafted a legalistic protest dripping with contempt and sent it to Meade requesting that an official correction be filed with the War Department. He told a private correspondent that he considered demanding a court of inquiry to secure proper credit for Williams and his division.[132] Meade eventually responded to Slocum's protest, apologizing for his failure to mention Williams and expressing regret for any disservice his report may have rendered. Although Williams accepted Meade's explanation, Slocum still harbored resentment, expressed later in condemnations of Meade's conduct at Gettysburg.[133]

A review of Twelfth Corps leadership on July 1–2 yields a mixed verdict. Slocum's own record has prospered from a lack of scrutiny. His vacillation and oversights on both days might have brought serious consequences. But because Ewell would not (or could not) exploit his advantages either day, Slocum generally has escaped censure from historical analysts. Among second- and third-level commanders, Williams and Greene stand out. Both performed splendidly under difficult circumstances requiring independent thinking. Thomas Ruger, George Cobham, Silas Colgrove, and Archibald McDougall reacted competently to increased responsibility. Charles Candy committed no serious error, and Henry Lockwood and his enthusiastic rookies made up in bravery and spirit what they lacked in polish and skill. John White Geary's inexplicable disappearance on the evening of July 2 dominates any evaluation of his generalship during the first two days at Gettysburg.

Regardless of the checkered record of its leadership and through no fault of its soldiers, the Twelfth Corps did not play a decisive role during these forty-eight hours. Its delayed appearance on July 1, though unwarranted and regrettable, did not materially affect the outcome of the fighting. Williams's contributions on the Union left on July 2 came after the die had been cast. Greene's tenacious defense of Culp's Hill possessed the most significance, but even there potential Confederate gains probably would have been transitory at best.

The Twelfth Corps left the Army of the Potomac in September 1863 for a new career in the West. It left behind a proud legacy earned on a half-dozen major battlefields. Gettysburg's first two days contributed but a modest portion to that distinguished record.

"No Troops on the Field Had Done Better"

John C. Caldwell's Division in the Wheatfield, July 2, 1863

D. Scott Hartwig

IN THE 128 YEARS SINCE THE BATTLE OF GETTYSBURG, VETERANS, students, and historians have filled volumes exploring the question of why the battle was lost or won. Such writers usually have focused on command at the army and corps level. There is nothing wrong with this emphasis, for the decisions and actions of senior officers shaped the battle and influenced thousands of lives. But these officers did not lead troops into battle. They managed resources, allocating men and material to obtain objectives. Command at this level can be likened to a sword. The hilt represents the army commander, the blade is the corps. The point of the sword represents those who directed soldiers in combat—the division, brigade, and regimental leaders. Although we know a great deal about what happened at the hilt and blade of the sword of command, we know relatively little about activity at the point. It is thus instructive to shift focus from the hilt and blade to the point. An examination of the experience of division command on July 2 illuminates the challenge of directing men in battle during the American Civil War.

The experience of Brig. Gen. John C. Caldwell and his First Division of the Second Corps, Army of the Potomac, illustrates the role of division leaders at Gettysburg. Caldwell's division serves as an excellent model for two reasons. First, Caldwell conducted the only division-sized Federal assault in what was almost exclusively a defensive battle for the Army of the

Potomac. Second, because defenders enjoyed significant advantages due to weaponry and tactics, it stands to reason that directing an attack was a division commander's most difficult mission. Caldwell faced the particularly challenging situation of managing an attack in an extremely fluid battle in which he literally knew nothing about the ground or enemy strength. Although perhaps not typical, Caldwell's experience reveals the problems with which division commanders contended in directing and coordinating an assault.

The First Division ranked among the outstanding units in the Army of the Potomac. It had been organized in the fall of 1861 by Maj. Gen. Edwin V. Sumner, who, despite limitations as a battlefield commander, understood how to train soldiers. When Sumner was promoted to corps command, the division passed to the equally tough Brig. Gen. Israel B. Richardson, who led it through the Seven Days battles and was mortally wounded during assaults against the Sunken Lane at Antietam. Brig. Gen. Winfield Scott Hancock succeeded Richardson, and the division fought magnificently under his direction in the grim attacks against Marye's Heights at Fredericksburg and during the Chancellorsville campaign. Sumner, Richardson, and Hancock left an indelible mark on the division, teaching the men sharp discipline and drill and imbuing them with an aggressive spirit. Hancock claimed at Gettysburg, without boast, that the division "had never flinched" on the field of battle.[1]

The First Division earned its enviable record at great cost. The only four-brigade division in the Union army at Gettysburg (none of the rest had more than three), it nonetheless counted a mere 3,200 effectives. Its largest brigade numbered 975 officers and men. The Second Brigade, famous as the Irish Brigade, mustered only 532 effectives. Four of its regiments were under one hundred men. Yet despite its skeleton strength, the division remained a formidable fighting unit because of excellent training and competent, respected leadership at every level. The First Division was a veteran organization in the best sense of the word. The term *veteran* often implies that all men so designated were "good" soldiers, yet many veteran units were quite marginal due to poor leadership, slack discipline, or heavy casualties. In contrast, a number of green outfits, notably Brig. Gen. George J. Stannard's brigade at Gettysburg, performed with distinction. Proficiency at battlefield drill, discipline, and leadership separated good and bad units in combat. In all of these categories the First Division had kept its fighting edge despite heavy losses. This was due, no doubt, to high standards for officers and men set by Sumner, Richardson, and Hancock.[2]

Hancock was promoted to command of the Second Corps following Chancellorsville, and Brig. Gen. John C. Caldwell replaced him by virtue of his seniority in the division. The thirty-year-old Caldwell hailed from Maine, where before the war he had been principal of Washington Academy at East Machias, a village in the northeastern corner of the state. He volunteered for service after the firing on Fort Sumter, and by April 28, 1862, had risen to the rank of brigadier general. When Oliver O. Howard was wounded at Seven Pines, his brigade was assigned to Caldwell, who led it competently in every battle that followed except Second Manassas. "Caldwell is an agreeable man and well liked," wrote one man who served with him before Gettysburg. "There is none of the assumed dignity and importance so common among officers. . . . He is much more familiar with his officers than General Meagher and is much better liked by them than M. by his." Despite his volunteer's background, Caldwell evidently enjoyed the confidence of Hancock, who otherwise would have supported someone else to command the First Division.[3]

Caldwell's experience in brigade leadership likely taught him that success on the battlefield depended on three basic factors—the ability to communicate, to move, and to engage the enemy. These factors also applied at the division level, but commanders faced larger responsibilities and far greater difficulty of application. In the era of muzzle-loading weapons and control of movements and firepower by voice or visual signals, a unit the size of the First Division posed complex challenges. Officers established control by maneuvering troops in dense formations so that commands by voice and signal could be heard or seen. Endless hours on the drill fields ingrained complex maneuvers that enabled a unit to move from column to line or line to column quickly and without disorder. The ultimate objectives of such training were to achieve maximum firepower on the firing line swiftly and to maintain cohesiveness in combat. In the noisy chaos of a Civil War battlefield, the best drilled and disciplined units minimized disorder and continued to deliver effective fire despite the hellish environment. Every man and officer grew accustomed to his place in a formation. A unit was a machine on the battlefield—soldiers were merely parts within it. With the exception of skirmishers, individuals received virtually no encouragement to demonstrate initiative and resourcefulness. The soldier's duty was to keep his place in the ranks and look to his officers for direction.

At the division level, Caldwell's task was to direct the movements of his brigades so that every rifle or musket in their ranks came to bear on the enemy. With four brigades, Caldwell's division was a formidable unit that could sustain itself in battle longer and perform more varied maneuvers than the typical two-brigade Federal division. But maneuvering four brigades in the deafening noise and smoky atmosphere of a battlefield

Brig. Gen. John Curtis Caldwell. Courtesy of the National Archives.

severely tested the limits of mid-nineteenth century military communications. Although the Civil War has been called the first modern war, the voice, signal (hand or flag), or written options for communicating available to Caldwell had changed little since the time of Alexander the Great. A competent staff was critical to Caldwell's ability to command and control his brigades. Through staff officers he could follow the flow of the battle and maintain communications, by verbal and written messages, with his brigadiers. Seven officers made up Caldwell's personal staff, five of whom (two majors and three first lieutenants), together with a cavalry corporal who served as an orderly, accompanied him into battle. One other means of communication was Caldwell's headquarters flag, a large banner that marked the division's administrative point of control on the battlefield.[4]

The primitive nature of communications severely limited Caldwell's ability to manage a battle. Once under fire, the division's brigades largely passed from his control to that of their respective commanders. Caldwell was fortunate that four good officers headed his brigades. Brig. Gen. Samuel K. Zook and Col. John R. Brooke had led brigades in battle; Col. Edward Cross and Col. Patrick Kelly, although new to brigade command, boasted extensive combat experience and had earned their positions through merit. All had learned their trade under the tutelage of Richardson and Hancock.

Like their former division commanders they were tough, aggressive, and confident, qualities that trickled down to their field and line officers as well as to the men on the firing line.

Unfortunately, the small arms of the division did not match the quality of its personnel. Six of the division's eighteen regiments were completely or partly armed with .69 caliber smoothbore muskets and two others carried .54 caliber Austrian muskets. At least six regiments carried two different caliber muskets. The variety of weapons made replenishing ammunition on the battlefield a time-consuming and complicated procedure, and at this late date in the war reflected badly on the Federal ordnance department. The large number of smoothbores also reduced Caldwell's tactical choices. Regiments armed with smoothbores could not break up Confederate formations with medium- or long-range fire; their only option was to close quickly to a range at which their weapons could be effective, a potentially costly business if the enemy were well posted and armed with rifles.[5]

The First Division bivouacked near the rear of Little Round Top following an exhausting march on July 1. Roused from their slumber on the morning of the second, the men underwent a "careful and rigid inspection" of arms in anticipation of action that day. The division then moved from its bivouac, taking up several different positions before marching to the southern end of Cemetery Ridge. Arriving at 7:00 A.M., Caldwell's troops massed in columns of regiments by brigades on the left of Brig. Gen. John Gibbon's Second Division of the Second Corps and the right of Maj. Gen. Daniel E. Sickles's Third Corps. This dense formation permitted close control and rapid mobility. Hancock undoubtedly ordered this alignment, for Gibbon's division and Brig. Gen. Alexander Hays's Third Division of the Second Corps deployed in the same formation. Facing a nebulous situation along his front (there was no guarantee that Lee would attack the Federals), Hancock wanted his divisions to move quickly if necessary.[6]

Caldwell placed the brigades of Cross, Kelly, and Brooke from left to right on the front line and held Zook in reserve behind Kelly. Capt. James Rorty's Battery B, 1st New York Artillery (four 10-pounder Parrotts) unlimbered between Cross's and Kelly's brigades to provide artillery support. First Lt. Josiah M. Favill, a young member of Zook's staff, recalled that the division's position provided not a particle of cover: "We were posted on broad, high, open ground, gently sloping in front towards a small brook called Plum Run, some three or four hundred yards in front." Because their officers expected movement or action momentarily, the Federals constructed no earthworks or other protection. Orders allowed the soldiers to stack arms and rest but not to remove their accouterments. "Our men sat or lay down in their ranks, while the officers gathered in little groups, and discussed the probable outlook for the day," wrote Favill. Officers informed the soldiers that they were to be held in reserve, an announcement that prompted a battle-wise Irishman in Kelly's brigade to quip, "In resarve; yis, resarved for the heavy fighting."[7]

The Irishman's prediction seemed to ring hollow as the morning passed without incident. "Our horses quietly browsed in the rich grass," wrote Lt. Col. St. Clair Mulholland of the 116th Pennsylvania, "and the men lay in groups, peacefully enjoying a rest after the rapid march of the day before." At 10:00 A.M. picket firing erupted beyond the Emmitsburg Road, continuing with varying intensity until after noon. "But 3 o'clock came and still no signs of the general engagement," noted Mulholland. There was, however, a disturbing development on Caldwell's left. Shortly before three o'clock, Sickles's Third Corps marched from its positions south of Caldwell to a point far in advance of the army's general line of battle. First Lt. W. S. Shallenberger of the 140th Pennsylvania observed "a division of the 3rd Corps . . . moving forward in line of battle by brigades. Beautifully the movement was executed—flags flying and bayonets glistening in the sunlight as they march[ed] against the foe." Caldwell watched the spectacle with Hancock, Kelly, and other officers who had gathered in front of the Irish Brigade. They could only guess at the meaning of the advance, but Hancock remarked with a smile, "Wait a moment, you will soon see them tumbling back."[8]

Whether Sickles should have moved forward is a question beyond the scope of this essay, but his new position forced Meade to modify his plans in order to support the exposed Third Corps. Sickles occupied a front too broad for his corps to defend properly; indeed, unsupported artillery held stretches of his line. This meant that units sent to reinforce Sickles would be broken up and rushed about to plug holes or respond to emergencies rather than entering the battle as organizations capable of delivering blows with their entire strength. Moreover, no single person coordinated the defense of the Union left—an arrangement that produced a critical void as troops from various corps hastened to support Sickles. It would be a battle on the Union side with no one at the hilt of the sword, a fact that would cost Caldwell and his men dearly.[9]

About 3:00 P.M., James Longstreet's Confederate artillery shattered the comparative tranquility of the battlefield with its pre-assault bombardment. "At half-past three the cannonade was furious," wrote Lt. Charles Hale of Colonel Cross's staff. The crash of musketry in the direction of Little Round Top carried to Caldwell's position by four o'clock. "It was a great relief," recalled Hale, "for the suspense was ended and we now knew that our lines out there in the front were fighting on the defensive."[10]

Longstreet's blow fell first at Devil's Den and Houck's Ridge, and within minutes Little Round Top also came under fierce attack. As more Southern brigades joined the battle, the action spread northward to John Rose's Wheatfield. Brig. Gen. George T. Anderson's brigade of eighteen hundred Georgians passed south of Rose's buildings, entered Rose Woods, and shouldered their way forward down a slope toward the open field of wheat. Opposing them were parts of two brigades from Sickles's corps—three regiments of Col. Regis de Trobriand's Third Brigade of Maj. Gen. David Bell Birney's First Division reinforced by elements of Col. William R. Brewster's Second Brigade of Brig. Gen. Andrew A. Humphreys's Second Division. Two brigades of Brig. Gen. James Barnes's First Division of the Fifth Corps further bolstered these defenders just before Anderson's assault struck. Barnes's brigades crowded upon a stony hill, sparsely covered with trees, situated near the southwestern side of the Wheatfield. Their fire and that of the Third Corps units drove Anderson back after a fierce contest of musketry.[11]

Even before Anderson's repulse, Barnes observed trouble on his right flank. The New Englander had been uneasy about his position from the first, instructing his brigade commanders to look for lines of retreat almost as soon as they arrived on Stony Hill. A large stretch of apparently unprotected ground to his right worried Barnes. Indeed, there was no infantry between him and the Peach Orchard. Sickles held the front from the orchard to Rose Woods with a line of artillery batteries unlimbered along the Wheatfield Road.[12]

The trouble looming on Barnes's flank came from Brig. Gen. Joseph B. Kershaw's brigade of South Carolinians, more than two thousand strong, which heralded the entry into the battle of Maj. Gen. Lafayette McLaws's division. As Kershaw passed the Emmitsburg Road, he split his brigade, sending his left wing, under Col. John D. Kennedy of the 2d South Carolina, in a northerly direction to attack the Peach Orchard and batteries along the Wheatfield Road. With his remaining two regiments, the 3d and 7th South Carolina, directly under his control, Kershaw swept through and around the Rose farm buildings and made straight for the Stony Hill. The Confederates paused briefly after passing the Rose farm buildings because the 3d had lapped over part of the 7th. Kershaw ordered the 7th to move by the right flank to uncover the 3d; this order somehow reached Kershaw's left wing, then threatening to overrun the guns along the Wheatfield Road. Without hesitation, the regiments under Colonel Kennedy broke off their attack and moved by the right flank, exposing their own left to guns along the Wheatfield Road. Quick to seize the opportunity, Federal cannoneers blasted the South Carolinians with canister and shrapnel, inflicting dreadful losses and sowing utter disorder in the ranks. Many of Kennedy's survivors made for the cover of a finger of Rose Woods that jutted out toward the Wheatfield Road. This brought them directly toward Barnes's flank, and he promptly ordered a retreat several hundred yards north to Trostle Woods, which ran along the northern border of the Wheatfield Road.[13]

Barnes's departure left de Trobriand's hard-pressed regiments alone to confront Anderson's renewed advance on their front and Kershaw's presence on their flank. Unable to stop the Confederates, de Trobriand pulled his men back. Part of his brigade halted on a knoll in the center of the Wheatfield to support Capt. George B. Winslow's Napoleons of Battery D, 1st New York Light Artillery. Canister from Winslow's guns sent Anderson's Georgians scrambling back for the cover of Rose Woods, but Kershaw's men soon brought fire to bear on the battery's right and a portion of Anderson's brigade worked through the eastern side of Rose Woods to menace its left. Winslow had no alternative but to withdraw. Confederates controlled the Wheatfield and Rose Woods, the center of Birney's front had been cracked wide open, and Federals at the Peach Orchard and Humphreys's line along the Emmitsburg Road occupied perilous positions.[14]

In the midst of this crisis, Sickles requested reinforcements from Meade. Meade sent a courier speeding to Hancock with instructions that he send a division to report to Maj. Gen. George Sykes—clear evidence that Meade lacked confidence in Sickles. The courier found Hancock still in the company of Caldwell in front of Kelly's brigade. According to Lieutenant Colonel Mulholland, who was present at the meeting, Hancock quietly remarked, "Caldwell, you get your division ready." The First Division would report to Sykes "for service in the direction of Little Round Top." The order to "fall in" and "take arms" brought the four brigades to their feet, and in minutes the division was ready to move.[15]

"The direction we were to take was to the front and left," recalled Lt. Charles A. Fuller of the 61st New York. "There was no time to countermarch so as to bring the men right in front, so we simply left faced and started." The right of a regiment usually led the column of march, but to have accomplished this with the entire division, as Fuller noted, would have entailed a tedious countermarch of every regiment in the division. Caldwell dispensed with the familiar to save precious minutes. The division moved to the left in mass by column of regiments—a formation seldom employed within range of enemy small arms or artillery fire. It was the same formation all the brigades had assumed when they arrived on Cemetery Ridge, except each regiment in each brigade had simply faced to the left, formed into columns of fours, and commenced movement. This formation somewhat resembled the Greek phalanx, a huge moving mass, or "chunck," of men, many ranks deep. The disadvantages of the formation when exposed to artillery fire were too grim to contemplate. A single round of solid shot, case, or shell could fell dozens of men. Caldwell knew the risks but also appreciated the necessity for speed. Under the circumstances it was a risk worth taking. A movement in mass brought his division to the point of crisis quickly and in strength that could be applied against the enemy immediately. It also made the division easier to manage by drastically cutting the length of the column and hence the time it would take Caldwell to communicate with his brigade commanders.[16]

Cross's brigade took the lead, followed in turn by Kelly, Brooke, and Zook. The men moved rapidly, frequently at the double-quick, in the direction of Little Round Top. Caldwell placed his headquarters at the front of the column, a position that allowed him to exert maximum control over his division. From there he could receive instructions from Sykes, whom he sent Lt. Daniel K. Cross of his staff to locate, and transmit them down the length of his column to each brigade commander without any disruption in the flow of information. He also could move the head of the column, and hence the entire division, in any direction with a single order.[17]

The wisdom of Caldwell's movement in mass became more apparent as the division neared the battle zone. Lieutenant Favill remembered that as the division marched forward "the tumult became deafening, the mountain side echoed back the musketry, so that no word of command could be heard, and little could be seen but long lines of flame, and smoke and struggling masses of men." Noise, carnage, confusion, and smoke—all were factors that historians who sit in judgment of soldiers like Caldwell often neglect to take into account. Yet he and his subordinates had to make instant decisions within this hostile environment. If they erred, and circumstances and means of communication ensured that they would, the consequences might be grim. Caldwell's situation was all the more difficult because, even with Sykes's orders, he knew virtually nothing about the ground, enemy positions and strength, or Federal dispositions in the area toward which he moved.[18]

The division passed by the George Weikert farm, through Weikert's Woods, over two stone walls, and into an open and slightly marshy pasture near the northernmost end of the Plum Run Valley (also known as the "Valley of Death"). The column crossed the pasture toward Trostle Woods, which screened the Wheatfield. Lieutenant Cross had failed to locate Sykes,

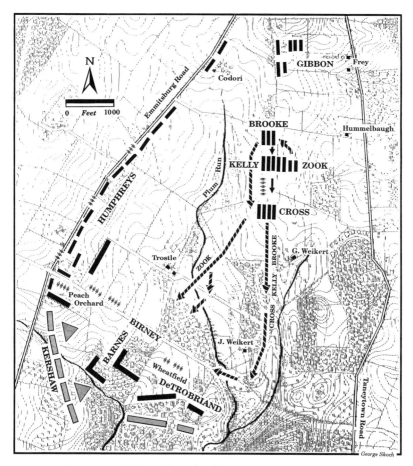

Caldwell's Division Shifts to the Left, July 2

and Caldwell had dispatched Lt. William P. Wilson to search for the Fifth
Corps commander. Wilson enjoyed better luck (although he never said
where he found Sykes) and returned with a member of Sykes's staff. They
met Caldwell at the head of the column as it entered Trostle Woods. Caldwell learned that he should take his division to Rose's Wheatfield rather
than toward Little Round Top. The instructions from Sykes called for the
First Division "to advance to the south side of the Wheat-field, drive the
enemy back, and if possible establish the original line on the crest." Sykes's
staff officer rode a young horse, and every Confederate shell that screamed
into the vicinity set the animal "to plunging furiously." Lt. Charles Hale,
who accompanied Colonel Cross and attempted to hear the orders carried
by Sykes's staff officer, recalled that the horse kicked so furiously "that
we had to give him all the room there was." Hale could pick up only the

officer's last statement, delivered as his horse gave a plunge: "The enemy is breaking directly on your right—Strike him quick." Now at least vaguely aware of the enemy's position, Caldwell could formulate a plan for committing his own men. But his battle report suggests that he still knew little of the ground and general disposition of friendly troops.[19]

Caldwell confronted a knotty tactical problem in attempting to strike swiftly against Confederates on the right. With the left of each regiment at the head of each column, deployment in the formation they were trained to assume in combat would entail moving the regiments by the left flank, then facing them to the right into the line of battle. The units would then have to march by the right flank to get back into the vicinity of the Wheatfield. Caldwell deemed all of this an unnecessary loss of time and instructed Colonel Cross to move his men onto the Wheatfield Road by the right flank, which brought them into line along the northern edge of the Wheatfield and southern edge of Trostle Woods. When each of Cross's regiments had deployed in a brigade front, they left-faced. This left the file closers in front of the line of battle and placed the rear rank in front and front rank in rear. "Of course there was instant confusion," observed Lieutenant Hale, "for it brought the line of battle facing by the rear rank, with the file closers pushing and crowding through." The 148th Pennsylvania "found itself in the anomalous condition of being not only faced by the rear rank, but inverted by wings—companies A and B in the center, and center companies far out of place at the extreme." The right guide of the regiment was in the center and the colors were in the rear rank on the right. "To any but well drilled and disciplined troops" this odd formation "would have been disastrous," wrote Col. Daniel Bingham of the 64th New York. A member of the 148th recalled that "this eccentricity of formation, I am happy to say, did not, in the slightest manner, affect the conduct of our regiment. Previous drill and discipline had provided for just such condition." Caldwell had gambled that his men possessed the training and discipline to fight effectively despite being employed in an awkward and unfamiliar formation. The situation demanded additional Federals on the firing line, and Caldwell's improvisation placed them there quickly.[20]

Cross's advance through Trostle Woods onto the Wheatfield Road and then into the Wheatfield was, as Lieutenant Hale testified, "all done without a halt, and without the loss of a minute in maneuvering." "The entire brigade moved with the mobility of a single battalion: four regiments, closed intervals, four sets of field officers—an aggregated strength of about one thousand," stated Hale admiringly. "Just in the nick of time it was hurled against the enemy and struck a tremendous blow. That was the very way the brigades of the First Division had been trained to fight." Cross

Col. Edward E. Cross. From Miller's *Photographic History* 8:102.

advanced his brigade to the brow of a slight ridge cutting across nearly the center of the Wheatfield. Most of the soldiers stood in the open, except for those of the 5th New Hampshire and two-thirds of the 148th Pennsylvania, who enjoyed cover along the eastern side of Rose Woods. Lt. Charles A. Fuller, a file closer in the 61st New York, recalled that as the brigade reached the crest of this ridge he saw in front "one or two men come toward us on a run, and throw themselves down behind this partial stone wall (which bordered the southern end of the Wheatfield). But a brief time passed when a solid line of men in gray appeared and placed themselves as had the first comers." It was Anderson's Georgians. "Here the battle opened with great energy," a member of the 148th Pennsylvania recollected. Cross's regiments opened a fire described by Caldwell as "terrific" on the gray-clad line in front. They drew a heavy fire in return and also felt pressure on their right flank from members of the 7th South Carolina, who had refused their right flank and were concealed by the arm of Rose Woods bordering the western edge of the Wheatfield. "The Rebs had their slight protection, but we were in the open," noted Lieutenant Fuller, "without a thing better than wheat straw to catch a minnie bullet that weighed an ounce. Of course our men began to tumble." Smoke quickly blanketed the field, and many men in the brigade lay down to gain some protection and to look for targets under the grimy canopy.[21]

While Cross's men slugged it out with Anderson, Kershaw, and perhaps elements of Semmes's brigade, Caldwell brought up his Second Brigade.

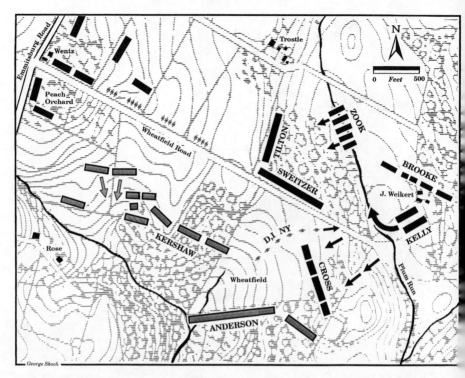

Cross's Brigade Enters the Wheatfield

Kelly's regiments also faced by the rear rank in their formation; due to the rapidity with which the brigade went into action, it pushed into the Wheatfield on Cross's right. It was probably while bringing Kelly into action that Caldwell learned he had lost control over Zook's brigade. Despite precautions to maintain control over his command, the limits of battlefield communications left Caldwell powerless to prevent others from seizing a major element of his force.[22]

Zook's brigade had occupied the rear of the First Division as it marched south to enter the battle. It was intercepted en route by Maj. Henry E. Tremain of Sickles's staff. Because Birney clamored for reinforcements in the area of the Wheatfield, Sickles had dispatched Tremain to find Hancock and hurry Caldwell's division forward if it had not already started. Tremain spotted fresh troops marching to the front and rode straight to them. Informed that they belonged to the First Division, Tremain considered trying to locate Caldwell but decided that it would take too long. The captain knew minutes were precious because of the crisis near the Wheatfield. On learning from a regimental commander that Zook led the brigade, Tremain spurred to the head of the column and asked the general if he would detach his brigade and go into action immediately. Tremain later recorded what transpired next:

> He replied, politely but with soldierly mien, that his orders were to follow the column. Repeating the request I asked him to assume the responsibility of compliance, promising to protect him and to return him as soon as possible with a formal order from the proper officer.
>
> It was a critical interview. There was no time to parley. . . . It was obvious, too, that Zook, as well as myself, fully appreciated that neither the request nor instant compliance with it could be deemed within the strict limits of military regularity. "Sir," said General Zook, with a calm, firm look, inspiring me with its significance, "if you will give me the order of General Sickles I will obey it." My response then was: "General Sickles' order, general, is that you file your brigade to the right and move into action here.". . . Few men would have acted as Zook did. Yet had he acted otherwise it might have changed the fate of the day. Who knows? It was such acts of sagacity and nobleness that won Gettysburg.

One might be tempted to add that such acts can just as well lose battles. It was fortunate for the Federals that Sickles and Sykes, though not working together in coordinating the battle, at least recognized the Wheatfield as the point needing immediate reinforcement. This brought Zook into battle with his own division quite by chance, and, equally by chance, on the right of the division line Caldwell was then forming. What Caldwell might have done with Zook had Tremain not intervened is purely speculative. The strongest brigade of the First Division with 975 effectives, Zook's command probably would have been held in reserve. But the actions of Tremain and Zook could not be undone, and Caldwell lived with the arrangement.[23]

In less than ten minutes Caldwell had placed three brigades totaling 2,350 men on the firing line. He had assistance from Captain Tremain, but given the noise, smoke, and poor communications, it was still an impressive performance. Control at the battle front now passed to the hands of Cross, Zook, and Kelly. As division commander, Caldwell would keep his finger on the pulse of action to determine when and where to commit Brooke's brigade, which constituted his reserve, while also looking beyond the immediate battle his men were fighting. Were his flanks adequately protected? Was support available to sustain his division's momentum?

Brig. Gen. Samuel
Kosciuszko Zook.
From Miller's *Photographic
History* 10:135.

How would he secure what had been gained already? What was the nature
of the ground? What were the dispositions of friendly troops in the area?
These were questions for which Caldwell sought answers while the battle
raged in front.[24]

The action had developed in promising fashion until fierce resistance by
the brigades of Kershaw, Anderson, and Semmes slowed Federal progress
to a near halt. Zook's regiments had passed over and through the brigades
of Barnes's division in Trostle Woods, crossed the Wheatfield Road and
its fences, and entered the "rocky woodland" of Rose Woods on the western edge of the Wheatfield. Perhaps forty yards to Zook's left rear was
Kelly's brigade, moving forward to go into action on Cross's right. Lieutenant Colonel Mulholland, whose 116th Pennsylvania occupied the right
of Kelly's line, noted that as Zook's troops "approached the line of timber
covering the hill they received a withering fire from the concealed enemy,
which staggered them for a moment." Josiah M. Favill of Zook's staff recalled that "we soon came to a standstill and a close encounter, when the
firing became terrific and the slaughter frightful. We were enveloped in
smoke and fire, not only in front, but on our left, and even at times on the
right." Among the first to fall was Zook, who sustained a mortal wound.

Col. Patrick Kelly. Courtesy of MOLLUS-MASS/U.S. Army Military History Institute, Carlisle, Pennsylvania.

Command passed to Lt. Col. C. G. Freudenburg of the 52d New York. He ordered the brigade to press forward before falling wounded himself. "Our men fired promiscuously, steadily pressing forward," wrote Lieutenant Favill, "but the fighting was so mixed, rebel and Union lines so close together, and in some places intermingled, that a clear idea of what was going on was not readily obtainable."[25]

Because Kershaw's men focused on Cross's right and on Zook, Kelly's Irish Brigade was able to close to within fifty feet of the Confederates. As the Federals approached Kershaw's line, wrote Mulholland, "suddenly someone in the ranks cried out 'there they are.'" Kelly's Irishmen had been fortunate. Every regiment but the 28th Massachusetts carried smoothbores, but at fifty feet even their inferior weapons could inflict significant damage. Mulholland believed that "the effect of our fire was deadly in the extreme, for under such circumstances a blind man could not have missed his mark." Yet the Irishmen made no headway against Kershaw's 7th and 3d South Carolina. Stubborn Confederate resistance helped check the Northern advance, but disorder on the Union side abetted the South Carolinians. The brigades of Zook and Kelly converged as they pushed into the woods; their left and right, respectively, overlapped and became hopelessly intermingled in "a deplorable state of confusion." The "dense woods" and "large bowlders of rocks" that strewed the woods also retarded efforts

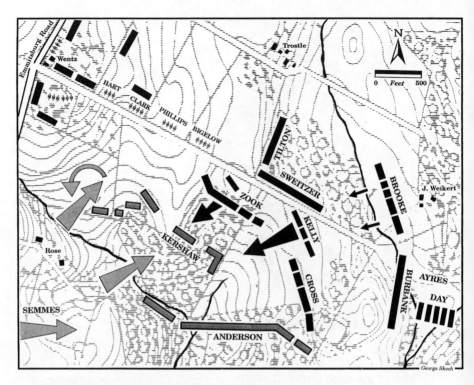

Zook's and Kelly's Brigades Enter the Wheatfield

to maintain forward momentum, as did the proximity of Anderson's Georgians, posted along the southern edge of the Wheatfield where they could bring fire on Kelly's flank.[26]

Cross's brigade might have relieved the pressure on Anderson; however, by the time Zook had been shot, so too had Cross. Before the New Hampshire colonel could launch an assault, he was mortally wounded at a point near the left of his brigade. Command in these difficult circumstances devolved on the senior officer, Col. Boyd McKeen, a good soldier who proved unable to establish control over the brigade and mount an offensive. McKeen also learned that cartridges were running low, which he reported to division headquarters.[27]

Caldwell responded promptly to McKeen's report by ordering Brooke to relieve the First Brigade. Just ten minutes had elapsed since the division had entered the battle, which attests to the rapidity of Cross's fire. Brooke quickly moved his brigade into action, passing into the Wheatfield and replacing the right of Cross's brigade. Only the 61st New York, 81st Pennsylvania, and right seven companies of the 148th Pennsylvania withdrew. The left three companies of the 148th and the 5th New Hampshire re-

Col. John Rutter Brooke.
From Miller's *Photographic History* 10:303.

mained in the woods trading fire with Anderson's men and elements of the 1st Texas and 15th Georgia. Brooke's regiments halted on the ridge, by then liberally sprinkled with the dead and wounded of the First Brigade, and returned the fire of Anderson's Georgians. While his men blazed away at their front, Brooke made his way over to Kelly's brigade, which was stalled somewhat to his right rear. At Brooke's encouragement, Kelly started his men forward and Brooke ordered his own soldiers to charge. "That was the right thing at the right time and we were off with a yell," wrote Stephen A. Osborne of the 145th Pennsylvania on Brooke's right. But from the point of view of Col. Daniel Bingham of the 64th New York, on Brooke's left center, the order was not so easily executed. "The men were firing as fast as they could load," asserted Bingham, "the din was almost deafening, it was very difficult to have orders understood, and it required considerable effort to start the line forward into another charge. The officers and non-commissioned officers displayed the greatest gallantry." So too did the color guards; indeed, it may have been the movement of the 64th New York's color guard that enabled Brooke to get his brigade moving. According to Colonel Bingham, the two color bearers of his regiment "rushed several rods ahead" of the regimental line "so that they were dimly perceivable through the cloud of smoke." This act started the 64th New York and 2d Delaware forward "with a cheer"—which may have inspired the rest of the brigade to advance.[28]

Brooke's surging line received a volley from Anderson's Georgians as it neared Rose Woods and the southern border of the Wheatfield. "It staggered us," wrote Stephen Osborne, "but only for a moment, then on we went right over the Johnnies, leaving almost as many prisoners as there were of us." After nearly an hour of intense fighting, Anderson's men were physically exhausted and too disorganized to stop Brooke's fresh regiments. "Pressing forward, firing as we went," reported Brooke, his regiments steadily advanced into Rose Woods. Elements of Anderson's regiments made a stand across Rose's Run among a "hornet's nest of rocks and underbrush" along the ridge that rises south of the run. The Georgians delivered a "deadly" fire into Brooke's advancing line from their position of cover. But the Federals were not to be stopped, as they "swept onward loading and firing" and rolled over the point of resistance, netting more than one hundred prisoners.[29]

At this rocky ledge Brooke's assault confronted part of Semmes's brigade drawn up in line "within pistol range." Sheltering themselves among rocks and behind the lip of the ridge, the Federals drove the Southerners to cover but proved unable to press their attack farther. Brooke paused to assess his situation. His assault into Rose Woods had precipitated a forward movement by the entire division. When Anderson's men withdrew on the southern end of the field, Kelly's Irish could advance against Kershaw's right. A gap extending for nearly one hundred yards between Kershaw's 7th South Carolina and the 50th Georgia of Semmes (which had come into the ravine at the base of the Stony Hill in response to a request from Kershaw) presented an opportunity. Kelly's men discovered the gap and worked around the flank of the Carolinians while their comrades and Zook's brigade, who were jumbled together "in one confused mass," pressed Kershaw's front. The 7th fought until the right and left wings were nearly doubled on each other. "This was some of the most severe fighting our division had ever done," wrote Lieutenant Colonel Mulholland. At last the 7th gave way, leaving the 3d South Carolina, reinforced by about fifty men of the 50th Georgia, to fight on desperately until overwhelmed and forced to retire with Kershaw to the Rose Farm. Kelly's and Zook's men swarmed over the position defended by Kershaw's men, taking "a great many prisoners" from the 3d and 7th and finding "many dead" Confederates "nearly all hit in the head or upper part of the body."[30]

While Brooke, Kelly, and Zook ground their way forward, the extreme left of the division, Cross's 5th New Hampshire and seven companies of the 148th Pennsylvania, also pressed ahead. They gained a position in Rose Woods overlooking the ravine on Brooke's left rear and sparred with elements of Henry L. Benning's and Jerome B. Robertson's brigades. Brooke,

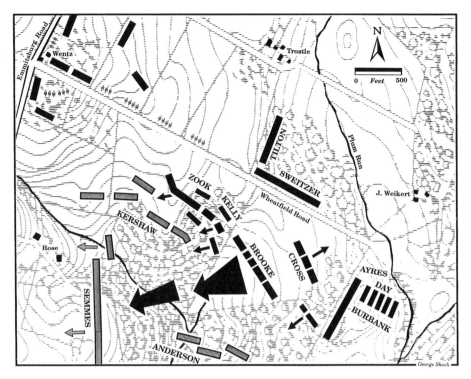

Brooke's Brigade Enters the Wheatfield

meanwhile, found his situation not yet desperate but growing perilous. In its fight for possession of the Stony Hill, Kelly's brigade had diverged to the right and lost connection with Brooke's right, leaving it in the air. Despite the efforts of the 5th and 148th, Brooke's left also was exposed. He sent a runner (or rider) back to apprise Caldwell of the situation and request support for his brigade's threatened flanks.[31]

Caldwell reacted promptly to Brooke's call for help. He sent Lieutenant Wilson of his staff over to some troops visible in Trostle Woods along the northern boundary of the Wheatfield Road. It was Col. Jacob B. Sweitzer's brigade of Barnes's division. Wilson made no headway with Sweitzer, so Caldwell rode over in person. Sweitzer recalled that Caldwell rode up "in haste and said his brigade [sic] was driving the enemy like H—l over yonder in the woods, pointing . . . beyond the Wheatfield, and asked if I would give him the support of my brigade." Sweitzer did not know Caldwell (he could see that he was a general) but referred the stranger to Barnes with the assurance that he would obey his commander's orders "with pleasure." Caldwell repeated his request to Barnes, who agreed to release Sweitzer, then proceeded to waste precious minutes by shouting a few "patriotic remarks" to Sweitzer's men before he ordered them forward. Sweitzer marched forward armed only with the knowledge that friendly troops were in the woods at the southern end of the Wheatfield and he was to support them. Caldwell sent no staff officer to direct Sweitzer—probably because they all were employed elsewhere. Even if a staff officer had been available, it might not have helped Sweitzer reach the point of most desperate need. Given the combination of intense confusion and primitive communications, Caldwell's simple request that Sweitzer's brigade support the troops fighting in the woods probably conveyed all that was necessary and possible at this stage of the battle.[32]

Caldwell looked to his left flank once Sweitzer's line had moved forward. While Caldwell's division had advanced through the Wheatfield and Rose Woods, Brigadier General Romeyn B. Ayres and two brigades of U.S. regulars from the Second Division of the Fifth Corps descended the northern shoulder of Little Round Top, crossed the Plum Run Valley, and climbed Houck's Ridge. Ayres's mission was to clear the ridge of Confederates, whose sniping fire was "annoying" Federals on Little Round Top. Unfortunately for Ayres, he fell victim to the absence of a controlling hand in this area of the battlefield. His division faced due west, whereas to his front Caldwell's general orientation was southwest—placing the two formations nearly at right angles to each other. Ayres also worried about deadly fire against his exposed left from Confederates concealed in high ground above Devil's Den. He responded to this emergency by refusing the left of his left regiment, the 17th U.S., and ordering the rest of the division to lie down. Pinned on the left and blocked by Caldwell's and Sweitzer's troops in their front and left front, Ayres's regulars endured the unnerving and maddening experience of taking fire without the ability to contribute materially to the fight.[33]

Caldwell sought to free the regulars. From Sweitzer's position he galloped over to Ayres, whom he found behind a stone wall that ran south from the Wheatfield Road. The two generals arranged to have Ayres's Second Brigade wheel to its left to come into line with the First Division's general orientation. This would secure Caldwell's left flank. "Thus far everything had progressed favorably," wrote Caldwell. "I had gained a position which, if properly supported on the flanks, I thought impregnable from the front."[34]

Caldwell had performed with commendable ability to this point. His soldiers entered the battle with speed and power, checked the penetration in Birney's front, threw three Southern brigades back in disorder, and gained ground beyond the original line. He had sought to protect gains by communicating to Barnes and Ayres his need for support while seeking coordination at least between the regulars and his own division. Barnes and Ayres, in contrast, made no effort to communicate with Caldwell. Nor did the commander of the First Division receive much help from Fifth Corps headquarters, though he acted under Sykes's orders. Caldwell alone attempted to exert some semblance of control over the struggle for the Wheatfield. But this effort at the division level—at the point of the sword—suffered from lack of direction at the corps level because neither Sykes nor Sickles applied a firm hand to the contest. In consequence, a confusing battle went from heady success to disaster in a matter of minutes.

About the time Caldwell's drive reached its high-water mark, Brig. Gen. William Barksdale's brigade of Mississippians slammed into the hinge of Sickles's line at the Peach Orchard and broke it wide open. While Barksdale swung north to roll up the Federals along Emmitsburg Road, Brig. Gen. W. T. Wofford's brigade of Georgians, which had followed in support of Barksdale, passed through the orchard and continued straight east, guiding on the Wheatfield Road. They picked up Kershaw's shattered left wing along their advance and bore down on Caldwell's exposed right. Caldwell knew nothing of this approaching Confederate storm. By the time he appreciated the danger, the situation had developed beyond his capacity to influence events—or to save his command.

While conversing with Ayres at the stone wall that sheltered regulars of the Second Brigade, Caldwell saw parties of troops falling back across the Wheatfield. Lt. William H. Powell of Ayres's staff observed this phenomenon with concern and warned Ayres, "General, you had better look out, the line in front is giving way." Powell recalled that Caldwell turned and remarked "in rather a sharp manner, 'That's not so sir; those are my troops being relieved.'" The two generals went on with their conversation, but Powell interrupted them again a few minutes later, advising Ayres "to look out for your command. I don't care what any one says, those troops in front are running away." Caldwell and Ayres paused to scan the front. Without a further word, Caldwell spurred his horse north along the stone wall to the Wheatfield Road, then west in the direction of his right flank. He could not have traveled far before discovering "that all the troops on my right had broken and were fleeing to the rear in great confusion." Caldwell and his orderly, Cpl. Uriah N. Parmelee—apparently the only member of his staff still accompanying the division commander—sought in vain to check the fleeing fugitives. Soon they were borne along with the flotsam of retreat and defeat.[35]

Zook's and Kelly's brigades dissolved under pressure applied against their flank by regiments under Wofford and Kershaw. The Confederates harassed retreating Federals with "terrific" and "most destructive" musketry, according to Lieutenant J. J. Permeus of the 140th Pennsylvania, who added that "neither valor nor discipline could withstand such a fire and such odds." Federals rushed to the rear to escape the trap closing on them. Permeus recalled that "as we fell back through the Wheatfield we suffered dreadfully, losing more, I think, than on the advance." Col. Patrick Kelly reported that his command "narrowly escaped being captured." As Confederates crushed the right of the First Division, Lieutenant Wilson of Caldwell's staff, either on his own or at his chief's direction, rode rapidly to warn Brooke of impending disaster that threatened to isolate and destroy his brigade. Brooke promptly ordered a retreat. "We went back, if not as fast and noisy as we went, still the most of us made fair time," wrote Stephen A. Osborne. Confederate troops were in the Wheatfield by the time Brooke's men emerged from Rose Woods. "I found the enemy had nearly closed in my rear," Brooke reported, "and had the movement not been executed at the time it was, I feel convinced that all would have been lost by death, wounds, or capture."[36]

The collapse of the First Division unleashed the fury of the Southern assault first on Sweitzer's brigade and then on Ayres's regulars. The regulars attempted to steady the crumbling Wheatfield line by changing the Second Brigade's front to the south-southwest. This brought the right of the brigade out into the Wheatfield and exposed it to a flank fire from Wofford's soldiers. The regulars hastily pulled out of danger, removing the last island of organized resistance against the triumphant Confederate tide in the Wheatfield.[37]

Caldwell reported that his men fell back "generally in good order, but necessarily with some confusion." Lt. Col. C. H. Morgan of Hancock's staff exhibited less charity when he wrote that he encountered the First Division, "or the remnants of it flying to the rear, without no shadow of an organization." Morgan's efforts to stop the fleeing troops duplicated Caldwell's earlier failure: "All attempt to rally them [elements of Third Corps] or any of Caldwell's division within reach of the enemy's bullets was useless."[38]

The First Division finally regrouped along Taneytown Road, but it was well into the night before officers restored order and organization. Losses had been severe—177 killed, 880 wounded, and 208 missing, or nearly 40 percent of the division. Brigade commanders Cross and Zook would die of their wounds, and Brooke lay painfully disabled. Only Kelly emerged from the battle unscathed. George Sykes complained to Hancock that the division had "done badly"; however, the record spoke otherwise. The First Division fought with courage and spirit. Only the depth of its penetration into the Wheatfield and Rose Woods exposed it to disaster when the Peach Orchard fell.[39]

Nor could it be said that Caldwell handled his division poorly. Indeed, he contributed a nearly flawless performance. When the call came for help on Sickles's hard-pressed front, Caldwell put his soldiers in motion within minutes. Risking casualties by moving his men in mass, he delivered them to the point of crisis rapidly and in strength. Caldwell labored under severe constraints: Sykes provided only sketchy instructions, the ground was unfamiliar, and information about Confederate strength and dispositions consisted of vague gestures by a staff officer. Exhibiting a flexible mind and translating decisions into action, Caldwell placed three brigades into the battle in ten minutes, a notable feat given the available communications. He saved precious minutes by deploying his brigades into battle faced by the rear rank, a formation that might have led to disaster with mediocre troops. Caldwell gambled that his well-drilled troops would not be adversely affected, and their stout performance vindicated his judgment. As already noted, no other Federal general in the Wheatfield battle area attempted to achieve control by coordinating with adjacent division commanders. When disaster struck, limitations of communication rendered Caldwell powerless to extricate his men from the field in better order. Even modern communications might not have made a great difference. If Caldwell's experience taught anything, it was that the Federals desperately needed someone above division command to monitor the battle and exercise a controlling influence. Such a presence likely would have spared not only Caldwell's First Division but also the divisions of Barnes and Ayres their bitter defeats.

Caldwell endured criticism by Sykes and some of his own subordinates for not putting his men "into action very handsomely"—a comment related to the facing-by-the-rear-rank deployment. "Much incensed" by Sykes's accusation, Hancock ordered an investigation into the conduct of the First Division. "Subsequent investigation showed that no troops on the field had done better," wrote Lieutenant Colonel Morgan. Although the investigation exonerated Caldwell, Hancock may have harbored a seed of doubt about his lieutenant. In the reorganization of the army in March 1864, Caldwell lost his command. Alexander Webb, a brigadier in the Second Corps painfully sparing in his praise for anyone, wrote on March 26, 1864, "Caldwell leaves in [?]. He feels very badly. I am very fond of him and am sorry to see him owsted."[40]

Caldwell had executed the basic principles of command in combat admirably. He had communicated as effectively as possible, moved his men skillfully, and engaged them with positive results. But another element of command applied particularly to those who led, not ordered, men into battle—an element that could be neither taught nor learned but had to be accepted. How Caldwell mastered it is unknown. Chaplain J. W. Stuckenberg of the First Division offered a graphic example in his wartime diary:

> In [the] 1st Division there were two operating stands, where the Surgeons were constantly consulting about operations and were performing amputations. Heaps of amputated feet & hands, arms & legs were seen lying under the tables and by their sides. Go around among the wounded and you witness the most saddening and sickening sights. Some are writhing with pain, and deeply moaning and groaning and calling for relief which cannot be afforded them. The finest forms are horribly disfigured & mutilated. Wounds are found in all parts of the body. . . . Some of the wounds are dressed, some not. From some the blood still oozes in others maggots are perhaps found. Perhaps they are poorly waited on, there not being nurses enough. No physician may have examined their wounds and dressed them. Their physical wants may not have been attended to. They long for home & their friends, but they cannot get to the one, the other cannot come to them. Through neglect, perhaps, they die. They are buried in their clothes, without shroud, without coffin, perhaps without religious services and a board to mark their resting place.[41]

Like any division, brigade, or regimental commander, Caldwell had to watch his men die in large numbers. Perhaps the most difficult challenge of command was to acknowledge this grim fact and persevere.

Day Three

"Rarely Has More Skill, Vigor, or Wisdom Been Shown"

George G. Meade on July 3
at Gettysburg

Richard A. Sauers

THE CONDUCT OF THE FEDERAL ARMY OF THE POTOMAC
at Gettysburg has received increasing attention in recent years. So too has
the generalship of its commander, Maj. Gen. George G. Meade. Historians
have scrutinized his actions on the field and have reached a wide variety of
conclusions. Meade's role on July 3, however, has received less attention
than have other aspects of his service at Gettysburg. In contrast, historians
have examined in great detail Robert E. Lee's decisions and movements of
that day. The result has fostered the impression that Lee stood at the center of events while Meade lurked somewhere in the background. In fact,
Meade remained active throughout July 3, rendering excellent service to the
army and the republic. This essays seeks to place Meade in his proper position as a crucial actor in the final day's fighting at Gettysburg.

Five days after taking charge of the army on June 28, Meade found his
command battered into the fishhook-shaped line extending from Culp's
Hill on the right to Round Top on the left. Two days of fighting had resulted
in more than eighteen thousand Union casualties, a figure exceeding the
butcher's bill at Chancellorsville (the total would rise to 23,049 officers and
men for the entire battle). Losses among general officers had been very
heavy. Maj. Gen. John F. Reynolds, commander of the First Corps, had been
killed on July 1, and Maj. Gen. Daniel E. Sickles, the former politician in
charge of the Third Corps, had been severely wounded on July 2. The First,

Second, Third, and Eleventh Corps had suffered heavy casualties, as had certain brigades in the Fifth Corps.[1]

With these conditions in mind, Meade summoned his principal subordinates to his headquarters for a conference on the evening of July 2. Crowded into a small room in the Leister house were Generals Daniel Butterfield (chief of staff), Gouverneur K. Warren (chief engineer), John Newton (First Corps), Winfield Scott Hancock (Second Corps), David B. Birney (Third Corps), George Sykes (Fifth Corps), John Sedgwick (Sixth Corps), Oliver O. Howard (Eleventh Corps), and Henry W. Slocum (Twelfth Corps). Because Hancock and Slocum were acting as wing commanders, Meade also ordered Brigadier Generals John Gibbon (Second Corps) and Alpheus S. Williams (Twelfth Corps) to attend. Cavalry Corps chief Alfred Pleasonton and artillery chief Henry J. Hunt were absent, as was Artillery Reserve commander Robert O. Tyler.

The conference opened with a general review of the battle's progress and reports on losses and the condition of the troops. Then followed discussion about the strength of the Federal position. Newton, one of the army's most experienced engineers, declared that Gettysburg was no place to fight a battle. After some debate, however, he clarified his opinion by stating that he would only rectify the line, rather than retreat. With Meade's assent, Butterfield next placed three questions before the officers. First, under existing circumstances should the army remain where it stood or retire to another position nearer its base of supplies? A decision to remain on the field led to the second question, namely, should the Federals attack or await another offensive move from the enemy? Finally, if the majority favored staying on the tactical defensive, for how long should they do so?

Nine officers voted on these questions. Meade and Butterfield took no part, and Warren, slightly wounded during the day, had fallen asleep in a corner. The voting commanders unanimously agreed to remain in position, with Gibbon, Newton, and Hancock suggesting that the lines be changed slightly. Everybody also voted to let the Confederates attack; there was a variety of answers as to how long to wait.[2]

Meade's role in this conference has been the subject of lengthy historical debates. Controversies spawned by the battle inspired a mountain of vituperative literature that has clouded accurate research. Proponents of Dan Sickles argued that Meade never wanted to fight at Gettysburg, that the battle was forced on him, and that he wanted to retreat on the afternoon of July 2 but was prevented from doing so by the bold advance of the Third Corps. Sickles's supporters also insisted that Meade seized another chance to retreat by holding a "council of war" that evening.[3]

Maj. Gen. George Gordon Meade. From Miller's *Photographic History* 10:169.

What did Meade wish to do? Accounts of the conference on the evening of July 2 vary. Butterfield stated to the Committee on the Conduct of the War that Meade told his officers Gettysburg was no place to fight a battle but that he would abide by the council's decision. General Birney said Meade only wanted to fight on the most favorable terms, while Brig. Gen. Albion P. Howe recalled that Sedgwick told him the possibility of retreat came up during the discussions. In an 1883 letter to Abner Doubleday, Slocum quoted Meade as saying, "Well, gentlemen, the question is settled. We will remain here, but I wish to say that I consider this no place to fight a battle."[4]

Meade's own testimony to the committee noted that "[t]he opinion of the council was unanimous, which agreed fully with my own views, that we should maintain our lines as they were then held, and that we should wait the movements of the enemy and see whether he made any further attack before we assumed the offensive." Other officers present at the conference remembered hearing Meade express no reservations about continuing the battle. In 1864, Sedgwick, Sykes, Newton, Williams, and Gibbon all denied ever having heard Meade counsel retreat. Hancock, Gibbon, and Sedgwick

The Leister house, site of Meade's headquarters. From *Battles and Leaders of the Civil War* 3:294.

told the committee the same thing, and Newton, Gibbon, Sykes, and Howard wrote postwar accounts defending Meade's honor.[5]

Meade apparently believed that the council of war was not important enough to mention in his official report. Indeed, he had already determined to remain and fight it out. At eight o'clock that evening, he sent
the following dispatch to General in Chief Henry W. Halleck: "The enemy
attacked me about 4 P.M. this day, and, after one of the severest contests
of the war, was repulsed at all points. We have suffered considerably in
killed and wounded. . . . We have taken a large number of prisoners. I shall
remain in my present position tomorrow, but am not prepared to say, until
better advised of the condition of the army, whether my operations will be
of an offensive or defensive character."[6]

Some historians have erroneously concluded that Meade sent this
telegram out as the council of war met.[7] However, the council did not start
while the battle was still in progress. Once the enemy attack on Cemetery
Hill had been repelled and the action on Culp's Hill sputtered to a close,
Meade's corps commanders were able to leave their troops to meet at the
Leister house. The eight o'clock telegram was composed and sent long
before the generals gathered. Having already determined to remain on the
battlefield, Meade only wished his subordinates to report on the condition
of their troops before making a decision to attack or defend.[8]

Meade reiterated this point in his committee testimony. Heavy losses on
the first two days, he stated, together with "my ignorance of the condition
of the corps, and the moral condition of the troops, caused me to send for
my corps commanders to obtain from them the exact condition of affairs in
their separate commands, and to consult and advise with them as to what,
if anything, should be done on the morrow." Himself a corps commander
only five days previously, Meade had yet to assemble all his chief subordi-

nates in one place. The three o'clock conference ordered the previous day had come to nothing, because Sickles's forward movement had jeopardized the position at Gettysburg and demanded quick thinking on Meade's part. The night of the second offered an opportunity for Meade to hear advice from his officers and see whether they agreed with his view that the army should remain on the field.[9]

A recent study has cast additional light on this conference. Two of the Army of the Potomac's intelligence officers, Col. George H. Sharpe and John C. Babcock, had analyzed the regiments from which Confederate prisoners had been taken on the first two days of battle, concluding that every brigade in Lee's army except those in George E. Pickett's division was represented. Sharpe and Babcock believed that this intelligence meant Lee's only fresh troops for the third day of fighting were Pickett's brigades.[10]

Before the council convened, Meade sent for Sharpe and asked him about an earlier note to Butterfield that detailed the information gleaned from prisoners. Generals Slocum and Hancock had already arrived at the Leister house. In an 1899 newspaper article, Sharpe recalled that Hancock, upon hearing his report, sat straight up from a reclining position and exclaimed, "General, we have got them nicked!" Both Sharpe and Babcock later thought it was their report that influenced the council to vote in favor of remaining at Gettysburg.[11]

The council broke up about midnight, by Gibbon's reckoning. Before he left, Gibbon expressed doubt to Meade about the propriety of his being part of the council. "That is all right," replied Meade pleasantly, "I wanted you here." Meade then added, "If Lee attacks tomorrow, it will be in your front." Surprised, Gibbon asked why his chief thought so. "Because," said Meade, "he has made attacks on both our flanks and failed and if he concludes to try it again, it will be on our centre."[12]

After the council adjourned, Slocum and Williams returned to the lines of the Twelfth Corps. They received reports that Confederates now occupied a large section of the breastworks erected by the corps on July 2, making reoccupation of the works by returning Federal troops impossible in the darkness. Slocum immediately informed Meade of the situation. The commanding general authorized Slocum to attack at daybreak and drive the enemy out of the works. Meade then got what sleep he could.[13]

When Meade awoke later in the morning, he decided to tour his battle line. He rode to the right, where he witnessed the beginning stage of the fighting on Culp's Hill, then continued along other sections of his line.[14] Lt. Frank A. Haskell of Gibbon's staff saw Meade as he passed through the Second Corps area. "He was early on horseback this morning, and rode along the whole line, looking to it himself," wrote Haskell, "and with glass in hand sweeping the woods and fields in the direction of the enemy, to see if ought of him could be discovered. His manner was calm and serious, but earnest. There was no arrogance of hope, or timidity of fear discernible in his face; but you would have supposed he would do his duty, conscientiously all well, and would be willing to abide the result. You would have seen this in his face."[15]

Concerned about the heavy attacks against Slocum's position, Meade instructed Sedgwick to send Brig. Gen. Alexander Shaler's brigade to reinforce the right. Meade then directed Slocum to hold Shaler's men in a central position so that his brigade could be quickly moved to any threatened spot of the line.[16]

Meade also fired off a number of orders and circulars that morning. At seven o'clock he sent a dispatch to Maj. Gen. William H. French, whose troops occupied Frederick, Maryland. Should the army have to fall back, instructed Meade, French would withdraw to Washington. In the event of a Confederate retreat, French should reoccupy Harpers Ferry and harass Lee's communications. In an eight o'clock order to Sedgwick Meade advised that information received from Warren and Howard indicated the Rebels would "make the attempt to pierce our center." Meade wished Sedgwick to mass any spare troops he had in a central position so they could be dispatched to any portion of the line as circumstances might require. Half an hour later, Meade sent a message to Maj. Gen. Darius N. Couch, commanding the Department of the Susquehanna. Couch's militia lay in the Harrisburg area; Meade alerted the general that prompt cooperation would be necessary if Lee retreated. Should Meade have to retire, Couch would defend Harrisburg.[17]

A letter to his wife, the first since the battle began, was marked 8:45 A.M. "All well and going on well with the Army," Meade wrote simply. "We had a great fight yesterday, the enemy attacking and we completely repulsing them; both Armies shattered. To-day at it again, with what result remains to be seen. Army in fine spirits and every one determined to do or die. George and myself well. Reynolds killed the first day. No other of your friends or acquaintances hurt."[18]

At 9:15 A.M., Meade issued a circular to all corps commanders. Having noticed that troops not actively engaged had shed their equipment, he directed his subordinates to keep their troops under arms at all times and be ready to move at a moment's notice. Another circular addressed the problem of stragglers and others absent from the ranks; Meade urged that the "utmost exertion" be used to keep all soldiers in the ranks. He also directed ordnance officers to see that all arms and equipment scattered over the battlefield be picked up and sent to the rear via empty ammunition wagons.[19]

Meade then left headquarters and headed south along Cemetery Ridge. He encountered Hancock and had a brief chat with his Second Corps commander. Accounts of this conversation are sketchy, but it appears that the two generals discussed the possible target of a Confederate assault. Meade now doubted that the enemy would attack his center, because Union artillery posted there had excellent fields of fire. Lee's favorite point of attack was often on his opponent's left, so Meade expected action there. If Lee did attack Hancock's position, Meade assured his lieutenant, he would use the Fifth and Sixth Corps to assail the Rebel right flank.[20]

Meade's exact movements for the remainder of the morning are controversial, because of contradictory accounts. The general's grandson wrote that Meade returned to headquarters and stayed there until General Gibbon appeared and urged the army commander to join him for breakfast. Meade then visited the lines of Brig. Gen. Alexander Hays's Third Division of the Second Corps. He next rode south to Little Round Top, talking with Generals Newton and Sedgwick en route. Meade joined Warren on the crest of the hill and surveyed the massing lines of Confederate batteries, a sure indication that an attack would come that day, before returning to army headquarters.[21]

General Gibbon recalled events differently. After his servants had located and stewed "an old and tough rooster," Gibbon went to Meade's headquarters. There he found the general "looking worn and haggard" and impressed upon Meade the importance of eating. Meade accompanied Gibbon, ate a "hasty breakfast," and immediately returned to the Leister house. Gibbon and some fellow officers remained seated on the ground, chatting about the battle and the future. "How long we sat there it is impossible to say," wrote Gibbon, before the sudden commencement of the great artillery bombardment scattered the group.[22]

Gibbon's aide, Lieutenant Haskell, gave yet another version of what transpired. Haskell wrote that two persons—one an officer—procured some chickens, butter, and an oversized loaf of bread, the last being rescued from a runaway pig that had eaten off an end. Hancock soon joined the festivities; Meade and a staff member then appeared and were invited to eat. Newton and Pleasonton eventually joined the group as well. After this meal, the generals lit cigars and, shaded by a small tree, discussed events. Meade still believed, wrote Haskell, that Lee would attack on the left, while Hancock thought the center. The commanding general discussed the fact that many good soldiers were serving as provost guards and would be more useful in the ranks; he thus gave an order for all men on this duty to rejoin their regiments. Meade soon left for headquarters, and the other officers followed suit, leaving only Gibbon and his staff.[23]

Shortly after one o'clock, the line of Confederate batteries stretching northeast from the Peach Orchard and north along Seminary Ridge began its now-famous barrage. Union infantrymen scurried for whatever cover they could find; Federal batteries waited a short time then opened fire. The noise was deafening—so loud, in fact, that civilians as far away as Philadelphia later claimed they could hear the distant echoes. Fortunately for the Union defenders, Confederate artillery shooting was not much better than average for the Civil War. Smoke hid the results of the Rebel bombardment from the Southern gunners, who could not see that their pieces were elevated too high to hit the line of Union infantry on Cemetery Ridge. Hancock's artillery suffered heavy casualties during the prolonged artillery duel, which occupied most of two hours and involved approximately 120 Confederate guns and 118 Union pieces. Because the Rebels overshot their targets, Meade's headquarters, only a few hundred yards behind the crest of Cemetery Ridge, became the unintentional recipient of a steady stream of projectiles. The commanding general and his staff were lucky to avoid serious casualties. Meade himself was standing in the doorway, observing the chaos outside, when a solid shot crashed into a box and grazed him. The unfortunate horses of his staff officers, tethered to a hitching rail outside, suffered badly; sixteen were killed and mangled during the cannonade.[24]

The constant threat of death or wounding from shells terrified Meade's staff. Maj. James C. Biddle confided to his wife that "it was horrible, they burst all around us & were going over our heads every second." Biddle wrote that the staff remained at headquarters about an hour. During that period, projectiles literally riddled the tiny farmhouse. One shot tore up the front steps, and another crashed through the porch supports. A third ball passed through the garret, while a fourth flew through the open doorway. "It was the most fearfully magnificent scene imaginable," wrote engineer Capt. William H. Paine.[25]

Meade clearly could not stay at headquarters. He was loath to relocate, however, because he worried that messengers would be unable to find him. In an effort to avoid the myriad flying splinters, however, he did consent to move out of the house and into the yard. Even outside, the general and his staff remained in jeopardy. Meade paced back and forth, deep in thought, waiting for information from his lines of battle. He watched as most of his staff nervously edged from the yard to shelter in the rear of the house. "Gentlemen, are you trying to find a safe place?" called out the amused general. "You remind me of the man who drove the ox-team which took ammunition from the heavy guns on to the field of Palo Alto. Finding himself within range, he tilted up his cart and got behind it. Just then General

[Zachary] Taylor came along, and seeing his attempt at shelter, shouted, 'You damned fool, don't you know you are no safer there than anywhere else?' The driver replied, 'I don't suppose I am, general, but it kind o' feels so.'"[26]

During the bombardment, Meade ordered several subordinates to send troops to reinforce Hancock's position. He dispatched Capt. Chauncey B. Reese, who served on Warren's staff, to General Slocum with an order to detach a brigade to the rear of Cemetery Hill; from that position the unit could move to any threatened part of the line. Meade had earlier directed Brig. Gen. John C. Robinson, commanding the depleted Second Division of the First Corps, to shift from his lines in reserve behind the Twelfth Corps back to his old position in rear of Cemetery Hill. Meade expected an attack there, recalled Robinson. During the bombardment, Meade ordered Robinson to move his two brigades to the right of the Second Corps. Alexander's Shaler's First Brigade of the Sixth Corps's Third Division was ordered from Culp's Hill, while Col. Henry L. Eustis's Second Brigade of the same division left the area of Little Round Top to support Hancock. Several Third Corps units also moved north to assist.[27]

One of the controversies associated with the battle began during the bombardment. In his committee testimony, Meade stated that "after I became fully satisfied of the object of the enemy's fire, I directed my artillery to cease firing in order to save their ammunition, and also with the view of making the enemy believe that they had silenced our guns, and thus bring on their assault the sooner." Earlier in the day, artillery chief Hunt had started at Culp's Hill and ridden the entire length of the line to Little Round Top. Along the way, he watched the massing Southern artillery batteries along Seminary Ridge. The general wondered, what was their purpose? Was the massing offensive or defensive in nature? As Hunt progressed along Cemetery Ridge he stopped at each battery and instructed its commander to withhold fire for fifteen or twenty minutes, then concentrate on the most destructive enemy batteries. Fire slowly, Hunt ordered, to conserve ammunition and allow the enemy to exhaust his own supply.[28]

Hunt was on Little Round Top when the Confederate artillery opened fire. The scene was "indescribably grand," thought Hunt. After giving orders to the Artillery Reserve, the general rode north along Cemetery Ridge. He found that even with a slow rate of fire ammunition chests were running low, so he hastened to Meade's headquarters to suggest that the guns cease fire. Meade had already departed for the cemetery, Hunt learned from a messenger left behind. The artillerist hastened to Cemetery Hill, but Meade was not there. Hunt shared his concerns with General Howard, who concurred with him.[29]

The artillery chief then rode south, ordering each battery in turn to cease fire. He ordered crippled batteries to the rear, to be replaced by fresh units. While looking for the replacement batteries, Hunt met Maj. Henry H. Bingham of Hancock's staff. Bingham reported that Meade had sent messengers in search of Hunt with orders to have the artillery cease firing to induce a rebel assault. A gratified Hunt later wrote, "I had only anticipated his wishes."[30]

Meade was sending out messengers, but he apparently was not receiving a steady stream of information from his subordinates. The general had resisted entreaties from his staff to vacate the area around the Leister house and seek safety, but now he saw the folly of remaining. He learned there was a signal corps officer at Slocum's headquarters on Powers Hill, a small knoll located south of the Baltimore Pike behind the Twelfth Corps position.[31] Still, Meade tried to remain close to the Leister house. Accompanied by some of his staff, he rode south along the Taneytown Road to the shelter of a barn on the opposite side of the road. Many staff officers failed to accompany the general. Major Biddle and about a dozen comrades crawled into the small cellar under the Leister house to escape the shelling. Captain Paine faced a dilemma. A servant had taken one of his two horses away to water before the bombardment began and had not returned; Paine's second animal, terrified by the din, had broken his tether and galloped away. Unable to follow Meade, Paine decided to remain at headquarters and direct any messengers to Meade's new location.[32]

Meade did not linger at the barn along the Taneytown Road, because Confederate artillery fire rendered the area unsafe. General Butterfield was wounded by a shell fragment and taken off the field. Meade now went to Powers Hill in search of the signal officer. Captain Meade could not accompany his father—one of his horses had been killed, and an orderly had disappeared with his spare animal. In company with Lt. Charles W. Woolsey, one of Adj. Gen. Seth Williams's aides, young Meade set off on foot toward Powers Hill.[33]

General Meade reached Power's Hill and found the signal corps officer, but when that officer attempted to communicate with the signalman at the Leister house he received no reply. The general concluded that the latter had departed. Meade believed he therefore could not remain on Power's Hill and must return to his original headquarters.[34]

Captain Meade was making his way toward Power's Hill when he met his father riding back toward Cemetery Ridge. The general told one of his orderlies to give his horse to his son, who then rode to Power's Hill to locate his own horse, which apparently had been taken to Slocum's headquarters. Young Meade found his horse and galloped off to find his father.[35]

By the time General Meade reached the Leister house, artillery firing had ceased and the sound of "heavy musketry" swelled directly ahead. The general encountered stragglers heading for the rear. Realizing that a Confederate infantry assault had come, Meade rode rapidly to the front. As he crested the ridge, Captain Meade caught up with him. The captain later wrote that he saw his father receive a message, then dispatch a mounted aide. No one else was with the general. Artillery on the ridge was firing rapidly, and the drifting smoke hid the state of affairs on the battle front. The general turned and smiled when his son rode alongside: "Hello George, is that you? I am glad you are here, you must stick by me now, you are the only officer left." Captain Meade recalled that his father mentioned something about it being a lively place, then said, "Lets go up here and find out what is going on."[36]

The Meades turned to the right to get out of the smoke. General Meade kept asking his son if he saw anyone he knew. "Let's find Hays," stated the general. The younger Meade assumed his father meant Brig. Gen. Alexander Hays, head of the Third Division of the Second Corps, because he had visited Hays's portion of the line earlier in the day. The two officers soon came across Lt. Jonathan Egan, commanding a section of Lt. Carle A. Woodruff's Battery I, 1st United States Artillery; Captain Meade recognized Egan and told his father so. The general asked Egan if he knew Hays's wherabouts. Egan pointed to the stone wall in his front. Just a few moments earlier the mounted Hays had led his troops over the wall as the rebels in front faltered. Meade inquired, had the enemy turned back? "Yes," replied Egan, "See, General Hays has one of their flags." "I don't care for their flag," snapped Meade, repeating, "Have they turned?" When Egan, who described Meade as "mighty cross too," replied in the affirmative, Meade moved toward the left.[37]

After riding a short distance, Meade ran headlong into a large body of Confederate prisoners trudging over the ridge. The beaten men in gray recognized Meade as a general and crowded around him, asking where they should go. Now in "fine spirits," Meade pointed to the rear, laughingly saying, "Go along that way and you will be well taken care of." In danger of shells from their own artillery, the prisoners dutifully scampered over the ridge to the provost guards on the reverse slope.[38]

Meade then encountered Lt. Frank A. Haskell, General Gibbon's aide. Haskell penned the following description of the victor of Gettysburg: "The [general] was no bedizened hero of some holy day review, but he was a plain man, dressed in a serviceable summer suit of dark blue cloth, without badge or ornament save the shoulder-straps of his grade, and a light, straight sword of a General, a General Staff, officer. He wore heavy, high top-boots and buff gauntlets; and his soft black felt hat was slouched down his eyes. His face was very white, not pale, and the lines were marked, and earnest, and full of care."

Meade recognized the lieutenant and asked "in a sharp, eager voice," "How is it going here?" When Haskell said he believed the attack had been repulsed, an incredulous Meade responded, "What? Is the assault entirely repulsed?" A glance over the field corroborated Haskell's brief reply, and a relieved Meade said simply, "Thank God." The usually impassive general caught himself as he was about to doff his hat and cheer, choosing instead merely to wave his hand and say "hur-rah!" George, however, threw off his hat and cheered loudly three times.[39]

The general then learned from Haskell that both Hancock and Gibbon had been wounded. Meade instructed Haskell to re-form the troops and prepare to resist another attack. Still followed by his son, Meade rode south some distance, peering at the front and observing events. Satisfied that the enemy assault had been repelled, the general told his son that he was going to see O. O. Howard. As Captain Meade turned to go with his father, a piece of shell struck his horse's hindquarters, felling the beast. The general kept on, apparently without noticing his son's predicament.[40]

General Meade next rode north to Cemetery Hill to ascertain the situation at that important position. Captain Meade met his father returning south along the ridge. The captain recalled that the general by now had his entire staff and several other mounted officers with him. Meade proceeded south to a point on the ridge opposite the Leister house, where he crossed the line of battle and continued all the way to Little Round Top. The general's cavalcade was treated to a thunderous roar of cheers along the entire distance. Although Confederates could watch Meade's progress, they did not fire a single artillery round at his party.[41]

At Little Round Top, Meade met General Sykes. According to Meade:

I went immediately to the extreme left of my line, with the determination of advancing the left and making an assault upon the enemy's lines. So soon as I arrived at the left I gave the necessary orders for the pickets and skirmishers in front to be thrown forward to feel the enemy, and for all preparations to be made for the assault. The great length of the line, and the time required to carry these orders out to the front, and the movement subsequently made, before the report given to me of the condition of the forces in the front and left, caused it to be so late in the evening as to induce me to abandon the assault which I had contemplated.[42]

Confusion inherent in mixing troops from several corps apparently caused much of this delay. Precious time slipped by, and in the end just one brigade of the Pennsylvania Reserves, supported by troops from the Sixth Corps, advanced against the rebels. Col. William McCandless's Yankees encountered Hood's withdrawing division and mauled some units in the area of the Wheatfield before both sides disengaged. This was the last infantry fighting at Gettysburg.

At 8:35 that night, Meade sent a telegram to Halleck announcing the results of the day's fighting. It included the following statement: "After the repelling of the assault, indications leading to the belief that the enemy might be withdrawing, an armed reconnaissance was pushed forward from the left, and the enemy found to be in force. . . . The army is in fine spirits."[43]

That night Meade and his staff slept among rocks in a small patch of woods along the Taneytown Road. The Leister house had been so badly pummeled as to be useless as a headquarters. Nine projectiles had hit the house, and the carcasses of sixteen horses lay outside. Later that night, a heavy thunderstorm drenched the victor of Gettysburg.[44]

In three days of hard fighting, the Army of the Potomac had beaten the Army of Northern Virginia. George G. Meade's presence had contributed significantly to the Federal success. Although his detractors, and historians relying upon their writings, have denigrated Meade's performance, the general did rather well. His work on July 3 continued his steady, if unspectacular, guidance of the first two days. Meade used his interior lines to shift reinforcements quickly to threatened areas of the battle line. Troops dispatched to Culp's Hill as support for Slocum's men were later moved elsewhere when it became apparent that Lee meant to assault the Union center. By the time Pickett's troops approached the Second Corps line, Meade and his aides had moved approximately thirteen thousand soldiers into position. Any Confederate breakthrough would have been easily contained and repelled.

Critics have lambasted as timidity and bad generalship Meade's failure to counterattack after Pickett's repulse. As Edwin B. Coddington has pointed out, however, these armchair generals have failed to consider the situation at the time.[45] Meade used interior lines to advantage, but by late afternoon on July 3 units from various corps were intermixed. Sedgwick's Sixth Corps, although lightly engaged during the three days of battle, was dispersed along Cemetery Ridge and unavailable for use in a counterattack. A large portion of the army was hungry, its supplies in arrears as the battle raged. In short, the army possessed high morale but was tired, hungry, and disorganized. Moreover, Meade had lost three corps commanders and many subordinates. The tenor of his evening dispatch to Halleck indicated uncertainty as to the morrow: Lee might be withdrawing, but he might stay and fight. Wishing to husband his resources, Meade decided to wait and see.

Promoted from corps command less than a week before, Meade had the good fortune to lead the Army of the Potomac in its first true victory over Lee's vaunted legions. Artillery chief Henry J. Hunt, in a postwar letter to Alexander Webb, heartily agreed with all Meade did on the battlefield. In researching his articles for the "Battles and Leaders" series in *Century Magazine*, Hunt concluded that Meade had made all the right decisions: "Rarely has more skill, vigor, or wisdom been shown under such circumstances as he was placed in."[46] His detractors and counterfactual history notwithstanding, George Gordon Meade had performed well beyond anyone's expectations.

James Longstreet's
Virginia Defenders

Carol Reardon

LT. GEN. JAMES LONGSTREET HAS WORN THE MANTLE OF
scapegoat for the South's defeat at Gettysburg for so long that it is difficult
to recall a time when this was not the case. Only in the last few decades have
students of the battle begun to find wanting the traditional evidence offered up by a host of seemingly unimpeachable sources from the Army
of Northern Virginia who condemn Longstreet for the failure of Pickett's
Charge. Once-silenced voices now ring out to challenge the accusation
that on July 3, 1863, "Old Pete" played the role of the Confederacy's Judas.
Among those voices are those of the survivors and friends of George E.
Pickett's Virginia division in Longstreet's First Corps. The sons of the Old
Dominion closest to that great charge on that hot summer day in south-
central Pennsylvania have long remained quiet in the historical debates
swirling around Lee and Longstreet's leadership at Gettysburg, and their
memories of that great day deserve greater illumination.

As William Garrett Piston has explained, any attempt to relieve James
Longstreet of the burden of blame for what happened that last day at
Gettysburg faces a daunting task.[1] Allegations of professional misconduct
lodged in the 1870s by Lee's own staff officers and former senior leaders of
the Army of Northern Virginia rang with authority then, and the legacy
of their efforts to transfer responsibility for the South's defeat from Lee
to Longstreet still colors historical narratives more than a century later.

Worse, those same staunch partisans of Lee tried hard to silence those who saw things differently, many of Pickett's men among them.

Certainly the veterans of the First Corps's Virginia division never planned to remain silent about what happened to them on July 3. Right after the battle they certainly had much to say about the misfortunes that had befallen them. Even as they mourned their dead and trumpeted the gallantry of Pickett's division, they also wanted to know why so many of their friends had died. This question held paramount importance for them in July 1863, but they did not accuse Old Pete of leading them to slaughter.

Even before the Army of Northern Virginia recrossed the Potomac to safety, Pickett's men figured they knew who had let them down. Uniformly, they blamed the troops under Brig. Gen. James Johnston Pettigrew and Maj. Gen. Isaac R. Trimble from Lt. Gen. A. P. Hill's Third Corps, commands that the Virginians believed had been ordered to support them on their left flank. Some additionally blamed the weak efforts of Brig. Gen. Cadmus M. Wilcox's Alabamians and Col. David Lang's Floridians on Pickett's right flank.

This prevailing sentiment proved so strong that William Cocke of the 9th Virginia could write home with confidence that he and his comrades did all they could do but that their supports had "run like sheep—thanks to Gracious they were NOT Va. troops." Pickett's men had driven the Yankees from their works "but for want of assistance couldn't turn the guns upon them." Maj. Charles S. Peyton of the 19th Virginia registered dismay in his after-action report, observing that his men had "hoped for a support on the left (which had started simultaneously with ourselves), but hoped in vain." Maj. James Dearing, whose battalion of Virginia batteries supported the advance of Pickett's men, concurred: "Well! We took those heights but could not hold them. Pickett's little division of 4000 Virginians took them by themselves unsupported and unassisted. Gen'l Heth's division started on his left but never reached their works," and thus "we were disappointed in the fruits of our Campaign." In a letter home, Lt. Col. Edward Porter Alexander, who served on July 3 as acting artillery chief of Longstreet's First Corps, offered similar sentiments: "Pickett's division was to make the charge—unsupported it afterward appeared in the rear, & Pettigrew's division of A. P. Hill's Corps was to go on his left, but when Pettigrew's division fell back under fire, the assault failed." If only the Third Corps troops had done their job, Alexander argued, "the result would have been very different, for the charge was as gallant as was ever made."[2]

In short, Pickett's men and those who served in close association with the Virginia division very quickly made up their minds that lack of support from A. P. Hill's Third Corps had caused their defeat. If there is virtue in

Brig. Gen. James Johnston Pettigrew, whose soldiers received considerable criticism for their role in the grand Confederate assault on July 3, 1863. From *Battles and Leaders of the Civil War* 3:429.

consistency, Pickett's men ranked among the most virtuous of all former Confederates: they held Longstreet blameless in July 1863, and they never changed their minds.

Indeed, at least at first it seemed that most Virginians in Lee's army concurred with Pickett's men. Without blaming any one command by name, a Virginian in Lt. Gen. Richard S. Ewell's Second Corps wrote home that "Pickett's division was ordered to charge—& did so—most gallantly & gained the works, but not being supported had to fall back. . . . Our loss was terrible—Pickett's division was almost annihilated." Charles Minor Blackford, another son of the Old Dominion who served outside the Virginia division, wrote home simply that he grieved deeply over the fate of Pickett's division, in which he had many friends, and added that "Poor Virginia bleeds again at every pore. There will be few firesides in her midst where the voice of mourning will not be heard when the blacklettered list of losses is published."[3] Not one word of censure against James Longstreet appears in these comments, and they represent the prevailing perception of most Virginians in Lee's beaten army as it retreated south.

Reporters for Richmond's five newspapers and writers for other Southern dailies leaned heavily on the soldiers' judgments to inform their own accounts of the defeat of the Army of Northern Virginia in Pennsylvania. Correspondent Jonathan Albertson, who penned one of the most vivid accounts of the July 3 charge, praised with florid prose the steadfastness of Pickett's Virginians, but of the Third Corps's advance he wrote that "I saw by the wavering of this line as they entered the conflict that they wanted the firmness of nerve and steadiness of tread which so characterized Pickett's men, and I felt that these men would not, could not stand the tremendous ordeal to which they would soon be subjected." Results soon bore out his fears. As Albertson saw the Virginians "plant their banner in the enemy's works" and heard "their glad shout of victory," he looked over toward Pettigrew's command. What he saw shocked him: "There all over the plain, in utmost confusion is scattered this strong division. Their line is broken; they are flying, apparently panic stricken, to the rear." A Georgia general's letter, widely reprinted all through the Confederacy, colorfully described the collapse of Pettigrew's line: it "wavers—it pauses—all is lost—it falls back—it runs. . . . Helter skelter, pell-mell, here they come."[4] A Richmond editor demanded satisfaction: "There is fault to be attached to someone—let our high officers, the proper ones, say to whom."[5]

Although there would be no formal investigation to determine what went wrong on July 3, correspondents did not shy away from pointing the finger of blame at those they considered responsible. Cavalry chief "Jeb" Stuart drew criticism for his absence during much of the battle. Second Corps head Ewell and Third Corps division commander Richard H. Anderson became targets for heated invective as well. But James Longstreet did not number among the commanders subjected to the closest scrutiny. Instead, Richmond's editors mourned Virginia's dead who served under him. They expressed relief when early rumors in Northern papers declaring him to be dead or a prisoner proved false. They printed and reprinted the story of Pickett's gallant men and damned the commands of Pettigrew and Trimble, and sometimes even Wilcox's Alabamians and Lang's Floridians, for their failure to support the Virginia division. By the end of July 1863, Richmond's newspapers had helped to ensure that the postbattle perceptions of the survivors of Pickett's division was the story that all Virginians embraced. James Longstreet still commanded their respect.

The bond between Longstreet and Pickett's men extended into the immediate postwar years. In the late 1860s Porter Alexander began research on a proposed history of the First Corps, and he asked James L. Kemper, Pickett's only surviving brigadier, about Longstreet's conduct that day. The Virginian recalled with pride how Old Pete had shared their danger: "Longstreet rode slowly and alone immediately in front of our entire line. He sat his large charger with a magnificent grace and composure I never before beheld. His bearing was to me the grandest moral spectacle of the war."[6]

Even into the early 1870s, Virginians willingly expressed good feelings about James Longstreet. In *Pickett's Men: A Fragment of War History*, one of the earliest Civil War unit histories, Walter Harrison of Pickett's staff allowed his respect for his corps commander to enliven his Gettysburg narrative. Early on July 3, Harrison had carried a question from Armistead to Longstreet as the corps commander rode along his lines with Lee. Harrison noted that "the great 'war horse' of the army, or as he was more familiarly called, 'Old Peter,' seemed to be in anything but a pleasant humor at the prospect 'over the hill.'" Harrison did not hint at any lack of will on Longstreet's part; indeed, after getting his own first glimpse of the field of impending battle he agreed entirely that "truly it was no cheering prospect." Harrison even recalled with embarrassment a "little trespass on military etiquette," in arriving abruptly and breaking the general's concentration on military matters. Longstreet had spoken to him sharply, but as Harrison rode off he was surprised to hear the general call him back to apologize for his brusqueness, apparently believing that "perhaps, in his usual kindheartedness, he had unnecessarily snubbed a poor subordinate."[7]

Harrison knew who deserved blame for what happened to Pickett's men. When "the critical moment for SUPPORT had arrived to this little band of so-far victors, . . . [a]nother wedge must be driven in, another sledge-hammer mauling given to this one." If help did not come, "this devoted forty-five hundred, this VERY forlorn hope, must succumb at once." When Pettigrew's and Trimble's men did not come up, Harrison made the case plainly: "I am recording the final discomfiture of Pickett's Men at Gettysburg, after their well-known charge—and I state simply the fact, that these other troops *were ordered* to support them, which, I believe it is quite as well known they did *not*." He named names: Pettigrew's and Trimble's men had failed Pickett's Virginians. He acknowledged that these Third Corps troops had gone into the charge greatly understrength after losing heavily on July 1 and had advanced on July 3 under leaders they did not know, but he did not excuse their conduct. "The overwhelming force of the enemy now having in reality no one else to contend with, soon closed in from every point upon the insignificant few, and poured in a direct as well as cross fires upon them." In none of this did Harrison offer a hint of censure against James Longstreet. Unfortunately, these were among the last kind words any Virginian publicly accorded Old Pete for several decades.[8]

Longstreet and his reputation fell victim not only to the well documented domination of Lee's partisans over the writing of Confederate history but also to forces inside postwar Virginia he could not have foreseen or controlled.[9] Virginia's Confederate veterans became a contentious and highly politicized lot. They rarely presented a united front, dividing repeatedly on sensitive local interests and an ever-changing array of political concerns that proved stronger than the ties that once had bound them as brothers-in-arms in a common cause. These political squabbles helped to shape the ways in which Virginia would remember its Confederate past, and few events attracted as much special attention as did the great Confederate charge of July 3, 1863, at Gettysburg.

The division in the Virginia Confederate veteran community became apparent in the late 1860s. Southern soldiers from the western part of the state and the Shenandoah Valley successfully wrested much of the control over veterans affairs from their former comrades who lived in the traditional seats of power in Virginia—the Piedmont, Tidewater, and Richmond areas. Jubal A. Early became an early and vocal leader of this western Virginia group. Because Lee himself spent his final years at Lexington in the Valley, some of his military staff and closest associates, such as Walter H. Taylor, A. L. Long, and former Army of Northern Virginia artillery chief and Episcopal minister William Nelson Pendleton of Lexington, allied themselves with this clique.

From the immediate postwar years and for many reasons, Pickett and his men, many of whom came from Richmond or the Tidewater, worked warily with this upstart western crowd. While they shared the bond of military service to the Confederacy and joined at first in a variety of veterans organizations, differing perspectives on the Commonwealth's political future ultimately helped to split them apart.

Most of the western Virginians—including a number of antebellum Whigs, such as Early—pledged loyalty to the Democratic party after the war. As unreconstructed a bunch of Southerners as one could find, they cultivated and cherished the memory of the Lost Cause and refused to embrace the concept of sectional reconciliation in any way. Even as the centennial of 1876 neared, some would come out against Virginian participation in any elaborate national celebration. Other Virginians supported the state's self-styled Conservatives, including George Pickett, governor-to-be James L. Kemper, and a number of other prominent veterans in Richmond and the eastern part of the state. These men joined their western counterparts in not apologizing for their service to Virginia and the South during the war. In peacetime, however, they had embraced what they considered to be practical economic and political programs that would restore the Old Dominion to prominence and wealth within a national framework. The Conservatives made clear that they were not members of the hated Republican party, but Virginia's Democratic veterans did not see much difference.

Two examples from 1875 illustrate the nature of the intrastate political split and its application to issues that touched Virginia's Confederate veterans. When George Pickett died in 1875, family and friends in Richmond began planning a military procession to bear his remains to his burial site in Hollywood Cemetery. When the arrangements were made public, Early and other western Virginians in the Confederate veteran community balked at the inclusion of black militia units. Conservative Kemper and his allies struck back hard, citing the stated wishes of the Pickett family to allow *all* Virginia military units, and they won the day. Just a few days later, however, organizing a similar parade to dedicate a statue in Richmond saluting Stonewall Jackson, the western Virginians reasserted their clout, and no black Virginia militia participated in the proceedings.[10]

Many elements of Longstreet's postwar career linked him philosophically with the Virginia Conservatives. His leadership of the mostly black militia and Metropolitan Police Force of New Orleans, his participation at their head in a riot against the Crescent City White League—an organization made up chiefly of Confederate veterans—and his acceptance of a variety of state and federal appointments from prominent state and national Republican leaders painted him in the minds of western Virginia Democrats as a political heretic, much like Pickett and Kemper. In time, Virginia's western group would make both Pickett's division and Longstreet pay for their political apostasy.

In early 1869, even before these splits appeared, prominent Virginia Confederate veterans of differing political sentiments, including both Jubal Early and George Pickett, helped to establish the Southern Historical Society. A few years after Lee died in 1870, the western Virginia faction—dubbed by some modern scholars the "Lee cult"—began publishing the *Southern Historical Society Papers.* They tightly controlled the content of this journal, which sought to preserve Confederate history in ways that glorified the great Southern military chieftain. The defeat at Gettysburg posed an especially tough problem for them until they determined to shift the blame for the reversal of the South's fortunes there from Lee to James Longstreet.

Longstreet's selection as their target was an easy and popular one. Even more disturbing to them than his political activities was another unforgivable sin: as early as 1866, Old Pete had criticized Lee openly in an interview with Northern journalist William Swinton, who promptly published the general's comments for a national audience. Lee's friends decided that they could not let Longstreet's attacks on their hero go unpunished.[11]

At first key leaders of the Lee cult, such as Early and Taylor, lodged against Longstreet serious allegations of slowness and recalcitrance on July 2. Buoyed by some success in that effort, they soon extended their accusations to blame him for the failure of Pickett's Charge on July 3. This would be no easy task—Lee's earliest biographers had made much of his meeting the survivors of Pickett's division with the acknowledgment "It is all my fault." The Lee cult decided on a simple tactic: drown out Lee's own self-effacing comment with a much louder and firmer "No, it was not."[12]

Consider the accusations they soon leveled against Old Pete. Armistead Long, once Lee's military secretary, asserted that "the attack of Pickett's division on the third has been more criticized, and is still less understood, than any other act of the Gettysburg drama. General Longstreet did not enter into the spirit of it, and consequently did not support it with his wonted vigor." Walter Taylor of Lee's staff explained the battle plan as he recalled it: Longstreet "was ordered to renew the fight early on the 3d; Ewell was to co-operate. Ewell ordered Johnson to attack at an early hour, anticipating that Longstreet would do the same. Longstreet delayed." Even when Longstreet finally advanced, wrote Taylor, "the attack was not made as designed." When Pickett's fresh division from the First Corps went forward, the divisions of Maj. Gen. John B. Hood and Maj. Gen. Lafayette McLaws stayed behind, and only elements of two divisions from Hill's Third Corps advanced with it. Thus, as Taylor argued, there "were nine divisions in the army; seven were quiet while two assailed the fortified line of the enemy." He wondered, "Was it designed to throw these few brigades . . . upon the fortified stronghold of the enemy, while, full half a mile away, seven ninths of the army, in breathless suspense, in ardent admiration and fearful anxiety, watched, but moved not? I maintain that such was not the design of the commanding general." In Taylor's mind, if Hood and McLaws had advanced as ordered, Southern arms could have resisted all efforts to repulse them. Taylor stopped just short of accusing Longstreet of insubordination for expressing his military opinion that "he would have stayed the execution" of the charge "had he felt that he had the privilege to do so."[13]

Longstreet's conduct on July 3 now drew heated criticism from fellow generals aligned with the Lee cult. Jubal Early fumed that Old Pete's lack of enthusiasm for Lee's plans prevented him from executing his orders "with the spirit of confidence so necessary to success." In another attack, he added that Longstreet, "who was entrusted with the conduct of the attack from our right, and who failed to begin it at the designated time," and even "shifted the responsibility for the final order for his charge, that properly attached to himself, to the shoulders of a colonel of artillery and then withheld two divisions intended and directed to cooperate in the charge, has no right to complain that the charge was hopeless from the beginning. It was his own conduct that contributed to making it so." Cadmus Wilcox, whose Alabama brigade entered the fray as Pickett's Virginians began their retreat, understood personally what Longstreet's weakness had meant for his own men. Pointing out that Old Pete had only nodded when he ordered

Pickett forward, lest "his voice should betray his want of confidence," Wilcox could not understand how, despite "this conviction of useless sacrifice of his men," he could order eleven hundred Alabamians to advance when "[s]uch a reinforcement to Pickett could have availed nothing." Wilcox's brigade "could only be sacrificed; and yet it was by this order that it advanced" to the slaughter.[14]

Old Pete always had his supporters. When William Nelson Pendleton criticized Longstreet's performance at Gettysburg before an audience in Galveston, he found that "his charges had rather created a feeling of indignation against him, and especially among soldiers" of the Texas Brigade "who had fought and bled" under Old Pete on July 2 at Gettysburg. Both McLaws and Brig. Gen. Benjamin G. Humphreys, who had served in Barksdale's Mississippi brigade at Gettysburg, also had spoken up in support of their commander's actions that day.[15]

But few defenders rose quickly to counter accusations lodged against Longstreet for his performance on July 3. Years later, Porter Alexander explained how Lee's friends had mounted what seemed to be an authoritative attack on Longstreet. He knew that Lee had been forced to revise his first plan for July 3—which would have continued the previous day's assault on both Union flanks—for a second plan that called for an attack on the Union center. As Alexander wrote, "For awhile, Longstreet's critics tried to make it appear that he disobeyed an order to put McLaws's & Hood's divisions also in the storming column with Pickett." But Alexander cited Lee's own battle report to make clear that "although there had been at first a desire on his part, to use some of these troops in Pickett's charge"—a sloppy reference to the first plan of attack—that design "had been abandoned." Alexander even argued that Lee had been correct to defer to Longstreet's concerns in this case. If Hood and McLaws had joined the assaulting column, "they could only have been withdrawn under observation, & fire from the enemy upon Round Top, & a cloud of skirmishers could have followed their withdrawal & soon driven back a large part of our firing line." Alexander dismissed as entirely wrongheaded Longstreet's critics who accused him of disobeying Lee's orders to include Hood and McLaws in the great assault. He expressed special concern because even "some of Gen. Lee's staff officers have written letters" suggesting this to be true.[16] But when Alexander reached these conclusions in the 1890s, the Lee cult had a nearly two-decade start on trashing Old Pete's good name.

During that time, one other key constituency of Confederate veterans in the Old Dominion had remained remarkably quiet as the blame for Gettysburg shifted from Lee to Longstreet. These were Pickett's men. Much to the dismay and anger of the Lee cult, the survivors of the Virginia division did not close ranks with their western brothers and participate in the vilification of their former corps commander. Pickett's men had not rallied to Old Pete's side to snub the Lee cult either, but Lee's partisans simply could not tolerate anything short of complete and willing compliance.

So they punished Pickett's men, in two ways. First, as Thomas L. Connelly and William Garrett Piston have documented, Lee's friends kept up their own heavy barrage of literary attacks on Longstreet. They so successfully baited Old Pete with their accusations in the *Southern Historical Society Papers* that the general's intemperate responses provided additional grist for subsequent exchanges. Second, in an effort both more subtle and more telling, the Lee cult effectively silenced Pickett's men by barring them from the pages of the Society's increasingly authoritative journal. The editors of the *Southern Historical Society Papers* controlled so completely the writing of Confederate history in Virginia that they could enforce such a ban. If Pickett's men would not blame Old Pete for the destruction of the Virginia division at Gettysburg, they could not expect the journal to trumpet their own glories for all posterity. Instead, the editors routinely celebrated the gallantry of Virginia units from the western part of the state and enshrined for all time as their second-greatest hero the martyred Stonewall Jackson. They expounded at length about the accomplishments of the Second and Third corps, the commands in which Jackson's men had served after the general's mortal wounding at Chancellorsville. Virginians who had taken no part in the July 3 charge but agreed nonetheless to blame Longstreet for mishandling it could also get a hearing from the editors.

But only a few authors from the Virginia division in Longstreet's corps appear in the journal's pages. They offered a few unremarkable company rosters from Pickett's fifteen Virginia regiments to fill an occasional two or three pages. Some of Pickett's men, such as Charles T. Loehr of the "Old First" Virginia Infantry, wrote short pieces about prison life or some other subject far removed from Gettysburg. The publication of such brief pieces suggests that veterans of Pickett's division won a few concessions in the apparent proscription against them. But they failed to tell the story they most wanted to tell. During the first two decades of the influential journal's long run, the editors did not allow any of them to publish a single feature article about the charge of July 3, 1863, the greatest moment in the history of Pickett's division.

As if to make sure that Pickett's men understood the price of noncooperation, the journal's pro-Lee editorial board actively solicited contributions from survivors of Pettigrew's and Trimble's commands—those whom Pickett's men had always blamed for leaving them alone to be slaughtered. The editors allowed Virginia-born James H. Lane, former commander of one of Trimble's North Carolina brigades, to challenge some of Walter Taylor's general comments about the performance of the Third Corps troops that day, but those criticisms led up to Lane's most vehement assertions. He knew, "*personally*, that my old brigade, in all its glorious achievements, never behaved more gallantly than on that terrible and bloody battle-field." He felt so strongly on this point as to conclude that "my brigade were as much the 'heroes of Gettysburg' as *any other* troops that took part in it"—an open slight of Pickett's Virginians.[17]

The editors personally invited Col. Burkett D. Fry of Archer's Tennessee and Alabama brigade to submit his account of "Pettigrew's Charge," and they did not edit out his criticisms of the conduct of Pickett's men and the absence of active leadership by Longstreet. General Wilcox fell in line completely with the editorial board's wishes, by lambasting Longstreet personally: "I never believed the attack made by Longstreet on the 3d was strong enough in numbers. I did not know that he had failed to attack as ordered." How did Wilcox learn about Longstreet's disobedience in executing Pickett's Charge? Revealing overt tampering by Lee's partisans, Wilcox cited his source as Col. Charles Venable of Lee's wartime staff, who had told him about Lee's initial July 3 order that called for the advance of Hood's and McLaws's men. Apparently not realizing that the orders to launch Pickett's Charge followed the abandonment of that first plan, Wilcox related Venable's memories: "I heard [Lee] give the orders when arranging the fight; and called his attention to it long afterward, when there was discussion about it. He said, 'I know it! I know it!'"[18] Against such organized partisanship, Longstreet never stood a chance if he could not find vocal defenders who could speak with equal authority. Pickett's men would have filled that bill most admirably, but their voices remained noticeably silent.

Buoyed by their initial successes, the Lee cult became ever more ambitious, and even a bit sloppy, in their effort to do in Longstreet and Pickett's men. The editors tried to enlist the aid of Virginian Henry Heth, a move that seemed to make good sense. Heth had suffered a head wound on July 1, and his division had marched into the July 3 assault under Pettigrew. Because his men lost so heavily and Pettigrew had been mortally wounded on the retreat back to Virginia, Heth certainly should have been willing to champion his division at the expense of Pickett's men. He started out well, explaining briefly that he believed his own troops had fought hard under adverse circumstances. But he ended his usefulness to the editors abruptly when he blamed Lee for the defeat, explaining that "the fight of the 3d of July was a mistake" and that "General Lee should have so manœuvred as to have drawn Meade down from his stronghold." Moreover, he cast no aspersions on Longstreet. In the end, somebody may have remembered that Heth was George Pickett's cousin.[19]

A similar invitation to Lafayette McLaws also backfired. Because Longstreet had ordered McLaws to be court-martialed, the editors believed McLaws would jump at an opportunity to prepare a rousing condemnation of Old Pete. McLaws, however, wrote: "If General Longstreet did not attack early on the 3d, as General Lee says he was ordered to do, his reasons for not doing so appear to have been perfectly satisfactory to General Lee." Longstreet had been right to convince Lee to keep McLaws and Hood in place to secure the Confederate right flank, and, McLaws continued, "as the same causes were in existence when Pickett's charge was made, it is not to be disputed that General Lee could not have expected Longstreet's two right divisions to take part in the charge." McLaws, too, quickly found his tenure as a contributor to the *Southern Historical Society Papers* at an end.[20]

By 1880 few bridges between the most ardent Lee partisans and Pickett's men remained. The editorial board of the *Papers* had learned that it could not count on former Confederate officers presumed to be unfriendly to Longstreet to blame him for Gettysburg, and they simply refused to give Pickett's men, who had served so well under Old Pete, even the slightest opportunity to slip in a positive comment about him. The proscription against their admission to those hallowed pages continued to be so strong that the testimony of Pickett's men remained uncourted even when it might have been useful. In 1881, for example, Union general Abner Doubleday published *Chancellorsville and Gettysburg*, a quirky little book replete with self-serving commentary and factual inaccuracies. In his discussion of July 3, Doubleday displayed a special talent for role reversal, placing Maj. Gen. Winfield S. Hancock's Second Corps in a supporting role to his own First Corps troops. He also asserted that mortally wounded General Armistead of Pickett's division had fought for the Union at First Manassas, and then at Gettysburg apologized for turning against his country to fight for the Confederacy. With Armistead's dying breath, wrote Doubleday, the Southern general had begged for forgiveness from his loyal friend, Hancock.[21]

When this story circulated the whole South screamed at the perceived slander, and the Southern Historical Society rose up to deliver Armistead from his detractor. Virginians stepped forward in droves to protect the general's good name. The editors of the *Southern Historical Society Papers* themselves refuted in several issues of the journal Doubleday's claim that Armistead fought on the Union side at First Manassas. They further disputed Armistead's deathbed apology by allowing the journal's subscribers to hear contrary evidence from Union General Hancock, his aide Henry Bingham, and even Maine minister Theodore Gerrish (who could only pro-

A nineteenth-century engraving depicting Lewis A. Armistead, his hat on the tip of his sword, just before he received a mortal wound among Union guns on Cemetery Ridge. From Louis Shepheard Moat, ed., *Frank Leslie's Illustrated History of the Civil War* (New York, 1895), 418.

vide hearsay evidence from one of his congregants who found himself in the same hospital as the wounded Confederate general). But only one of Armistead's own men from Pickett's division, former Col. Rawley Martin, won the privilege of offering testimony, and the editors accorded him only a single sentence. The refusal of Pickett's men to cooperate with the Lee cult thus banned them from the South's most influential military history journal even when they—before all others—might best clear Armistead's reputation.[22]

Pickett's men tried to fight back. Rarely taking on the Southern Historical Society's leadership directly, they mounted a slow but steady counter-attack against their silencers. First and foremost, to be sure, they wanted to make certain that their division's sacrifices on July 3 would not be forgotten. They defended their good name and praised the timeless virtues of these bravest of Virginians in privately published personal and unit reminiscences, in articles for nationally circulating popular magazines, in Northern veterans newsletters, and even in *St. Nicholas*, the foremost children's magazine of the day.

In each case, the story they told remained the same as they had recounted in July 1863: they had behaved nobly. A veteran of the 7th Virginia reminded his brothers-in-arms of the confidence with which they went into the July 3 attack, certain that "victory was sure to perch upon their banners." Despite the horrors of "guns, swords, haversacks, human flesh and bones, flying through the air," they answered Pickett's call: "Up, men, and to your posts! Don't forget today that you are from old Virginia!" They also had not been to blame for the outcome of the battle. As readers of the 1st Virginia's regimental history learned about the fate of their division, "The reinforcement has not dared to enter this death-trap, and 'Pickett's Division,' or all that is left of it, being about one-tenth, slowly returns to the point from when it issued, 'to do or die.'"[23] The Virginians were made of the finest stuff, the young readers of *St. Nicholas* read, while Pettigrew's North Carolinians, who had failed to support them, came from common clay.[24] As it happened, Northern audiences and even Young America heard more about Pickett's men, heard it first, and heard it with less slander of Longstreet than did most former Confederates.

Although this literary war eventually took a toll on Pickett's men, they did not ignore a second point they wanted to make. When considering command responsibilities for the July 3 charge, they did not respond directly to the allegations that Lee's partisans lodged against them or their senior leaders. Most often they resorted to the tale they had always told and threw back into the faces of the Lee cult the Southern chieftain's own acceptance of blame for the events of July 3. As the 1st Virginia's regimental history recorded it, Lee had met Pickett with the remnants of his battered division and told him, "General, your men have done all that men could do, the fault is entirely my own."[25]

In the short term, this is as far as Pickett's men dared to venture. If they chose to praise Longstreet, they did so for his leadership or character at a battle other than Gettysburg. When it came to discussing the latter, it seemed safer to protect him passively with silence rather than offering him up yet again to fellow Virginians who might find a way to turn their good words for Old Pete against him. Their inability to launch a more active defense of their general cannot be construed as a weakening of their loyalty. Many still recalled him with respect. The veterans of the First Virginia Infantry Association even invited Longstreet to a regimental reunion in Richmond in 1883. He sent his regrets, but the author of the unit's history felt so strongly about his praise for the 1st Virginia's conduct in their initial battle that he included it verbatim: at Blackburn's Ford, "the heavy part of this fight was made by the old First Regiment, so that it can well claim to have done more towards the success of the First Manassas than any one regiment. This, too, was their first battle, and I can say that the officers and men did their duties as well, if not better, than any troops whose service came under my observation."[26] Just as it praised the gallant "Old First," Longstreet's comment may have served as well to challenge the reputation of the Stonewall Brigade of western Virginians, who bore the sobriquet that Jackson had won in this fight.

Pickett's men had to find a way to do more than snipe at their critics and to loosen the grip of the Lee cult on Virginia's, and the Confederacy's, military history. They finally discovered it in the late 1880s, but it took three events in 1887 and 1888 to show them how they might overcome the efforts to relegate them to the shadows of history.

In early 1887, the veterans of the Philadelphia Brigade that had defended the stone wall at the Angle on July 3, 1863, invited the survivors of Pickett's division—and only those Virginians—to return to Gettysburg that summer for a reunion on the twenty-fourth anniversary of the battle. Notwithstanding the condemnation of Virginia's more ardent Lost Cause partisans ringing in their ears, several hundred members of the new Pickett's Division Association went to Pennsylvania. Newspapers across the nation covered the event and heralded the meeting as solid evidence of the dawning of a new era of sectional reconciliation. Pickett's men became models to be emulated.[27]

Longstreet did not join them there in 1887, but he shared their commitment to national reunion and used this bond to strengthen his ties to his old command. When he came to Gettysburg in 1888 for the silver anniversary ceremonies, he found only a small contingent of Pickett's men attending, because many former Confederates had been put off by organizers' plans to make it a Northern—and not a national—affair. Still, Longstreet drew the lion's share of attention as he made the rounds of the veterans' camps with Union general Daniel Sickles, another Gettysburg apostate. Longstreet took every opportunity to heap praise on Pickett's division. He spoke to one gathering of Union veterans of the "gallant Pickett at the head of my own old division," made up of "troops whose half-concealed smiles expressed pleasure in their opportunity [to] fill the measure of a soldier's pride." They had done their job "with that confidence that commands success where it is possible." Longstreet grew quiet only when he drew near the field of the charge itself, and several reporters commented upon his silence, his grim visage, and his contemplative mood.[28]

He tried to avoid comment about his ongoing clashes with fellow Southerners over the truth of history, suggesting instead that more and more former Confederates would come to Gettysburg in the true spirit of reunion as Pickett's men had come the year before. At one point, a man hollered from the crowd to ask if Jubal Early would be among the returnees. Longstreet "stoked his side whiskers thoughtfully as a smile appeared at the corners of his mouth. Finally he said: 'I don't think Early will come.'" When somebody asked why, Longstreet said, "Early might think the people of Chambersburg might not care to see him," and he wondered aloud if "Early's experience in Pennsylvania might weigh heavily on his conscience." But mostly he spoke of Pickett's men, and with words of profuse praise built a strong foundation for a new relationship with his Virginia veterans.[29]

Perhaps one more event in 1888 showed Pickett's men where their true loyalties must lie. That October the Pickett's Division Association planned to unveil a monument over their late commander's grave at Hollywood Cemetery. Democratic governor and former Confederate general Fitzhugh Lee declined an invitation to speak at the ceremony, which was timed to coincide with Veterans Day at the annual Virginia Exposition. (Curiously enough, Lee quickly accepted a speaking invitation for the very next day of that gathering—Democratic Party Day.)[30] Former general Eppa Hunton, Garnett's successor after Gettysburg and a rare prominent Democrat among Pickett's senior officers, also turned down his old comrades. One of Pickett's former staff officers finally accepted the charge. When organizers sent out invitations to march in the procession to the cemetery, many Virginia Confederate veteran groups from Richmond and the Tidewater accepted, but others, such as the Pegram Artillery Battalion Association—an organization comprising mostly Third Corps veterans—refused to send delegations. Moreover, other former Confederates announced their refusal to attend as a sign of protest against the decision of the Pickett's Division Association to allow former Union soldiers of the Philip Kearny GAR post of Richmond and the men of the Philadelphia Brigade to participate in the event. The unveiling took place with great ceremony, but only a slice of the Virginia Confederate veteran community attended.[31]

Pickett's men found in these reunion ceremonies and monument dedications the confidence they needed to acknowledge more openly their loyalty to Longstreet, and the general reciprocated. By 1890, Longstreet had agreed to return to Richmond for the dedication of Robert E. Lee's statue on Monument Avenue. Although the Washington Artillery of Louisiana served as his official hosts, the general took great pleasure in the adulation of all his old command. Longstreet's former chief of staff Moxley Sorrel wrote to Thomas J. Goree, who also had served the general well, to describe

Maj. Gen. George Edward
Pickett. Courtesy of the
Library of Congress.

a photograph taken at a First Corps dinner after the dedication, a snapshot that included "Longstreet, [Joseph B.] Kershaw, [Charles] Field, Alexander, [Osmun] Latrobe, [Cullen] Barksdale, some Washington artillery men, and several Virginians." Sorrel reported with satisfaction that in the procession Longstreet "received a splendid and well deserved ovation from the old soldiers." Longstreet himself took pleasure in recounting how "my carriage attracted more attention, I suppose, than was expected," while his critics Fitzhugh Lee and John B. Gordon were "but little noticed by the troops in line."[32]

In the early 1890s, Pickett's men began to speak with louder voices. More important, they began to make an impact on the writing of Confederate history. Pickett's former staff officers led the way, and LaSalle Corbell Pickett, the general's widow, also responded early and positively to Longstreet's overtures of friendship. They more than anyone else understood the depths of the personal ties that had bound the two men for decades. They knew that the pair had served in the same regiment in Mexico, and that when Lieutenant Longstreet had fallen wounded while bearing forward the Stars and Stripes, Lieutenant Pickett had caught it and carried it over the enemy breastworks. They knew that when Longstreet had lost several children to scarlet fever early in 1862, Pickett had made the funeral arrangements to spare the bereaved parents that burden. Finally, they agreed that the time had come to cast off the protective mantle of silence with which they had shielded Old Pete and replace it with an open defense of his leadership at Gettysburg and elsewhere.[33]

Longstreet no doubt welcomed their support. As he wrote his former commissary chief Raphael Moses in 1891, "My arm is paralyzed; my voice that once could be heard all along the lines is gone. I can scarcely speak above a whisper; my hearing is very much impaired." Yet, added Longstreet, "I have some misrepresentations of my battles that I wish to correct, so as to have my record correct before I die."[34]

Pickett's men initially used the avenues with which they had become most familiar. They went directly to Northern audiences, authors, and literary outlets. One early success came in 1892, when Northern historian J. H. Stine reprinted letters from several of Pickett's staff and senior regimental officers in his *History of the Army of the Potomac*. As Stine wrote to former Capt. Robert A. Bright, "Pickett's staff is mentioned prominently." Although letters from Bright, fellow staff officer Capt. W. Stuart Symington, and Col. William R. Aylett of the 53d Virginia seem to have been intended to correct Stine's slight misperceptions about the organization of Pickett's attacking force on July 3, none of the accounts pictured a reluctant or despondent Longstreet. Naming his corps commander specifically, Bright portrayed an officer entirely involved in the proper execution of his duties. Sent by Pickett to inform Longstreet that the Virginians needed immediate reinforcement, he easily located Old Pete, met no difficulty obtaining a positive response to Pickett's request, and lodged no criticism against him. James Crocker, former adjutant of the 9th Virginia, restated strongly that which Pickett's men always believed: their attack was repulsed only when the "North Carolina troops broke and left the line of Garnett and Kemper unsupported on the left."[35]

Throughout the 1890s, the bond between Pickett's men and Longstreet strengthened. Old Pete contacted Charles Pickett, the general's brother and former adjutant, for assistance in writing his memoirs. Longstreet acknowledged that "the Pickett charge was the crowning point of Gettysburg & Gettysburg of the war—so regarded at least," and he wanted George Pickett's original report of the July 3 action. As Longstreet recalled it, Pickett had criticized "the lot assigned him" and Lee had returned it to him with orders to revise it and limit his comments to losses only. "Pickett's report was not so strong against the attack as mine before the attack was made," Longstreet commented, "but his was made in writing."[36] As part of Pickett's chain of command, Longstreet knew its contents. If he sought it now from the general's own brother, clearly he remembered that Pickett had not blamed him for any wrongdoing. Charles Pickett likely would have been glad to produce it, but he doubted the document still existed. As he explained to another correspondent, most of the general's wartime papers had been destroyed when Richmond burned or when the division's head-quarters wagons were captured on the road to Appomattox.[37]

As a show of good faith, however, Charles Pickett encouraged the rest of his brother's staff to help Longstreet as much as they could. The more information Longstreet could gather the more he might learn, wrote Charles Pickett, for after all, "each one sees the shield from his point of view." All of Pickett's surviving staff officers who served with him at Gettysburg agreed to cooperate. Captain Bright, along with fellow captains Symington and Edward R. Baird, agreed that Old Pete had conducted himself on July 3 in ways appropriate to his rank and position. Bright recalled Longstreet's genuine concern for Pickett's flanks, citing his frequent question, "Where are the men who were on your left?"—Pettigrew's and Trimble's men. At one point or another, Pickett had sent Bright, Symington, and Baird to hurry Wilcox and Lang onto the field, but all recalled that they went on that mission armed with Longstreet's specific authority. They blamed the defeat on the same troops Pickett's men always blamed, and as Symington recalled it, the cowardly supports that ran came from North Carolina. "I say North Carolina because when I carried one of their flags trying to get them to rally, the few who did stand said they were North Carolinians. I finally tore the flag off the staff & later carried it to Longstreet's headquarters," an unlikely action if Bright had held his corps commander responsible for the destruction of Pickett's division.[38]

Longstreet repaid Pickett's Virginians for their kindness and their loyalty. In *From Manassas to Appomattox*, he continued to blame Lee for not heeding his warnings against the July 3 charge, noting that the great chieftain "was impatient of listening, and tired of talking, and nothing was left but to proceed." But for Pickett's men, he had nothing but praise. He recalled the "elastic springing step" of the men of the Virginia division, credited Pickett himself for his wisdom in pulling back his troops when their line was flanked, and remembered "no indication of panic among them. The broken files marched back in steady step. The effort was nobly made, and failed from blows that could not be fended." It almost seems as if Longstreet finally had come to agree with Pickett, who, years before, in one of his two recorded comments about the failure of his charge, had said, "I believe the Yankee army had something to do with it." (The other comment, which won Pickett the further enmity of many diehard Lee partisans, was reported long after the war by John Mosby. The former Confederate partisan leader alleged that after accompanying him to see their former chieftain in 1870, Pickett cried out that Lee "had my division massacred at Gettysburg.")[39]

Longstreet and his Virginia friends quickly formed a mutual admiration society. Just as Longstreet saluted the gallantry of Pickett and his Virginians, Sallie Pickett, the general's widow, breathed new life into Old Pete's reputation. In her own book *Pickett and His Men*, for which Longstreet wrote an introduction, she did not suggest that Old Pete's reluctance to give the order to charge reflected poorly on either his generalship or his character. For Sallie, that single moment more than any other consummated the general's sense of military professionalism. She believed that Longstreet may have looked at Pickett with "an expression which seldom comes to any face. In that solemn silence memories of the long friendship may have flooded his soul." But then, she noted, Old Pete did his duty and personally gave the order to advance. Sallie cherished a note allegedly written to her by Longstreet in which he admitted that he could not speak the order and had only nodded in assent to Pickett's request to move forward: "As I watched him, gallant and fearless as any knight of old, riding to certain doom, I said a prayer for his safety and made a vow to the Holy Father that my friendship for him, poor as it is, should be your inheritance."

If Jubal Early had not already been dead for five years when Sallie published these lines, such words might have killed him. At the very least, he would have scowled to read that Sallie did not blame the failure of the great charge on James Longstreet but on the absence of close artillery support, promised and then not delivered. In a pointed attack on army artillery chief William Nelson Pendleton, one of the most stalwart of Lee's partisans and one of the first to attack Longstreet for his performance at Gettysburg, she bluntly asked, "Where were the guns?"[40]

It took until the end of the century for Pickett's men finally to rediscover their voices. In doing so, they accomplished two things. First and foremost, they secured for themselves and their posterity a special place in American history that shed glory on their supreme courage under fire at the highwater mark of the rebellion at Gettysburg. They also found ways to carve out an honored place for James Longstreet in the stories that they told. Some of these changes could not take place until nearly all of Virginia's most virulent Lost Cause advocates had died or retired from public life. For other former Confederates, it took time to accept the reality that the cause of national reunion—and not the Lost Cause—had captured the national imagination.

Perhaps the most startling change, beginning in the mid-1890s, came when new editors of the *Southern Historical Society Papers* opened their pages to the memoirs of Pickett's men, accounts of their great charge, and effusive belated eulogies to slain regimental and brigade commanders. Pickett's men proceeded carefully but purposefully to take full advantage of their new opportunities. They saluted their own military prowess and mourned their dead, as they always had done. But they now took care to praise Lee as fulsomely as the general's partisans had always wanted them to do. As Col. Joseph C. Mayo of the 3d Virginia wrote, "The commanding general had assigned our division the post of honor that day. He was a Virginian; so were they." When Lee rode along their lines, he seemed "a very anointed king of command, posing for the chisel of a Phidias, and looking on him we knew that the army was safe."[41]

Pickett's veterans stopped reminding readers that Lee had accepted responsibility for the charge and its repulse, and more than ever they pointed the finger of blame at Pettigrew, Trimble, and sometimes Wilcox and Lang. As Captain Baird told an audience of United Daughters of the Confederacy at Tappahannock, Virginia, "Personally I know that some troops on our left gave way for I was sent with Captain Symington of Pickett's staff to rally them." Captain Bright praised the memory of Col. James K. Marshall of the 52d North Carolina, who pressed on after taking a serious wound. But even as he honored the one, Bright damned the many, asserting that if all the men on Pickett's left had followed Marshall's example, "history would have been written another way."[42]

Through such memoirs, Pickett's staff officers repeatedly made clear that they had not blamed Longstreet in 1863 for what had happened to the Virginia division, and they did not do so now. Captain Bright, in his wonderful account of the charge published in the *Southern Historical Society Papers* in 1904, expressed this sentiment most unequivocally. His introductory comments explicitly expressed regret that he had been unable to publish his paper before the death in January of that year of "my corps commander, the brave General Longstreet." Other old friends also stated their views in the public press. Moxley Sorrel, who remained critical of his chief's performance on July 2, acknowledged that while Old Pete did not approve of the plans for the July 3 charge, "his soldierly eye watched every feature of it. He neglected nothing that could help it and his anxiety for Pickett and the men was very apparent."[43]

Sallie Pickett sealed the bond. As the golden anniversary of the battle drew near, she penned a dreadfully romantic novel, *The Bugles of Gettysburg*, and a number of short stories. For the new women's magazine *Cosmopolitan* she serialized the Pickett family's wartime experiences and glorified her husband's closest friends, including Ulysses S. Grant and even Abraham Lincoln. But she saved some of her most unrestrained prose for James Longstreet. In *The Heart of a Soldier*, presented to the public as a compilation of George Pickett's wartime letters to Sallie—although historians now tend to agree that Sallie was their true author—James Longstreet appears strong, if troubled, on July 3. When Pickett rode to "Old Peter" for orders, he found him "like a great lion at bay. I have never seen him so grave and troubled." Although Longstreet could not utter the words to advance, Pickett had understood clearly the meaning of his nod and turned to lead his men forward. He suddenly had turned around, however, and written on the envelope bearing this letter, "If Old Peter's nod means death then good-by and God bless you, little one." Pickett then handed it over to "the dear old chief" with the request that it be mailed to Sallie if he fell in the upcoming battle. Even as Sallie's fabricated letters revealed Longstreet's human frailties, they never allowed her soldier to render his commander anything less than full honors due a respected superior.[44]

Indeed, the Virginia widow made much of the close personal relationship the two men had shared. Her sons and grandsons stood for photographs with Longstreet's descendants at the golden anniversary celebrations at Gettysburg.[45] Journalists fawned over them, and one correspondent noted with satisfaction that when a band struck up the national anthem, "the Picketts, the Longstreets, the daughter of General [A. P.] Hill, the Meades," and long rows of veterans of both armies "became silent, rose to their feet, and uncovered."[46]

Sallie grew especially fond of telling about a time a few months after Gettysburg when Pickett expressed a desire for a furlough to marry her. Longstreet had told him that he could not grant leaves just then "but added with the twinkle in his eye which those who knew him so well remember: 'I might detail you for special duty, and you could, of course, stop off and get married if you wanted to.'"[47] Few Virginians would have dared to endow Old Pete with such kindness just a few years earlier.

Sallie succeeded so well in softening Longstreet's image that she outdid the general's own widow. As a guest of the state of Pennsylvania, Helen Dortch Longstreet went to Gettysburg as a *New York Times* special correspondent at the golden anniversary ceremonies. As combative as Old Pete himself when responding to a slight against his good name, she managed to strike a discordant note during the reunion by complaining that the battle's most "famed charge was Longstreet's." Citing Dan Sickles's comment that "it is improper to call it Pickett's charge," because Lee had named Old Pete as its tactical commander, she won few fans among the Virginians: she diminished the glory of their sacrifice by turning them into hapless victims of a tragic blunder her husband had tried to stop. She wrote of gazing out over the field of the charge and sharing her own soldier's feelings of "dumb agony as he looked upon the marching columns and knew that it was their death march."[48] Sallie had also written something like this about

Longstreet, but she had manipulated Old Pete's moments of grief as emotional expressions that ennobled him.

How can this literary war shed light on James Longstreet on July 3 at Gettysburg? Perhaps the most important lesson is that students of the 1863 Pennsylvania campaign must treat traditional sources about Longstreet, Pickett, and the great charge with greater care and considerable skepticism. It remains important to follow the chain of evidence. The letters and diaries of Pickett's survivors explain only what happened within the writer's limited view. They only rarely provide insights about the command level that would carry the authority to challenge testimony from staff officers close to the generals. But collectively, they do reveal one important fact: in the search for scapegoats to blame for an unexpected defeat, James Longstreet did not figure prominently in the Army of Northern Virginia's post-battle gossip.

Reporters wove together the disconnected threads of dozens of soldiers' stories. The coverage in Southern newspapers in July 1863 included very little negative commentary on the performance of James Longstreet at Gettysburg. The newspapers certainly contain no accusations of culpability for the failure of the great charge of July 3.

The years immediately following Lee's death in 1870 marked a turning point in Gettysburg historiography. Almost anything written about the battle after the Southern Historical Society's postwar literary assault on James Longstreet in the late 1870s must be judged in light of the stated intentions of some of its members—men who tried to rewrite history in ways that filled their own needs for a Gettysburg scapegoat. It is important not to ignore the potential damage to historical truth the Southern Historical Society's efforts could cause. For example, when Longstreet tried to defend himself, Walter Taylor wrote, "From the course pursued by General Longstreet, I now feel he should be handled with ungloved hands."[49] The tampering with the record by men such as Taylor still reveals itself in Gettysburg battle studies today, and over the years it has thickened the fog of war the military historian seeks to lift.

Pickett's men have helped to make it possible to see James Longstreet the soldier rather than James Longstreet the Confederate Judas. But they could not deliver him completely from the accusations of his harshest critics. Most of Pickett's men were not well placed to controvert the Lee cult's accusations against their old corps commander. The regimental colonel and the color bearer could not speak with the same authority on command issues as could the generals or the staff officers who served at the side of the great Confederate chieftain.

Because Lee's closest associates could not bring themselves to admit it, that left only Longstreet himself to make clear that on July 3, 1863, he played the same role he had performed on many previous battlefields. He was Lee's second in command. As Lee's most experienced and most trusted subordinate, one who had offered advice on other fields, he performed his duties on July 3 as faithfully as he always had. Douglas Southall Freeman erred when in his assessment of Second Manassas he wrote, "The seeds of much of the disaster Gettysburg were sown . . . when Lee yielded to Longstreet and Longstreet discovered that he would." Lee had not always accepted Longstreet's advice, but it is important to note that he always listened to it. If Longstreet had failed to voice his opposition to Lee's plan, he would have failed his general. Lee himself would not have expected Old Pete to hold back. Thus, Longstreet was just doing his job when he made his famous comment: "I have been a soldier all my life. I have been with soldiers engaged in fights by couples, by squads, companies, regiments, divisions, and armies, and should know, as well as any one, what soldiers can do. It is my opinion that no fifteen thousand men ever arrayed for battle can take that position."[50] His Virginia critics served neither Longstreet nor history well when they willfully turned Old Pete's legitimate professional opinion into a form of insubordination, and Pickett's men could say little to defend him from such slander.

Those who accused Old Pete of purposely entering the fight with too small a force failed to acknowledge that Lee himself already had made many decisions about the upcoming assault. Lee designated the point of attack. Lee selected the assault troops, and he chose to include units from both Longstreet's First Corps and A. P. Hill's Third Corps. Lee decided upon a pre-assault artillery bombardment. But when Lee turned over the execution of the plan to Longstreet, he had not done all he could or should have done to increase the likelihood of victory. Corps staffs—and that of Hill's Third Corps operated as such for the first time in this battle—were not planning staffs as they are in modern armies. Longstreet explained quite rightly that Lee should have provided "the benefit of his presence and his assistance in getting the troops up, placing them, and arranging the batteries; but he gave no orders or suggestions after his early designation of the point for which the column should march."[51] Pickett's men could not speak with sufficient authority to sustain Longstreet's assertions on these points either.

In the end, despite their best efforts to defend their corps commander, Pickett's men never found their fullest voice. Their foes had picked their fight carefully, choosing to attack James Longstreet in ways his own men could not refute. His critics did not attack his physical courage that day; too many eyewitnesses in Pickett's ranks could have contested that notion. His critics did not accuse him of failing to take specific actions that would have enhanced the likelihood of victory; too many saw Longstreet ride the lines and check artillery deployments and the like. His critics only charged him with those things that could not be challenged authoritatively by anybody—especially by his own soldiers who remained most devoted to him. Longstreet once wrote that many Southerners considered Lee's only fault as a general to be "his tender generous heart." But, he noted, "a heart in the right place looks more to the cause intrusted to its care than for hidden ways by which to shift the responsibilities to the shoulders of those whose lives hang upon his word."[52] Old Pete believed that Lee had not personally blamed him for what happened at Gettysburg; all he could do is hope his chieftain's most ardent partisans, in time, would also come to that conclusion. Longstreet worried about how history would remember him. But even if Pickett's men could not make their voices heard loudly enough to matter when he needed them the most, he never had to worry about where he stood in the eyes of his soldiers who had stormed Cemetery Ridge at his order. Pickett's Virginians never broke faith with Old Pete, and in time they proved it.

"Every Map of the Field Cries Out about It"

The Failure of Confederate Artillery at Pickett's Charge

Peter S. Carmichael

ROBERT E. LEE'S TACTICAL MASTERPIECE AT CHANCELLORSVILLE electrified the Army of Northern Virginia. The rank and file boasted of their invincibility, proclaimed their leader unbeatable, and assured the nation that final victory lay within reach. No branch of the army exhibited more confidence before Gettysburg than Lee's "long arm." Confederate gunners helped consummate victory at Chancellorsville when they overwhelmed Federal batteries at Fairview, shattering the backbone of Joseph Hooker's defense on May 3. Their remarkable performance marked the emergence of Lee's cannoneers. Long considered inferior to their counterparts in the Army of the Potomac, Southern artillerists pointed to Chancellorsville as irrefutable proof that they could out-duel their adversary. They attributed their success to a newly implemented battalion system that effectively concentrated firepower. "The most noteworthy feature of the Battle was the efficiency of our Artillery," observed a Confederate cannoneer after Chancellorsville. "Owing to the issue of good guns replacing bad & the organization into Battalions we massed it & produced effects unknown [and] unhoped before."[1]

Success at Chancellorsville led Lee's cannoneers to conclude mistakenly that organizational problems, a persistent weakness in the long arm, had been solved with the battalion system. Gettysburg shattered this illusion. The massive, but largely ineffective, cannonade preceding Pickett's Charge failed because of a technical issue—a convoluted chain of command that did not encourage cooperation among the chiefs of corps artillery and army headquarters.[2] Moreover, the improved battalion system could not overcome the incompetence of William Nelson Pendleton, the army's nominal chief of artillery. His battlefield failures had become notorious by the time of Gettysburg, earning him the nickname "Old Mother Pendleton." He clearly lacked the skill to get the most out of Lee's ordnance on July 3. Only the army's commanding general could have forged a shared purpose among his cannoneers while coordinating the efforts of the artillery and infantry; however, Lee did not provide such leadership on Gettysburg's final day. Although he believed the infantry's success ultimately hinged on the cannonade's effectiveness, Lee paid little attention to his artillery at Gettysburg. He gave too much latitude to Pendleton, who neither ensured cooperation among his chiefs of corps artillery nor provided proper support for the infantry once the attack began.

On paper Pendleton possessed the necessary credentials to become a successful chief of artillery. He had graduated fifth in the West Point class of 1830, receiving a brevet second lieutenant's commission in the 4th Regiment of Artillery. He subsequently left the army to become an ordained Episcopal priest.[3] When Virginia seceded from the Union he returned to the military, serving as captain of the famous Rockbridge Artillery. Controversy immediately followed. After First Manassas, rumors alleged that he had cowered on the ground instead of personally leading his battery.[4] Doubts about Pendleton's leadership increased during the Seven Days battles, when he seemingly disappeared with the Reserve Artillery at Malvern Hill. At Second Fredericksburg subordinates criticized his tactical judgment, and Pendleton vainly demanded a court of inquiry from Lee. None of these battlefield mishaps sparked more controversy than the collapse of the Confederate rear guard near Shepherdstown, Virginia, during Lee's retreat from Antietam. Lee had assigned Pendleton the critical task of defending Boteler's Ford while the rest of the army withdrew to Virginia. A small Union force crossed the river, stormed the Confederate position, and nearly captured thirty-three guns of the Reserve Artillery.[5]

Pendleton's frequent mishaps, well known and documented throughout the army, caused many to wonder why Lee did not banish the artillerist to a less important theater. Confederate gunner John H. Chamberlayne voiced the concerns of his comrades when he described Pendleton as "Lee's weakness." The artillery chief was, added Chamberlayne, "like the elephant, we have him & we don't know what on earth to do with him, and it costs a devil of a sight to feed him."[6] Lee recognized Pendleton's deficiencies, but refused to assign him to a less critical post. Pendleton probably avoided a

Brig. Gen. William Nelson
Pendleton. From *Battles
and Leaders of the Civil
War* 3:329.

humiliating transfer largely because of his close ties with Jefferson Davis
and Lee's desire to protect the feelings of an old friend. Although the commanding general never took the bold step of removing Pendleton, he tried
to restrict his duties to bureaucratic matters.[7] He rarely gave Pendleton
meaningful control of the artillery in battle. Without centralized leadership from above, Lee's artillery corps repeatedly struggled to operate as
a cohesive force on the battlefield, proving unable to focus on a single
purpose.

As an administrator, Pendleton figured prominently in the artillery's
reorganization that followed Antietam and Fredericksburg, overseeing
reforms that greatly enhanced the effectiveness of Lee's ordnance. During
the winter of 1862–1863 Pendleton consulted with Col. Stapleton Crutchfield and Col. Edward Porter Alexander before implementing a plan that
organized batteries into independent battalions, a system that had been
partially formulated in the autumn of 1862. The old system assigned an
individual battery to a brigade, giving infantry officers virtually unlimited
control over the placement of guns in battle. Because brigade commanders
were possessive of their batteries, artillery officers could not work as an
independent arm without tremendous difficulty. Overall, the old organiza-

tion made it nearly impossible for the artillery of the Army of Northern Virginia to apply its full weight against the enemy. Pendleton offered a partial remedy by assigning batteries to battalions of about sixteen guns. Instead of answering to a brigadier general of infantry, the officer in charge of the battalion would follow the instructions of his corps chief of artillery. Batteries could be detached systematically, allowing Lee's army to concentrate its artillery fire without brigade and division commanders working at cross-purposes with artillery officers.[8]

The unveiling of the battalion system at Chancellorsville produced remarkable results. Porter Alexander concentrated more than forty guns at Hazel Grove, silencing Hooker's artillery at Fairview and giving Lee's cannoneers a rare counterbattery victory over the Army of the Potomac. But success masked a serious flaw in the new organization: the chief of artillery for each corps could receive conflicting orders from his corps commander and from Pendleton. Moreover, the battalion system did not foster communication and cooperative action among artillery officers of different corps.[9]

Battalion commanders of different corps usually did not have to worry about coordinating their fire, but the Union "fishhook" line at Gettysburg presented a unique opportunity for such collaboration. Before Pickett's Charge, a concentrated deployment of Second Corps guns north of Cemetery Hill could have raked the Union line along Cemetery Ridge while the batteries in the First and Third Corps struck Meade's front. This would have produced a crossfire that might have damaged, if not crippled, the Union center. A significant reduction in Union ordnance would have enabled Confederate units to reach Cemetery Ridge with fewer casualties and with their formations intact.

Instead of working in unison before Pickett's Charge, the artillery chiefs of each corps acted independently. A lack of coordination contributed to the dilution of Confederate firepower. Even the massing of some 160 Confederate guns against Cemetery Ridge failed to generate a concentrated fire. When a handful of Southern and Northern officers gathered informally at Appomattox, Union artillerist Henry J. Hunt initiated a discussion about Gettysburg. He told Confederate staff officer Armistead L. Long that the "fire, instead of being concentrated on the point of attack, as it ought to have been, and as I expected it would be, was scattered over the field." Long, who had served under Hunt in a mounted battery before the war, seemed amused by the memory, replying, "When the fire became so scattered, [I] wondered what you would think about it!"[10]

Operating on an exterior line largely caused this dispersal of Confederate artillery fire. Most of Lee's batteries that participated in the July 3 bombardment occupied the arc of an enveloping line; in other words, they fired along a straight line toward Cemetery Ridge. Because of the shallowness of the Union target, Southern cannoneers enjoyed little room for error. A Confederate shell needed to explode directly over the crest of the ridge, above the main Union line, to be effective. Furthermore, the top of the ridge resembled a narrow spinal column; it did not allow for dense formations. A broad, flat plateau atop Cemetery Ridge would have significantly increased Confederate chances of striking their target.[11]

Precision firing was impossible in the black-powder era. Guns recoiled after every shot. They needed to be repositioned and realigned, which disrupted aim. Enemy fire and a blinding smoke impeded cannoneers from finding the correct range. Confederate artillerists also contended with unreliable fuses. Much of the Southern ordnance exploded prematurely or did not detonate at all.[12] In this instance the rounds either sailed harmlessly over Meade's lines or fell short, buried in the face of Cemetery Ridge. An artillery officer in the Union Fifth Corps reported that the enemy's fire "was by no means as effective as it should have been, nine-tenths of their shot passing over our men. Officers tell me that the case and pieces of shell came down like hail, so high over their head did they burst."[13]

Although Pendleton lacked direct line authority to move individual battalions on the battlefield, he had the power and responsibility to define the artillery's role in the overall tactical scheme. As chief of artillery, he surveyed the entire field and should have seen the best opportunities to employ Lee's ordnance. Before Pickett's Charge the artillery commanders of each corps did not have the time to examine each other's ground for possible cooperative action, nor was it their duty. Only Pendleton could have orchestrated a combined artillery attack. Porter Alexander blamed Pendleton for not using more Second Corps guns north of Cemetery Hill to enfilade the Union center. "The great criticism which I have to make on the artillery operations of the day [July 3]," observed Alexander, "is upon the inaction of the artillery of Ewell's Corps." The temporary commander of First Corps artillery, Alexander claimed that he only knew "his own ground" and "had but the vaguest notion of where Ewell's corps was. And Ewell's chief doubtless had as vague ideas of my situation & necessities." "Gen. Lee's chief [Pendleton] should have known," Alexander averred, "& given every possible energy to improve the rare & great chance to the very utmost." With the luxury of hindsight, Alexander concluded after the war that the failure to use Ewell's batteries "was a serious loss. Every map of the field cries out about it."[14]

Only one of the five battalions in the Second Corps fired at the shank of the fishhook, achieving a crossfire with the Southern guns on Seminary Ridge. Ewell's enfilading fire lasted briefly, and no more than a few dozen shots were expended, but they achieved spectacular results. Meade's line quivered as Confederate rounds slammed into the flanks of the Union regiments and batteries on Cemetery Hill. Gen. Oliver O. Howard reported that "shells burst in the air, in the ground to the right and left, killing horses, exploding caissons, overturning tombstones, and smashing fences. There was no place for safety. In one regiment 27 were killed and wounded by one shell." The effect of Ewell's guns on Cemetery Hill also impressed the chief of Eleventh Corps artillery, who noted that "they caught us square in flank. . . . They raked the whole line of batteries, killed and wounded the men and horses, and blew up the caissons rapidly." If fewer than fifty rounds inflicted such damage, it is no wonder that Alexander raved about the possibilities of concentrating Ewell's full ordnance against Cemetery Ridge.[15]

Responsibility for the failure to enfilade Meade's line must rest primarily with Pendleton, who lacked the vision to employ Ewell's ordnance effectively. Although Lee recognized Pendleton's liabilities as a combat officer, he neither intervened in his subordinate's affairs nor selected another officer to advise him informally on the overall use of artillery. Lee should have compensated for Pendleton, especially in light of his belief that proper support from the long arm would pave the way for Pickett's and Pettigrew's attacking soldiers. Lee determined that Longstreet's guns, from their advanced position at the Peach Orchard, would render the Union line helpless. "A careful examination was made of the ground secured by Longstreet," he wrote in his official report, "and his batteries placed in positions, which, it was believed would enable them to silence those of the enemy." Once Meade's artillery was dismantled and Confederate infantry moved forward, Lee expected, Longstreet's and A. P. Hill's guns would follow in support. "The batteries were directed to be pushed forward as the infantry progressed," the commanding general asserted, "protect their flanks, and support their attacks closely."[16]

For Confederate artillery to destroy Union batteries on Cemetery Ridge and then follow Pickett and Pettigrew's infantry required a strong guiding hand from above. Lee, however, seemed reluctant to assert himself on July 3. He left complicated questions of coordination to his subordinates without facilitating joint action between two different arms of service and two different corps.[17] From dawn until the start of the attack, some nine hours, Lee and his staff observed the dispositions. The commanding general must have had detailed information regarding every brigade and battalion. He should have noticed that Longstreet's guns occupied unfavorable ground. From the Peach Orchard the terrain generally sloped toward the

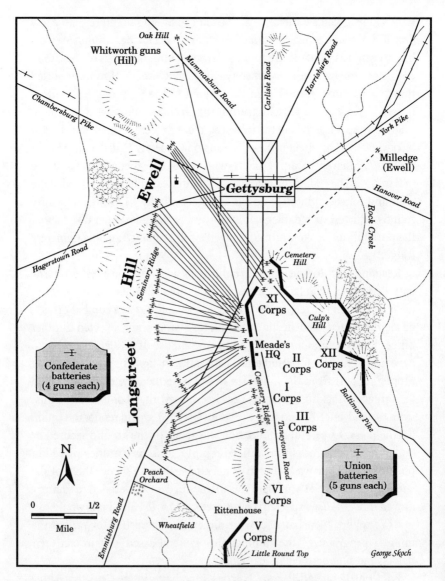

The following labels appear on the map:

Oak Hill
Whitworth guns (Hill)
Mummasburg Road
Carlisle Road
Harrisburg Road
Chambersburg Pike
York Pike
Ewell
Milledge (Ewell)
Gettysburg
Hanover Road
Rock Creek
Hagerstown Road
Seminary Ridge
Hill
Cemetery Hill
Confederate batteries (4 guns each)
Longstreet
XI Corps
Culp's Hill
Meade's HQ
II Corps
XII Corps
Cemetery Ridge
I Corps
Taneytown Road
III Corps
Baltimore Pike
N
Peach Orchard
Union batteries (5 guns each)
VI Corps
0   1/2
Mile
Emmitsburg Road
Wheatfield
Rittenhouse
V Corps
Little Round Top
George Skoch

The Confederate Cannonade That Preceded Pickett's Charge

Federals, exposing cannoneers, caissons, and horses to enemy fire. Although Lee roamed the field freely, he did not ensure that infantry and artillery officers in the First and Third corps worked together. Lee's disconnectedness from the battlefield puzzled Alexander, who wrote in retrospect: "It must be remembered that the preparations for this charge were made deliberately, & under the observation of Gen. Lee himself, & of all of his staff." Alexander thought "if there was one thing they might be sup-

Col. Edward Porter
Alexander. From
Miller's *Photographic History*
5:61.

posed to take an interest in, it would be in seeing that the troops which were
to support the charge were in position to do it." Longstreet echoed Alexander's concerns, criticizing Lee for not giving the "benefit of his presence
and his assistance in getting the troops up, posting them, and arranging the
batteries; . . . he gave no orders or suggestions after his early designation of
the point for which the column should march."[18]

Lee made matters worse by issuing vague instructions to his corps commanders and their respective artillery chiefs. On the night of July 2, Alexander learned that Longstreet would resume the attack with Pickett's division at daylight somewhere to the left of the Peach Orchard. But the exact
point was not designated. Alexander's orders the next morning also lacked
important specifics. He simply was "to post the artillery for an assault upon
the enemy's position." After arranging his guns, he learned "that it was to
be led by Pickett's division" and directed on Cemetery Ridge. He spent the
remainder of the morning "waiting for Pickett's division, and possibly
other movements of infantry." Longstreet had told Alexander to drive the
enemy off Cemetery Ridge and advance as many guns as possible to aid
the attack. Beyond that, headquarters had not defined Alexander's role in
the overall scheme of the assault. Isolation from the army's high command
forced Alexander to base his preparations on the rumor that "General Lee

had said that he was going to send every man he had upon the hill." "At any rate," Alexander concluded, "I assumed that the question of supports had been well considered, and that whatever was possible would be done."[19] Gen. R. Lindsay Walker, A. P. Hill's chief of artillery, did not leave a detailed account of July 3, but fragmentary evidence suggests that he had little communication with either Lee or Pendleton.[20]

Lee's orders to his artillerists were both vague and contradictory. They revealed a tension between the primary goals of breaking Union resistance on Cemetery Ridge and closely following Pickett's infantry advance. Lee and Pendleton must have realized that the magnitude of the artillery barrage would drain ammunition reserves. Yet if Walker and Alexander emptied their limber chests during the preliminary bombardment, they would be unable to advance with Pickett and Pettigrew, let alone cover the army's eventual retreat to Virginia (or whatever movement that might follow action on July 3). Neither Lee nor Pendleton advised Walker or Alexander on this matter, nor did they take precautions to prevent a waste of precious rounds. "Though no one cautioned me about it," Alexander wrote, "my own good sense made me appreciate that it would be very imprudent not to keep to the last extremity enough ammunition."[21]

A. P. Hill and Lindsay Walker failed to display the same good judgment. Confederate and Federal skirmishing around the Bliss barn during the morning of July 3 dragged more than sixty guns of the Third Corps into a pointless thirty-minute duel with Federal artillery. Longstreet's seventy-five guns remained quiet, under strict orders from Alexander, but Hill and Walker inexplicably permitted their cannoneers to burn their ammunition needlessly. Alexander could not believe that Hill had squandered powder on such a meaningless target, observing after the war, "I would not [have] let one of my guns fire a shot."[22]

Preparations for the charge became more muddled and confused without strong leadership from James Longstreet. Instead of energetically seeking to carry out Lee's orders on July 3, he transferred duties normally reserved for a corps commander to Alexander, a colonel of artillery. Before the bombardment commenced, Alexander had been instructed to gauge the effect of his fire and determine the optimal moment for Pickett to make the advance. Alexander decided that it would take some twenty or thirty minutes of firing before Pickett should advance. "I had no expectation whatever of seeing anything special happen in the enemy during the cannonade," the Georgian wrote, "either to make me lengthen or shorten this period." The enemy's superior weaponry, ammunition, and position should have challenged Alexander's confidence, but "the fact is that like all the rest of the army I believed that it would come out right, because Gen. Lee had planned it."[23]

Just before the bombardment commenced, a note from Longstreet tempered Alexander's optimism. In this dispatch the First Corps commander shifted the burden of the assault on Alexander, asking the artillerist to call off Pickett's advance if the Confederate cannonade did not drive off or demoralize the enemy. "That presented the whole business to me in a new light," Alexander admitted after the war. "It was no longer Gen. Lee's inspiration . . . , but my cold judgment to be founded on what I was going to see."[24]

When Longstreet's note arrived, artillerist John C. Haskell noticed that Alexander "seemed very much worried" as he read the communiqué. Alexander turned to Haskell and "expressed his disgust at having such a responsibility put on him and asked what I thought." Haskell agreed that Longstreet had acted inappropriately and suggested that Alexander "should reply to Longstreet that he had better come in and decide for himself."[25]

Alexander vainly tried to shift responsibility back to his superior. He realized that once the cannonade began, the resulting smoke would make it difficult to decide whether Meade's guns had been silenced—the critical factor in sending the infantry forward. The impasse between Longstreet and Alexander was broken when the artillerist considered that "Lee had originally planned" the attack and "half the day had been spent in preparation." Unwilling to cause a "loss of time by any indecision on my part," Alexander sent Longstreet a final reply: "General. When our artillery fire is at its best I shall order Gen. Pickett to charge." Overall, neither Lee nor Longstreet left his personal imprint on this assault, which faced nearly insurmountable odds and ranked among the most difficult in the history of the Army of Northern Virginia. The commanding general's nephew, Fitzhugh Lee, complained after the war: "[That] the responsibility and fate of a great battle should be passed over to a lieutenant colonel of artillery, however meritorious he might be, is, and always will be, a subject of grave comment."[26]

Any possibility of Alexander's extending his sphere of influence to Walker's guns ended when Longstreet required his artillerist to decide the timing of the infantry assault. Alexander consequently spent his time consulting with Pickett and Longstreet before the attack and never met with Walker. The only discussion of cooperative action occurred during an early morning conference in which Pendleton offered Alexander nine howitzers from the Third Corps. These guns, under Maj. Charles Richardson, lacked sufficient range to participate in the preliminary bombardment, and Walker told Pendleton that he had no use for them. When Pendleton asked Alexander if he could employ them, the Georgian "jumped at the idea, & thanked him & said, 'yes, I had the very place for them.'" Alexander decided to hold

Richardson's cannon out of the bombardment, keeping the guns "under cover & out of view, so that with fresh men, & uninjured horses, & full chests of ammunition, these nine light howitzers might follow Pickett's infantry in the charge." Alexander directed Richardson's batteries to a protective hollow behind some woods with the explicit orders to wait until ordered forward.[27]

Alexander had thus devised an ingenious scheme for supporting the assault with artillery, but for some reason he did not relate the details to Pendleton. The latter probably assumed that Alexander would station Richardson's guns along the firing line. Poor communication between the two men would ultimately ruin an intriguing possibility to provide close support for Pickett's infantry. Just before the bombardment, Alexander sent a staff officer to move Richardson's hidden cannon closer to the front lines, but neither the major nor his guns could be found. When the staff officer reported the guns missing, Alexander sternly said: "He [Richardson] would not dare to leave there without orders. You go again & find him & don't you come back without him." After another search, the staff officer again reported that he could not locate the pieces. Alexander subsequently discovered that Pendleton had removed at least four cannon; the remaining guns, Richardson admitted, were moved a short distance because of enemy fire. "God knows where he went to," Alexander complained, "but it was where he could not be found." Richardson's disobedience infuriated Alexander, who considered preferring charges. In a postwar letter, Alexander hinted at the difficulty of cooperating with artillery battalions outside his own corps: "I feel bitterly about that [loss of Richardson's guns] to this day. It was such a beautiful chance to handle Arty [artillery] & to show what it can do & I was only a fool not to have selected some of my own old battalion for it, being tempted to try this command as their guns were better adapted to close quarters."[28]

Not only had Pendleton interfered with Alexander's plan for Richardson's guns, but he also hindered the long arm by relocating Longstreet's reserve artillery train farther behind the lines. Although such a move might have been necessary because incoming enemy rounds posed an occasional threat, the added distance made it impossible to resupply efficiently. Just as he had failed to inform Alexander about moving Richardson's guns, so also did Pendleton overlook the necessity of telling his subordinates that their ordnance wagons had been relocated. Much confusion arose and time was wasted as men searched for their elusive wagons. Many of Alexander's gunners, who quickly burned their long-range shot and shell, could only watch the cannonade and the charge.[29] "One half hour before Pickett's Division was put in motion," reported the captain of the Fauquier Artillery, "almost all the artillery ammunition was exhausted along the line, and none could be obtained from the ordnance train in time to be of service." When Longstreet encountered a battalion commander who had nearly expended his ammunition, he asked "why orders to keep caissons filled had not been obeyed." The officer responded that "the caissons had been away nearly, three-quarters of an hour, and there was a rumor that General Pendleton had sent the reserve artillery ammunition more than a mile in rear of the field."[30]

Although Pendleton's misuse of the ordnance wagon severely undermined Confederate efforts, he should not bear responsibility for all the troubles with ammunition. Neither Longstreet nor Lee concerned himself with this vital issue, even though they had ordered one of the most massive cannonades of the entire war. Their subordinates had failed to inform them about the ammunition shortages, but the army commander and his senior lieutenant had the responsibility to check the ordnance levels themselves. Moreover, both officers knew that a wagon road connected the army to its arsenals and depots at Staunton, some two hundred miles to the south. The tenuousness of this supply line, lightly guarded, extending over treacherous ground, and vulnerable to enemy cavalry raids, exacerbated shortages in the artillery. If Longstreet had asked Alexander about the ammunition situation earlier in the morning of July 3, "he would," as historian Edwin B. Coddington has pointed out, "have found his best argument against Lee's plans for a grand charge." Not until Picket's men began their advance did Longstreet check supply levels. When Alexander explained that the fire wavered because ammunition was running low, Longstreet "spoke at once, & decidedly, 'Go & halt Pickett right where he is, & replenish your ammunition.'" Alexander bluntly replied, "We can't do that. We nearly emptied the trains last night. Even if we had it, it would take an hour or two, & meanwhile the enemy would recover from the pressure he is now under. Our only chance is to follow it up now—to strike while the iron is hot."[31]

In his official report on Gettysburg, Lee admitted that the artillery's problems with ammunition were "unknown to me," even after the protracted cannonade. He should have anticipated problems, considering that the army had been heavily engaged for two days. His negligence is especially difficult to understand because Lee had stated that Pickett's assault depended on a well sustained, closely supported artillery barrage. Overlooking such a vital component of the attack stands as Lee's most serious mistake on July 3. Meade, in contrast, inquired about his ammunition supply as soon as he arrived in Gettysburg. After the battle, Col. Eppa Hunton of Pickett's division explained that "our artillery did splendid service that day. . . . The efficiency was destroyed by want of ammunition."

A Virginia war correspondent offered a similar analysis, complaining that "just as Pickett was getting well under the enemy's fire our batteries ceased firing." Why the guns remained "silent as death," he observed, "is the inquiry that rises upon every lip." The quick exhaustion of ammunition, he concluded, "would seem to demand investigation."[32]

Ammunition depletion in the First Corps did not stop the resourceful Alexander from closely supporting Pickett's right flank. He advanced those of his guns that possessed a reserve of at least fifteen rounds; only eighteen of his seventy-five cannon met this criterion. As Alexander moved his detachment toward the Emmitsburg Pike, firing over the heads of the charging infantrymen, he saw George J. Stannard's Vermont brigade in front of the main enemy line, menacing the Confederate right flank. Alexander immediately wheeled some of his batteries at the Peach Orchard into action, delivering a destructive oblique fire. One of Alexander's cannoneers reported that the enemy "melted away promptly."[33]

While Alexander dispersed the Vermonters, a Union flanking party tore into Pettigrew's left flank. The Federals met little resistance, because Lindsay Walker's guns remained fixed on Seminary Ridge instead of trailing Pettigrew's infantry. Many of Walker's limbers had been nearly emptied during the early morning bombardment of the Bliss barn. This useless expenditure of ammunition came back to haunt the Confederates; Third Corps cannoneers had too few remaining rounds to move forward. Although the terrain probably limited Walker's possibilities for maneuvering, it appears that he did not even attempt a modest advance with his batteries. Walker's subordinate and battalion commander, Maj. William T. Poague, claimed that "not a word was said about following the infantry as they advanced to the attack."[34]

The machinery of Lee's long arm had malfunctioned badly on July 3. Poor communication among artillery chiefs and between them and army headquarters undermined collective action. Alexander, Longstreet, and Lee worked under the assumption that the infantry would advance in conjunction with artillery that would continue firing during the charge. For some unexplainable reason, A. P. Hill and Lindsay Walker never grasped the importance of this assignment. Keeping the Third Corps guns in a stationary position, Lee explained in his official report, largely caused the collapse of Pettigrew's men. Because Hill's artillery battalions did not provide sustained support, wrote Lee, "the enemy was enabled to throw a strong force of infantry against our left, already wavering under a concentrated fire of artillery from the ridge in front, and from Cemetery Hill, on the left."[35]

Many complicated and interconnected factors conspired against the Confederate bombardment that opened Pickett's Charge. At the most fundamental level, the chain of command did not encourage cooperation among artillery officers of various corps. This technical problem muted the firepower of Lee's long arm. Without strong direction from the army's high command, Ewell's Second Corps guns missed a magnificent opportunity to enfilade the Union line. Each corps artillery chief managed a well-defined section of the battlefield; as Lee's senior artillery officer, William Nelson Pendleton had the overall perspective and power to fit the pieces together and facilitate communication. But "Old Mother Pendleton" assumed a passive approach on July 3, doing little or nothing to apply broad pressure against the Federals. On the two occasions he did take decisive action, moving Richardson's guns and the First Corps ordnance wagons, the effects proved detrimental to the army. Regarding Pendleton's performance at Gettysburg, Thomas J. Goree of Longstreet's staff later wrote, "Although nominally *Chief of Artillery*, yet he was in the actual capacity of Ordnance Officer, and, as I believe, miles in the rear. I know that I did not see him on the *field* during the battle. It was a notorious fact and general[ly] remarked that he was almost entirely ignored by Genl. Lee, as Chief of Artillery, and the management of it given to the Corps Chiefs of Artillery."[36]

Lee bears responsibility for allowing a man so stupendously incompetent as Pendleton to rule the artillery. He might have compensated for his subordinate's shortcomings or sufficiently shielded him from the army. But he did neither. In fact, he seemed uninterested in his artillery at Gettysburg, failing even to check on the supply of ammunition available prior to the bombardment. This unconscionable oversight nearly doomed the charge. He further distanced himself from the battlefield when he gave Longstreet too much control over the preparations for Pickett's Charge. Complicating the situation, the First Corps commander behaved in a manner bordering on insubordination. Longstreet's trying to shift responsibility for the attack to Porter Alexander distracted the young Georgian from his primary responsibilities as an artillerist. But Lee was on the field. He had the authority to dictate affairs, ensuring that his subordinates executed his precise instructions for an attack that he must have considered one of the defining moments of his army. When Lee told the survivors of Pickett Charge that the failure of their effort was all his fault, he should have made a similar admission to his artillerists.

"I Do Not Believe That Pickett's Division Would Have Reached Our Line"

Henry J. Hunt and the Union Artillery on July 3, 1863

Gary M. Kross

HENRY JACKSON HUNT COMPILED A RECORD OF GREAT accomplishment as an artillerist in the United States Army. A gifted man widely known among his contemporaries as the leading authority on light artillery, he combined calmness under fire, a splendid eye for terrain, and mastery of the technical side of gunnery to achieve superior results on the battlefield.[1] Yet despite his unquestioned abilities, Hunt frequently found himself embroiled in debates over questions of his command responsibilities and the proper relationship between various branches of the service. Those problems surfaced in dramatic form at Gettysburg on July 3, 1863.

Hunt's military service honored a well-established tradition within his family. The son and grandson of officers, he graduated from West Point in 1839 and subsequently fought in Mexico as a lieutenant of artillery. In the 1850s he was promoted to captain and, toward the end of the decade, served on a three-man board that produced a revised set of light artillery tactics that received wide use during the Civil War. Following the outbreak of war in April 1861 he was promoted to major in May, participated in the Battle of First Bull Run in late July, and then received assignment as chief of artillery in the Washington defenses. His commission as colonel dated from September 28, 1861.[2]

Maj. Gen. George B. McClellan began building the Army of the Potomac after First Bull Run. Destined to be the principal Union field force in the eastern theater, this army would spend the better part of four years defending Washington, D.C., attempting to capture Richmond, and fighting what would later be christened the Confederate Army of Northern Virginia.[3] Hunt would be a leading influence in the Army of the Potomac from 1862 to war's end. McClellan's force contained a strong Artillery Reserve consisting of one-third of the field batteries; the other two-thirds were distributed among the infantry divisions. Under this organization, Brig. Gen. William F. Barry, a West Point classmate of Hunt's, served as chief of artillery for the army. Hunt commanded the Artillery Reserve, devoting considerable time to the task of training its gunners.[4]

In June 1862, McClellan redistributed his guns, taking half the artillery from the infantry divisions to form a reserve for each infantry corps. Officers designated by the corps commanders, and subject to their direct orders, took charge of the corps reserves. This reorganization also affected the army's chief of artillery, who henceforth would perform strictly administrative duties unless ordered by the commanding general to take charge of batteries in the field. This separation of command and administration existed in no other army in the world. It prompted many qualified artillery officers, who feared slow promotion and then only to an administrative post, to seek positions in other branches of the service—a loss that dealt a serious blow to the "long arm" of the Army of the Potomac.[5]

On September 5, 1862, Hunt succeeded Barry as chief of artillery. Promotion to brigadier general of volunteers soon followed, to date from September 15. At the time of Hunt's advancement, the artillery in the Army of the Potomac consisted of approximately ten thousand men, nine thousand horses, and four hundred guns. Although a body of men equivalent to an infantry corps, the artillery included just one brigadier general—Hunt himself—and only six other officers above the grade of captain. Hunt complained throughout his military career about both the anomalous separation of command and administration in the artillery and his being subject to the whim of whoever might be in command of the army.[6]

Hunt's experience with George McClellan in 1861 created an expectation of more field command and greater responsibility. The artillerist gave his superior unqualified support early in the war and continued to do so for the rest of his life. Just prior to the Battle of Antietam, McClellan entrusted Hunt with control of all the artillery in the field, with full power to invoke the name of the commanding general when dealing with officers superior in rank. The arrangement worked well initially, but Hunt proved unable to maintain tight control over fifty-five batteries during the fighting on

Brig. Gen. Henry Jackson Hunt. Courtesy of Cal Packard, Mansfield, Ohio.

September 17. Although McClellan was pleased with his artillery chief's performance, Hunt himself was not. He had no doubt thrived on wielding overall control of nearly three hundred guns, but the inability of those guns to coordinate and concentrate their fire during the Battle of Antietam displeased him.[7]

For the next two months, Hunt tried in vain to wrest control of artillery from infantry commanders and to consolidate the field batteries into a single corps under his authority. Abraham Lincoln's replacement of McClellan with Ambrose E. Burnside on November 7, 1862, hurt Hunt's efforts. Although Burnside retained Hunt in overall artillery command, the latter's responsibilities became largely advisory. Hunt found himself counseling infantry officers as to the possible placement and use of their guns— a job made more difficult when Burnside divided his infantry into three "Grand Divisions" operating independently of one another.[8]

Six weeks after the Union disaster at the Battle of Fredericksburg in December 1862, Joseph Hooker succeeded Burnside as commander of the Army of the Potomac. "Fighting Joe" almost immediately redefined Hunt's responsibilities as purely administrative. During the fighting at Chancellorsville in May 1863, Hunt played a secondary role as no more than the titular head of Union artillery on the field. Shortly after his defeat at Chancellorsville, Hooker wisely issued Special Order No. 129, which not only restored Hunt to field command but also officially recognized the artillerist's authority to bring about the unified control over Union guns he so desperately wanted.[9]

Hunt immediately restored a strong Artillery Reserve under loyal officers of his choosing who would be accountable only to him and the army's commanding general. He then set about replacing officers he believed had been appointed to their positions as a result of the political cliques that dominated Hooker's army. Late in May, Hunt named Capt. John G. Hazard commander of the Second Corps artillery. This appointment of a staunch Hunt supporter infuriated Maj. Gen. Winfield Scott Hancock, chief of the Second Corps.[10] Best described as an infantry chauvinist, Hancock joined many other infantry officers in believing that artillery could not exert as much influence on a battlefield as infantry. For proof of this, they maintained, one need only look at the much higher percentage of wounds created by infantry than by artillery. Hancock would argue over the next twenty-three years that an operation's success or failure was not subject to the decisions of artillery officers, who never bore responsibility for a battle's outcome. Under no circumstances would Hancock willingly give up control of the artillery assigned to his corps.[11]

In contrast to Hancock's attitude, Henry Hunt, John Hazard, and other artillerists insisted that if given a chance and properly used, their arm could inflict fearful damage on an opponent. But proper liaison between infantry and artillery rarely existed, and the efficiency of the artillery almost always suffered as a result. Infantry commanders seldom realized that they must take prompt advantage of opportunities presented them by the artillery, a failing that promoted distrust among gunners and fed a relationship of skepticism and contempt between the two branches. Hunt revealed his bias against infantry commanders in a journal kept during the Spotsylvania campaign. He described the "crude notions of advantage of position" held by Maj. Gen. David Bell Birney, whose Third Corps artillery Hunt helped place on July 2 at Gettysburg. In a more damning assessment, Hunt observed that "it may be added that in the management of the Artillery Gen. [G.K.] Warren has managed worst than Gen. Hancock."[12] In light of their very different perceptions about artillery, it is not surprising that communication between Hunt and Hancock would be almost nonexistent at Gettysburg or that the coordination between the two would suffer as a result.

On June 28, 1863, Maj. Gen. George Gordon Meade was appointed to replace Hooker as army commander, a change that delighted Hunt. Meade was a topographical engineer by training who appreciated the importance of terrain in promoting the most efficient use of prearranged fire from both infantry and artillery. Hunt believed that Meade had been appointed as a result of McClellan's influence; if true, the chief of artillery could expect no diminution of his own status in the army. On July 28 Hunt informed his wife that the president "wrote McC the facts and asked him who he should appoint, to which McC replied 'Meade' and so luckily Meade was appointed, for if Hooker had been retained we would have been at this hour a ruined people."[13] Hunt undoubtedly watched closely for any order or posturing from Meade, stated or implicit, that might affect his own role as absolute commander of all field artillery in the Army of the Potomac.

During hearings held by the Joint Committee on the Conduct of the War on April 4, 1864, a questioner asked Hunt: "When were you restored to the full command of the artillery?" "General Meade took command on the 28th of June, I think, and moved the next morning," replied Hunt. "I had no opportunity then of saying anything whatever to him about my position. I proceeded to do everything I could, as I always had done, to forward whatever was necessary to be done. At Taneytown I received orders from General Meade with the regard to selecting positions for the artillery at Pipe Creek and examining the country there, and I accompanied him to Gettysburg, which place we reached about one o'clock at night."

After officers on the ground at Gettysburg had explained the army's position to Meade, he directed Hunt "to immediately select the positions for the artillery, which I proceeded to do, so far as the darkness would permit. I could see our own ground, but not that of the enemy. General Meade accompanied me." Around dawn on July 2, Maj. Gen. Henry W. Slocum, the Twelfth Corps commander, reported to Meade that there was a gap in his line and that the Confederates seemed to be preparing to attack. "I was lying down near the root of a tree there," continued Hunt. "General Meade immediately asked for me; and when I reported to him he gave me directions to take immediate measures for stopping the gap, and if an attack was made to repulse it. I looked upon that as no opportunity to come to an explanation with him; but I regarded it, and his previous order to look to the positions of the batteries, as, in fact, recognizing the position I had held both under General McClellan and General Burnside. At all events, I proceeded at once to act upon that assumption; ordered artillery from wherever I could find it, where I thought it could be spared, without any regard to the commands of others, except to inform them that it was necessary; took possession of all the ground that covered the position, put the batteries on it [forty-nine guns], and covered that gap until the troops took their position there, when I distributed the artillery back to its former positions."[14]

Hunt contended that from this time on he "exercised all the duties of commander of the artillery, as recognized in modern armies, in the same way as at Antietam, where General McClellan told me on the field that he held me responsible for everything in connection with the artillery."[15] Although Meade's actions persuaded Hunt that he exercised command over all Union artillery at Gettysburg, the army's commander issued no written order or made any other reference to this subject to his infantry corps commanders.

When Hunt arrived at Gettysburg with Meade, a third of the battle had already been fought. Hunt quickly perceived that Union infantry commanders had not used their supporting artillery to its full potential. During the first day's fight, many Union batteries had been placed in untenable positions for the sole purpose of supporting infantry units that also held ground inferior to that occupied by the enemy. Any converging fire was impractical, because the Federal units fought independently rather than cooperating with one another. Most of the Federal artillery spent a good part of the day defending itself with counterbattery fire.[16]

As dawn broke on July 2, Hunt made a reconnaissance of the ground on which his artillery would fight for the next two days. A substantial portion of the Union position followed Cemetery Ridge, which formed the shank of the famous "fishhook" (or shepherd's crook or bishop's crosier, depending on who described the line), running generally from north to south.

Fighting on July 2 sustained the notion that Hunt controlled all Federal artillery on the field. Maj. Gen. Daniel E. Sickles, the Third Corps commander, called to Meade's headquarters for assistance in determining a line of defense as early as 11:00 A.M. "I had just come into headquarters from an inspection of the ground," Hunt later recalled, "when General Meade sent for me and told me that General Sickles, who was there at the time, wished me to examine his line, or the line that he wanted to occupy." Meade instructed Hunt to find appropriate artillery positions. Sickles insisted that the guns be placed in front of the existing fishhook line. Sickles's artillery moved as much as three-quarters of a mile forward to positions selected by Hunt.[17] As action progressed on July 2, Hunt placed much of the Artillery Reserve in support of Sickles's advanced lines. Despite Hunt's considerable activity, he has seldom been viewed as a major factor in the day's outcome. Winfield Scott Hancock's actions, in contrast, have received wide attention and praise. The commander of the Second Corps rightly receives credit for shoring up much of the Union left flank after Sickles's line broke under the pressure of nearly twenty-one thousand assaulting Confederates. Hancock positioned much of his own Second Corps artillery, some of the Reserve Artillery, and their infantry supports that finally ended the threat to the Union left flank early on the evening of July 2.[18] Still, the day's action seemed to reaffirm in Hunt's mind his mandate as commander of all Federal artillery on the field.

Hunt spent an active night of July 2. Summoned to General Meade's council of war that evening, he arrived after the meeting broke up because he had, as he later explained, been devoting his energies "in great part to repairing damages, replenishing the ammunition chests, and reducing and reorganizing such batteries as had lost so many men and horses as to be unable efficiently to work the full number of guns."[19] Upon finally reaching Meade's headquarters, he learned that the army would stand and fight another day. Fully in agreement with this decision, Hunt left headquarters to ready the Union artillery for the next day's fight.[20] From 1:00 to 4:30 A.M. on July 3 he worked to bolster the Union right flank and ready an artillery barrage against Rebel forces that had gained a foothold at the base of Culp's Hill. By dawn Hunt had reviewed all the army's artillery positions, including those of the Second Corps in the Union center. Although Meade had surmised on the night of July 2 that the Second Corps might be the probable target of a Confederate attack on July 3, there is no indication that Hunt's predawn agenda included formulation of a plan for the defense of Hancock's part of the line. The artillerist returned to the Union right flank and remained there, viewing the action at Culp's Hill until sometime after 10:00 A.M.[21]

Hunt later wrote that "between ten and eleven A.M., everything looking favorable at Culp's Hill, I crossed over to Cemetery Ridge, to see what might be going on at other points. Here a magnificent display greeted my eyes. Our whole front for two miles was covered by [Confederate] batteries already in line or going into position. They stretched—apparently in one unbroken mass—from opposite the town to the Peach Orchard, which bounded the view to the left, the ridges of which were planted thick with cannon." Hunt surmised that it "most probably meant an assault on our center, to be preceded by a cannonade in order to crush our batteries and shake our infantry."[22]

Hunt described the Union position atop Cemetery Ridge in a letter written nearly a decade after the fact. "This space of 1600 or 1700 yards was an open well defined crest, the 2nd Corps occupied the northern part, the 1st and 3rd Corps the southern or shorter part which was in a decided re-entrant," he noted. "Any attempt to assault the 1st and 3rd Corps here would bend the enemy's [left] flank to the whole 2nd Corps and would lead to his certain destruction."[23] By this Hunt meant that the Second Corps occupied a portion of the fishhook that protruded farther toward the enemy than did the southern half of the Union line.

Although the preceding quotations were written with the benefit of hindsight, there is little doubt that Hunt correctly identified on July 3 the likely point of the Confederate infantry attack. An artillery commander of Hunt's superior ability could see what ground his enemy could cover effectively by the placement of batteries, as well as the routes of advance that permitted effective support from those guns. Even if his opponent's infantry dispositions remained obscure—which they did—and the situation was somewhat uncertain, the solution of the defensive problem was to cover the terrain in the immediate Union front. This Hunt set out to do.

The Second Corps line along Cemetery Ridge consisted of five brigades of infantry and twenty-eight cannon condensed into a half-mile front. It extended from a group of trees, known as Ziegler's Grove, to the decided bend, or re-entrant, in the Union line mentioned by Hunt. Brig. Gen. George J. Stannard's First Corps brigade continued the line southward, with Col. Freeman McGilvery's forty-nine guns in ten batteries (much of the Artillery Reserve), under the direct command of Hunt, south of Stannard's soldiers. What remained of the Union Third Corps after its hard fighting on July 2 stood in direct support of the Reserve Artillery line. Over-all, the Federals massed seventy-seven guns and infantry from three corps into a 1,600-yard front.[24]

Cemetery Ridge allowed placement of artillery and infantry in close proximity to each other. The ridge line was high enough for artillery, and its infantry supports could lie down, at least initially, in front of the Federal guns.[25] A six-gun artillery battery ideally occupied about seventy-five yards in a constricted formation; however, even this spacing was not the rule on July 3, especially on the Second Corps artillery front, where in some cases guns stood but fifteen feet apart. An entire battery could not change direction of fire to its right or left front easily, as the pivoting pieces would be masked by the rest of the carriages in line; it was necessary, therefore, to push half the battery forward and pull the other half back. Owing to the constraints imposed on the batteries by their infantry supports, arcs of fire among the artillery units ranged from a generous sixty degrees to a mere fifteen degrees.[26] Still, because of the sheer number of batteries involved, Hunt determined to coordinate the artillery's supporting fire. Forty-five guns posted on the flanks of the Second Corps and McGilvery's line enhanced the potential of his crossfire scenario.[27]

Hunt began riding from battery to battery, regardless of command, instructing each about his intention to coordinate a concentrated crossfire against any advancing enemy infantry. "From the great extent of ground occupied by the enemy's batteries," he explained, "it was evident that all the artillery on our west front, whether of the army corps or the reserve, must concur as a unit, under the chief of artillery, in the defense."[28]

Hunt anticipated that a Confederate cannonade to soften the Union defenses could draw his own batteries into a wasteful return of fire. In a postwar letter to William Tecumseh Sherman regarding the artillery's role at Gettysburg, he pointed out that the army's regulations in force during the Civil War stipulated that "in the attack the artillery is employed to silence the batteries that protect the position. In the defense it is better to direct its fire on the advancing troops." In line with this doctrine, Hunt determined to husband as much ammunition as possible. To that end he instructed every artillery commander he encountered to hold his fire for at least fifteen minutes after the Confederates commenced their cannonade, and then to reply "under all circumstances . . . deliberately."[29]

Concern about ammunition, especially among the Second Corps batteries, occupied much of Hunt's attention. A great deal of ordnance had been expended on July 2, when Hancock personally maneuvered his artillery to secure the Union left flank. Furthermore, according to Hunt's journal, only half of the Second Corps artillery train had arrived at Gettysburg. He had been repeatedly called upon to supply the Second Corps with ammunition from the Artillery Reserve train because of the "neglect or failures on the part of the Generals to keep their Artillery trains in hand. The Artillery Reserve and especially the special train . . . supplied the deficiencies."[30]

Hunt added that "there was a special wagon train with the Artillery Reserve carrying 20 rounds per gun for every gun in the Army over and above the allowance authorized by G. Orders. This was made by me in preparing for the Gettysburg campaign and unknown to Gen. Hooker. General Ingalls furnished the wagons." Even Meade did not learn about this special train until late November 1863, when Hunt told him about it in the midst of the Mine Run campaign. According to Hunt, Meade readily approved of what his chief of artillery had done at Gettysburg.[31] The special train was designed to supplement the ammunition supply of the army—not to be used for emergencies. It was not an inexhaustible source for generals who failed logistically with their own trains. As a consequence, on July 3 there was no extra ammunition to be had or wasted.

Still other problems diminished the Second Corps's supply of ammunition. Beginning about 8:00 A.M. on July 3, well before the Rebels revealed their intent for the day, Hancock's gunners dueled with some of A. P. Hill's Confederate batteries. This exchange provided support to infantry units skirmishing at the Bliss farm, which lay approximately six hundred yards directly in front of the Second Corps line. Second Lt. John Egan, a section commander in Lt. George A. Woodruff's Second Corps battery, recalled that "batteries opened at intervals from different points along the whole Rebel line upon the artillery of the 2nd Corps." Egan estimated that at least "ten or twelve distinct artillery fights" erupted that morning. In fact, as many as a hundred cannon may have dueled for supremacy at the Bliss farm. Hunt witnessed at least one of these exchanges. He was standing behind the third limber of Lt. Alonzo H. Cushing's Second Corps battery when an explosion took place. A Rebel shell hit one of the limbers; two more of Cushing's limbers detonated as a result of the exploding Union ammunition.[32] These exchanges drained ammunition from Second Corps batteries before the great artillery duel of July 3 commenced.

Hunt chose not to seek out and inform General Hancock of his crossfire scenario. During the council of war on the night of July 2, Meade had given Hancock charge of all troops in the Union center and Brig. Gen. John Gibbon command of the Second Corps. Whether Hunt choose the path of least resistance or truly considered his plan so sound that it would meet with no interference, his failure to inform Hancock boded ill. John Gibbon also may have figured in the decision not communicate with Hancock. An artillery instructor at West Point for five years prior to the outbreak of the war, Gibbon had published *The Artillerist's Manual* in 1860.[33] If Hunt believed that Gibbon controlled the Union center, he may have thought it unnecessary to explain his plan. Whatever Hunt's rationale, the Union artillery would not achieve exemplary execution against Pickett's Charge. The guns that Hunt controlled and those in Hancock's corps would cooperate neither during the Confederate bombardment nor against the infantry assault that followed.

Hunt had started his ride from battery to battery from the positions facing west atop Cemetery Hill, the northernmost point of his artillery line. He had proceeded south along Cemetery Ridge and, according to his postwar account, had reached "the last battery on Little Round Top, when . . . the enemy opened with all his guns." "From that point the scene was indescribably grand," he continued. "All their batteries were soon covered with smoke, through which the flashes were incessant, whilst the air seemed filled with shells, whose sharp explosions, with the hurtling of their fragments, formed a running accompaniment to the deep roar of the guns." According to Hunt, "Most of the enemy's projectiles passed overhead, the effect being to sweep all the open ground in our rear, which was of little benefit to the Confederates—a mere waste of ammunition, for everything here could seek shelter." Hunt described the Union infantry on Cemetery Ridge as "lying down on its reverse slope, near the crest, in open ranks, waiting events." The Confederate artillery was not trying to hit the rear of the Union position or the infantry on the reverse slope of Cemetery Ridge; its target was the Federal artillery along the ridge. However, even taking into consideration infantry supports both in front and rear of the guns, the Union position at its widest point presented a target just seventy-five yards deep. Once cannon smoke engulfed their artillery positions, Confederate gunners had no realistic opportunity to readjust their fire. As a result, sniffed Hunt, the enemy fire "was scattered over the whole field."[34]

Hunt wrote after the war that as "soon as the enemy opened his cannonade which was a furious one, Gen. Hancock as reported to me noticed that the batteries of his corps did not reply and directed Captain Hazard to open at once. Captain Hazard informed him of my orders and begged him not to insist upon his own, but to this he would not listen and compelled a rapid reply to the enemy." Hancock then rode over to Col. Freeman McGilvery at the Artillery Reserve position and ordered him to commence firing. Alluding to Hunt's fifteen-minute rule, McGilvery stated that he had "received special instructions, and the time was not come." Hancock asked for the source of these instructions, and McGilvery replied, "from the Chief of Artillery." Hancock next insisted that Hunt had not envisioned such a Confederate bombardment when he gave his orders, to which McGilvery

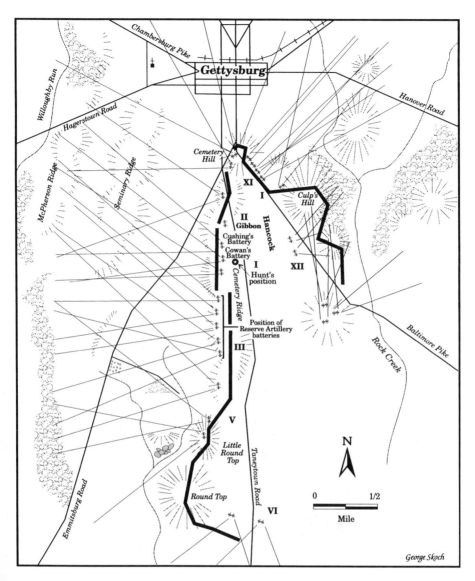

Hunt's Plan for Artillery Fire against Pickett's Charge

replied that the chief of artillery "had predicted just what was then occur-ring" and that his "orders were given to meet this very case." Hancock then remarked, "My troops cannot stand this cannonade and will not stand it if it is not replied to," and ordered McGilvery to open fire at once. Concerned about the morale of his infantry, Hancock told every battery commander that he encountered to open fire. McGilvery declined to do so "before the time set by his own commander."[35] But even after Hunt's order to cease fire

Maj. Gen. Winfield Scott Hancock. Courtesy of the Library of Congress.

in anticipation of the Confederate infantry assault, batteries of the Second Corps continued to fire, under Hancock's orders.

About 2:30 P.M., ninety minutes into the cannonade, Hunt began a cessation of fire along the Union front. "Finding our ammunition running low and that it was very unsafe to bring up loads of it, a number of caissons and limbers having been exploded," he wrote in his official report, "I directed that the fire should be gradually stopped, which was done, and the

Hunt (*seated at left*) and Hancock (*seated at the right of* Hunt) together in Warrenton, Virginia, on November 10, 1862. Courtesy of the U.S. Army Military History Institute, Carlisle, Pennsylvania.

enemy soon slackened his fire also. I then sent orders for such batteries as were necessary to replace exhausted ones, and all that were disposable were sent me." Hunt was on Cemetery Hill when he decided that enough was enough, and the first guns he ordered to cease firing were the nineteen atop that eminence.[36]

Cessation of this fire may have given Robert E. Lee the impression that his artillery bombardment had been at least partially successful. Capt. William Reese's Jeff Davis Artillery was the northernmost four-gun battery along Seminary Ridge. It was from this area, north of Lee's headquarters, that the Confederate commander viewed much of the artillery exchange. Lee had directed Reese to fire exclusively at the Union cannon on Cemetery Hill, indicating to the captain that those guns posed the greatest threat to enfilade the Confederate infantry assault. When the nineteen Union cannon abruptly ceased firing, it was reported, Lee rode up to Reese's men, saluted, and thanked them for "their unsurpassed chivalry."[37] Lee then rode south along his lines, encouraging his infantry for their fight to come. At approximately the same time Hunt also rode south, instructing his battery commanders to conserve long-range ammunition and open against the anticipated Rebel infantry assault at a range of about 1,200 yards.

Gibbon's manual stipulated that artillery worked best against infantry at a medium range, eight hundred to twelve hundred yards.[38] It was most effective at a thousand yards, or "not beyond the limit of distinct vision." Infantry should not be fired upon from much beyond a thousand yards, unless the ground was very favorable, hard and dry for ricochet fire. Confederate infantry would have to cross 1,200 yards of precisely this type of ground to get at the Second Corps. Considering the number of guns involved (122), the nature of the ground, and the range to target, Hunt had every reason to feel confident that his prearranged fire could create a considerable killing ground in front of the Second Corps infantry.

The presumption can be made that Hunt would have ordered a "grazing" fire against the advancing Confederate infantry. If the angle of incidence was too great, an artillery projectile buried itself in the ground; such "plunging fire" would not have been appropriate in this instance. "Grazing" or "rolling" fire can be achieved when the axis of the field piece is more horizontal to the ground, creating a number of low bounds or ricochets for best results. This would have been true for both Union shot and shell. When the ground was favorable for ricochets, solid shot from field guns could range as far as 1,700–1,900 yards, making a number of more-or-less extensive bounds and hitting not only the initial target but also supporting lines. Bursting shell could ricochet and disperse their deadly fragments as much as six hundred yards beyond and through their initial target. Shrapnel shells and case shots released their balls at the explosion, achieving more deadly effect the greater the velocity at the moment of bursting; the greatest velocity was achieved at a distance of about eight hundred yards. All Union batteries were encouraged to fire independently of one another, to avoid volley fire. Should the Union batteries fail to do this, Confederate infantry could take advantage of intervals between volleys to increase the rate of their advance.

After cessation of the cannonade, timed at about 3:10 P.M. by most official reports, the Confederate infantry emerged from the woods to form for the assault. Maj. Thomas W. Osborn, commanding the Union Eleventh Corps artillery and watching the Confederate charge from an oblique position on West Cemetery Hill, recorded one of the best descriptions of Union artillery versus Confederate infantry on July 3. "We had but a few minutes to wait after the artillery ceased firing for developments," wrote Osborn. "I think it was not more then ten minutes before the enemy's line of battle showed itself coming over Seminary Ridge at the point where we supposed Lee's troops were massed. As the line of battle came into view, it appeared to be about three-fourths of a mile in length and was moving in perfect line. The moment that the line appeared coming down the slope of Seminary Ridge, every battery on Meade's line opened on it. . . . The enemy's artillery kept up their fire on our line, but none of our batteries paid any further attention to it. They devoted their attention exclusively to the advancing line of battle."[39]

"From the very first minute our guns created sad havoc in that line," continued Osborn. "Lee's first line of battle had advanced about two hundred yards, after it came within sight, when another line in every way similar followed. These two lines of battle, nearly a mile distant, were then the sole object of fire of all the guns which could be made to bear upon them. The effects of this fire could very soon be seen." Osborn described how Federal batteries initially fired solid shot from Napoleons and percussion rounds from rifled pieces: "The artillerymen endeavored to roll the solid shot through the ranks and explode the percussion shells in front of the lines. This method was effective to a large degree, as we would see the ranks thinned at many points and here and there a wide gap made as from two to a dozen men were taken out by the men being shot down." The Confederates moved forward, however, "as steadily as if on dress parade. The entire field was open and the movement was in plain view on a nearly level plain."[40]

As the attack unfolded, Federal gunners switched to "time shells . . . and the killing and wounding was proportionately more severe." Southern ranks "had been a good deal cut out" by the time they traversed a third of the distance from Seminary Ridge. "They halted and closed their ranks from the right and left on the center and dressed their lines, which were materially shortened," stated Osborn. "This was done under a fearful artillery fire which was cutting them down by the hundreds every minute. They then moved forward as before, but the nearer they approached the more severe was their loss from our guns and the more seriously were the lines thinned. Still there was no hesitation or irregularity in the movement. The steady and firm step of the veteran soldiers continued." Passage of another third of the distance brought the Confederates within the reach of long-range canister from the artillery and musketry from the Union infantry. Their "lines again halted, closed up and dressed, still more depleted than before. The lines were then very materially shortened in comparison with what they were when they first came into view."[41]

Osborn noted that the "remainder of the charge upon Hancock's front was made upon the double quick over about an eighth of a mile and of course occupied but a very few minutes." The full force of canister and musket fire swept the attackers, as Union guns on the flanks fell silent. The Confederates "were so rapidly cut down that the regular lines of battle could not be maintained. As they approached Hancock's line, as is always the case in such charges, they took advantage of the slight irregularities of the ground, formed themselves into wedge shape and made a dash in this form to break Hancock's line."[42]

Although Osborn's account compliments the Union artillery effort, Hunt expected more damage from his crossfire scenario. "The weight of the assault fell upon the positions occupied by Hazard's batteries," he wrote. "I had counted on an artillery cross-fire that would stop it before it reached our lines, but, except a few shots here and there, Hazard's batteries were silent until the enemy came within canister range." Hunt laid much of the blame on Hancock for the failure to inflict more artillery damage. Union guns "had unfortunately exhausted their long range projectiles during the cannonade, under the orders of their corps commander, and it was too late to replace them," claimed Hunt. "Had my instructions been followed here, as they were by McGilvery, I do not believe that Pickett's division would have reached our line. We lost not only the fire of one-third of our guns, but the resulting cross-fire which would have doubled its value. The prime fault was in the obscurity of our army regulations as to the artillery, and the absence of all regulations as to the proper relations of the different arms of service to one another." On July 3, that obscurity cost the Union much blood and many lives, "and for a moment endangered the integrity of our line if not the success of the battle."[43]

A conversation at the end of the war with Confederate general Cadmus M. Wilcox bolstered Hunt's conclusions about the Federal artillery's role on July 3. Wilcox's Alabama brigade, as well as Col. David Lang's Florida brigade, were sent to the support of Maj. Gen. George E. Pickett's Virginians about fifteen minutes into the Confederate charge. The two brigades advanced south of Pickett's division directly in front of McGilvery's Artillery Reserve positions, and as they crossed the Emmitsburg Road were repulsed by Hunt's artillery alone. "I was told in April last by the Confederate General who commanded the second column of attack . . . that our artillery fire had broken the efficiency of the first assault," wrote Hunt in January 1866. "His (Wilcox['s]) assault was met by the full force of our artillery, on front, right and left, and broke it up before it could reach our lines, (this artillery had obeyed my instructions). I fully believe Gen. Wilcox's statement, and also that if the batteries of 2d Corps had been in the efficient condition that my orders contemplated; and in which they would have been, had their orders not been interfered with, that the enemy

Looking southwest toward the Cordori house from the Union line on Cemetery Ridge. In this 1882 photograph by William Tipton, the horse and rider mark the approximate location of Cushing's Battery. Courtesy of the Paul Phillipoteaux Series by William Tipton, Gettysburg National Military Park.

would not have reached our lines in condition to make the vigorous attack they did."[44] Hunt went to his grave believing that Hancock had prevented Federal artillery from achieving its full potential on the third day at Gettysburg.

During the charge, Hunt was to the left and rear of Capt. Andrew Cowan's battery just south of the "Clump of Trees." A few hundred Rebels— the wedge-shaped mass mentioned by Major Osborn—pushed forward toward Lieutenant Cushing's battery to Hunt's right. As the Confederates surged into Cushing's guns, observed Hunt, "the display of Secesh Battle flags was splendid and scarry [sic]."[45] But the breach in the Union line soon closed, as reinforcements charged through the battery and drove the Rebels back.

On Hunt's immediate front, the enemy got so close that Captain Cowan heard a Confederate officer yell, "Take that gun!" Rebels charging Cowan's guns were brought down by double charges of canister at ten yards. In the saddle on his horse "Bill," Hunt watched Confederates rush toward the battery. He fired his pistol and shouted "See em, See em!" Five bullets struck Bill, who reared and then collapsed, pinning Hunt beneath him. Members

McGilvery's Artillery Reserve positions along Cemetery Ridge
(Little Round Top and Round Top in the right background). Wilcox's and
Lang's Confederate brigades advanced against these guns. Courtesy of the
Gary M. Kross Collection.

of Cowan's battery pried Hunt free of the fallen animal. Soon mounted
again on one of the battery's horses, Hunt viewed the Confederate retreat
in his front. According to Cowan, Hazard also spent time near his battery.
"Here I first saw Col. Hazard," recalled Cowan after the war, "who came up
with Gen. Hunt to commend my course in taking this position." Hazard
likely stayed with Hunt only a few minutes before moving to his right, departing before the charge reached its zenith.[46]

A strength of the tactical defense during the Civil War was its extreme
resiliency. Defending units often absorbed hard blows, withstood heavy casualties, and maintained their cohesion.[47] Battle smoke sometimes acted
as a great nullifier of the tactical defense. A year before the battle of Gettysburg, Hunt had issued General Orders No. 94, which stated that "firing will
be deliberate and the greatest care will be taken to secure accuracy. Under
no circumstances will it be so rapid that the effect of each shot and shell
can not be noted when the air is clear." According to Col. Freeman McGilvery, he opened fire as Hunt directed, discharging his guns "slowly and
deliberately." Because of the smoke factor, it is unlikely that batteries sub-

ject to Hunt's direct control fired more than ten shots per minute against the advancing Southern infantry on July 3.[48]

In 1937, Capt. Victor A. Coulter of the Chemical Warfare Service Reserve examined smoke as a factor in Pickett's Charge in a paper titled "Smoke at Gettysburg." During World War I, the army had determined that a single company of infantry with smoke-making capabilities could effectively screen a front of 1,600 yards. Hunt reported that the Union front in question spanned 1,600 yards, so Coulter's findings are pertinent. Coulter himself averred "that Pickett's Charge, with little or no natural cover is a suitable engagement on which to superimpose a modern smoke screen." The captain further remarked "that the critical period of an infantry advance begins at about 800 yards from the objective. Musket fire at Gettysburg was not effective at that range, but direct fire from the Federal artillery tore gaping holes in the assaulting lines at about that distance. Since all the fire at Gettysburg was delivered following direct laying of the pieces, the experiments of the last ten years on the effect of covering riflemen with a smoke blanket apply properly." The army's experiments during the 1920s and 1930s showed that when the defensive position was covered with smoke, the percentage of hits they scored on silhouette targets decreased by 93 percent.[49]

Coulter concluded that a blanket of smoke enshrouding the Union line during Pickett's Charge would have helped Confederates maintain their planned alignment. The attackers (and their supports) would have taken fewer losses crossing the open fields, could have dismantled the fences along the Emmitsburg Road in relative safety, and might even have had an opportunity to maneuver into position east of the road. The longer the smoke hovered about the Union positions, the lower Confederate casualties during the assault would have been—ranging from 4 percent with a heavy smoke concentration to 50 percent if the Union fire was judiciously and accurately delivered.[50]

No officer on the field understood the importance of smoke better than Henry Hunt, and none was more qualified to deal with the problem. He had to balance the need for rapid fire with the desirability of limiting the accumulation of smoke along the Federal line—a difficult task under the best of circumstances. Hunt faced the added burden, as two students of the artillery at Gettysburg have put it, of overcoming "the resistance of high ranking infantry officers who failed to grasp the differences between artillery and infantry, or the principles Hunt sought to employ."[51] Just prior to and during the Confederate assault, Hunt urged all batteries he encountered to cease counterbattery fire and to expend their remaining rounds in a judicious manner. (Gouverneur K. Warren shared Hunt's

Looking south along Cemetery Ridge from just north of the "Clump of Trees." The x in 1882 William Tipton photograph marks the position of Cowan's Battery, from near which Hunt watched the climax of Pickett's Charge. Courtesy of the Paul Phillipoteaux Series by William Tipton, Gettysburg National Military Park.

sensitivity about smoke, suggesting to the artillerist shortly before the Confederate attack that "it was inexpedient to fill the valley with a screen of smoke.")[52] The different rates of fire along the Union line during Pickett's Charge underscored the practicality of Hunt's theory of central control over artillery support.

The Union center held on July 3 because of the powerful concentration of infantry and artillery along the defensive position and the long and open distance traversed by Confederate attackers. The precise effect of Union artillery during Pickett's Charge, the percentage of Confederate loss attributable to its fire, cannot be gauged with precision. Hunt certainly believed his guns had contributed to Union success. But if asked about the artillery's role, especially if the query came after the war, he would have stated without equivocation that Union cannon should have inflicted greater damage on the attacking Rebels.

After the Battle of Gettysburg, a troubled Hunt speculated about the future in a letter to his wife. "It is now possible I shall remain long with the Army in my present position," he said. "There will probably and pos-

sibly be trouble between Gen. M[eade] and myself. I have asked to be relieved from his staff and will insist upon it unless he meets my views as
to my department and if he does meet them, it will bring him to War with
many of his Generals." Whatever happened in that regard, Hunt intended
to do his duty: "I shall save myself for the campaign of 1864."[53]

Hunt remained the chief gunner of the Army of the Potomac through
the rest of the war. Under Ulysses S. Grant, he oversaw siege operations at
Petersburg in 1864–1865. Yet he never believed that he received his full
measure of credit for what he accomplished. He feuded with Winfield Scott
Hancock and other infantry commanders for the rest of his career. After
the war, he sometimes employed the advantage of hindsight to argue in
behalf of his branch of the service—and to win acknowledgment of what
he considered his proper place as a major figure in the history of the Army
of the Potomac.[54]

Appendix

Headquarters, June 22, 1863

Maj. Gen. J. E. B. STUART,

Commanding Cavalry:

GENERAL: I have just received your note of 7.45 this morning to General Long-street. I judge the efforts of the enemy yesterday were to arrest our progress and ascertain our whereabouts. Perhaps he is satisfied. Do you know where he is and what he is doing? I fear he will steal a march on us, and get across the Potomac before we are aware. If you find that he is moving northward, and that two brigades can guard the Blue Ridge and take care of your rear, you can move with the other three into Maryland, and take position on General Ewell's right, place yourself in communication with him, guard his flank, keep him informed of the enemy's movements, and collect all the supplies you can for the use of the army. One column of General Ewell's army will probably move toward the Susquehanna by the Emmitsburg route; another by Chambersburg. Accounts from him last night state that there was no enemy west of Frederick. A cavalry force (about 100) guarded the Monocacy Bridge, which was barricaded. You will, of course, take charge of [A. G.] Jenkins' brigade, and give him necessary instructions. All supplies taken in Maryland must be by authorized staff officers for their respective departments—by no one else. They will be paid for, or receipts for the same given to the owners. I will send you a general order on this subject, which I wish you to see is strictly complied with.

I am, very respectfully, your obedient servant

R. E. LEE
General.

Headquarters,
Millwood, June 22, 1863—7 p.m.

Maj. Gen. J. E. B. STUART,

Commanding Cavalry:

GENERAL: General Lee has inclosed to me this letter to you,* to be forwarded to you, provided you can be spared from my front, and provided I think that you can move across the Potomac without disclosing our plans. He speaks of your leaving, via Hopewell Gap, and passing by the rear of the enemy. If you can get through by that route, I think that you will be less likely to indicate what our plans are than if you should cross by passing to our rear. I forward the letter of instructions with these suggestions.

Please advise me of the condition of affairs before you leave, and order General Hampton—whom I suppose you will leave here in command—to report to me at Millwood, either by letter or in person, as may be most agreeable to him.

Most respectfully,

JAMES LONGSTREET,
Lieutenant-General.

N. B.—I think that your passage of the Potomac by our rear at the present moment will, in a measure, disclose our plans. You had better not leave us, therefore, unless you can take the proposed route in rear of the enemy.

Headquarters Army of Northern Virginia,
June 23, 1863—5 p.m.

Maj. Gen. J. E. B. STUART,

Commanding Cavalry:

GENERAL: Your notes of 9 and 10:30 a.m. to-day have just been received. As regards the purchase of tobacco for your men, supposing that Confederate money will not be taken, I am willing for your commissaries or quartermasters to purchase this tobacco and let the men get it from them, but I can have nothing seized by the men.

If General Hooker's army remains inactive, you can leave two brigades to watch him, and withdraw with the three others, but should he not appear to be moving northward, I think you had better withdraw this side of the mountain to-morrow night, cross at Shepherdstown next day, and move over to Fredericktown.

You will, however, be able to judge whether you can pass around their army without hinderance, doing them all the damage you can, and cross the river east of the mountains. In either case, after crossing the river, you must move on and feel the right of Ewell's troops, collecting information, provisions, &c.

*Of same date.

Give instructions to the commander of the brigades left behind, to watch the flank and rear of the army, and (in the event of the enemy leaving their front) retire from the mountains west of the Shenandoah, leaving sufficient pickets to guard the passes, and bringing everything clean along the Valley, closing upon the rear of the army.

As regards the movements of the two brigades of the enemy moving toward Warrenton, the commander of the brigades to be left in the mountains must do what he can to counteract them, but I think the sooner you cross into Maryland, after to-morrow, the better.

The movements of Ewell's corps are as stated in my former letter. Hill's first division will reach the Potomac to-day, and Longstreet will follow to-morrow.

Be watchful and circumspect in all your movements.

I am, very respectfully and truly, yours,

R. E. LEE
General.

Notes

R. E. Lee and July 1 at Gettysburg

1. Douglas Southall Freeman, ed., *Lee's Dispatches: Unpublished Letters of General Robert E. Lee, C.S.A., to Jefferson Davis and the War Department of the Confederate States of America, 1862–1865* (1915; rev. ed., ed. Grady McWhiney, New York: G. P. Putnam's Sons, 1957), xxxvii.

2. Maj. Gen. Sir Frederick Maurice, ed., *An Aide-de-Camp of Lee, Being the Papers of Colonel Charles Marshall* (Boston: Little, Brown, 1927), 190. Although concerned with the overland campaign of 1864–65, Andrew A. Humphreys's discussion of the water route alternative illuminates the considerations affecting the choice of routes toward Richmond. See Humphreys, *The Virginia Campaign of '64 and '65: The Army of the Potomac and the Army of the James* (New York: Charles Scribner's Sons, 1883), 6–9.

3. Robert K. Krick, "Why Lee Went North," in Morningside Bookshop, *Catalogue Number Twenty-Four* (Dayton, Ohio, 1988), 10.

4. Edward Porter Alexander, *Fighting for the Confederacy: The Personal Recollections of General Edward Porter Alexander*, ed. Gary W. Gallagher (Chapel Hill: Univ. of North Carolina Press, 1989), 415.

5. U.S. War Department, *The War of the Rebellion: A Compilation of the Official Records of the Union and Confederate Armies*, 128 vols. (Washington, D.C.: GPO, 1880–1901), ser. 1, vol. 27, pt. 3:932 (hereafter cited as OR; all references are to volumes in series 1); Clifford Dowdey and Louis H. Manarin, eds., *The Wartime Papers of R. E. Lee* (Boston: Little, Brown, 1961), 816.

6. OR, vol. 29, pt. 1:405; ibid., vol. 51, pt. 2:761; Dowdey and Manarin, eds., *Wartime Papers*, 675.

7. Dowdey and Manarin, eds., *Wartime Papers*, 388–89.

8. Ibid., 508.

9. Ibid., 843–44.

10. These data are taken from Thomas L. Livermore, *Numbers and Losses in the Civil War in America, 1861–65* (1901; reprint, Dayton, Ohio: Morningside House, 1986), 86, 88–89, 92, 98.

11. Krick, "Why Lee Went North," 11.

12. Richard E. Beringer, Herman Hattaway, Archer Jones, and William N. Still, Jr., *Why the South Lost the Civil War* (Athens, Ga.: Univ. of Georgia Press, 1986), 9, 16.

13. Lt. Col. George A. Bruce, "The Strategy of the Civil War," in *Papers of the Military Historical Society of Massachusetts*, 14 vols. and index (1895–1918; reprint, Wilmington, N.C.: Broadfoot Publishing Company, 1989–90), 13:469.

14. Maj. Gen. J. F. C. Fuller, *The Generalship of Ulysses S. Grant* (1929; reprint, Bloomington: Indiana Univ. Press, 1958), 365.

15. On the question of Northern morale in the early summer of 1864, see Lt. Col. Alfred H. Burne, *Lee, Grant and Sherman* (New York: Charles Scribner's Sons, 1939), 65, and William H. Swinton, *Campaigns of the Army of the Potomac: A Critical History of Operations in Virginia, Maryland and Pennsylvania, from the Commencement to the Close of the War, 1861–1865* (New York: Charles Scribner's Sons, 1882), 494–95. Swinton's perceptive study argued that after Cold Harbor the outlook in the North was so gloomy "that there was at this time great danger of a collapse of the war. The history of this conflict truthfully written will show this."

16. *OR*, vol. 27, pt. 2:308; Herman Hattaway and Archer Jones, *How the North Won: A Military History of the Civil War* (Urbana: Univ. of Illinois Press, 1983), 398.

17. Dowdey and Manarin, eds., *Wartime Papers*, 505; *OR*, vol. 27, pt. 2:305.

18. *OR*, vol. 27, pt. 3:868–69; ibid., vol. 40, pt. 2:703.

19. Maurice, ed., *Aide-de-Camp of Lee*, 73, 68.

20. Fuller, *Generalship of Grant*, 377.

21. *OR*, vol. 27, pt. 2:316; Maurice, ed., *Aide-de-Camp of Lee*, 217.

22. *OR*, vol. 27, pt. 2:313.

23. Ibid., 295–97.

24. Ibid., pt. 3:913, 931.

25. Edwin B. Coddington, *The Gettysburg Campaign: A Study in Command* (New York: Charles Scribner's Sons, 1968), 594–95.

26. *OR*, vol. 27, pt. 3:913. Lee's orders to Stuart and Longstreet's transmittal letter are reproduced in the Appendix.

27. *OR*, vol. 27, pt. 3:915.

28. It is apparent that the word "not" was unintended. Read literally, the orders of June 23 set forth different movements for Stuart depending on the same facts: "if General Hooker's army remains inactive" and "should he [Hooker] not appear to be moving northward." This almost certainly represented a careless ambiguity, but it seems not to have been a critical one. In both of the orders printed in the *Official Records*, Stuart was to feel Ewell's right and give him information. Virtually all writers have ignored this seemingly misplaced "not" in Lee's instructions to Stuart. An exception is Coddington, who in *The Gettysburg Campaign*, 108, overlooks the possibility of a simple error and speculates that perhaps Lee "considered it possible that Hooker would move southward to threaten Richmond, in which case Stuart's occupation of Frederick, a town equidistant from Baltimore and Washington, would be an effective deterrent."

29. *OR*, vol. 27, pt. 3:923.

30. Maurice, ed., *Aide-de-Camp of Lee*, 208 n.

31. *OR*, vol. 27, pt. 3:207–8; Kenneth P. Williams, *Lincoln Finds a General: A Military Study of the Civil War*, 5 vols. (New York: Macmillan, 1949–59), 2:666.

32. Coddington, *Gettysburg Campaign*, 207; Maurice, ed., *Aide-de-Camp of Lee*, 191.

33. *OR*, vol. 27, pt. 2:308.

34. Ibid., 307, 607; Coddington, *Gettysburg Campaign*, 264.

35. *OR*, vol. 27, pt. 2:444.

36. Coddington, *Gettysburg Campaign*, 280; Walter H. Taylor, *Four Years with General Lee* (1877; reprint, Bloomington: Indiana Univ. Press, 1962), 280; A. L. Long, *Memoirs of Robert E. Lee: His Military and Personal History* (New York: J. M. Stoddart, 1886), 275–76; *OR*, vol. 27, pt. 2:348–49.

37. Coddington, *Gettysburg Campaign*, 309.

38. Alexander, *Fighting for the Confederacy*, 233–34.

39. Ibid., 234; *OR*, vol. 27, pt. 2:317.

40. These postwar recollections by John B. Gordon, Henry Kyd Douglas, James Power Smith, Isaac R. Trimble, Jubal A. Early, Walter H. Taylor, and others are cited in Douglas Southall Freeman, *Lee's Lieutenants: A Study in Command*, 3 vols. (New York: Charles Scribner's Sons, 1942–44), 3:92–102.

41. OR, vol. 27, pt. 1:721, 277, 283, 704, 758–59, 777, 825; Harry W. Pfanz, *Gettysburg—The Second Day* (Chapel Hill: Univ. of North Carolina Press, 1987), 38–39.

42. OR, vol. 27, pt. 2:555, 445.

43. Ibid., 470, 607, 445.

44. Freeman, *Lee's Lieutenants*, 3:97–98.

45. OR, vol. 27, pt. 2:317–18.

46. Freeman, *Lee's Lieutenants*, 3:90–105.

Confederate Corps Leadership on the First Day at Gettysburg: A. P. Hill and Richard S. Ewell in a Difficult Debut

1. Much of the controversial writing about Gettysburg appeared in the pages of J. William Jones et al., eds., *Southern Historical Society Papers*, 52 vols. and 2-vol. index (1876–1959; reprint, Millwood, N.Y.: Kraus Reprint Company, 1977–80) (hereafter cited as SHSP); see especially vols. 4–6 for the opening arguments by Jubal A. Early, James Longstreet, and other principals in the debate. Important modern works include Thomas L. Connelly, *The Marble Man: Robert E. Lee and His Image in American Society* (New York: Knopf, 1977), especially chaps. 2 and 3; Connelly and Barbara Bellows, *God and General Longstreet: The Lost Cause and the Southern Mind* (Baton Rouge: Louisiana State Univ. Press, 1982), especially chap. 1; Glenn Tucker, *Lee and Longstreet at Gettysburg* (Indianapolis: Bobbs-Merrill, 1968), which devotes considerable attention to Richard S. Ewell; William Garrett Piston, *Lee's Tarnished Lieutenant: James Longstreet and His Place in Southern History* (Athens, Ga.: Univ. of Georgia Press, 1987); and Gaines M. Foster, *Ghosts of the Confederacy: Defeat, the Lost Cause, and the Emergence of the New South* (New York: Oxford Univ. Press, 1987), especially chaps. 3–7.

2. On the reorganization of the army and the importance of Jackson's legacy, see Freeman, *Lee's Lieutenants*, 2:683–714.

3. Spencer Glasgow Welch, *A Confederate Surgeon's Letters to His Wife* (1911, reprint, Marietta, Ga.: Continental Book Company, 1954), 66–67 (the 13th South Carolina was in Abner Perrin's brigade of Dorsey Pender's division); Henry Heth, "Letter from Major-General Henry Heth, of A. P. Hill's Corps, A.N.V.," in SHSP 4:155.

4. Jedediah Hotchkiss, *Virginia*, vol. 4 of Clement A. Evans, ed., *Confederate Military History* (1899; reprint, Wilmington, N.C.: Broadfoot Publishing Company, 1987), 403; Edward Porter Alexander, *Military Memoirs of a Confederate: A Critical Narrative* (1907; reprint, Dayton, Ohio: Press of Morningside Bookshop, 1977), 381; John S. Mosby, *Stuart's Cavalry in the Gettysburg Campaign* (1908; reprint, Gaithersburg, Md.: Olde Soldier Books, 1987), 141, 155.

5. Jennings C. Wise, *The Long Arm of Lee; or, The History of the Artillery of the Army of Northern Virginia, With a Brief Account of the Confederate Bureau of Ordnance*, 2 vols. (1915; reprint, Richmond, Va.: Owens Publishing Company, 1988), 2:615; Warren W. Hassler, *Crisis at the Crossroads: The First Day at Gettysburg* (University, Ala.: Univ. of Alabama Press, 1970): 153; Coddington, *Gettysburg Campaign*, 273–74; Freeman, *Lee's Lieutenants*, 3:170–71.

6. William Starr Myers, ed., "The Civil War Diary of General Isaac Ridgeway Trimble," *Maryland Historical Magazine* 17 (March 1922):11 (Trimble's use of "Cemetery Hill" and "Culp's Hill," local place names that he almost certainly did not know at the time of the battle, suggests that he revised his diary after the fact); Isaac R. Trimble, "The Battle and Campaign

of Gettysburg, from the Original MS. Furnished by Major Graham Daves of North Carolina," in SHSP 26:123–24. A more dramatic version of the meeting between Ewell and Trimble is in Randolph H. McKim, "The Gettysburg Campaign," in SHSP 40:273.

7. Glenn Tucker, *High Tide at Gettysburg: The Campaign in Pennsylvania* (Indianapolis: Bobbs-Merrill, 1958), 186 (quoting Stikeleather's letter, which was published in the *Raleigh* [N.C.] *Semi-Weekly Standard* on August 4, 1863); W. H. Swallow (a pseudonym), "The First Day at Gettysburg," *Southern Bivouac*, N.S., 1 (December 1885):441–42.

8. Henry Kyd Douglas, *I Rode with Stonewall, Being Chiefly the War Experiences of the Youngest Member of Jackson's Staff from the John Brown Raid to the Hanging of Mrs. Surratt* (Chapel Hill: Univ. of North Carolina Press, 1940), 247; John B. Gordon, *Reminiscences of the Civil War* (New York: Charles Scribner's Sons, 1903), 154–55.

9. Transcript of conversation between R. E. Lee and William Allan, April 15, 1868, pp. 13–14, and February 19, 1870, p. 21, William Allan Papers, Southern Historical Collection, Wilson Library, University of North Carolina, Chapel Hill, North Carolina (repository hereafter cited as SHC). An editorial note preceding the text of the transcripts states that the "conversations were held in General Lee's office, usually in the morning, and Colonel Allan made his memoranda the same day."

10. Robert E. Lee, Jr., *Recollections and Letters of General Robert E. Lee* (1904; reprint, Wilmington, N.C.: Broadfoot Publishing Company, 1988), 415–16. These quotations are as remembered by Cassius Lee's son Cazenove Lee, who passed them along to Robert E. Lee, Jr.

11. Freeman, *Lee's Lieutenants*, 3:172–73; Clifford Dowdey, *Death of a Nation: The Story of Lee and His Men at Gettysburg* (New York: Knopf, 1958), 152–53; Hassler, *Crisis at the Crossroads*, 155; Coddington, *Gettysburg Campaign*, 320–212. For a treatment of Ewell on July 1 that generally accepts the traditional interpretation (and differs markedly from the present essay), see Gary W. Gallagher, "In the Shadow of Stonewall Jackson: Richard S. Ewell in the Gettysburg Campaign," *Virginia Country's Civil War* 5 (1986):54–59.

12. A glaring example of Gordon's confident dissembling may be found on page 160 of his *Reminiscences of the Civil War*, where he states that "impartial military critics, after thorough investigation, will consider . . . [it] as established . . . [that] General Lee distinctly ordered Longstreet to attack early the morning of the second day" at Gettysburg. By the time Gordon wrote this in the early twentieth century, a mass of evidence, much of it from the pens of Lee's own staff, left little doubt that Lee had given Longstreet no such order.

13. Jubal A. Early, *The Campaigns of Gen. Robert E. Lee: An Address by Lieut. General Jubal A. Early, Before Washington and Lee University, January 19th, 1872* (Baltimore: John Murphy, 1872), 45. For some of the richest collections of postwar testimony by Confederate participants, see Robert Underwood Johnson and Clarence Clough Buel, eds., *Battles and Leaders of the Civil War*, 4 vols. (New York: Century, 1887) (hereafter cited as B&L); *The Annals of the War Written by Leading Participants North and South, Originally Published in the Philadelphia Weekly Times* (Philadelphia: Times Publishing Company, 1879); and the periodicals *The Land We Love* (published 1866–69), *Our Living & Our Dead* (published 1874–76), *Southern Bivouac* (published 1882–85), and *Confederate Veteran* (published 1892–1932).

14. See "Letter from General Winfield Scott Hancock," in SHSP 5:168–72 (quotation on page 168). Among the many Confederates who quoted Hancock to prove that Ewell should have mounted assaults against Cemetery Hill were John B. Gordon, *Reminiscences of the Civil War*, 156, and Fitzhugh Lee, *General Lee* (New York: D. Appleton, 1894), 272–73. As careful a student as Coddington, *Gettysburg Campaign*, 318, 320–21, states that Hancock's letter indicated that to "achieve complete success after smashing the Union positions north and west of the town the Confederates would have had to continue their drive through the streets and up Cemetery Hill without a letup." Jackson might have accomplished this, observes Coddington, but Ewell could not.

15. Lee to Jefferson Davis, October 2, 1862, in OR, vol. 19, pt. 2:643; Lee to Davis, May 20, 1863, ibid., vol. 25, pt. 2:810–11.

16. Lee to A. P. Hill, June 5, 1863, ibid., vol. 27, pt. 3:859–60.

17. Ibid., vol. 27, pt. 2:307.

18. J. S. D. Cullen to James Longstreet, May 18, 1875, quoted in James Longstreet, *From Manassas to Appomattox: Memoirs of the Civil War in America* (Philadelphia: J. B. Lippincott, 1896), 383; OR, vol. 27, pt. 3:943–44 (letter from Lee to Ewell dated June 28 should be dated June 29; see Coddington, *Gettysburg Campaign*, p. 189).

19. OR, vol. 27, pt. 2:607, 637; Henry Heth, "Letter from Major-General Henry Heth, of A. P. Hill's Corps, A.N.V.," in SHSP 4:157.

20. Louis G. Young, "Pettigrew's Brigade at Gettysburg, 1–3 July, 1863," in Walter Clark, ed., *Histories of the Several Regiments and Battalions from North Carolina in the Great War, 1861–'65*, 5 vols. (1901; reprint, Wendell, N.C.: Avera Press for Broadfoot's Bookmark, 1982), 5:116–17 (cited hereafter as N.C. Regiments); Heth, "Letter from Major-General Heth," 157; OR, vol. 27, pt. 2:607. A somewhat different version of the episode involving Hill, Heth, and Pettigrew appears in Henry Heth, *The Memoirs of Henry Heth*, ed. James L. Morrison (Westport, Conn.: Greenwood Press, 1974), 173. The memoirs were written in 1897, some twenty years after the letter published in SHSP.

21. Walter Kempster, "The Cavalry at Gettysburg," in Ken Bandy and Florence Freeland, comps., *The Gettysburg Papers*, 2 vols. (Dayton, Ohio: Press of Morningside Bookshop, 1978), 1:402; OR, vol. 27, pt. 2:607. In his paper, originally presented in 1913, Kempster quoted a postwar conversation between himself and Heth.

22. Lieutenant Colonel Arthur James Lyon Fremantle, an English officer accompanying Longstreet at Gettysburg, recorded his impressions of Hill about 4:30 that afternoon: "General Hill now came up and told me he had been very unwell all day, and in fact he looks very delicate" (Fremantle, *Three Months in the Southern States: April–June, 1863* [1863; reprint, Lincoln: Univ. of Nebraska Press, 1991], 254). Both of Hill's biographers make the excellent point that Hill would have accompanied Heth's advance on July 1 if he thought there was any chance of a major engagement. See William Woods Hassler, *A. P. Hill: Lee's Forgotten General* (Richmond: Garrett and Massie, 1962), 158–59; James I. Robertson, Jr., *General A. P. Hill: The Story of a Confederate Warrior* (New York: Random House, 1987), 215.

23. OR, vol. 27, pt. 2:607, 637; Taylor, *Four Years with Lee*, 92–93. Lee had told Ewell on the morning of July 1 that "he did not want a general engagement brought on till the rest of the army came up" (OR, vol. 27, pt. 2:444). He likely communicated the same sentiment to Hill.

24. Taylor, *Four Years with Lee*, 93; Heth, *Memoirs*, 175; OR, vol. 27, pt. 2:348.

25. Taylor, *Four Years with Lee*, p. 93. Heth went to Lee rather than Hill for permission to continue the assaults when Robert Rodes's division of Ewell's corps appeared on the Federal right (Heth, *Memoirs*, 175). Coddington discusses Heth's failure to go through channels (i.e, through Hill) in *Gettysburg Campaign*, 309. Hill's uncertain health and Heth's friendship with Lee might help to explain the division commander's actions. Robertson, *General A. P. Hill*, 215, argues that Hill should not be held responsible for initiating the action between Heth and Buford, but he "did become culpable once Heth became locked in combat."

26. OR, vol. 27, pt. 2:317–18.

27. Fremantle, *Three Months*, 254; OR, vol. 27, pt. 2:607.

28. Welch, *Surgeon's Letters*, 66; Perrin's letter is reproduced in Milledge L. Bonham, Jr., ed., "A Little More Light on Gettysburg," *Mississippi Valley Historical Review* 24 (March 1938): 523; Young, "Pettigrew's Brigade at Gettysburg," 121.

29. William Woods Hassler, "A. P Hill at Gettysburg: How Did He Measure Up as Stonewall Jackson's Successor?", *Virginia Country's Civil War* 5 (1986):51.

30. For rumors about Jackson's deathbed preference for Ewell, see Douglas Southall Freeman, *R. E. Lee: A Biography*, 4 vols. (New York: Charles Scribner's Sons, 1934–35), 3:8; Freeman, *Lee's Lieutenants*, 2:690; William Dorsey Pender, *The General to His Lady: The Civil War Letters of William Dorsey Pender to Fanny Pender*, ed. William Woods Hassler (Chapel Hill: Univ. of North Carolina Press, 1965), 237.

31. OR, vol. 25, pt. 2:810; transcript of conversation between R. E. Lee and William Allan, March 3, 1868, p. 8, Allan Papers, SHC.

32. OR, vol. 27, pt. 2:443–44.

33. Ibid., 444–45, 468–69, 552–55. For examples of postwar claims that Ewell frittered away this crucial opportunity (all of which compare Ewell to Jackson in the most unfavorable terms), see Douglas, *I Rode with Stonewall*, 247; Gordon, *Reminiscences*, 154–56; and James Power Smith, "General Lee at Gettysburg, A Paper Read Before the Military Historical Society of Massachusetts, on the Fourth of April, 1905," in SHSP 33:143–44. Douglas and Smith had served on Jackson's staff.

34. George Campbell Brown Memoir, p. 57, Brown-Ewell Papers, Tennessee State Library and Archives, Nashville, Tennessee.

35. This and the two following paragraphs are based on ibid., 59–61.

36. OR, vol. 27, pt. 2:469–70. See also Early's account in Jubal A. Early, *Lieutenant General Jubal Anderson Early, C.S.A.: Autobiographical Sketch and Narrative of the War Between the States* (1912; reprint, Wilmington, N.C.: Broadfoot Publishing Company, 1989), 269–71, which conforms closely to his official report.

37. OR, vol. 27, pt. 2:555.

38. Ibid., 445; Jedediah Hotchkiss, *Make Me a Map of the Valley: The Civil War Journal of Stonewall Jackson's Topographer*, ed. Archie P. McDonald (Dallas: Southern Methodist Univ. Press, 1973), 157; John B. Gordon to "My own precious wife," July 7, 1863, Gordon Family Papers (MS 1637), University of Georgia Special Collections, Athens, Georgia.

39. Taylor, *Four Years with Lee*, 95–96.

From Chancellorsville to Cemetery Hill:
O. O. Howard and Eleventh Corps Leadership

1. John Tyler Butts, ed., *A Gallant Captain of the Civil War* (New York: F. Tennyson Neely, 1902), 67 (this is the memoir of Captain von Fritsch, a member of Colonel Leopold von Gilsa's staff); Louise W. Hitz, ed., *The Letters of Frederick C. Winkler, 1862–1865* (Madison, Wisc.: Privately printed, 1963), 51; Oliver Otis Howard, "Gen. O. O. Howard's Personal Reminiscences of the War of the Rebellion," *National Tribune*, June 12, 1884.

2. The best recent examination of the Eleventh Corps on May 2 is Donald C. Pfanz, "Negligence on the Right: The Eleventh Corps at Chancellorsville," in *The Morningside Notes* (Dayton, Ohio: Morningside Bookshop, 1984), 1–8.

3. Coddington, *Gettysburg Campaign*, 306; James S. Pula, *For Liberty and Justice: The Life and Times of Wladimir Krzyzanowski* (Chicago: Polish American Congress Charitable Foundation, 1978), 92; Alanson H. Nelson, *The Battles of Chancellorsville and Gettysburg* (Minneapolis: Privately printed by the author, 1899), 78.

4. Charles W. McKay, "Bushbeck's Brigade," *National Tribune*, October 8, 1908. The Twelfth Corps, part of which also was identified with Pope's army, suffered some of the same ostracism.

5. Carl Schurz, *The Autobiography of Carl Schurz*, abridged in one volume by Wayne Andrews (New York: Charles Scribner's Sons, 1961), 247–48.

6. Quoted in Alfred C. Raphelson, "Alexander Schimmelfennig: A German-American Campaigner in the Civil War," *Pennsylvania Magazine of History and Biography* 87 (April 1963): 172.

7. *The Battle of Chancellorsville and the Eleventh Army Corps*, unattributed pamphlet (New York: G. B. Teubner, 1863), 43.

8. Schurz, *Autobiography*, 249–51.

9. Ibid., 252–54; Hitz, ed., *Winkler Letters*, 52 (first quotation); Pula, *For Liberty and Justice*, 73–74, 89 (second quotation).

10. Frank J. Welcher, *The Union Army, 1861–1865: Organization and Operations, The Eastern Theater* (Bloomington: Indiana Univ. Press, 1989), 459. The officers were Schurz and Adolph von Steinwehr.

11. Pula, *For Liberty and Justice*, 74; John A. Carpenter, *With Sword and Olive Branch: Oliver Otis Howard* (Pittsburgh: Univ. of Pittsburgh Press, 1964), 50.

12. Oliver O. Howard, "After the Battle," *National Tribune*, December 31, 1885; Carl Schurz, "The Battle of Gettysburg," *McClure's Magazine* 29 (July 1907):273; Charles W. Howard, "The First Day at Gettysburg," in Military Order of the Loyal Legion of the United States (hereafter cited as MOLLUS), Illinois Commandery, *Papers* 4 (Chicago: Cozzens & Beaton, 1907), 256.

13. William Simmers, *The Volunteers Manual* (Easton, Pa.: D. H. Neiman, 1863), 26–27 (first quotation); Francis C. Barlow to his mother and brothers, May 8, 1863, typescript in the collections of Gettysburg National Military Park (hereafter cited as GNMP) (second quotation).

14. Schurz, *Autobiography*, 259; Butts, ed., *Gallant Captain*, 74. Simmers, *Volunteers Manual*, 28, offers a different explanation for von Gilsa's arrest: at Middletown, Barlow "was frantic because our worthy brigade commander had dared to await orders from Major-General Howard (by whose order he had been detached), before acting on his [Barlow's] order to rejoin the division."

15. Stewart Sifakis, *Who Was Who in the Civil War* (New York: Facts on File, 1988), 421. Two good sources on Ames are Blanche Butler Ames, comp., *Chronicles from the Nineteenth Century* (Clinton, Mass.: Privately printed, 1957), and Blanche Ames, *Adelbert Ames, 1835–1933: General, Senator, Governor* (New York: Argosy-Antiquarian, 1964).

16. Sifakis, *Who Was Who*, 678–79; Ezra J. Warner, *Generals in Blue: Lives of the Union Commanders* (Baton Rouge: Louisiana State Univ. Press, 1964), 530–31; Adolphus F. Vogelbach, "Honor to Whom Honor Is Due," *National Tribune*, October 11, 1888; Adin B. Underwood, *The Three Years' Service of the Thirty-Third Mass. Infantry Regiment, 1862–1865* (Boston: A. Williams, 1881), 117.

17. Vogelbach, "Honor to Whom Honor Is Due"; Sifakis, *Who Was Who*, 146, 606; Pula, *For Liberty and Justice*, 73; Francis C. Barlow to his mother and brothers, May 8, 1863, GNMP.

18. Schurz, *Autobiography*, passim; Sifakis, *Who Was Who*, 574; Warner, *Generals in Blue*, 426–28.

19. Raphelson, "Alexander Schimmelfennig," provides the best biographical treatment of its subject. See also Butts, ed., *Gallant Captain*, 70, and Pula, *For Liberty and Justice*, 58–59.

20. Pula's *For Liberty and Justice* is a full-length biography of Krzyzanowski. See page 59 for a discussion of Krzyzanowski's style of command.

21. Coddington, *Gettysburg Campaign*, 306.

22. Simmers, *Volunteers Manual*, 26. Although the evidence is often contradictory, many writers believe that morale in the Eleventh Corps improved rapidly after Chancellorsville. See, for example, Theodore A. Dodge, *The Campaign of Chancellorsville* (Boston: James R. Osgood, 1881), 104; Owen Rice, *Afield with the Eleventh Army Corps at Chancellorsville* (Cincinnati: H. C. Sherrick, 1885), 38; and Edwin B. Coddington, "The Role of the 153rd Pennsylvania Volunteer Infantry in the Civil War," copy of article from unidentified journal in Vertical File, GNMP.

23. Schurz, "Battle of Gettysburg," 272.

24. Pula, *For Liberty and Justice*, 91; Butts, ed., *Gallant Captain*, 71 (quotation).

25. Howard, "Gen. O. O. Howard's Personal Reminiscences," *National Tribune*, June 26 (quotation), July 3, 1884.

26. Albert Wallber, "From Gettysburg to Libby Prison," in MOLLUS, Wisconsin Commandery, *Papers* 4 (Milwaukee: Burdick & Allen, 1914), 191; Simmers, *Volunteers Manual*, 27; Andrew J. Boies, *Record of the Thirty-Third Massachusetts Volunteer Infantry* (Fitchburg, Mass.: Sentinel Printing Company, 1880), 31.

27. Carpenter, *Sword and Olive Branch*, 50; O. O. Howard, "Campaign and Battle of Gettysburg," *Atlantic Monthly Magazine* 38 (July 1876):51; Schurz, *Autobiography*, 255; Alfred E. Lee, "Reminiscences of the Gettysburg Battle," *Lippincott's Magazine*, N.S., 6 (July 1883):54.

28. Boies, *Thirty-Third Massachusetts*, 32; Edward S. Salomon, *Gettysburg* (San Francisco: Shannon-Conmy Printing Company, 1913), 5.

29. Howard, "Campaign and Battle of Gettysburg," 52; Pula, *For Liberty and Justice*, 93; Oliver Otis Howard, *The Autobiography of Oliver Otis Howard*, 2 vols. (New York: Baker and Taylor, 1908), 1:402; Schurz, "Battle of Gettysburg," 272.

30. OR, vol. 27, pt. 3:414–15; ibid., pt. 1:733, 739.

31. Charles Howard, "First Day at Gettysburg," 239; OR, vol. 27, pt. 1:701; Howard, "Gen. O. O. Howard's Personal Reminiscences," *National Tribune*, November 27, 1884; Howard, *Autobiography*, 1:402–3; O. O. Howard to Jacobs, July 23, 1864, photocopy in the collections of GNMP.

32. Howard, "Campaign and Battle of Gettysburg," 52.

33. Warren W. Hassler, "The First Day's Battle at Gettysburg," *Civil War History* 6 (September 1960):263; Howard, *Autobiography*, 1:408–9; Howard, "Campaign and Battle of Gettysburg," 53; OR, vol. 27, pt. 1:701; Hassler, *Crisis at the Crossroads*, 30; Marshall D. Krolick, "The Union Command: Decisions That Shaped a Battle," *Blue and Gray Magazine* 5 (November 1987):15.

34. Mark H. Dunkelman and Michael J. Winey, *The Hardtack Regiment: An Illustrated History of the 154th Regiment, New York State Infantry Volunteers* (Rutherford, N.J.: Fairleigh Dickinson Univ. Press, 1981), 71; Howard, "Gen. O. O. Howard's Personal Reminiscences," *National Tribune*, November 27, 1884; Howard, *Autobiography*, 1:408–9; Alfred E. Lee, "The Eleventh Corps: The Disadvantages Under Which It Fought at Gettysburg," *Philadelphia Weekly Press*, January 26, 1887; Coddington, *Gettysburg Campaign*, 280.

35. Howard, *Autobiography*, 1:409; Charles Howard, "First Day at Gettysburg," 239–40. Coddington, *Gettysburg Campaign*, 268–69, affirms that Major William Riddle of Reynolds's staff first contacted Howard.

36. OR, vol. 27, pt. 1:701; Howard, *Autobiography*, 1:409; Howard, "Campaign and Battle of Gettysburg," 53; Howard, "Gen. O. O. Howard's Personal Reminiscences," *National Tribune*, November 27, 1884.

37. Howard, "Campaign and Battle of Gettysburg," 53; Howard, *Autobiography*, 1:409; OR, vol. 27, pt. 1:701.

38. Howard, *Autobiography*, 1:409–10; Howard, "Campaign and Battle of Gettysburg," 53.

39. See Coddington, *Gettysburg Campaign*, 702–3 n. 90, for a discussion of Howard's claim that he rather than Reynolds selected Cemetery Hill. J. Max Mueller, a member of von Steinwehr's staff, accorded the honor to his chief in "Hancock at Gettysburg: The Claim That He Selected the Battle-ground Disputed by a Staff Officer," *New York Times*, October 16, 1880.

40. Howard, "Gen. O. O. Howard's Personal Reminiscences," *National Tribune*, November 27, 1884; Howard, *Autobiography*, 1:411. See also *Army and Navy Journal*, April 16, 1864, for a positive statement supporting Howard's selection of the position. Identified only as "A.S.," the author of this statement probably was von Steinwehr.

41. Edward C. Culp, *The 25th Ohio Vet. Vol. Infantry in the War for the Union* (Topeka, Kan.: George W. Crane, 1885), 77.

42. Howard, "Campaign and Battle of Gettysburg," 54; Howard, *Autobiography*, 1: 412; OR, vol. 27, pt. 1:701–2; Howard, untitled typescript of article from unidentified journal, p. 29, in the collections of GNMP (cited hereafter as Howard, "Untitled Typescript"). Charles Howard, "First Day at Gettysburg," 244, remembered Skelly's given name as William.

43. Howard, "Untitled Typescript," 30–31; Howard, *Autobiography*, 1:413; and Charles Howard, "First Day at Gettysburg," 244, all identify the messenger as Hall. In his report in OR, vol. 27, pt. 1:702, Howard mentions Riddle by name, while in "Campaign and Battle of Gettysburg," 54, he calls the officer "Biddle."

44. Hassler, *Crisis at the Crossroads*, 65.

45. OR, vol. 27, pt. 1:742; Pula, *For Liberty and Justice*, 95–96; Wallber, "From Gettysburg to Libby Prison," 191–92.

46. OR, vol. 27, pt. 1:727; Schurz, *Autobiography*, 256–57; James Beale, *The Statements of Time on July 1 at Gettysburg, Pa. 1863* (Philadelphia: James Beale Printer, 1897), 25–26.

47. D. Scott Hartwig, "The 11th Army Corps on July 1, 1863—'The Unlucky 11th.'" *Gettysburg Magazine* 2 (January 1990):35. Hartwig's work is by far the best tactical study of the Eleventh Corps on July 1.

48. Hartwig, "11th Corps on July 1," 33, 35. Other estimates vary: OR, vol. 27, pt. 1:151, counts 9,893 officers and men equipped and present for duty on June 30; Hassler, *Crisis at the Crossroads*, 64, puts Howard's strength at 9,500; John W. Busey and David G. Martin, *Regimental Strengths at Gettysburg* (Hightstown, N.J.: Longstreet House, 1982), 78, offers the figure of 8,477 Eleventh Corps Infantry engaged at Gettysburg.

49. The artillery of the Eleventh Corps was organized as follows: Battery G, Fourth U.S. Artillery, Lt. Bayard Wilkeson, six light 12-pounders; Battery I, First Ohio Artillery, Capt. Hubert Dilger, four light 12-pounders; Battery K, First Ohio Artillery, Capt. Lewis Heckman, four light 12-pounders; Battery I, First New York Artillery, Capt. Michael Wiedrich, six 3-inch rifles; Thirteenth New York Independent Battery, Lt. William Wheeler, four 3-inch rifles (OR, vol. 27, pt. 1:747).

50. Howard, "Campaign and Battle of Gettysburg," 54; OR, vol. 27, pt. 3:702 (quotation). In OR, vol. 27, pt. 1:727, and "The Battle of Gettysburg," 274, Schurz credits First Corps division commander James Wadsworth rather than Doubleday with dispatching the information about a Confederate threat west of Gettysburg.

51. Charles Howard, "First Day at Gettysburg," 248; OR, vol. 27, pt. 1:702. In his *Autobiography*, 1:416, Howard credited his brother with bringing news of Southern forces forming to the north.

52. OR, vol. 27, pt. 1:702; Hassler, "First Day's Battle at Gettysburg," 269–70; Coddington, *Gettysburg Campaign*, 282.

53. Joseph A. Gaston, "The Gettysburg Campaign, to include the Fighting on the First Day, July 1, 1863," unpublished paper (prepared at the Army War College, 1911–12), 72, U.S. Army Military History Institute, Carlisle Barracks, Pennsylvania (first quotation); Coddington, *Gettysburg Campaign*, 301 (second quotation); Louis Fischer, "At Gettysburg. First Day's Work of the Eleventh Corps, July 1, 1863." *National Tribune*, December 12, 1889.

54. Howard, "Untitled Typescript," 33.

55. Coddington, *Gettysburg Campaign*, 301–2.

56. Howard, "Campaign and Battle of Gettysburg," 55; Chapman Biddle, *The First Day of the Battle of Gettysburg: An Address Before the Historical Society of Pennsylvania, March 8, 1880* (Philadelphia: J. B. Lippincott, 1880), 39. In his *Autobiography*, 1:414, Howard states that he rode with Barlow "through the city, and out to what is now Barlow Hill"; however, no other source supports this claim. See Hartwig, "11th Corps on July 1," 39, for a discussion of how far Howard advanced.

57. Sidney G. Cooke, "The First Day at Gettysburg," in MOLLUS, Kansas Commandery, *War Talks in Kansas* (Kansas City, Mo.: F. Hudson, 1906), 282. Cooke served in the 147th New York Infantry.

58. Hassler, *Crisis at the Crossroads*, 68; Raphelson, "Alexander Schimmelfennig," 174; OR, 27, pt. 1:728.

59. OR, vol. 27, pt. 1:721; Hassler, *Crisis at the Crossroads*, 69.

60. Howard, "Campaign and Battle of Gettysburg," 56; Howard, *Autobiography*, 1:414; Coddington, *Gettysburg Campaign*, 282; Krolick, "Union Command," 17; OR, vol. 27, pt. 1: 702–3; Hassler, *Crisis at the Crossroads*, 111.

61. OR, vol. 27, pt. 1:728; Schurz, "Battle of Gettysburg," 276 (quotation).

62. Hartwig disagrees in "11th Corps on July 1," 49, concluding that "there is not sufficient evidence to form a reasonable opinion." But see ibid., 43, which seems to ascribe the decision to Barlow after all.

63. Howard, *Autobiography*, 1:416.

64. Schurz, "Battle of Gettysburg," 276; Schurz, *Autobiography*, 259; OR, vol. 27, pt. 1:728; Francis C. Barlow to his mother, July 7, 1863, copy in the collections of GNMP; Butts, ed., *Gallant Captain*, 75; Edward C. Culp, "Gettysburg: Reminiscences of the Great Fight by a Participant," *National Tribune*, March 19, 1885.

65. Hartwig, "11th Corps on July 1," 40; Coddington, *Gettysburg Campaign*, 291; Fred Tilberg to Warren Hassler, January 16, 1951, Vertical File, GNMP.

66. Raphelson, "Alexander Schimmelfennig," 174, advances this theory, which is persuasive but unprovable. In "11th Corps on July 1," 40, Hartwig speculates that Barlow's motives were purely defensive.

67. Henry J. Hunt, "The First Day at Gettysburg," in B&L, 3:281; Hassler, *Crisis at the Crossroads*, 70; Hassler, "First Day's Battle at Gettysburg," 270; Schurz, "Battle of Gettysburg," 276; OR, vol. 27, pt. 1:728; Schurz, *Autobiography*, 259.

68. Hartwig, "11th Corps on July 1," 43; George Campbell Brown, "My Confederate Experiences," typescript in the collections of GNMP.

69. Hartwig, "11th Corps on July 1," 43–44; Hassler, *Crisis at the Crossroads*, 88; Krolick, "Union Command," 18; Coddington, *Gettysburg Campaign*, 291. Krolick and Coddington characterize the Confederate assault as a surprise.

70. C. D. Grace, "Rodes's Division at Gettysburg," *Confederate Veteran* 5 (December 1897): 614–15.

71. Hartwig, "11th Corps on July 1," 44–47, provides a detailed account of this phase of the fighting. See also Hassler, *Crisis at the Crossroads*, 81; quotation from Francis C. Barlow to his mother, July 7, 1863, GNMP.

72. Hunt, "First Day at Gettysburg," 281; G. W. Nichols, *A Soldier's Story of His Regiment and Incidentally of the Lawton-Gordon-Evans Brigade, Army of Northern Virginia* (1898; reprint, Kennesaw, Ga.: Continental Book Company, 1961), 116; Hartwig, "11th Corps on July 1," 45.

73. Hartwig, "11th Corps on July 1," 45; Lee, "Reminiscences," 56 (quotation).

74. Hartwig, "11th Corps on July 1," 45, 47.

75. OR, vol. 27, pt. 1:925. Buford transmitted this information to Meade via Alfred Pleasonton, commander of the cavalry in the Army of the Potomac.

76. Howard, "Campaign and Battle of Gettysburg," 56–57; Charles Howard, "First Day at Gettysburg," 253–56. In *Gettysburg Campaign*, 311–13, Coddington discusses Slocum's lack of activity.

77. OR, vol. 27, pt. 1:703; Howard, "Campaign and Battle of Gettysburg," 57 (quotation).

78. Hartwig, "11th Corps on July 1," 47; OR, vol. 27, pt. 1:703; Howard, *Autobiography*, 1:417.

79. Hartwig, "11th Corps on July 1," 47–48; Daniel B. Allen to J. B. Bachelder, April 5, 1864, copy in the collections of GNMP. Allen commanded the 154th New York of Coster's brigade; the 73d Pennsylvania was detached at the depot. See also Mark H. Dunkelman, "Coster Avenue Mural, Gettysburg," 4, typescript in the collections of GNMP.

80. Schurz, Autobiography, 260; Hartwig, "11th Corps on July 1," 48; Dunkelman and Winey, Hardtack Regiment, 72–73; John F. Sullivan, letter to the Ellicotville (N.Y.) Post, September 5, 1888, copy in the collections of GNMP.

81. Dunkelman and Winey, Hardtack Regiment, 75; Hartwig, "11th Corps on July 1," 48.

82. Schurz, Autobiography, 260 (first quotation); Dunkelman and Winey, Hardtack Regiment, 75 (second quotation); Dunkelman, "Coster Avenue Mural," 6; Mark H. Dunkelman, "Address at the Dedication of the Coster Avenue Mural, July 1, 1988," copy of unpublished address in the collections of GNMP.

83. OR, vol. 27, pt. 1:729.

84. Howard, "Campaign and Battle of Gettysburg," 57; Howard, Autobiography, 1:417; Hassler, "First Day's Battle at Gettysburg," 271; Charles Howard, "First Day at Gettysburg," 257–58; Hassler, Crisis at the Crossroads, 123. As is typical concerning times of day on a battlefield, the sources disagree as to when the Union army began its wholesale withdrawal. For example, Hartwig, "11th Corps on July 1," 49, states that the Eleventh Corps retreated "through the streets of Gettysburg" no later than 3:45 P.M.

85. James Beale, "Gettysburg: A Review of Gen. Howard's Account of the Battle," National Tribune, January 1, 1885. It is possible that Beale referred to Barlow's rather than Schimmelfennig's division.

86. William F. Fox, ed., New York Monuments Commission for the Battlefields of Gettysburg and Chattanooga: Final Report on the Battlefield of Gettysburg, 3 vols. (Albany, N.Y.: J. B. Lyon, 1900, 1902), 1:380.

87. See, for example, OR, vol. 27, pt. 2:317 (R. E. Lee's report), 607 (A. P. Hill's report).

88. Schurz, Autobiography, 261; Underwood, Three Years' Service, 118; Culp, "Gettysburg Reminiscences."

89. Pula, For Liberty and Justice, 105; Coddington, Gettysburg Campaign, 295–96; Hunt, "First Day at Gettysburg," 283; Howard, "Gen. O. O. Howard's Personal Reminiscences," National Tribune, November 27, 1884; Underwood, Three Years' Service, 119.

90. Carl Schurz, The Reminiscences of Carl Schurz, 3 vols. (New York: McClure, 1907–8), 3:35–37; Butts, ed., Gallant Captain, 78; "The General's Tour," Blue and Gray Magazine 5 (November 1987):53; Fox, Final Report on Gettysburg, 3:25, 43; Raphelson, "Alexander Schimmelfennig," 176.

91. Hartwig, "11th Corps on July 1," 49.

92. Howard, "Campaign and Battle of Gettysburg," 58; Krolick, "Union Command," 17–18; Coddington, Gettysburg Campaign, 303.

93. Schurz, Autobiography, 261; OR, vol. 27, pt. 1:704; Culp, "Reminiscences." Some accounts state that Howard did not achieve effective control of the situation on Cemetery Hill until 5:00 P.M.

94. Charles Howard, "First Day at Gettysburg," 264, 358–59; Coddington, Gettysburg Campaign, 296–97; Howard, "Campaign and Battle of Gettysburg," 58 (quotations); Pula, For Liberty and Justice, 105, 107.

95. Hassler, Crisis at the Crossroads, 134; Schurz, "Battle of Gettysburg," 277; Hunt, "First Day at Gettysburg," 283; Schurz, Autobiography, 263.

96. Schurz, Autobiography, 264.

97. Krolick, "Union Command," 11–12, 19; Coddington, Gettysburg Campaign, 284–85; Howard, "Campaign and Battle of Gettysburg," 58; Howard, "Gen. O. O. Howard's Personal Reminiscences," National Tribune, November 27, 1884; Schurz, Autobiography, 262.

98. Eminel P. Halstead, "The First Day of the Battle of Gettysburg," in MOLLUS, District of Columbia Commandery, *Papers* 1 (Washington, D.C.: 1887), 7–8.

99. Howard, "Campaign and Battle of Gettysburg," 58–59; Howard, *Autobiography*, 1:418; OR, vol. 27, pt. 1:704; Howard, "Gen. O. O. Howard's Personal Reminiscences," *National Tribune*, November 27, 1884.

100. David M. Jordan, *Winfield Scott Hancock: A Soldier's Life* (Bloomington: Indiana Univ. Press, 1988), 83.

101. Beale, "Gettysburg," severely questions Howard's veracity on this and other points.

102. Schurz, *Autobiography*, 262–63.

103. OR, vol. 27, pt. 1:696–97.

104. Charles Howard, "First Day at Gettysburg," 264. In OR, vol. 27, pt. 1:705, and his *Autobiography*, 1:423, O. O. Howard gives slightly different versions of this exchange; he includes Slocum and Sickles as part of the group in *Autobiography*.

105. Schurz, *Autobiography*, 266.

106. Determining precise casualties is virtually impossible. The Eleventh Corps reported 3,801 casualties at Gettysburg (OR, vol. 27, pt. 1:183); Hartwig estimates 2,850 lost on July 1, including 250 killed, 1,200 wounded, and 1,400 missing and captured ("11th Corps on July 1," 49); Hassler, who provides casualties by regiment, gives the figures as 1,768 killed and wounded and 1,427 missing or captured for a total of 3,195 (*Crisis at the Crossroads*, 147–48).

107. Pula, *For Liberty and Justice*, 107, 101; OR, vol. 27, pt. 2:492 (first quotation); A. R. Barlow, "A Defense of the Eleventh Corps," *National Tribune*, January 15, 1885 (second quotation).

108. Francis C. Barlow to Robert Treat Paine, August 12, 1863, Francis C. Barlow to his mother, July 7, 1863, typescripts in the collections of GNMP.

109. Coddington, *Gettysburg Campaign*, 305; Hartwig, "11th Corps on July 1," 49; Hassler, *Crisis at the Crossroads*, 147–49.

110. O. O. Howard to his wife, July 16, 1863, copy in the collections of GNMP; D. Henson, "Ohio Troops in the Eleventh Corps," *National Tribune*, March 13, 1890; Robert Underwood Johnson and Clarence Clough Buel, "Hancock and Howard in the First Day's Fight," B&L, 3:289.

111. Charles Howard, "First Day at Gettysburg," 262.

112. Krolick, "Union Command," 17–18, 20, is Howard's most recent and eloquent critic. See also Coddington, *Gettysburg Campaign*, 300.

113. For a more sympathetic treatment of Howard's generalship, see Hassler, *Crisis at the Crossroads*, 154.

114. Schurz, *Autobiography*, 265; Howard, "Campaign and Battle of Gettysburg," 59.

Three Confederate Disasters on Oak Ridge:
Failures of Brigade Leadership on the First Day at Gettysburg

Robert K. Krick enjoyed invaluable archival assistance from the splendid historian of Gettysburg National Military Park, Kathy Georg Harrison, in doing the research for his article. Harrison's files include the unpublished John B. Bachelder maps (ca. 1883), which provide wonderfully detailed approximations of positions and movements on the first day at Gettysburg.

1. Samuel Merrifield Bemiss to "My dear Children," April 10, 1863, in the Bemiss Family Papers, Virginia Historical Society, Richmond, Virginia (MSS 1B4255d23). Bemiss was tending Lee because Lafayette Guild, the army's chief surgeon, was himself sick. Apparently un-

aware of the need to await postwar deification of Lee in some mythological process, Bemiss enthused in unbridled fashion about the character of his patient and hoped his children would someday "imitate his actions and arrive at his excellencies."

2. W. W. Blackford, *War Years with Jeb Stuart* (New York: Charles Scribner's Sons, 1945), 230; T. Michael Parrish, ed., *Reminiscences of the War in Virginia, by David French Boyd* (Austin, Tex.: Jenkins, 1989), 19–21.

3. Louis G. Young, "Gettysburg Address," in *Addresses Delivered before the Confederate Veterans' Association, of Savannah, Ga., 1898–1902* (Savannah: Savannah Morning News Print, 1902), 35–36.

4. Heth, *Memoirs*, xli.

5. OR, vol. 25, pt. 2:633, 644–45.

6. Freeman, *Lee's Lieutenants*, 2:507.

7. *Official Register of the Officers and Cadets of the U.S. Military Academy* (New York: W. L. Burroughs, 1847), 7–8, 21; and publications of identical title and imprint dating from 1844, 1845, and 1846.

8. Henry Heth, *A System of Target Practice for the Use of Troops When Armed with the Musket, Rifle-Musket, Rifle, or Carbine. . . . Published by Order of the War Department* (Philadelphia: Henry Carey Baird, 1858). The reprint (Washington, D.C.: GPO, 1862) is identical, excepting the deletion of Heth's name, and probably was printed from the same plates.

9. J. W. Benjamin, "Gray Forces Defeated in Battle of Lewisburg," *West Virginia History* 20 (October 1958):32; Rose W. Fry, *Recollections of the Rev. John McElhenney, D.D.* (Richmond: Whittet & Shepperson, 1893), 181.

10. John A. Fite, *Memoirs of Colonel John A. Fite . . . 1832–1925* (N.p., 1935), 95.

11. OR, vol. 27, pt. 2:637; W. H. Bird, *Stories of the Civil War* (Columbiana, Ala.: Advocate Print, n.d.), 7–8.

12. Compiled Service Record of Joseph R. Davis in M331, Roll 72, National Archives, Washington, D.C.; L. M. Blackford to "My Dear Mother," March 11, 1863, in Blackford Family Papers (MS 1912), SHC. For an amusing, if minor, example of avuncular intervention, see the excuse for tardiness supplied by President Davis on behalf of General Davis in George L. Christian, "General Lee's Headquarters Records and Papers—The Present Location of Some of These," in SHSP 44:232–33.

13. J. E. B. Stuart to G. W. Custis Lee, December 18, 1862, Stuart Papers, Perkins Library, Duke University, Durham, North Carolina.

14. Robert K. Krick, *Lee's Colonels: A Biographical Register of the Field Officers of the Army of Northern Virginia*, rev. ed. (Dayton, Ohio: Press of Morningside Bookshop, 1984), 43–44, 47, 83, 117, 172, 232, 242, 302, 310; John M. Stone to Joseph R. Davis, undated typescript in John B. Bachelder Papers, in the collections of GNMP.

15. OR, vol. 25, pt. 2:648–49.

16. Draft map for 11 A.M., July 1, compiled by John B. Bachelder, ca. 1883, revising his earlier published versions, in the collections of GNMP.

17. Dunbar Rowland, *The Official and Statistical Register of the State of Mississippi* (Nashville: Press of the Brandon Printing Company, 1908), 433.

18. Manuscript Bachelder map and bound volume containing Cope survey notes, p. 18, both in the collections of GNMP; John M. Stone to Joseph R. Davis, undated typescript in Bachelder Papers, GNMP.

19. Charles M. Cooke, "Fifty-Fifth Regiment," in *N.C. Regiments*, 3:297; Samuel Hankins, *Simple Story of a Soldier* (Nashville: Confederate Veteran, 1912), 43; LeGrand J. Wilson, *The Confederate Soldier* (Memphis: Memphis State Univ. Press, 1973), 116–17; J. V. Pierce (147th New York Infantry) to J. B. Bachelder, November 1, 1882, Bachelder Papers, GNMP (hereafter cited as Pierce letter, GNMP).

20. Hankins, *Simple Story of a Soldier*, 44; Wilson, *Confederate Soldier*, 117; Cooke, "Fifty-Fifth Regiment," 297.

21. *Galveston Daily News*, June 21, 1896, p. 1 (this article by a veteran of the 55th plagiarizes the account in N.C. *Regiments* but adds a few interesting personal notes); Pender, *The General to His Lady*, 244; Cooke, "Fifty-Fifth Regiment," 279; manuscript Bachelder map and bound volume containing Cope survey notes, p. 18, GNMP.

22. OR, vol. 27, pt. 2:650; W. B. Murphy (Co. A, 2d Mississippi Infantry) to F. A. Dearborn, June 29, 1900, copy in the collections of GNMP (this vivid and important source hereafter cited as Murphy letter, GNMP).

23. OR, vol. 27, pt. 2:649; Murphy letter, GNMP; Pierce letter, GNMP.

24. *Galveston Daily News*, June 21, 1896, p. 1; John M. Stone to Joseph R. Davis, undated typescript in Bachelder Papers, GNMP; Pierce letter, GNMP.

25. Cooke, "Fifty-Fifth Regiment," 297; Murphy letter, GNMP; Cope survey notes, p. 18, GNMP.

26. OR, vol. 27, pt. 2:649; Cope survey notes, p. 18, GNMP; John M. Stone to Joseph R. Davis, undated typescript in Bachelder Papers, GNMP.

27. Accounts by John A. Kellogg, A.A.G. of Cutler's brigade, and Dawes himself, in Bachelder Papers, GNMP, agree on the matter of the corking detachment.

28. Wharton J. Green, *Recollections and Reflections* (Raleigh: Edwards and Broughton, 1906), 176.

29. *Publications of the Mississippi Historical Society* 9 (1906):27; Murphy letter, GNMP.

30. Cooke, "Fifty-Fifth Regiment," 298.

31. Murphy letter, GNMP; Hankins, *Simple Story of a Soldier*, 47. For a splendid account of Federal operations against Davis, see D. Scott Hartwig, "Guts and Good Leadership: The Action at the Railroad Cut, July 1, 1863," *Gettysburg: Historical Articles of Lasting Interest* 1 (July 1989):5–14.

32. Wilson, *Confederate Soldier*, 118; R. T. Bennett, "Fourteenth Regiment," in N.C. *Regiments*, 1:719; John R. King, *My Experiences in the Confederate Army* (Clarksburg, W. Va.: Stonewall Jackson Chapter, United Daughters of the Confederacy, 1917), 13.

33. OR, vol. 27, pt. 1:638.

34. Henry Kyd Douglas manuscript marginalia in his copy of G. F. R. Henderson, *Stonewall Jackson and the American Civil War*, 2 vols. (London: Longmans, Green, 1898), 1:576, original in the collections of Antietam National Battlefield, Sharpsburg, Maryland.

35. James Power Smith to "My dearest sister," January 21, 1863, in the collections of Fredericksburg and Spotsylvania National Military Park, Fredericksburg, Virginia; Francis Smith Robertson, "Reminiscences of the Years 1861–1865," *Historical Society of Washington County, Va., Bulletin*, ser. 2, no. 23 (1986):15; Thomas H. Carter to D. H. Hill, July 1, 1885, in the Lee Papers, Virginia Historical Society; B. T. Lacy recollections, file folder titled Jackson's Staff, Roll 39, Jedediah Hotchkiss Papers, Library of Congress.

36. OR, vol. 27, pt. 2:552, 596.

37. James M. Thompson, *Reminiscences of Autauga Rifles* (Autaugaville, Ala: Printed for the author, 1879), 7; OR, vol. 27, pt. 2:552.

38. OR, vol. 27, pt. 2:602. The timing here, as for all other events under discussion, is from Bachelder's manuscript maps, ca. 1883, revising his earlier and less detailed published maps, originals in the collections of GNMP. The 1:00 P.M. map shows the three brigades abreast on the nose of Oak Ridge just above Forney's house.

39. OR, vol. 27, pt. 2:602, 592, 601, 553; Robert E. Park, "War Diary of Capt. Robert Emory Park, Twelfth Alabama Regiment, January 28th, 1863–January 27th, 1864," in SHSP 26:12–13.

40. OR, vol. 27, pt. 2:552.

41. R. E. Rodes to A. P. Hill, May 13, 1863, in Edward A. O'Neal's Compiled Service Record, Microcopy M331, Roll 190, National Archives; R. E. Lee to Jefferson Davis, May 26, 1863, in Freeman, ed., *Lee's Dispatches*, 95.

42. Circular letter in Edward A. O'Neal's Compiled Service Record; R. E. Rodes to Maj. W. H. Taylor, August 1, 1863, in Cullen A. Battle's Compiled Service Record, Microcopy M331, Roll 18, National Archives.

43. Edward A. O'Neal's Compiled Service Record.

44. R. E. Lee to Jefferson Davis, April 6, 1864, Lee to Secretary of War James A. Seddon, June 11, 1864, in Freeman, ed., *Lee's Dispatches*, 146–47, 225–26. O'Neal's letter of May 29, 1864, in his Compiled Service Record proposed the financial need criterion.

45. OR, vol. 27, pt. 2:553, 595–96.

46. W. H. May, "Reminiscences of the War Between the States," 5, typescript at the Georgia Department of Archives and History, Atlanta; OR, vol. 27, pt. 2:595–600, 592.

47. OR, vol. 27, pt. 2:553–54

48. Ibid., 553; C. C. Wehrum to John B. Bachelder, January 21, 1884, Bachelder Papers, GNMP.

49. John D. Vautier, "At Gettysburg," *Philadelphia Press*, November 10, 1886.

50. OR, vol. 27, pt. 2:553, 601; Park, "War Diary," 13; Krick, *Lee's Colonels*, 267.

51. OR, vol. 27, pt. 2:553.

52. Ibid., 596–97, 603.

53. Ibid., 601, 592–93.

54. V. E. Turner and H. C. Wall, "Twenty-Third Regiment," in *N.C. Regiments*, 2:235.

55. John Stanley Brooks Letters (M-3094), SHC. Brooks's letters covering the controversy with Iverson include January 4, 1863, to "Dear Brother"; January 14, 1863, to "Dear Parrents"; March 1, 1863, to "Dear Sister"; and March 8, 1863, to "Dear Parrents and Sister M."

56. OR, vol. 27, pt. 2:579, 554; Turner and Wall, "Twenty-Third Regiment," 235–36.

57. Walter A. Montgomery, "Twelfth Regiment," in *N.C. Regiments*, 1:636; James C. MacRae and C. M. Busbee, "Fifth Regiment," ibid., 287; Turner and Wall, "Twenty-Third Regiment," 235; John Stanley Brooks to "Dear father," July 12, 1863, in Brooks Letters, SHC.

58. Turner and Wall, "Twenty-Third Regiment," 235; J. D. Hufham, Jr. [pseudonym], "Gettysburg," *Wake Forest Student* 16 (1897):454; George Campbell Brown memoir, p. 53, Brown-Ewell Papers, Tennessee State Library and Archives.

59. Turner and Wall, "Twenty-Third Regiment," 235; Montgomery, "Twelfth Regiment," 634–35; Isaac Hall to J. B. Bachelder, August 15, 1884, Bachelder Papers, GNMP.

60. Turner and Wall, "Twenty-Third Regiment," 235; Vautier, "At Gettysburg."

61. Vautier, "At Gettysburg."

62. Samuel D. Marshbourn Reminiscences, North Carolina State Archives; Thomas F. Toon, "Twentieth Regiment," in *N.C. Regiments*, 1:119; Turner and Wall, "Twenty-Third Regiment," 238.

63. Henry Robinson Berkeley, *Four Years in the Confederate Artillery* (Chapel Hill: Univ. of North Carolina Press, 1961), 50.

64. OR, vol. 27, pt. 2:444, 579–80.

65. Turner and Wall, "Twenty-Third Regiment," 236–37; J. L. Wallace Reminiscences, North Carolina State Archives; Jonathan Fuller Coghill to "Dear Pappy, Ma, and Mit," July 17, 1863, from a copy in the possession of John R. Bass, Spring Hope, North Carolina. Coghill's letters dated July 9, July 31, and August 1 (copies of which are in the possession of Mr. Bass) also supply details about the July 1 disaster.

66. C. C. Wehrum to John B. Bachelder, January 21, 1884, Bachelder Papers, GNMP; Vautier, "At Gettysburg."

67. Montgomery, "Twelfth Regiment," 635; Don P. Halsey, Jr., *A Sketch of the Life of Capt. Don P. Halsey of the Confederate States Army* (Richmond: Wm. Ellis Jones, 1904), 10–12; OR, vol. 27, pt. 2:445, 451, 554.

68. Memoir of Colonel Charles Christopher Blacknall by his son, in the Oscar W. Blacknall Papers, North Carolina State Archives.

69. OR, vol. 27, pt. 2:554; George Campbell Brown Memoir, p. 53, Brown-Ewell Papers, Tennessee State Library and Archives; Toon, "Twentieth Regiment," 111.

70. Montgomery, "Twelfth Regiment," 636–37.

71. May, "Reminiscences"; Compiled Service Record of Major James C. Bryan, Microcopy M311, Roll 38, National Archives. Bryan's papers include extensive transcripts from a court of inquiry that supply interesting material on the retreat, notably times of entry into various villages and routes taken by the trains.

72. Diary of Edward A. O'Neal, Jr., in John Coffee and Family Papers, Library of Congress; L. Minor Blackford, *Mine Eyes Have Seen the Glory* (Cambridge, Mass.: Harvard Univ. Press, 1954), 217–19.

73. Transcript of conversation between William Allan and R. E. Lee, February 19, 1870, p. 21, William Allan Papers, SHC.

"If the Enemy Is There, We Must Attack Him":
R. E. *Lee and the Second Day at Gettysburg*

1. Joan K. Walton and Terry A. Walton, eds., *Letters of LeRoy S. Edwards Written During the War Between the States* (N.p., [1985]), [57]; Arthur James Lyon Fremantle, *Three Months in the Southern States: April–June, 1863* (1863; reprint, Lincoln: Univ. of Nebraska Press, 1991), 231–32.

2. Randolph H. McKim, *A Soldier's Recollections: Leaves from the Diary of a Young Confederate* (1910; reprint, Washington, D.C.: Zenger Publishing, 1983), 182; Stephen Dodson Ramseur to Ellen Richmond, Aug. 3, 1863, folder 7, Stephen Dodson Ramseur Papers, Southern Historical Collection, Wilson Library, University of North Carolina, Chapel Hill, North Carolina (repository hereafter cited as SHC).

3. Robert Garlick Hill Kean, *Inside the Confederate Government: The Diary of Robert Garlick Hill Kean*, ed. Edward Younger (New York: Oxford Univ. Press, 1957), 84; Wade Hampton to Joseph E. Johnston, July 30, 1863, quoted in Herman Hattaway and Archer Jones, *How the North Won: A Military History of the Civil War* (Urbana: Univ. of Illinois Press, 1983), 414.

4. James Longstreet to Augustus Baldwin Longstreet, July 24, 1863, reproduced in part in J. William Jones et al., eds., *Southern Historical Society Papers*, 52 vols. and three-vol. index (1876–1959; reprint, Wilmington, N.C.: Broadfoot Publishing, 1990–92), 5:54–55 (hereafter cited as SHSP). This letter also appeared in the *New Orleans Republican* on Jan. 25, 1876, in the *New York Times* four days later, and in Longstreet's article "The Campaign of Gettysburg" in the *Philadelphia Weekly Times*, Nov. 3, 1877 (the *Weekly Times* article also appeared under the title "Lee in Pennsylvania" in Editors of the *Philadelphia Weekly Times*, *The Annals of the War Written by Leading Participants North and South* [Philadelphia, 1879], 414–46 [the last work cited hereafter as *Annals of the War*]).

5. William Swinton, *Campaigns of the Army of the Potomac: A Critical History of Operations in Virginia, Maryland and Pennsylvania, from the Commencement to the Close of the War, 1861–1865* (1866; rev. ed., New York: Charles Scribner's Sons, 1882), 340–41. Swinton credited "a full and free conversation" with Longstreet as his source for "revelations of the purposes and sentiments of Lee." In Editors of the *Philadelphia Weekly Times*, "Lee in Pennsylvania," 433, Longstreet used almost precisely the same language as Swinton when he observed: "There is no doubt that General Lee, during the crisis of that campaign, lost the matchless equipoise

that usually characterized him, and that whatever mistakes were made were not so much matters of deliberate judgment as the impulses of a great mind disturbed by unparalleled conditions."

6. Edward A. Pollard, *The Lost Cause: A New Southern History of the War of the Confederates* (New York: E. B. Treat and Company, 1866), 406–7. Pollard's assessment of Lee is a bit harsher in his *Lee and His Lieutenants, Comprising the Early Life, Public Services, and Campaigns of General Robert E. Lee and His Companions in Arms, with a Record of Their Campaigns and Heroic Deeds* (New York: E. B. Treat and Company, 1867).

7. James D. McCabe, Jr., *Life and Campaigns of General Robert E. Lee* (St. Louis: National Publishing, 1866), 393–95.

8. Jubal A. Early, *The Campaigns of Gen. Robert E. Lee. An Address by Lieut. General Jubal A. Early, before Washington and Lee University, January 19th, 1872* (Baltimore: John Murphy and Company, 1872), 30–32. Fitzhugh Lee, J. William Jones, and William Nelson Pendleton were among Longstreet's chief critics. For the early arguments in the Gettysburg controversy, see vols. 4–6 of the SHSP. Useful modern treatments include Thomas L. Connelly, *The Marble Man: Robert E. Lee and His Image in American Society* (New York: Alfred A. Knopf, 1977); William Garrett Piston, *Lee's Tarnished Lieutenant: James Longstreet and His Place in Southern History* (Athens: Univ. of Georgia Press, 1987); and Glenn Tucker, *Lee and Longstreet at Gettysburg* (Indianapolis: Bobbs-Merrill, 1968).

9. Frank E. Everett, Jr., "Delayed Report of an Important Eyewitness to Gettysburg—Benjamin G. Humphreys," *The Journal of Mississippi History* 46 (Nov. 1984): 318.

10. U.S. War Department, *The War of the Rebellion: A Compilation of the Official Records of the Union and Confederate Armies*, 127 vols., index, and atlas (Washington, D.C.: GPO, 1880–1901), ser. 1, vol. 27, pt. 2:318 (hereafter cited as OR; all references are to volumes in series 1).

11. Ibid., 318–19.

12. Robert E. Lee, Jr., *Recollections and Letters of General Robert E. Lee* (1904; reprint, Wilmington, N.C.: Broadfoot Publishing, 1988), 102. Lee wrote to Maj. William M. McDonald of Berryville, Virginia.

13. Transcript of conversation between R. E. Lee and William Allan, Apr. 15, 1868, pp. 13–15, William Allan Papers, SHC. Lee apparently misconstrued Longstreet's comment about an agreement not to fight an offensive battle, interpreting it as a claim that Lee had agreed to fight no battle at all.

14. Transcript of conversation between R. E. Lee and William Allan, Feb. 18, 1870, pp. 20–21, William Allan Papers, SHC.

15. John D. Imboden, "The Confederate Retreat from Gettysburg," in *Battles and Leaders of the Civil War*, ed. Robert Underwood Johnson and Clarence Clough Buel, 4 vols. (New York: Century, 1887), 3:421 (this set hereafter cited as B&L); Henry Heth, "Letter from Major-General Henry Heth, of A. P. Hill's Corps, A.N.V.," in SHSP 4:154–55.

16. Fremantle, *Three Months*, 269. For other eyewitness versions of Lee's accepting full responsibility for the defeat while greeting survivors of the Pickett-Pettigrew assault, see Charles T. Loehr, *War History of the Old First Virginia Infantry Regiment, Army of Northern Virginia* (1884; reprint, Dayton, Ohio: Press of Morningside Bookshop, 1978), 38 (Loehr recalls Lee saying to Pickett, "General, your men have done all that men could do, the fault is entirely my own."), and Robert A. Bright, "Pickett's Charge. The Story of It as Told by a Member of His Staff," in SHSP 31:234 (Bright has Lee say, "Come, General Pickett, this has been my fight and upon my shoulders rests the blame ."").

17. R. E. Lee to Jefferson Davis, Aug. 8, 1863, in OR, vol. 51, pt. 2:752. Lee also alluded to public disapproval in his talk with John Seddon: "Major Seddon, from what you have observed, are the people as much depressed at the battle of Gettysburg as the newspapers appear to indicate?" Seddon answered in the affirmative, whereupon Lee stated forcefully that

popular sentiment misconstrued events on the battlefield—Fredericksburg and Chancellorsville were hollow victories yet lifted morale, whereas Gettysburg accomplished more militarily
but lowered morale. Heth, "Letter from Major-General Henry Heth," 153–54.

18. Heth, "Letter from Major-General Henry Heth," 159–60; Thomas Jewett Goree to
James Longstreet, May 17, 1875, in Thomas Jewett Goree, *The Thomas Jewett Goree Letters*, vol. 1,
The Civil War Correspondence, ed. Langston James Goree V (Bryan, Texas: Family History Foun-
dation, 1981), 285–86. Longstreet asked Goree for his recollections of Gettysburg in a letter of
May 12, 1875. A portion of Goree's reply of May 17 (with several errors of transcription) ap-
pears on p. 400 of Longstreet's *From Manassas to Appomattox: A Memoir of the Civil War in America*
(Philadelphia: J. B. Lippincott, 1896).

19. James Power Smith, "General Lee at Gettysburg," in *Papers of the Military Historical Society of Massachusetts*, 14 vols. and index (1895–1918; reprint, Wilmington, N.C.: Broadfoot
Publishing, 1989–90), 5:393. The charge that Lee considered Longstreet slow was common in
Lost Cause literature. For example, Fitzhugh Lee's "A Review of the First Two Days' Operations at Gettysburg and a Reply to General Longstreet by Fitzhugh Lee," in SHSP 5:193, quotes
an unnamed officer who stated that Lee called Longstreet "the hardest man to move I had in
my army"; and Douglas Southall Freeman, *R. E. Lee: A Biography*, 4 vols. (New York: Charles
Scribner's Sons, 1934–36), 3:80, cites W. Gordon McCabe, who in old age remarked to Freeman that Lee had told his son Custis that Longstreet was slow. Nothing in Lee's own writing supports this contention; however, William Preston Johnston made a memorandum of
a conversation with Lee on May 7, 1868, in which he claimed that Lee, in the context of a discussion of the second day of the Battle of the Wilderness, observed that "Longstreet was often
slow." William G. Bean, ed., "Memoranda of Conversations Between General Robert E. Lee
and William Preston Johnston, May 7, 1868, and March 18, 1870," *Virginia Magazine of History
and Biography* 73 (Oct. 1965):478. Because it is impossible to confirm when Johnston reconstructed his conversations with Lee, his undated memorandum should be used with care.

20. Longstreet, *From Manassas to Appomattox*, 384. The best analysis of Longstreet's part in
the Gettysburg controversy is Piston, *Lee's Tarnished Lieutenant*, esp. chaps. 7–9. Piston concludes (p. 150) that "Longstreet's efforts to defend his military reputation had been futile."

21. Edward Porter Alexander, *Fighting for the Confederacy: The Personal Recollections of General
Edward Porter Alexander*, ed. Gary W. Gallagher (Chapel Hill, N.C.: Univ. of North Carolina
Press, 1989), 277–78. See also idem, *Military Memoirs of a Confederate: A Critical Narrative* (New
York: Charles Scribner's Sons, 1907), 387–89.

22. Freeman, *R. E. Lee* 3:81–82.

23. Ibid., 82–84, 159–60. Douglas Southall Freeman offered a significantly different
analysis in *Lee's Lieutenants: A Study in Command*, 3 vols. (New York: Charles Scribner's Sons,
1942–44), 3:173–74, finding that Longstreet's "attitude was wrong but his instinct was correct. He should have obeyed orders, but the orders should not have been given."

24. Clifford Dowdey, *Death of a Nation: The Story of Lee and His Men at Gettysburg* (New York:
Alfred A. Knopf, 1958), 155, 239–40. The reviewer was Richard B. Harwell, whose blurb appears on the dustjacket of Dowdey's *Lee* (Boston: Little, Brown, 1965).

25. Frank E. Vandiver, "Lee During the War," in *1984 Confederate History Symposium*, ed.
D. B. Patterson (Hillsboro, Tex.: Hill Junior College, 1984), 17. Vandiver listed a series of
physical factors: "Lee at Gettysburg was infirm, had been thrown from his horse a couple of
weeks before and had sprained his hands; he may have been suffering from infectious my-
ocarditis, did have diarrhea and stayed mainly in his tent." There is slim evidence to support
such a catalog of ailments.

26. J. F. C. Fuller, *Grant and Lee: A Study in Personality and Generalship* (1933; reprint, Bloomington: Indiana Univ. Press), 197. Fuller disliked Lee's tactical plan because it "depended on
the earliest possible attack and the most careful timing to effect co-operation; further, Lee's

troops were by no means concentrated, and to make things worse he issued no written orders."

27. H. J. Eckenrode and Bryan Conrad, *James Longstreet: Lee's War Horse* (1936; reprint, Chapel Hill: Univ. of North Carolina Press, 1986), 213.

28. Edwin B. Coddington, *The Gettysburg Campaign: A Study in Command* (New York: Charles Scribner's Sons, 1968), 362.

29. Harry W. Pfanz, *Gettysburg: The Second Day* (Chapel Hill: Univ. of North Carolina Press, 1987), 26–27; Alan T. Nolan, *Lee Considered: General Robert E. Lee and Civil War History* (Chapel Hill: Univ. of North Carolina Press, 1991), 98.

30. Walter H. Taylor, *Four Years with General Lee* (1877; reprint, Bloomington: Indiana Univ. Press, 1962), 93.

31. For discussions of Lee on the first day at Gettysburg, see Alan T. Nolan, "R. E. Lee and July 1 at Gettysburg," and Gary W. Gallagher, "Confederate Corps Leadership on the First Day at Gettysburg: A. P. Hill and Richard S. Ewell in a Difficult Debut," in *The First Day at Gettysburg: Essays on Confederate and Union Leadership*, ed. Gary W. Gallagher (Kent, Ohio: Kent State Univ. Press, 1992).

32. The quotations are from the first of Longstreet's three accounts, in Editors of the *Philadelphia Weekly Times*, "Lee in Pennsylvania," 421. See also James Longstreet, "Lee's Right Wing at Gettysburg," in B&L 3:339–40, and Longstreet, *Manassas to Appomattox*, 358–59. Douglas Southall Freeman, among others who sought to discredit Longstreet, made much of the fact that each of the three narratives employed somewhat different language in recounting this episode. Freeman, *R. E. Lee* 3:74–75. The most important point, however, is that all three versions concur in juxtaposing Longstreet's defensive and Lee's offensive inclinations.

33. Smith, "General Lee at Gettysburg," 391. This account was reprinted under the same title in SHSP 33:135–60.

34. James Power Smith, "With Stonewall Jackson in the Army of Northern Virginia," in SHSP 43:57–58. Smith presented a slightly different version of the discussion between Lee and Longstreet here, adding: "I was the only other person present at this interview between Lee and Longstreet on the afternoon of the first day of the Battle of Gettysburg." The version cited in the preceding note does not mention's Lee's disappointment at Longstreet's reply.

35. G. Moxley Sorrel, *Recollections of a Confederate Staff Officer* (1905; reprint, Wilmington, N.C.: Broadfoot Publishing, 1987), 157; Raphael J. Moses, "Autobiography," pp. 60–61, No. 529, SHC; Fremantle, *Three Months*, 256.

36. The quotation is from Thomas J. Goree to My Dear Mother, July 12, 1862, in Goree, *Goree Letters*, 164. In *Lee and His Lieutenants*, 420, Edward A. Pollard described the relationship between Lee and Longstreet as "not only pleasant and cordial, but affectionate to an almost brotherly degree; an example of beautiful friendship in the war that was frequently remarked by the public."

37. Armistead L. Long to Jubal A. Early, Apr. 5, 1876, reproduced in "Causes of the Defeat of Gen. Lee's Army at the Battle of Gettysburg—Opinions of Leading Confederate Soldiers," in SHSP 4:66; transcript of conversation between R. E. Lee and William Allan, Apr. 15, 1868, pp. 13–14, William Allan Papers, SHC; Taylor, *Four Years with General Lee*, 96.

38. Jubal A. Early, "Leading Confederates on the Battle of Gettysburg. A Review by General Early," in SHSP 4:271–75. For descriptions of the ground in the official reports of Second Corps officers, see OR, vol. 27, pt. 2:445 (Ewell), 469–70 (Early), and 555 (Rodes).

39. Early, "A Review by General Early," 273–74.

40. George Campbell Brown Memoir, pp. 70–71, Brown-Ewell Papers, Tennessee State Library and Archives, Nashville, Tennessee. Brown admitted that he could not fix precisely the time of his meeting with Lee, suggesting that it might even have taken place on the night of July 2. His "strong impression" was that it was on the night of the first, however, and it seems

far more likely that Lee was considering a flanking movement then—with Longstreet's arguments fresh in his mind—rather than after the second day's fighting.

41. Early, "A Review by General Early," 272–73; OR, vol. 27, pt. 2:446.

42. OR, vol. 27, pt. 2:318–19.

43. Jedediah Hotchkiss, Make Me a Map of the Valley: The Civil War Journal of Stonewall Jackson's Topographer, ed. Archie P. McDonald (Dallas, Tex.: Southern Methodist Univ. Press, 1973), 157; OR, vol. 27, pt. 2:317.

44. Moses, "Autobiography," 61; OR, vol. 27, pt. 2:318.

45. Alexander, Fighting for the Confederacy, 233; David Gregg McIntosh, "Review of the Gettysburg Campaign. By One Who Participated Therein," in SHSP 37:140.

46. Jubal A. Early, Lieutenant General Jubal Anderson Early, C.S.A.: Autobiographical Sketch and Narrative of the War Between the States (1912; reprint, Wilmington, N.C.: Broadfoot Publishing, 1989), 257–58; George Templeton Strong, Diary of the Civil War, 1860–1865, ed. Allan Nevins (New York: Macmillan, 1962), 327.

47. For a sampling of this correspondence, see OR, vol. 27, pt. 3:494–508.

48. Alexander, Fighting for the Confederacy, 234.

49. Ibid.

50. Gideon Welles, Diary of Gideon Welles, Secretary of the Navy Under Lincoln and Johnson, ed. Howard K. Beale, 3 vols. (New York: W. W. Norton, 1960), 1:328, 330.

51. OR, vol. 27, pt. 1:61.

52. Heth, "Letter from Major-General Henry Heth," 160.

53. Fremantle, Three Months, 256; Justus Scheibert, Seven Months in the Rebel States During the North American War, 1863, ed. William Stanley Hoole (Tuscaloosa, Ala.: Confederate Publishing, 1958), 118.

54. Lee, Recollections and Letters, 109; OR, vol. 27, pt. 2:309.

55. Alexander, Fighting for the Confederacy, 91–92.

The Peach Orchard Revisited:
Daniel E. Sickles and the Third Corps on July 2, 1863

1. The most extensive treatment of Sickles's actions at Gettysburg on July 2, 1863, and the debate they provoked is Richard A. Sauers, A Caspian Sea of Ink: The Meade-Sickles Controversy (Baltimore, Md.: Butternut and Blue, 1989). Although openly pro-Meade and anti-Sickles, Sauers's work nevertheless is highly useful for its tracing of the controversy over time and its organization of the voluminous materials on the subject.

2. The fullest biographies of Sickles are Edgcumb Pinchon, Dan Sickles: Hero of Gettysburg and "Yankee King of Spain" (Garden City, N.Y.: Doubleday, Doran and Company, 1945), and W. A. Swanberg, Sickles the Incredible (New York: Charles Scribner's Sons, 1956). Pinchon is more dramatic, Swanberg more thoroughly researched and dependable. The preceding paragraphs are drawn from Swanberg, Sickles the Incredible, 77–87.

3. Swanberg, Sickles the Incredible, 88–105.

4. Ibid., 1–76; Pinchon, Dan Sickles, 67–137. A prominent member of Sickles's defense team was Edwin M. Stanton, soon to be Lincoln's secretary of war.

5. Swanberg, Sickles the Incredible, 106–46. Although troublesome to both men, the arguments between Sickles and Hooker involved relatively petty issues. See Walter H. Hebert, Fighting Joe Hooker (Indianapolis: Bobbs-Merrill, 1944), 66–67. One of these altercations led Hooker to write: "In my official intercourse with veteran politicians suddenly raised to high military rank, I have found it necessary to observe their correspondence with especial circumspection." OR 5:637. The vote to confirm Sickles's commission was 19 to 18.

6. Swanberg, *Sickles the Incredible*, 146–66. For the performance of Hooker's division, of which Sickles's brigade was a part, in the Peninsula campaign, see Hebert, *Fighting Joe Hooker*, 92–112.

7. Sickles's assignment to command the Third Corps was announced as temporary on February 5, 1863, then made permanent on April 15, 1863. OR, vol. 25, pt. 2:51, 211–12. Meade's letters expressing his opinion of Sickles can be found in George Meade, *The Life and Letters of George Gordon Meade*, 2 vols. (New York: Charles Scribner's Sons, 1913), 1:351, 354.

8. Swanberg, *Sickles the Incredible*, 177–90. The classic account of Chancellorsville is John Bigelow, Jr.'s, *The Campaign of Chancellorsville: A Strategic and Tactical Study* (New Haven: Yale Univ. Press, 1910); for portions especially relevant to Sickles's situation, see 279–81, 324–27, 344–46. Sickles's after-action report is in OR, vol. 25, pt. 1:384–95. His casualties are listed in ibid., 180. Meade's comment is in Meade, *Life and Letters* 1:373.

9. On the Hooker-Meade disagreement, see Swanberg, *Sickles the Incredible*, 195–96; Hebert, *Fighting Joe Hooker*, 218; Meade, *Life and Letters*, 377–78, 381–82. For Hooker's relief and replacement by Meade, see Hebert, *Fighting Joe Hooker*, 231–46; Freeman Cleaves, *Meade of Gettysburg* (Norman, Okla.: Univ. of Oklahoma Press, 1960), 115–25; and Coddington, *The Gettysburg Campaign*, 130–33.

10. Coddington, *The Gettysburg Campaign*, 210, 218–19; Edward J. Nichols, *Toward Gettysburg: A Biography of General John F. Reynolds* (State College: Pennsylvania State Univ. Press, 1958), 180–82; David M. Jordan, *Winfield Scott Hancock: A Soldier's Life* (Bloomington: Indiana Univ. Press, 1988), 81. Hancock's assignment to command the Second Corps had come only on June 24, 1863. OR, vol. 27, pt. 3:299.

11. Coddington, *The Gettysburg Campaign*, 224–28; Sauers, *Caspian Sea of Ink*, 11–12; OR, vol. 27, pt. 3:395–96, 399. The rebuke to Sickles can be found in OR, vol. 27, pt. 3:399. Coddington argues that Meade was correct in his censure of Sickles but that Hancock did not merit such treatment, even though he also failed to attain his target and thereby delayed another corps. Coddington, *The Gettysburg Campaign*, 669 n. 99. Although there are some differences in the two cases, it is difficult not to see a double standard at work in the mind of the new army commander.

12. OR, vol. 27, pt. 3:420. Again, the tone taken with Sickles is quite different from that taken with other corps commanders, most of whom fell short of Meade's goal for June 29.

13. OR, vol. 27, pt. 3:419, 424–25, 458–59, 463–66, 468; Henry Edwin Tremain, *Two Days of War: A Gettysburg Narrative and Other Excursions* (New York: Bonnell, Silver and Bowers, 1905), 1–20; Swanberg, *Sickles the Incredible*, 202–3; Coddington, *The Gettysburg Campaign*, 231–32; Sauers, *Caspian Sea of Ink*, 19–21. The brigades left behind were Col. P. Regis de Trobriand's Third Brigade of the First Division and Col. George C. Burling's Third Brigade of the Second Division.

14. OR, vol. 27, pt. 1:482, 531; Sauers, *Caspian Sea of Ink*, 22–24; Swanberg, *Sickles the Incredible*, 204–6.

15. George Gordon Meade, *With Meade at Gettysburg* (Philadelphia: John C. Winston, 1930), 96–100; Sauers, *Caspian Sea of Ink*, 25–27; Coddington, *The Gettysburg Campaign*, 330, 337–41; Pfanz, *Gettysburg: The Second Day*, 58–59. For a division commander's comments on the drafting of the contingency plan, see John Gibbon, *Personal Recollections of the Civil War* (New York: G. P. Putnam's Sons, 1928), 139–40.

16. Meade, *With Meade at Gettysburg*, 100–102; Sauers, *Caspian Sea of Ink*, 27–28; Coddington, *The Gettysburg Campaign*, 343–44; Pfanz, *Gettysburg: The Second Day*, 82–83; OR, vol. 27, pt. 1:482, 531.

17. OR, vol. 27, pt. 3:486–87; Joint Committee on the Conduct of the War, *Report of the Joint Committee on the Conduct of the War, at the Second Session Thirty-eighth Congress* (Washington,

D.C.: GPO, 1865), 1:331–32, 449 (hereafter cited as *CCW*); Meade, *With Meade at Gettysburg*, 105–6; Meade, *Life and Letters* 2:354; Coddington, *The Gettysburg Campaign*, 344; Sauers, *Caspian Sea of Ink*, 29; Pfanz, *Gettysburg: The Second Day*, 60, 93.

18. *CCW* 1:449–50; Henry J. Hunt, "The Second Day at Gettysburg," in *B&L* 3:301–3. Hunt's analysis of Meade's and Sickles's positions is as follows: "The direct short line through the woods, and including the Round Tops, could be occupied, intrenched, and made impregnable to a front attack. But, like that of Culp's Hill, it would be a purely defensive one, from which, owing to the nature of the ground and the enemy's commanding position on the ridges at the angle, an advance in force would be impracticable. The salient line proposed by General Sickles, although much longer, afforded excellent positions for our artillery; its occupation would cramp the movements of the enemy, bring us nearer his lines, and afford us facilities for taking the offensive. It was in my judgment tactically the better line of the two, provided it were strongly occupied, for it was the only one on the field from which we could have passed from the defensive to the offensive with a prospect of decisive results. But General Meade had not, until the arrival of the Sixth Corps, a sufficient number of troops at his disposal to risk such an extension of his lines; it would have required both the Third and Fifth corps, and left him without any reserve. Had he known that Lee's attack would be postponed until 4 P.M., he might have occupied this line in the morning; but he did not know this, expected an attack at any moment, and, in view of the vast interests involved, adopted a defensive policy, and ordered the occupation of the *safe* line." For a most judicious modern analysis of both the ground and the Sickles-Hunt colloquy, see Pfanz, *Gettysburg: The Second Day*, 93–97.

19. OR, vol. 27, pt. 1:482–83, 515, 531–32; *CCW* 1:297–98, 390–91. Humphreys placed the time of his advance at about 4:00 P.M., but this seems much too late. For Sickles's motivation in making the advance, see also Swanberg, *Sickles the Incredible*, 209–11; Coddington, *The Gettysburg Campaign*, 346; Pfanz, *Gettysburg: The Second Day*, 102–3; and Sauers, *Caspian Sea of Ink*, 30, 35–36. The Confederate unit discovered by Berdan was Cadmus M. Wilcox's brigade of R.H. Anderson's division of the Confederate Third Corps, not part of Longstreet's First Corps.

20. *CCW* 1:298–99; Tremain, *Two Days of War*, 56–65; Meade, *With Meade at Gettysburg*, 107–9, 114–15; Coddington, *The Gettysburg Campaign*, 345–46; Sauers, *Caspian Sea of Ink*, 36–38; Swanberg, *Sickles the Incredible*, 212–19; Pfanz, *Gettysburg: The Second Day*, 139–44. The exact details of these Sickles-Meade encounters are hopelessly snarled among the accounts of various participants and partisans. Nevertheless, the results are the same.

21. *CCW* 1:304; Swanberg, *Sickles the Incredible*, 220–35; OR, vol. 27, pt. 1:16.

22. *CCW* 1:295–394 (Sickles), 305–12 (Doubleday), 329–58 (Meade), 417–35 (Butterfield), 435–39 (Meade); OR, vol. 27, pt. 1.122–39; ibid. 33:3; Swanberg, *Sickles the Incredible*, 247–58; Sauers, *Caspian Sea of Ink*, 41–58. The identity of Historicus is unknown, although he must have been close to Sickles, if not the general himself. W. A. Swanberg believed Sickles to be Historicus, as did Coddington, in *The Gettysburg Campaign*, 721–22 n. 98. For another candidate, John B. Bachelder, see Cleaves, *Meade of Gettysburg*, 229–30.

23. The most exhaustive treatment to date of Sickles's arguments is Sauers, *Caspian Sea of Ink*, and the sources cited therein. Chapters 4 and 5 delineate the postwar development of the controversy and the changing arguments of participants, partisans, and historians. Chapters 6–9 explore Sickles's four main arguments. Sauer's discussion has a strong (and admitted) pro-Meade bias, which on occasion tends to reduce the strength of his case.

24. Although biased against Meade because he believed the army commander had treated him badly at Gettysburg, Maj. Gen. Abner Doubleday stated the truth before the Joint Committee on the Conduct of the War when he testified: "General Meade is in the habit of violating the organic law of the army to place his personal friends in power." *CCW* 1:311. Few could quarrel with the choice of Reynolds, but Hancock had been only a division commander as late as Chancellorsville and did not outrank those corps commanders placed under his

charge by Meade. Of course, Hooker had rewarded his own friends such as Sickles when he had held army command. This natural human practice nevertheless tended to polarize the Army of the Potomac into warring factions, to the detriment of successful prosecution of the public business.

25. Sickles's testimony and arguments on the weakness of his original position are digested and summarized in Sauers, *Caspian Sea of Ink*, 121–26. This position apparently stretched from Patterson Woods in the north to just beyond the location of the First New Jersey Brigade monument in the south. A walking tour of this area and that immediately in front of it is highly instructive. The ground is indeed low, is partially masked in front, and is clearly lower than the Peach Orchard ridge to the west. Standing in the area just north of the G. Weikert House, it is easy to see why Sickles was so attracted to the Peach Orchard position. The best defensive solution to the terrain puzzle presented to Sickles is elusive even today. An excellent description of the terrain in which Sickles had to operate can be found in Hunt, "The Second Day at Gettysburg," 295–96. As for Meade's inattention to his left, even his biographer finds this lapse to be an error. Cleaves, *Meade of Gettysburg*, 146.

26. Henry J. Hunt's "The Second Day at Gettysburg," 302–3 provides the clearest statement of the issues and a judicious analysis of both protagonists.

27. For the respective frontages of the Second and Third corps, see Sauers, *Caspian Sea of Ink*, 128. Strengths of the two corps are carefully estimated in John W. Busey and David G. Martin, *Regimental Strengths and Losses at Gettysburg* (Hightstown, N.J.: Longstreet House, 1986), 16. In his vigorous attack on Sickles's action, Coddington argued that the Third Corps was actually stronger than the Second Corps. Coddington, *The Gettysburg Campaign*, 725 n. 132. As for Warren, both he and Meade went to the left only in response to Sickles's advance. Had Sickles remained in the position favored by Meade, it is likely that the army commander's focus would have remained on his right. *CCW* 1:377.

"*If Longstreet . . . Says So, It Is Most Likely Not True*":
James Longstreet and the Second Day at Gettysburg

1. *Petersburg Index-Appeal* of undetermined date cited in a clipping in Reel 59, Frame 91, Jedediah Hotchkiss Papers, Library of Congress, Washington, D.C. (repository hereafter cited as LC).

2. Thomas Jewett Goree to his mother, Dec. 14, 1861, in Goree, *Goree Letters*, 111.

3. W. W. Blackford, *War Years with Jeb Stuart* (New York: Charles Scribner's Sons, 1945), 47; diary of Matilda Hamilton of "Prospect Hill," near Fredericksburg, Dec. 28, 1862, typescript in author's possession.

4. A. P. Stewart in "Soldier's Note Book," *Atlanta Journal*, Nov. 13, 1890; *Official Register of the . . . U.S. Military Academy . . . June, 1842* (New York: J. P. Wright, Book, Job and Law Printer, 1842), 8.

5. [Francis Grose], *Advice to the Officers of the British Army* (London: Printed by W. Richardson, 1783), 8; Sir Edward Thornton and James A. Garfield as quoted in William S. McFeely, *Grant: A Biography* (New York: W. W. Norton, 1981), 383, 434.

6. Gallagher's observation quoted above, p. 122; Freeman, R. E. Lee 3:331.

7. James Longstreet to Joseph E. Johnston, Oct. 5, 1862, Longstreet Papers, Perkins Library, Duke University, Durham, North Carolina (repository hereafter cited as PLD).

8. Moses, "Autobiography," 54; Sorrel, *Recollections*, 54; James Longstreet to Joseph E. Johnston, Oct. 5, 1862, Longstreet Papers, PLD.

9. Freeman, *Lee's Lieutenants* 2:620 n. 60 (where the year is misdated by typographical error); Cadmus M. Wilcox to E. P. Alexander, March 10, Feb. 6, 1869, Alexander Papers, SHC.

10. Lafayette McLaws to Charles Arnall, Feb. 2, 1897, Roll 34, Hotchkiss Papers, LC.

11. Ibid.; Freeman, *Lee's Lieutenants* 1:259–60.

12. Longstreet, *Manassas to Appomattox*, 196; James Longstreet to T. T. Munford, Nov. 8, 13, 1891, Box 26, Munford-Ellis Family Papers, PLD.

13. James Longstreet to Fitz John Porter, Apr. 1878, Porter Papers, LC; Longstreet, *Manassas to Appomattox*, 187.

14. James Longstreet to Lafayette McLaws, June 3, 1863, McLaws Papers, SHC.

15. James Longstreet, "Lee's Invasion of Pennsylvania," in B&L 3:246; James Longstreet, "The Mistakes of Gettysburg," in *Annals of the War*, 620.

16. OR, vol. 27, pt. 2:358; John Bell Hood to James Longstreet, June 28, 1875, in SHSP 4:148.

17. Undated transcript of Samuel R. Johnston's letter to Lafayette McLaws, in the latter's hand, McLaws Papers, PLD.

18. Ibid.; Alexander, *Fighting for the Confederacy*, 236.

19. Longstreet, "Lee in Pennsylvania," 423; George Campbell Brown Memoir, p. 83; Henry Herbert Harris Diary, July 14, 1863, typescript at Fredericksburg and Spotsylvania National Military Park from original owned by a descendant living in Fredericksburg.

20. Alexander, *Fighting for the Confederacy*, 278; A. L. Long, *Memoirs of Robert E. Lee* (Richmond, Va.: B. F. Johnson & Co., 1886), 281–82.

21. Alexander, *Fighting for the Confederacy*, 237.

22. John Bell Hood to James Longstreet, June 28, 1875, in SHSP 4:149.

23. Sorrel, *Recollections*, 169; Longstreet, *Manassas to Appomattox*, 368.

24. Longstreet, *Manassas to Appomattox*, 368.

25. Sorrel, *Recollections*, 157–58.

26. Lafayette McLaws to My Dear Wife, July 7, 1863, McLaws Papers, SHC.

27. For considerable detail on this episode, see Lafayette McLaws to I. R. Pennypacker, July 31, 1888, A. K. Smiley Public Library, Redlands, California. After the war, when it suited him again, Longstreet reclaimed these orders to withdraw as his own.

28. Longstreet, "Lee in Pennsylvania," 414.

29. Undated newspaper clipping, Roll 59, Frame 83, Hotchkiss Papers, LC. Several similar clippings are in adjacent frames of the same source.

30. Lafayette McLaws to Lizzie Ewell, Feb. 29, 1864, Ewell Papers, LC; Lafayette McLaws to Charles Arnall, Feb. 2, 1897, Roll 34, Hotchkiss Papers, LC.

31. The only published summary of the charges is in Robert K. Krick, "The McLaws-Knoxville Court Martial," a short article without notes in *A Collection of Essays Commemorating the 125th Anniversary of the Siege of Knoxville* (Knoxville, Tenn.: Knoxville Civil War Round Table, 1988), 11–14. The important manuscripts are in the McLaws Papers, PLD and SHC.

32. Clifford Dowdey, *The Seven Days: The Emergence of Lee* (Boston: Little Brown, 1964), 84.

33. Evander M. Law to Lafayette McLaws, Apr. 29, 1864, McLaws Papers, SHC.

34. R. E. Lee to James Longstreet, Jan. 19, 1865, MS 1F1613a2, Virginia Historical Society, Richmond, Virginia.

35. Thomas Miller Ryland Diary, March 19, 1865, typescript in the author's possession from original owned by a descendant in Warsaw; Charles B. Fleet memoir in Elizabeth M. Hedges, *C. B. Fleet: The Man and the Company* [Lynchburg, Va.(?) 1985 (?)], 42.

36. Transcript of conversation between R. E. Lee and William Allan, Apr. 15, 1868, p. 15, William Allan Papers, SHC.

37. Hunter H. McGuire to Jedediah Hotchkiss, March 30, 1893, Jan. [day illegible], 1897, Roll 34, Hotchkiss Papers, LC.

38. Richard Taylor, *Destruction and Reconstruction* (New York: D. Appleton and Company, 1879), 231.

1. Historical image and historical reality can be entirely different. Howard, Sickles, and Schimmelfennig all have their Gettysburg defenders.

2. Charles E. Slocum, *The Life and Services of Major-General Henry Warner Slocum* (Toledo: Slocum Publishing, 1913), 112. Howard made these remarks at a memorial service for Slocum in Plymouth Church, Brooklyn, on April 24.

3. OR, vol. 25, pt. 1:185. The corps lost 2,822 men at Chancellorsville.

4. On Slocum's life and military career, see Ezra J. Warner, *Generals in Blue: Lives of the Union Commanders* (Baton Rouge: Louisiana State Univ. Press, 1964), 451–53; *Dictionary of American Biography* 17:216–17 (hereafter cited as DAB); and Coddington, *The Gettysburg Campaign*, 45.

5. Slocum, *Life and Services*, 292–93.

6. For information on Williams, see Warner, *Generals in Blue*, 559–60, and DAB 20:247–48. Warner speculates that Williams failed to retain corps command after Antietam because the authorities preferred to reserve such positions for regular army officers. Williams's letters appear in Alpheus S. Williams, *From the Cannon's Mouth: The Civil War Letters of General Alpheus S. Williams*, ed. Milo M. Quaife (Detroit: Wayne State Univ. Press, 1959).

7. OR, vol. 25, pt. 2:583; Warner, *Generals in Blue*, 272. Knipe commanded Pennsylvania militia during the Gettysburg campaign; McDougall returned to his regimental command shortly after the battle.

8. Warner, *Generals in Blue*, 415–16. The other Western regiments were the 27th Indiana and 5th, 7th, 29th, and 66th Ohio.

9. J. L. Cornet, "The Twenty-Eighth in Ten States and Twenty-Five Battles," *National Tribune*, Dec. 25, 1886; Warner, *Generals in Blue*, 169–70.

10. Stewart Sifakis, *Who Was Who in the Civil War* (New York: Facts on File, 1988), 104; Roger D. Hunt and Jack R. Brown, *Brevet Brigadier Generals in Blue* (Gaithersburg, Md.: Olde Soldier Books, 1990), 98. Candy's brigade included the 5th, 7th, 29th, and 66th Ohio and the 28th and 147th Pennsylvania.

11. Warner, *Generals in Blue*, 256–57; Hunt and Brown, *Brevet Brigadier Generals in Blue*, 119.

12. William M. Balch, "Did General George S. Greene Win the Civil War at the Battle of Gettysburg?" *National Tribune*, Aug. 20, 1931; Warner, *Generals in Blue*, 186–87; Wayne E. Motts, "To Gain A Second Star: The Forgotten George S. Greene," *Gettysburg: Historical Articles of Lasting Interest* 3 (July 1990):65–67. The only general officer at Gettysburg who had seen more sunrises than Greene was Brig. Gen. William "Extra Billy" Smith, a brigade commander in the Army of Northern Virginia.

13. John W. Busey and David G. Martin, *Regimental Strengths at Gettysburg* (Baltimore: Gateway Press, 1982), 88. Williams reported 3,770 men present in his division on June 30, and Geary stated that he took 3,922 soldiers into the battle. See Coddington, *The Gettysburg Campaign*, 713 n. 186; and OR, vol. 27, pt. 1:833.

14. OR, vol. 27, pt. 1:758; William F. Fox, "Slocum and His Men. A History of the Twelfth and Twentieth Army Corps," in *In Memoriam Henry Warner Slocum 1826–1894* (Albany, N.Y.: J. B. Lyon, 1904), 174; Williams, *From the Cannon's Mouth*, 224.

15. Oration of Capt. Joseph Matchett in John P. Nicholson, ed., *Pennsylvania at Gettysburg*, 2 vols. (Harrisburg, Pa.: E. K. Meyers, State Printer, 1893), 1:283–84; OR, vol. 27, pt. 1:758; ibid., pt. 3:420–21.

16. George K. Collins, *Memoirs of the 149th Regt. N.Y. Vol. Inft.* (Syracuse, N.Y.: Published by the Author, 1891), 133 (first quotation); Matchett in *Pennsylvania at Gettysburg* 1:284 (second quotation); OR, vol. 27, pt. 1:796; George A. Thayer, "Gettysburg, As We Men on the Right Saw

It," reprinted in Ken Bandy and Florence Freeland, comps., *The Gettysburg Papers*, 2 vols. (Dayton, Ohio: Press of Morningside House, 1978), 2:803; Charles F. Morse, *History of the Second Massachusetts Regiment of Infantry; Gettysburg: A Paper Read at the Officers Reunion in Boston, May 10, 1878* (Boston: George H. Ellis Printer, 1882), 6; William Henry Harrison Tallman, "Memoir," typescript in the vertical files at Gettysburg National Military Park (repository hereafter cited as GNMP). The precise time of departure and order of march from Littlestown to Two Taverns is difficult to establish. Williams says his troops left their camps "at daylight . . . my division leading." Various Second Division sources report they left Littlestown about 8:00 A.M., but Geary claims to have departed with his troops at 5:00 A.M. See OR, vol. 27, pt. 1:825; Williams, *From the Cannon's Mouth*, 224; Richard Eddy, *History of the Sixtieth New York State Volunteers* (Philadelphia: Published by the Author, 1864), 259.

17. Tallman, "Memoir."

18. OR, vol. 27, pt. 3:416; Jesse H. Jones, "Saved the Day. Greene's Brigade Behaves Nobly at Gettysburg," *National Tribune*, March 7, 1895 (quotation); Coddington, *The Gettysburg Campaign*, 311.

19. Morse, "History of the Second Massachusetts," 6; Eddy, *History of the Sixtieth New York*, 259; Thayer, "Gettysburg," 803; OR, vol. 27, pt. 1:825; Lt. Col. Charles P. Horton to John B. Bachelder, Jan. 23, 1867, typescript in Bachelder Papers, GNMP; Coddington, *The Gettysburg Campaign*, 707 n. 138.

20. Collins, *Memoirs of the 149th Regt.*, 134; Morse, *History of the Second Massachusetts*, 6; Julian Wisner Hinkley, *A Narrative of Service with the Third Wisconsin Infantry* (Madison: Wisconsin History Commission, 1912), 82.

21. Charles P. Horton to John B. Bachelder, Jan. 23, 1867, Bachelder Papers, GNMP; Eddy, *History of the Sixtieth New York*, 259; John Hamilton SeCheverell, *Journal History of the Twenty-Ninth Ohio Veteran Volunteers, 1861–1865* (Cleveland, 1883), 69.

22. Thayer, "Gettysburg," 803; *Maine at Gettysburg: Report of the Maine Commissioners Prepared by the Executive Committee* (Portland, Maine: Lakeside Press, 1898), 520; Henry W. Slocum to Messrs T. H. Davis & Co., Sept. 8, 1875, Samuel P. Bates Papers, copy at GNMP. See also Coddington, *The Gettysburg Campaign*, 311.

23. Edmund R. Brown, *The Twenty-Seventh Indiana Volunteer Infantry in the War of the Rebellion* (Monticello, Ind., 1899), 367; OR, vol. 27, pt. 3:463. It is difficult to determine the precise time or even the sequence of arrival for Howard's couriers and the unidentified civilian. Slocum failed to acknowledge the receipt of messages from Howard in his accounts of events at Two Taverns.

24. OR, vol. 27, pt. 3:458–59.

25. Slocum received along with the circular a communication from Maj. Gen. Daniel Butterfield, Meade's chief of staff, providing further instructions about executing the withdrawal should Reynolds trigger the movement. Ibid., 462.

26. Coddington, *The Gettysburg Campaign*, 311; William F. Fox, "Life of General Slocum," in *In Memoriam Henry Warner Slocum*, 77.

27. Slocum, *Life and Services*, 102 (quotations); Fox, "Life of General Slocum," 78–79. Howard would not have received a copy of the Pipe Creek Circular by the time he sent his messengers.

28. Samuel P. Bates, *The Battle of Gettysburg* (Philadelphia: T. H. Davis & Co., 1875), 93.

29. Henry W. Slocum to Messrs. T. H. Davis & Co., Sept. 8, 1875, copy in Samuel R. Bates Papers, GNMP (first quotation); Coddington, *The Gettysburg Campaign*, 708–9 n. 149 (second quotation); Oliver O. Howard, "Campaign and Battle of Gettysburg," *Atlantic Monthly Magazine* 38 (July 1876): 60; Abner Doubleday to Samuel P. Bates, Apr. 24, 1874, Samuel P. Bates Papers, copy at GNMP; Meade, *Life and Letters* 2:249.

30. Coddington, *The Gettysburg Campaign*, 312, 708 n. 142; OR, vol. 27, pt. 1:825. William Fox reported that he spoke with the hotel keeper at Two Taverns, a Mr. Snyder, after the battle. Snyder told Fox that Slocum and his staff were at dinner in the hotel when an orderly bearing Howard's dispatch appeared. Slocum read the message and left the table quickly. "In ten minutes they were all gone." It is uncertain if Snyder meant all the officers left the hotel or the entire corps left Two Taverns. Fox implies the latter, although this would have been highly unlikely. Slocum's departure from the hotel would not be tantamount to an instant march by the corps. Fox, "Slocum and His Men," 175–76.

31. Tallman, "Memoir."

32. Collins, *Memoirs of the 149th Regt.*, 134; Samuel Toombs, *Reminiscences of the War* (Orange, N.J.: Printed at the Journal Office, 1878), 72, 74–75; Morse, "History of the Second Massachusetts," 6–7.

33. Slocum, *Life and Services*, 102; Alpheus S. Williams to John B. Bachelder, Nov. 10, 1865, typescript in Bachelder Papers, GNMP. It is puzzling that Slocum would not have heard about Reynolds's death from one of Howard's couriers at Two Taverns.

34. Alpheus S. Williams to John B. Bachelder, Nov. 10, 1865, typescript in Bachelder Papers, GNMP; L. R. Coy to his wife, July 2, 1863, typescript copy in 123d N.Y. file at GNMP; Matchett in *Pennsylvania at Gettysburg* 1:284.

35. Alpheus S. Williams to John B. Bachelder, Nov. 10, 1865, typescript in Bachelder Papers, GNMP; Williams, *From the Cannon's Mouth*, 224–25; OR, vol. 27, pt. 1:811. It is curious that Williams would be directed to go to the right when the point of danger in the late afternoon of July 1 clearly lay on Cemetery Hill. Perhaps Slocum acted on information he received from Howard's couriers while en route to Gettysburg and issued before the Federal line collapsed north and west of town. Harry W. Pfanz has identified the road used by Williams to be the one that left the Baltimore Pike at the Horner Farm and led past the Deardorff Farm to the Hanover Road about one mile east of Benner's Hill. See *Atlas to Accompany the Official Records of the Union and Confederate Armies* (Washington, D.C.: GPO, 1891–95), Plate XL. See also Coddington, *The Gettysburg Campaign*, 709 n. 151.

36. OR, vol. 27, pt. 1:825, 848. The Second Brigade probably alighted at Powers Hill.

37. OR, vol. 27, pt. 1:825, 839; William F. Fox, ed., *New York Monuments Commission for the Battlefields of Gettysburg and Chattanooga. Final Report on the Battlefield of Gettysburg*, 3 vols. (Albany: J. B. Lyon, Printers, 1900, 1902), 2:634, 1:446–47, 2:628 (hereafter cited as N.Y. at Gettysburg); Maj. Moses Veale in *Pennsylvania at Gettysburg* 2:566.

38. Williams, *From the Cannon's Mouth*, 225; OR, vol. 27, pt. 1:773, 777, 811; Hinkley, *Third Wisconsin*, 83–84.

39. Coddington, *The Gettysburg Campaign*, 310, 302, 315. Coddington states that Howard "had a justifiable grievance against General Henry W. Slocum" for being "unnecessarily slow" on July 1. However, he adds that it was "questionable whether Slocum could have pushed on to Gettysburg in time to affect the outcome of the battle on July 1 even if he had not hesitated in his movements." The Twelfth Corps covered the four miles from its bivouacs north of Two Taverns to Rock Creek in less than two hours. Had Slocum ordered a departure when first notified of the battle at Gettysburg, it is reasonable to believe that Williams could have reached Cemetery and East Cemetery hills by 4:00 P.M. and supplemented Col. Orland Smith's Eleventh Corps brigade, which served as a lonely anchor around which the First and Eleventh corps rallied. Of course, had Slocum investigated the sounds of battle prior to the arrival of messengers at Two Taverns, the corps could have appeared at Gettysburg earlier.

40. OR, vol. 27, pt. 1:703; Oliver Otis Howard, *Autobiography of Oliver Otis Howard*, 2 vols. (New York: Baker & Taylor, 1908), 1:416. Although Howard's first message may be considered implicit, there is no question that the communication carried by Capt. Daniel Hall at

2:45 P.M. clearly called for Slocum's help. See Charles W. Howard, "The First Day at Gettysburg," in Military Order of the Loyal Legion of the United States, Illinois Commandery, *Papers* 4 (Chicago: Cozzens & Beaton, 1907), 253–54; OR, vol. 27, pt. 1:126.

41. Howard, "The First Day at Gettysburg," 258.

42. Col. C. H. Morgan's "Statement," typescript in Bachelder Papers, GNMP.

43. Edwin Eustace Bryant, *History of the Third Regiment of Wisconsin Veteran Volunteer Infantry* (Madison, Wisc.: Published by the Veteran Association of the Regiment, 1891), 183–84; Lewis A. Stegman, "Slocum at Gettysburg," *National Tribune*, June 17, 1915; Coddington, *The Gettysburg Campaign*, 313. For Slocum's explanation, see Howard's report in OR, vol. 27, pt. 1:704.

44. Morgan, "Statement"; OR, vol. 27, pt. 1:696, 704. Hancock stated that Slocum arrived between 5:00 and 6:00 P.M.; Howard placed the time at about 7:00 P.M. See OR, vol. 27, pt. 1:368–69, 704.

45. There is some question about Slocum's position subsequent to Meade's arrival. Clearly, he no longer commanded the army. Williams stated that in the late afternoon of July 1 he "had been notified that I was in command of the 12th Corps, Gen. Slocum temporarily taking command of the right wing, in place of Reynolds." At 9:20 P.M. Slocum sent a message to Meade as commander of the Twelfth Corps. At 3:40 A.M. on July 2, Slocum communicated to Williams instructing that officer to advance his "division." It appears that Slocum considered himself back in charge of the Twelfth Corps, and not a wing, during the predawn hours of July 2. Williams, *From the Cannon's Mouth*, 225; OR, vol. 27, pt. 3:468, 484.

46. Oration of Rev. J. Richards Boyle, in *Pennsylvania at Gettysburg* 2:592–93; OR, vol. 27, pt. 1:846–49; "Notes of a Conversation with General Kane," typescript in Bachelder Papers, GNMP.

47. Geary stated that "at 5 A.M. on the 2d, having been relieved by the Third Army Corps . . . the division was placed on the right of the main line of battle." Col. John H. Patrick of the 5th Ohio, also in command of the 147th Pennsylvania at this time, reported that he received orders at 5:00 A.M. from his brigade commander, Col. Candy, to "return to the brigade" from their advanced positions west of Little Round Top. This would suggest that Geary received orders to move prior to 5:00 A.M. Col. Henry A. Barnum of the 149th New York says that the division began its march at 4:00 A.M., but this seems too early. Sunrise on July 2 came at 4:15 A.M. OR, vol. 27, pt. 1:825, 839, 868; Pfanz, *Gettysburg: The Second Day*, 58.

48. Elevations and distances may be calculated from the U.S. Geological Survey topographical maps. Coddington, *The Gettysburg Campaign*, 330; OR, vol. 27, pt. 2:504. Except for a thicker understory today, the area looks much as it did in 1863.

49. Collins, *Memoirs of the 149th Regt.*, 136; Jones, "Saved the Day."

50. Motts, "To Gain a Second Star," 68. The 60th New York initially occupied Greene's left, but shortly after the original deployment a portion of the 78th New York moved to the 60th's left. The rest of the 78th New York served on the picket line near Rock Creek. OR, vol. 27, pt. 1:860, 862–63. Busey and Martin, *Regimental Strengths at Gettysburg*, 96, credit Greene's brigade with 1,350 men. The ravine below Greene's right is still readily discernable on the ground.

51. Moses Veale in *Pennsylvania at Gettysburg* 2:566–67; OR, vol. 27, pt. 1:854. Regimental monuments and markers on Culp's Hill, though not infallible, are of some use when placing regiments on the ground. Busey and Martin, *Regimental Strengths at Gettysburg*, 95, give Kane's strength as nine hundred; OR, vol. 27, pt. 1:833, credits the brigade with only seven hundred men in the engagement.

52. Henry E. Brown, *The 28th Regt. P.V.V.I., The 147th Regt. P.V.V.I., and Knap's Ind. Battery "E." at Gettysburg, July 1,2,3, 1863* (N.p., 1892), 5; J. L. Cornet, "The Twenty-Eighth in Ten States," *National Tribune*, Dec. 25, 1886; OR, vol. 27, pt. 1:836.

53. Williams, *From the Cannon's Mouth*, 226; OR, vol. 27, pt. 1:773, 777–78; Alpheus S. Williams to John B. Bachelder, Nov. 10, 1865, typescript in Bachelder Papers, GNMP. The Fifth Corps division that supported Williams belonged to Brig. Gen. James Barnes.

54. OR, vol. 27, pt. 1:778, 783. McDougall stated that his brigade did not leave for its new position until 11:00 A.M. Morse, "The Twelfth Corps at Gettysburg," in Military Order of the Loyal Legion of the United States, Massachusetts Commandery, *Papers* 14 (1918; reprint, Wilmington, N.C.: Broadfoot Publishing, 1990), 23, describes the swale as follows: "This so-called swale was a low, flat meadow, about a hundred yards wide, between the two rocky, wooded hills. Through this swale trickled a small stream, at that time nearly dry, which flowed into Rock Creek." The regimental positions behind the stone wall are given in OR, vol. 27, pt. 1:800. The regimental order on the front line is probably correct and conforms with the regimental monuments on the field.

55. Byrant, *History of the Third Regiment*, 185; OR, vol. 27, pt. 1:819; Edmund J. Raus, Jr., *A Generation on the March—The Union Army at Gettysburg* (Lynchburg, Va.: H. E. Howard, 1987), 76. For a synopsis of Carman's contributions to Antietam historiography, see Stephen W. Sears, *Landscape Turned Red: The Battle of Antietam* (New Haven: Ticknor & Fields, 1983), 373.

56. Thayer, "Gettysburg," 806; Morse, "The Twelfth Corps at Gettysburg," 23; Morse, "History of the Second Massachusetts," 7; OR, vol. 27, pt. 1:815, 823; Bryant, *History of the Third Regiment*, 185; Brown, *The Twenty-Seventh Indiana*, 370. Most of the battlefield tablets refer to the small rocky knoll south of the swale as "McAllister's Woods," although few of the memoirs or contemporary accounts assign it any specific name.

57. Sifakis, *Who Was Who*, 391–92.

58. OR, vol. 27, pt. 1:775; pt. 3:496–97; Pfanz, *Gettysburg: The Second Day*, 62–63; Raus, *A Generation on the March*, 29, 84; Busey and Martin, *Regimental Strengths at Gettysburg*, 92; N.Y. at Gettysburg 3:1030. Although the two Maryland regiments had been in service since mid-1861, only the 1st Maryland Potomac Home Brigade had seen any action and this of a limited nature. For a summary of the brigade's combat history prior to the Gettysburg campaign, see John C. Burns, "Maryland and the Struggle for the Union Right at Gettysburg," 11–12, typescript dated 1973, GNMP.

59. Stephen G. Cook and Charles E. Benton, eds., *The "Dutchess County Regiment" in the Civil War* (Danbury, Conn.: Danbury Medical Printing Co., 1907), 22, 26; N.Y. at Gettysburg 3:1032; John H. Shane, "Getting into the Fight at Gettysburg," *National Tribune*, Nov. 27, 1924.

60. Cook and Benton, *The "Dutchess County Regiment,"* 27, 29–30; N.Y. at Gettysburg 3:1032–33, 1039; Henry J. Hunt, "The Second Day at Gettysburg," in B&L 3:294; Williams, *From the Cannon's Mouth*, 227; Alpheus S. Williams to John B. Bachelder, Apr. 7, 1864, typescript in Bachelder Papers, GNMP.

61. OR, vol. 27, pt. 1:870; Burns, "Maryland and the Union Right at Gettysburg," 13. For Meade's role in determining the Twelfth Corps deployment on the morning of July 2, see OR, vol. 27, pt. 1:759.

62. OR, vol. 27, pt. 3:486–87; Coddington, *The Gettysburg Campaign*, 337; Hunt, "The Second Day at Gettysburg," 297; Toombs, *Reminiscences*, 75; Fox, "A History of the Twelfth and Twentieth Army Corps," 177–78.

63. Analyzing the command structure of the Twelfth Corps on the morning of July 2 can be a thorny undertaking. Although it may be argued that Slocum retained his position as a "wing commander" assigned him by Meade's Pipe Creek Circular on July 1, the circumstances anticipated by the circular never occurred, so Slocum did not exercise wing authority on July 1. Meade's communications to Slocum on the morning of July 2 addressed him as Twelfth Corps commander, not a wing leader, and Slocum responded in like fashion. See OR, vol. 27, pt. 3:486–87. General Ruger indirectly supported this understanding in ibid., pt. 1:778.

64. Brown, *The Twenty-Seventh Indiana*, 369; OR, vol. 27, pt. 1:778, 811–12, 815; Raus, *A Generation on the March*, 20.

65. Alpheus S. Williams to John B. Bachelder, Apr. 21, 1864, typescript in Bachelder Papers, GNMP; Williams, *From the Cannon's Mouth*, 228.

66. Collins, *Memoirs of the 49th Regt.*, 137; Jones, "Saved the Day"; *In Memoriam, George Sears Greene Brevet Major-General, United States Volunteers, 1801–1899* (Albany, N.Y.: J. B. Lyon, State Printers, 1909), 42. Geary mentioned nothing about hesitating to authorize construction of the works but stated instead that "breastworks were immediately thrown up along our entire line." OR, vol. 27, pt. 1:826.

67. Collins, *Memoirs of the 149th Regt.*, 137; Jones, "Saved the Day"; Balch, "General George S. Greene"; Charles P. Horton to John B. Bachelder, Jan. 23, 1867, typescript in Bachelder Papers, GNMP. Harry Pfanz called my attention to the fact that elements of Brig. Gen. James S. Wadsworth's division of the First Corps built earthworks on Culp's Hill during the evening of July 1. This circumstance reduces the innovation, if not the correctness, of Greene's desire to fortify his line.

68. Charles P. Horton to John B. Bachelder, Jan. 23, 1867, typescript in Bachelder Papers, GNMP; Collins, *Memoirs of the 149th Regt.*, 137; McKim, *A Soldier's Recollections*, 197.

69. OR, vol. 27, pt. 1:847, 849, 854; "Notes of a Conversation with General Kane," GNMP.

70. OR, vol. 27, pt. 1:773, 783, 798, 803; Henry C. Morhous, *Reminiscences of the 123d Regiment, New York State Volunteers* (Greenwich, N.Y.: People's Journal Book and Job Office, 1879), 47; John W. Storrs, *The Twentieth Connecticut* (Naugatuck, Conn.: Press of the Naugatuck Valley Sentinel, 1886), 82–83.

71. Williams, *From the Cannon's Mouth*, 226; OR, vol. 27, pt. 1:773, 778, 872; Morse, "The Twelfth Corps at Gettysburg," 24.

72. Thayer, "Gettysburg," 807 (quotation); Morse, "History of the Second Massachusetts," 8; Collins, *Memoirs of the 149th Regt.*, 138; Storrs, *The Twentieth Connecticut*, 83.

73. Coddington, *The Gettysburg Campaign*, 367; Hunt, "The Second Day at Gettysburg," 293–94.

74. Busey and Martin, *Regimental Strengths at Gettysburg*, 151; OR, vol. 27, pt. 2:286.

75. OR, vol. 27, pt. 2:543; Burns, "Maryland and the Union Right at Gettysburg," 14–15; Robert K. Krick, *Lee's Colonels* (Dayton, Ohio: Press of Morningside Bookshop, 1979), 212.

76. OR, vol. 27, pt. 2:543; Burns, "Maryland and the Union Right at Gettysburg," 15–16; Bryant, *History of the Third Regiment*, 186; OR, vol. 27, pt. 1:863.

77. Coddington, *The Gettysburg Campaign*, 428; OR, vol. 27, pt. 1:826, 870, 899.

78. *In Memoriam, George Sears Greene*, 40; OR, vol. 27, pt. 1:863, 773, 870; Bryant, *History of the Third Regiment*, 186–87; Coddington, *The Gettysburg Campaign*, 428; OR, vol. 27, pt. 2:544. Capt. Charles I. Raine replaced Latimer, who died on August 1.

79. See Pfanz, *Gettysburg: The Second Day*, for the definitive study of Longstreet's assaults against Sickles.

80. OR, vol. 27, pt. 3:489; Henry W. Slocum to Messrs. T. H. Davis & Co., Sept. 8, 1875, copy in Samuel P. Bates Papers, GNMP (Slocum responded to Samuel P. Bates's *The Battle of Gettysburg*, 191); *N. Y. at Gettysburg* 3:1335; *In Memoriam, George Sears Greene*, 41, 85; Fox, "A History of the Twelfth and Twentieth Army Corps," 178. Coddington, *The Gettysburg Campaign*, 764 n. 115, was among the first historians to analyze Slocum's actions carefully as well as critically.

81. Alpheus S. Williams to John B. Bachelder, Apr. 21, 1864, Nov. 10, 1865, typescripts in Bachelder Papers, GNMP.

82. Henry W. Slocum to Messrs. T. H. Davis & Co., Sept. 8, 1875, copy at GNMP.

83. OR, vol. 27, pt. 1:826.

84. Charles P. Horton to John B. Bachelder, Jan. 23, 1867, typescript in the Bachelder Papers, GNMP. Horton placed the Confederate attack against Culp's Hill considerably earlier than most other witnesses, calling into question the accuracy of his account.

85. Ibid.; Henry W. Slocum to Messrs. T H. Davis & Co., Sept. 8, 1875, copy at GNMP.

86. Alpheus S. Williams to John B. Bachelder, Apr. 21, 1864, Nov. 10, 1865, typescripts in Bachelder Papers, GNMP; Morse, "The Twelfth Corps at Gettysburg," 26; OR, vol. 27, pt. 1:783; L. R. Coy to his wife, July 2, 1863, typescript copy in 123d New York file, GNMP; Williams, From the Cannon's Mouth, 228.

87. Williams, From the Cannon's Mouth, 228; Coddington, The Gettysburg Campaign, 418, 757 n. 51.

88. Morhous, 123rd Regiment, New York, 48; N. Y. at Gettysburg 2:858; Morse, "History of the Second Massachusetts," 8–9. This woman was the same "crone" who encouraged the Third Brigade as it marched into position in the morning (see reference to Bryant in note 55). It is possible that this episode occurred after Ruger's division reached Cemetery Ridge.

89. Alpheus S. Williams to John B. Bachelder, Nov. 10, 1865, typescript in Bachelder Papers, GNMP; OR, vol. 27, pt. 1:806; Coddington, The Gettysburg Campaign, 757 n. 51; Burns, "Maryland and the Union Right at Gettysburg," 18.

90. Alpheus S. Williams to John B. Bachelder, Nov. 10, 1865, typescript in Bachelder Papers, GNMP; Williams, From the Cannon's Mouth, 228; OR, vol. 27, pt. 1:774; Morse, "The Twelfth Corps at Gettysburg," 27; N.Y. at Gettysburg 3:1042. McGilvery and Williams had served together at Cedar Mountain in 1862.

91. OR, vol. 27, pt. 1:804, 809; N.Y. at Gettysburg 3:1043; Williams, From the Cannon's Mouth, 228. In his official report, Williams implied that Lockwood did form a line of battle. OR, vol. 27, pt. 1:774. See Pfanz, Gettysburg: The Second Day, 408–9, for a summary of this action.

92. OR, vol. 27, pt. 1:766, 804–6; Cook and Benton, "The Dutchess County Regiment," 32. See Pfanz, Gettysburg: The Second Day, 341–46, for a description of the capture of Bigelow's guns.

93. OR, vol. 27, pt. 1:766, 774, 804; Morse, "The Twelfth Corps at Gettysburg," 27; Alpheus S. Williams to John B. Bachelder, Nov. 10, 1865, typescript in Bachelder Papers, GNMP; Jeffrey G. Charnley, "Neglected Honor: The Life of General A. S. Williams of Michigan (1810–1878)," (Ph.D. diss., Michigan State Univ., 1983), 188–89; Coddington, The Gettysburg Campaign, 419.

94. In OR, vol. 27, pt. 1:371, Maj. Gen. Winfield S. Hancock testified that "General Meade brought up in person a part of the Twelfth Corps, consisting of two regiments of Lockwood's brigade." However, neither Williams nor Lockwood mentioned Meade's presence before the advance and Meade himself claimed no such credit. In The Gettysburg Campaign, 758 n. 57, Coddington postulates that although Hancock knew both Meade and Williams well, in the smoke of battle Hancock or one of his staff officers probably confused Williams with the army commander due to their superficial physical similarities.

95. OR, vol. 27, pt. 1:826. Candy's brigade in reserve on Culp's Hill would have been closer to the Baltimore Pike than Cobham's brigade. The accounts of this march imply but do not specify that Candy took the lead.

96. OR, vol. 27, pt. 1:759; Bryant, History of the Third Regiment, 189; Morse, "The Twelfth Corps at Gettysburg," 26.

97. OR, vol. 27, pt. 1:826; Coddington, The Gettysburg Campaign, 764 n. 118. See Alpheus S. Williams to John B. Bachelder, Nov. 10, 1865, typescript in Bachelder Papers, GNMP, and OR, vol. 27, pt. 1:774 for possible origins of this order.

98. Coddington, The Gettysburg Campaign, 433–34. Capt. Horton testified that "staff officers and orderlies were sent in all directions to find the missing force." But the delay in

doing so speaks either to the timeliness or efficiency of these searchers. Charles P. Horton to John B. Bachelder, Jan. 23, 1867, typescript in Bachelder Papers, GNMP.

99. OR, vol. 27, pt. 2:504; Coddington, The Gettysburg Campaign, 430. Coddington describes Johnson's position as being "in the triangular shaped area between the York and Hanover roads and about a mile from Culp's Hill. Jones's brigade moved forward about half a mile when it was detached to support the artillery." Coddington, The Gettysburg Campaign, 762 n. 105.

100. See OR, vol. 27, pt. 2:446–47, 504, and Coddington, The Gettysburg Campaign, 428–29, 762 n. 101. In In Memoriam, George Sears Greene, 44–45, Capt. Lewis R. Stegman argues that when the Union skirmish line was weakened to prepare for the move to Cemetery Ridge, Confederate officers must have reported the departure to their superiors resulting in Johnson's attack on Culp's Hill. Stegman offers no evidence to support his opinion.

101. OR, vol. 27, pt. 2:504, 518–19; pt. 1:956. The Union cavalry belonged to Brig. Gen. David McMurtrie Gregg, commander of the Second Division.

102. OR, vol. 27, pt. 2:447; Burns, "Maryland and the Union Right at Gettysburg," 23. A dam across Rock Creek near McAllister's Mill had flooded some of the creek upstream into a virtual millpond. For a reference to the pond, see OR, vol. 27, pt. 1:856.

103. OR, vol. 27, pt. 1:862, 865, pt. 2:504; In Memoriam, George Sears Greene, 43; N. Y. at Gettysburg 2:627; Balch, "General George S. Greene." Von Hammerstein was a twenty-seven-year-old German native and veteran of the Austrian army. Raus, A Generation on the March, 71.

104. In Memorium, George Sears Greene, 43–44; Jesse H. Jones, "The Breastworks at Culp's Hill," in B&L 3:316.

105. OR, vol. 27, pt. 1:731, 856; In Memoriam, George Sears Greene, 86–87, 47; Morse, "The Twelfth Corps at Gettysburg," 28; Coddington, The Gettysburg Campaign, 431, 763 n. 108. Greene neglected to mention the 157th New York of the Eleventh Corps as coming to his assistance, but Maj. Gen. Carl Schurz specifically did so in his report. The total number of reinforcements comes from Greene, but such precise tabulations should be used with some caution. The other regiments involved were the 6th Wisconsin, 14th Brooklyn (84th New York), 147th New York, 82d Illinois, 61st Ohio, and 45th New York. Heavy casualties on July 1 had reduced the strength of these regiments.

106. OR, vol. 27, pt. 2:513; In Memoriam, George Sears Greene, 45–46. Map 9 in Coddington, The Gettysburg Campaign, between 412 and 413 reverses Jones and Nicholls (Williams), a mistake repeated on other Gettysburg maps. Johnson's regiments included the 10th, 21st, 23d, 25th, 37th, 42d, 44th, 48th, and 50th Virginia, First Maryland Battalion, 1st and 3d North Carolina, and 1st, 2d, 10th, 14th, and 15th Louisiana regiments.

107. Charles P. Horton to John B. Bachelder, Jan. 23, 1867, typescript in Bachelder Papers, GNMP.

108. Ibid.; Collins, Memoirs of the 149th Regt., 138; Jesse H. Jones, "A Story of the Fierce Fighting on the Right at Gettysburg," National Tribune, June 6, 1901.

109. Charles P. Horton to John B. Bachelder, Jan. 23, 1867, typescript in Bachelder Papers, GNMP.

110. S. Z. Ammen, "Maryland Troops in the Confederacy," unattributed newspaper articles, photocopies in the possession of Harry W. Pfanz; Fox, "A History of the Twelfth and Twentieth Army Corps," 179; OR, vol. 27, pt. 1:826, 856, 866; N. Y. at Gettysburg 1:451.

111. Coddington, The Gettysburg Campaign, 427, 761 n. 95. Brig. Gen. John Gibbon received Hancock's order and passed it along to Brig. Gen. Alexander S. Webb, who selected the 71st and 106th Pennsylvania regiments from his brigade.

112. George S. Greene, "The Breastworks at Culp's Hill," in B&L 3:317; OR, vol. 27, pt. 1:826, 866; Charles P. Horton to John B. Bachelder, Jan. 23, 1867, typescript in Bachelder Papers, GNMP. Horton claimed that Smith told him he had received orders to return the 71st

Pennsylvania to its position with the Second Corps. Smith made no such claim in his report, and in fact stated he returned to camp "against orders." OR, vol. 27, pt. 1:432. In *The Gettysburg Campaign*, 431, Coddington observes that "the disappearance of the 71st Pennsylvania in no way affected the outcome of the struggle."

113. OR, vol. 27, pt. I:866–88; Charles P. Horton to John B. Bachelder, Jan. 23, 1867, typescript in Bachelder Papers, GNMP; Winfield Peters, "A Maryland Warrior and Hero," in SHSP 29:247; Coddington, *The Gettysburg Campaign*, 431–32; Collins, *Memoirs of the 149th Regt.*, 139; *N. Y. at Gettysburg* 2:689.

114. Typical Confederate claims that the Federal works were carried by storm are in McKim, *A Soldier's Recollections*, 198, and OR, vol. 27, pt. 2:504; for a Union rejoinder, see Charles P. Horton to John B. Bachelder, Jan. 23, 1867, typescript in Bachelder Papers, GNMP. The 137th lost 137 men at Gettysburg, as many as the 149th, 60th, and 78th combined. The brigade experienced some losses on July 3, but most of the casualties in the 137th came on July 2. OR, vol. 27, pt. 1:185.

115. OR, vol. 27, pt. 1:868, 763, 861, 764 (second quotation); Eddy, *History of the Sixtieth New York*, 261; Collins, *Memoirs of the 149th Regt.*, 143 (first quotation). Few Union defenders performed more memorably than Color Sgt. William C. Lilly of the 149th, who repeatedly spliced his unit's fractured flagstaff and raised the tattered banner during the fighting. Lilly's gallant determination is memorialized in bronze relief on the regiment's monument on Culp's Hill.

116. Balch, "General George S. Greene"; John O. Foering in *Pennsylvania at Gettysburg* 1:189–90.

117. Eugene Powell, "Rebellion's High Tide Dashed Against the Immovable Rocks of Gettysburg. The Splendid Work on Culp's Hill by the 12th Corps," in *National Tribune*, July 5, 1900 (quotation); *In Memoriam, George Sears Greene*, 46; Alexander, *Fighting for the Confederacy*, 243; Slocum, *Life and Services*, 107. For other opinions about the consequences of Johnson's victory that night, see Morse, "The Twelfth Corps at Gettysburg," 28–29; Jones, "The Breastworks at Culp's Hill," in B&L 3:316; Greene, "The Breastworks at Culp's Hill," in B&L 3:317; McKim, *A Soldier's Recollections*, 198–99; Fox, "Life of Slocum," 81; and Motts, "To Gain a Second Star," 65.

118. Coddington, *The Gettysburg Campaign*, 432–33. Most assertions that Ewell missed an opportunity at Gettysburg concern July 1.

119. OR, vol. 27, pt. 1:759, 761, 778, 780; Alpheus S. Williams to John B. Bachelder, Apr. 21, 1864, typescript in Bachelder Papers, GNMP; Williams, *From the Cannon's Mouth*, 228.

120. OR, vol. 27, pt. 1:780, 813; Morse, "The Twelfth Corps at Gettysburg," 30; Morse, "History of the Second Massachusetts," 9–10; Toombs, *Reminiscences*, 79.

121. Morse, "The Twelfth Corps at Gettysburg," 30–32; OR, vol. 27, pt. 1:816–17, 820; Alonzo H. Quint, *The Record of the Second Massachusetts Infantry, 1861–65* (Boston: James P. Walker, 1867), 179–80; George A. Thayer, "On the Right at Gettysburg. A Survivor's Story of the Gallant But Unavailing Charge by the 2nd Mass. Infantry," *National Tribune*, July 24, 1902.

122. OR, vol. 27, pt. 1:783, 790–91; *N. Y. at Gettysburg* 2:858; Morhous, *123rd Regiment, New York*, 48; Matchett in *Pennsylvania at Gettysburg* 1:285; Storrs, *The Twentieth Connecticut*, 88. Storrs describes a full-blown battle around Spangler's Spring, a claim unsubstantiated by other evidence.

123. L. R. Coy to his wife, Sarah, July 6, 1863, typescript, GNMP; OR, vol. 27, pt. 1:774–75. See OR, vol. 27, pt. 1:780, for a slightly different regimental order.

124. OR, vol. 27, pt. 1:806, 809–10; *N. Y. at Gettysburg* 3:1033, 1040.

125. OR, vol. 27, pt. 1:827. Geary probably placed the time of this order somewhat early.

126. Ibid., 827–28, 847, 849, 851, 854, 857, 836; *Pennsylvania at Gettysburg* 1:204, 2:593; "Notes of a Conversation with General Kane"; William Rickards to John B. Bachelder,

Apr. 12, 1864, typescript in Bachelder Papers, GNMP; Coddington, *The Gettysburg Campaign*, 434–35, 765 n. 121; Greene, "Breastworks at Culp's Hill," 317; Collins, *Memoirs of the 149th Regt.*, 140.

127. Alpheus S. Williams to John B. Bachelder, Nov. 10, 1865, typescript in Bachelder Papers, GNMP. Meade would later forget that he had sent for Williams, or perhaps the staff officer invited Williams on his own accord.

128. Slocum, *Life and Services*, 109; Brown, *The Twenty-Seventh Indiana*, 376. See Coddington, *The Gettysburg Campaign*, 449–53, for a description of the council.

129. Williams, *From the Cannon's Mouth*, 229; *OR*, vol. 27, pt. 1:775, 870; Fox, "A History of the Twelfth and Twentieth Army Corps," 181; Coddington, *The Gettysburg Campaign*, 466–68.

130. Meade's report is in *OR*, vol. 27, pt. 1:114–19.

131. Williams, *From the Cannon's Mouth*, 272; Coddington, *The Gettysburg Campaign*, 772–73 n. 57. Slocum had written Col. Joseph Howland on July 17, 1863, that he thought highly of Meade and hoped that "he will continue to do as well as he has thus far." Miscellaneous Manuscripts of Col. Joseph Howland, New-York Historical Society. Coddington believes that Maj. Gen. Daniel Butterfield, a Sickles partisan and inveterate critic of Meade's generalship at Gettysburg, probably influenced Slocum against Meade when Butterfield and Slocum served together in Tennessee during the winter of 1863–64.

132. *OR*, vol. 27, pt. 1:764–65; Henry W. Slocum to LeRoy W. Morgan, quoted in Williams, *From the Cannon's Mouth*, 284–87.

133. *OR*, vol. 27, pt. 1:769–70; Alpheus S. Williams to John B. Bachelder, Nov. 10, 1865, typescript in Bachelder Papers, GNMP; Coddington, *The Gettysburg Campaign*, 773 n. 57.

"No Troops on the Field Had Done Better":
John C. Caldwell's Division in the Wheatfield, July 2, 1863

The author is deeply indebted to Col. Terrance McClain (U.S. Army, Ret.) for his keen insight into the challenge of command in combat, and to Eric A. Campbell for making available all of his files on Caldwell's division at Gettysburg.

1. Undated statement by C. H. Morgan to John B. Bachelder, Bachelder Papers, New Hampshire Historical Society, Concord, New Hampshire (hereafter cited as Bachelder Papers, NHHS).

2. Busey and Martin, *Regimental Strengths at Gettysburg*, 242.

3. J. W Stuckenberg Diary, Gettysburg College Library (repository hereafter cited as GCL).

4. Robert L. Brake, "List of Staff Officers, Army of the Potomac at the Battle of Gettysburg," GNMP. Included on Caldwell's staff were ambulance and ordnance officers, neither of whom accompanied him into battle.

5. Dean Thomas, *Ready, Aim, Fire: Small Arms Ammunition in the Battle of Gettysburg* (Gettysburg, Pa.: Thomas Publications, 1981), 60.

6. John P. Nicholson, ed., *Pennsylvania at Gettysburg: Ceremonies at the Dedication of the Monuments Erected by the Commonwealth of Pennsylvania*, 2 vols. (Harrisburg, Pa.: William S. Ray, State Printer, 1904), 1:727; *OR*, vol. 27, pt. 1:379.

7. Josiah M. Favill, *Diary of a Young Officer* (Chicago: R. R. Donnelly & Sons, 1909), 244–45; Nicholson, *Pennsylvania at Gettysburg* 1:683; Francis A. Walker, *History of the Second Army Corps in the Army of the Potomac* (New York: Charles Scribner's Sons, 1886), 543.

8. Nicholson, *Pennsylvania at Gettysburg* 1:622–23.

9. The need to coordinate the various units on the Union left eventually became apparent to Meade, who placed Hancock in command of both the Second and Third corps after Sickles was wounded. Hancock could do little with the Third Corps, however, because its organization was largely destroyed by that time.

10. Charles A. Hale, "With Colonel Cross in the Gettysburg Campaign," *Civil War Times Illustrated* 13 (August 1974):35.

11. For a more detailed description of this action, see chapter 11 in Pfanz, *Gettysburg: The Second Day.*

12. *OR*, vol. 27, pt. 1:601.

13. Ibid., pt. 2:368; Joseph B. Kershaw, "Kershaw's Brigade at Gettysburg," in B&L, 3:336.

14. New York Monuments Commission for the Battlefields of Gettysburg and Chickamauga, *Final Report on the Battlefield of Gettysburg*, 3 vols. (Albany, N.Y.: J. B. Lyon, 1900), 3:1206–7 (cover title, by which this item is hereafter cited, *New York at Gettysburg*); Major John P. Dunne to Pennsylvania State Adjutant General, July 29, 1863, RG 19, Pennsylvania State Archives (copy GNMP); John Haley to John B. Bachelder, Bachelder Papers, NHHS.

15. Nicholson, *Pennsylvania at Gettysburg* 1:623; William P. Wilson undated statement to John B. Bachelder, Bachelder Papers, NHHS.

16. Charles A. Fuller, *Personal Recollections of the War of 1861–1865* (Sherburne, N.Y.: New Job Printing House, 1906), 92; *OR*, vol. 27, pt. 1:391.

17. William P. Wilson undated statement to John B. Bachelder, Bachelder Papers, NHHS.

18. Favill, *Diary of a Young Officer,* 346.

19. William P. Wilson undated statement to John B. Bachelder, Bachelder Papers, NHHS; Hale, "With Colonel Cross," 35; *OR*, vol. 27; pt. 1:379. Caldwell reported that he was positioned "on the right of the Fifth and the left of the Third Corps." His position was actually between Ayres's and Barnes's divisions of the Fifth Corps and in the center of the line Birney's division had occupied.

20. Hale, "With Colonel Cross," 35; *New York at Gettysburg* 1:460; "From the 64th New York," *Cattaraugus Freeman,* July 30, 1863 (hereafter cited by title of newspaper only); Nicholson, *Pennsylvania at Gettysburg* 1:728–29; Joseph W. Muffly, *The Story of Our Regiment: A History of the 148th Pennsylvania Volunteers* (Des Moines, Iowa: Kenyon Printing, 1911), 734.

21. Hale, "With Colonel Cross," 36; Fuller, *Personal Recollections,* 94–95; Muffly, *History of the 148th Pennsylvania,* 537; *OR*, vol. 27, pt. 1:379; Kershaw "Kershaw's Brigade," 336.

22. *OR*, vol. 27, pt. 1:379.

23. Tremain, *Two Days of War,* 81–84.

24. J. W. Stuckenberg Diary, GCL.

25. Favill, *Diary of a Young Officer,* 246; Nicholson, *Pennsylvania at Gettysburg* 1:624, 694.

26. Nicholson, *Pennsylvania at Gettysburg* 1:624–25; *OR*, vol. 27, pt. 1:392, 398. See also Kershaw's account in "Kershaw's Brigade" and his report in *OR*, vol. 27, pt. 2:366–70.

27. Hale, "With Colonel Cross," 36; *OR*, vol. 27, pt. 1:381–82.

28. John R. Brooke to Francis A. Walker, Nov. 14, 1885, Bachelder Papers, NHHS; *OR*, vol. 27, pt. 1:382, 400; *Cattaraugus Freeman,* July 30, 1863; Stephen A. Osborne, "Recollections of the Civil War," *Shenango Valley News,* Apr. 2, 1915, copy at United States Military History Institute, Carlisle, Pennsylvania.

29. Osborne, "Recollections of the Civil War"; *Cattaraugus Freeman,* July 30, 1863; *OR*, vol. 27, pt. 1:400; Nicholson, *Pennsylvania at Gettysburg* 1:701; A. E. Clark, "A Yankee at Gettysburg," *National Tribune,* Oct. 10, 1918. The 145th Pennsylvania reported sending one hundred prisoners to the rear. Brooke stated simply that his brigade captured a "great number." It is likely that many of these prisoners escaped shortly after their capture when the Wheatfied was overrun by Wofford's and Kershaw's brigades. Col. W. W. White of the 7th Georgia, who wrote the report for Anderson's command, placed the number of missing in the brigade at

fifty-one. See reports in *OR*, vol. 27, pt. 1:413–16 (Capt. John W. Reynolds and Capt. Moses W. Oliver of the 145th), 400 (Brooke), and in ibid., pt. 2:397 (White).

30. D. Sheldon Winthrop, *The Twenty-Seventh (Conn.)* (New Haven, Conn.: Morris & Benham, 1866), 386; Nicholson, *Pennsylvania at Gettysburg* 1:625; *OR*, vol. 27, pt. 1:386–92, 398; Kershaw, "Kershaw's Brigade," 336; Joseph B. Kershaw to John B. Bachelder, Apr. 3, 1878, Bachelder Papers, NHHS. Kershaw reported a total of thirty-two missing and captured. *OR*, vol. 27, pt. 2:370.

31. William P. Wilson undated statement to John B. Bachelder; William P. Wilson to John B. Bachelder, March 25, 1884, Bachelder Papers, NHHS; *OR*, vol. 27, pt. 1:401.

32. Jacob B. Sweitzer account of operations, Joshua L. Chamberlain Papers, LC (copy at GNMP); *OR*, vol. 27, pt. 1:379, 602, 611.

33. *OR*, vol. 27, pt. 1:634. The fierce criticism of Sickles's handling of the battle on July 2 may have diverted attention from the performance of George Sykes, whose direction of his corps was mediocre at best.

34. Ibid., 379, 634.

35. William H. Powell, *The Fifth Army Corps* (New York: G. P. Putnam's Sons, 1896), 534–38; *OR*, vol. 27, pt. 1:379–80.

36. J. J. Permeus to John B. Bachelder, Nov. 3, 1871, Bachelder Papers, NHHS; Osborne, "Recollections of the Civil War"; *OR*, vol. 27, pt. 1:401.

37. *OR*, vol. 27, pt. 1:634.

38. Ibid., 380; C. H. Morgan undated statement to John B. Bachelder, Bachelder Papers, NHHS.

39. Busey and Martin, *Regimental Strengths at Gettysburg*, 242; C. H. Morgan undated statement to John B. Bachelder, Bachelder Papers, NHHS.

40. C. H. Morgan undated statement to John B. Bachelder, Bachelder Papers, NHHS; Alexander Webb to his wife, March 26, 1864, cited in Coddington, *The Gettysburg Campaign*, 751 n. 41.

41. J. W. Stuckenberg Diary, GCL.

"Rarely Has More Skill, Vigor, or Wisdom Been Shown":
George G. Meade on July 3 at Gettysburg

1. For an intelligent discussion of the casualties in both armies for the first two days, see John M. Vanderslice, *Gettysburg Then and Now* (New York: G. W. Dillingham, 1899), 112–32, 192–224.

2. For a description of this council of war, see Edwin B. Coddington, *The Gettysburg Campaign: A Study in Command* (New York: Scribner's, 1968), 449–53; and Richard A. Sauers, *A Caspian Sea of Ink: The Meade-Sickles Controversy* (Baltimore: Butternut & Blue, 1989), 135–43.

3. For an analysis of the Meade-Sickles controversy, see Sauers, *Caspian Sea of Ink*, which includes a thorough investigation of both primary sources and secondary literature on this subject.

4. Sauers, *Caspian Sea of Ink*, 140.

5. U.S. Congress, Joint Congressional Committee on the Conduct of the War, *Report of the Joint Congressional Committee on the Conduct of the War, at the Second Session Thirty-eighth Congress. Army of the Potomac. Battle of Petersburg* (Washington, D.C.: GPO, 1865), 350 [hereafter cited as *CCW*]; Sauers, *Caspian Sea of Ink*, 140–41.

6. U.S. War Department, *The War of the Rebellion: A Compilation of the Official Records of the Union and Confederate Armies* 128 vols. (Washington, D.C.: GPO, 1880–1901), ser. 1, vol. 27, pt. 1:72 [hereafter cited as *OR*; all references are to series 1].

7. See, for example, Freeman Cleaves, *Meade of Gettysburg* (Norman: Univ. of Oklahoma Press, 1960), 156–57.

8. In his committee testimony, General Butterfield recalled that the fighting on Culp's Hill was still audible as the council assembled. *CCW*, 425.

9. Ibid., 350.

10. Edwin C. Fishel, *The Secret War for the Union* (Boston: Houghton Mifflin, 1996), 526–27.

11. Ibid., 528–29. Did Sharpe and Babcock exaggerate their influence in later years? None of the conference participants, especially Hancock and Slocum, mentioned the intelligence report in their testimony before the Committee on the Conduct of the War. It is worth noting, however, that both generals had a good reason not to bring this up before the committee— any mention would be a breach of the secrecy surrounding Sharpe's activities. Sharpe also failed to mention Gibbon's presence at the council, and Gibbon presumably had accompanied Hancock to the Leister house (see John Gibbon, *Personal Recollections of the Civil War* [New York: Putnam's, 1928], 140). Fishel represented Meade as a vacillating general who still wanted to withdraw to Pipe Creek, a portrait not in keeping with most accounts of the general at Gettysburg.

12. Gibbon, *Personal Recollections*, 144–45. Although this book was not published until 1928, Gibbon completed the manuscript by 1885, as evidenced by the date found on the last page. Sections of his Gettysburg chapters were published as articles in the July 6, 13, and 20, 1887, editions of the *Philadelphia Weekly Press*.

13. George Gordon Meade, *The Life and Letters of George Gordon Meade, Major General United States Army*, ed. George Meade, 2 vols. (New York: Scribner's, 1913), 2:98.

14. Meade's favorite horse, Old Baldy, had been wounded the previous day. The general rode a steed named Blackey. See George Meade to John B. Bachelder, May 6, 1882, Bachelder Papers, New Hampshire Historical Society, Concord [repository hereafter cited as NHHS].

15. Frank L. Byrne and Andrew T. Weaver, *Haskell of Gettysburg: His Life and Civil War Papers* (Madison: State Historical Society of Wisconsin, 1970), 142.

16. Henry W. Slocum to L. R. Morgan, January 2, 1864, in Alpheus S. Williams, *From the Cannon's Mouth: The Civil War Letters of General Alpheus S. Williams*, ed. Milo M. Quaife (Detroit: Wayne State Univ. Press, 1959), 285. In this letter, Slocum complained that Meade sent the Sixth Corps troops to him "without visiting me or any portion of the line."

17. OR, vol. 27, pt. 3:501–2; vol. 51, pt. 1:1068; vol. 27, pt. 3:499.

18. Meade, *Life and Letters* 2:103.

19. Ibid.

20. Coddington, *Gettysburg Campaign*, 483–84; Byrne and Weaver, *Haskell of Gettysburg*, 142–43; *CCW*, 408. Ample evidence suggests that Meade thought of his center as being Cemetery Hill rather than the line of the Second Corps.

21. Meade, *Life and Letters* 2:104–5. This section of the text was written by the general's grandson. At the time of his death, Colonel Meade had gotten as far as describing the fighting on Culp's Hill. His son, also named George Meade, wrote the remainder of volume 2, basing his work on Meade's committee testimony, the *Official Records*, and private correspondence in the family's possession. See Meade's note on page 102.

22. Gibbon, *Personal Recollections*, 146.

23. Byrne and Weaver, *Haskell of Gettysburg*, 144–47. Haskell's details suggest that this meal took place earlier in the morning than in Gibbon's recollections, which seem to place the meal closer to noon.

24. Coddington, *Gettysburg Campaign*, 496; Meade, *Life and Letters* 2:106.

25. Meade, *Life and Letters* 2:106; James C. Biddle to wife, July 8, 1863, Biddle Letters, Historical Society of Pennsylvania, Philadelphia [repository hereafter cited as HSP]; William H.

Paine Diary, July 3, 1863, Paine Papers, New-York Historical Society, New York City [repository hereafter cited as NYHS].

26. Meade, *Life and Letters* 2:106–7.

27. Ibid., 107; *OR*, vol. 27, pt. 1:290; Chauncey B. Reese to Gouverneur K. Warren, March 11, 1866, Warren Papers, New York State Library, Albany. For a detailed summary of units maneuvered into position to support the front line if needed, see Isaac R. Pennypacker, *General Meade* (New York: D. Appleton, 1901), 193–94.

28. *CCW*, 333; Henry J. Hunt, "The Third Day at Gettysburg," in Robert Underwood Johnson and Clarence Clough Buel, eds., *Battles and Leaders of the Civil War*, 4 vols. (New York: Century, 1887–1888), 3:371–72.

29. Ibid., 373–74.

30. Ibid., 374. No one on Cemetery Hill except Maj. Thomas W. Osborn recalled seeing Meade there. In a postwar article, Osborn wrote that Meade appeared during the height of the shelling and asked him if the batteries could stay on the hill. Meade remained only two or three minutes. Osborn described Meade as "perfectly cool and collected in his judgment, but in his manner excited and nervous." He compared Meade with Maj. Gen. Edwin V. Sumner, former Second Corps commander, who was also high-strung in the heat of battle. See Osborn, "The Artillery at Gettysburg," in *Philadelphia Weekly Times*, May 31, 1879. After Hunt had instructed the Second Corps batteries to cease firing, Hancock ordered his guns to open fire again in order to help the morale of his foot soldiers. Hancock's interference, said Hunt, depleted ammunition and enabled the attacking force to cross the fields with fewer casualties than might have occurred. Hunt and Hancock engaged in a vituperative postwar argument about this.

31. Meade, *Life and Letters* 2:107; George Meade to John B. Bachelder, December 4, 1869, Bachelder Papers, copy in Peter F. Rothermel Papers, Pennsylvania State Archives, Harrisburg [repository hereafter cited as PSA].

32. James C. Biddle to wife, July 8, 1863, Biddle Letters, HSP; William H. Paine Diary, July 3, 1863, Paine Papers, NYHS; George Meade to John Bachelder, December 4, 1869, copy in Peter F. Rothermel Papers, PSA.

33. George Meade to John B. Bachelder, May 6, 1882, Bachelder Papers, NHHS; Meade, *Life and Letters* 2:107–8.

34. George Meade to John B. Bachelder, December 4, 1869, copy in Peter F. Rothermel Papers, PSA.

35. George Meade to John B. Bachelder, May 6, 1882, Bachelder Papers, NHHS; George Meade to John B. Bachelder, December 4, 1869, copy in Peter C. Rothermel Papers, PSA.

36. George Meade to John B. Bachelder, May 6, 1882, Bachelder Papers, NHHS. Captain Meade thought that the messenger who galloped up to his father was Lt. Ranald S. Mackenzie, one of Warren's aides.

37. George Meade to John B. Bachelder, May 6, 1882, John Egan to George Meade, February 8, 1870, Bachelder Papers, NHHS.

38. George Meade to John B. Bachelder, May 6, 1882, Bachelder Papers, NHHS.

39. Byrne and Weaver, *Haskell of Gettysburg*, 173–74; undated letter of Lt. Col. Charles H. Morgan to John B. Bachelder filed among Bachelder's 1886 correspondence, Bachelder Papers, NHHS [hereafter cited as Morgan letter to Bachelder].

40. George Meade to John B. Bachelder, May 6, 1882, Bachelder Papers, NHHS; Byrne and Weaver, *Haskell of Gettysburg*, 174–75; Morgan letter to Bachelder. Colonel Morgan observed that after Hancock was wounded he dictated a message to Meade, stating that if the general would advance the Fifth and Sixth corps he would win a glorious victory. Hancock also repeated this statement in his committee testimony (*CCW*, 408.)

41. Meade, *Life and Letters* 2:109–10; George Meade to John B. Bachelder, December 4, 1869, copy in Peter C. Rothermel Papers, PSA; George Meade to John B. Bachelder, May 6,

1882, Bachelder Papers, NHHS; Cleaves, *Meade of Gettysburg*, 167. At some point during the period after Pickett's repulse, Meade placed General Newton in charge of the entire line from the right of the Fifth Corps to Cemetery Hill. See Newton's report in OR, vol. 27, pt. 1:263. It seems natural that Meade would have done this while riding south along the line. Newton had his headquarters with the First Corps troops stationed on Gibbon's left.

42. CCW, 333. Meade did not mention any of this in his official report.

43. OR, vol. 27, pt. 1:75.

44. William H. Paine Diary, July 3, 1863, Paine Papers, NYHS; Pennypacker, *General Meade*, 201.

45. Coddington, *Gettysburg Campaign*, 532–34.

46. Hunt's letter to Webb, dated January 12, 1888, is in William H. Powell, *The Fifth Army Corps (Army of the Potomac). A Record of Operations During the Civil War in the United States of America, 1861–1865* (New York: Putnam's, 1896), 559.

James Longstreet's Virginia Defenders

1. See William Garrett Piston, "Cross Purposes: Longstreet, Lee, and Confederate Attack Plans for July 3 at Gettysburg," in Gary W. Gallagher, ed., *The Third Day at Gettysburg and Beyond* (Chapel Hill: Univ. of North Carolina Press, 1994), 31–55.

2. William Henry Cocke to William Cocke, July 11, 1863, Cocke Family Papers, Virginia Historical Society, Richmond [repository hereafter cited as VHS]; U.S. War Department, *The War of the Rebellion: A Compilation of the Official Records of the Union and Confederate Armies*, 128 vols. (Washington, D.C.: GPO, 1880–1901), ser. 1, vol. 27, pt. 2:386 [hereafter cited as OR; all references are to volumes in series 1]; James Dearing to Mother, July 20, 1863, Dearing Family Papers, Alderman Library, University of Virginia, Charlottesville [repository hereafter cited as UVA]; Edward Porter Alexander to Father, July 17, 1863, Alexander-Hillhouse Papers, Southern Historical Collection, Wilson Library, University of North Carolina, Chapel Hill [repository hereafter cited as SHC].

3. H. T. Holladay to [?], July 7, 1863, Holladay Family Papers, UVA; Susan Leigh Blackford, comp., *Letters from Lee's Army* (New York: Scribner's, 1947), 188.

4. "The Battle of Gettysburg," *Richmond Enquirer*, July 23, 1863; Ambrose Wright to his wife, July 7, 1863, printed in Augusta (Ga.) *Daily Constitutionalist*, July 23, 1863, and reprinted in *Richmond Daily Dispatch*, July 28, 1863.

5. *Richmond Sentinel*, July 20, 1863.

6. William Garrett Piston, *Lee's Tarnished Lieutenant: James Longstreet and His Place in Southern History* (Athens: Univ. of Georgia Press, 1987), 60.

7. Walter Harrison, *Pickett's Men: A Fragment of War History* (New York: D. Van Nostrand, 1870), 91–92.

8. Ibid., 98–100.

9. On the material covered in this and the following three paragraphs, see chapter 4 of Carol Reardon, *Pickett's Charge in History and Memory* (Chapel Hill: Univ. of North Carolina Press, 1997), especially 84–88.

10. See Virginius Dabney, *Richmond: The Story of a City* (New York: Doubleday, 1976), 232–33.

11. On the Lee cult and Longstreet, see chapter 7 of Piston, *Lee's Tarnished Lieutenant*.

12. For an entire chapter devoted to Lee after the charge, see John Esten Cooke, *A Life of Gen. Robert E. Lee* (New York: D. Appleton, 1871), 325 ff.

13. A. L. Long, "Letter from General A. L. Long, Military Secretary to General R. E. Lee," in J. William Jones and others, eds., *Southern Historical Society Papers*, 52 vols. (1876–1959;

reprint, Wilmington, N.C.: Broadfoot, 1990–1992), 4:123 [hereafter cited as SHSP]; Walter H. Taylor, "Memorandum of Colonel Walter H. Taylor of General Lee's Staff," in SHSP 4:84–85; Walter H. Taylor, "The Campaign in Pennsylvania," in [A. K. McClure, ed.], The Annals of the War Written by Leading Participants North and South (Philadelphia: The Times Publishing Company, 1879), 312–16.

14. Jubal A. Early, "Letter from Gen. J. A. Early," in SHSP 4:64; Jubal A. Early, "Reply to General Longstreet's Second Paper," in SHSP 5:284–85; Cadmus M. Wilcox, "General Cadmus M. Wilcox on the Battle of Gettysburg," in SHSP 6:120–21.

15. Thomas J. Goree, Longstreet's Aide: The Civil War Letters of Major Thomas J. Goree, ed. Thomas W. Cutrer (Charlottesville: Univ. Press of Virginia, 1995), 159.

16. Edward Porter Alexander, Fighting for the Confederacy: The Personal Recollections of General Edward Porter Alexander, ed. Gary W. Gallagher (Chapel Hill: Univ. of North Carolina Press, 1989), 252, 280.

17. James H. Lane, "Letter from General James H. Lane," in SHSP 5:39–40.

18. B. D. Fry, "Pettigrew's Charge at Gettysburg," in SHSP 7:91–93; Wilcox, "Battle of Gettysburg," in SHSP 6:121.

19. Henry Heth, "Letter from Major-General Heth of A. P. Hill's Corps, A.N.V.," in SHSP 4:159–60.

20. Lafayette McLaws, "Gettysburg," in SHSP 7:82.

21. Abner Doubleday, Chancellorsville and Gettysburg (New York: Scribner's, 1881), 195.

22. Several installments of "Notes and Queries" in SHSP (10:284, 335, 423–29; 11: 284–86) address questions relating to Armistead's mortal wounding in the Angle.

23. David E. Johnston, Four Years a Soldier (Princeton, W.V.: n.p., 1887), 244–64; Charles T. Loehr, War History of the Old First Virginia Infantry Regiment, Army of Northern Virginia (1884; reprint, Dayton, Ohio: Morningside, 1978), 36.

24. Quoted in William R. Bond, Pickett or Pettigrew? An Historical Essay (Weldon, N.C.: Hall & Sledge, 1888), 7.

25. Loehr, War History, 38.

26. Ibid., 11.

27. See Reardon, Pickett's Charge, 93–103.

28. National Tribune, July 12, 1888.

29. New York Times, July 4, 1888.

30. Richmond Dispatch, August 28, 1888. See also Reardon, Pickett's Charge, 104–7.

31. Richmond Dispatch, August 30, October 4, 1888.

32. Goree, Longstreet's Aide, 171, 177.

33. See Jeffry D. Wert, General James Longstreet: The Confederacy's Most Controversial Soldier, A Biography (New York: Simon & Schuster, 1993), 48–49, 97.

34. Mel Young, comp. and ed., Last Orders of the Lost Cause: The Civil War Memoirs of a Jewish Family of the "Old South" (Lanham, Md.: Univ. Press of America, 1995), 211.

35. See James H. Stine, History of the Army of the Potomac (Philadelphia: J. B. Rodgers, 1892), 538–40, for the full texts of the letters from Pickett's staff.

36. James Longstreet to Major Nash, October 3, 1892, copy in Charles Pickett Papers, VHS; Charles Pickett to James Longstreet, October 12, 1892, James Longstreet Papers, SHC.

37. Charles Pickett explained what he believed happened to the family's papers in a letter to Miss Lida Perry, March 24, 1896, George E. Pickett Papers, William R. Perkins Library, Duke University, Durham, N.C.

38. Charles Pickett to James Longstreet, October 12, 1892, James Longstreet Papers, SHC; W. Stuart Symington to Charles Pickett, October 17, 26, 1892, Robert A. Bright to Charles Pickett, October 15, 1892, Charles Pickett Papers, VHS.

39. James Longstreet, *From Manassas to Appomattox: Memoirs of the Civil War in America* (Philadelphia: Lippincott, 1896), 390–96; LaSalle Corbell Pickett, "My Soldier," *McClure's Magazine* (1908): 569; John Singleton Mosby, *The Memoirs of Col. John S. Mosby*, ed. Charles W. Russell (1917; reprint, Bloomington: Indiana Univ. Press, 1959), 381–83.

40. LaSalle Corbell Pickett, *Pickett and His Men* (Atlanta: Foote and Davies, 1899), 301, 310–14.

41. Joseph C. Mayo, "Pickett's Charge at Gettysburg," in *SHSP* 34:328, 335.

42. Edward R. Baird, "Gettysburg," an address delivered to the Essex chapter, United Daughters of the Confederacy, Tappahannock, Virginia, copy in Edward R. Baird Papers, Museum of the Confederacy, Richmond, Va.; Robert A. Bright, "Pickett's Charge," in *SHSP* 31:231.

43. Bright, "Pickett's Charge," in *SHSP* 31:228; G. Moxley Sorrel, *Recollections of a Confederate Staff Officer*, ed. Bell I. Wiley (1958; reprint, Wilmington, N.C.: Broadfoot, 1991), 163.

44. LaSalle Corbell Pickett, *The Heart of a Soldier* (New York: Seth Moyle, 1913), 98–99.

45. These photographs may be found inserted throughout *Fiftieth Anniversary of the Battle of Gettysburg, Report of the Pennsylvania Commission, December 31, 1913, Revised Edition, April 1915* (Harrisburg, Pa.: William Stanley Ray, 1915).

46. Herbert Francis Sherwood, "Gettysburg Fifty Years Afterward," *Outlook* 104 (July 19, 1913): 612.

47. Pickett, *Pickett and His Men*, 319.

48. *New York Times*, July 4, 1913.

49. Quoted in Piston, *Lee's Tarnished Lieutenant*, 130.

50. Douglas Southall Freeman, *R. E. Lee: A Biography*, 4 vols. (New York: Scribner's, 1934–1935), 2:235; James Longstreet, "Lee in Pennsylvania," in [McClure, ed.], *Annals of the War*, 429.

51. Longstreet, *Manassas to Appomattox*, 388.

52. Ibid., 405–6.

"Every Map of the Field Cries Out about It":
The Failure of Confederate Artillery at Pickett's Charge

The author would like to thank Shawn Gaddis of Western Carolina University, Robert E. L. Krick of Richmond, Va., and Robert K. Krick of Fredericksburg, Va., for their research assistance and advice in the preparation of this article.

1. John H. Chamberlayne, *Ham Chamberlayne-Virginian: Letters and Papers of an Artillery Officer in the War for Southern Independence, 1861–1865*, ed. C. G. Chamberlayne (1932; reprint, Wilmington, N.C.: Broadfoot, 1992), 176. On Confederate artillery on May 3 at Chancellorsville, see Jennings C. Wise, *The Long Arm of Lee; or, The History of Artillery of the Army of Northern Virginia . . . .*, 2 vols. (Lynchburg, Va.: J. P. Bell, 1915), 2:505–29; Douglas Southall Freeman, *Lee's Lieutenants: A Study in Command*, 3 vols. (New York: Scribner's, 1942–44), 2:444–66.

2. On the Army of Northern Virginia's battalion system, see Wise, *Long Arm of Lee* 1: 412–25. For discussions of Confederate artillery as it related to Pickett's Charge, see Edwin B. Coddington, *The Gettysburg Campaign: A Study in Command* (New York: Scribner's, 1968), 484–502; Kathleen R. Georg and John W. Busey, *Nothing But Glory: Pickett's Division at Gettysburg* (Gettysburg, Pa.: Thomas Publications, 1987), 22–37; George R. Stewart, *Pickett's Charge: A Microhistory of the Final Attack at Gettysburg, July 3, 1863* (1959; reprint, Dayton, Ohio: Morningside, 1983), 32–35, 45–47, 127–61.

3. There is no modern biography of William Nelson Pendleton. The best source on his prewar and Confederate careers, which includes much of his personal correspondence, is

Susan P. Lee, *Memoirs of William Nelson Pendleton, D.D.* (1893; reprint, Harrisonburg, Va.: Sprinkle Publications, 1991).

4. William Nelson Pendleton to Thomas J. Jackson, April 25, 1862, Thomas J. Jackson Papers, Southern Historical Collection, Wilson Library, University of North Carolina, Chapel Hill [repository hereafter cited as SHC].

5. For the best treatments of Pendleton's near-disaster at Shepherdstown, see Freeman, *Lee's Lieutenants* 2:226–35; Peter S. Carmichael, "'We Don't Know What on Earth to Do with Him': William Nelson Pendleton and the Affair at Shepherdstown, September 19, 1862," in Gary W. Gallagher, ed., *The Antietam Campaign* (Chapel Hill: Univ. of North Carolina Press, 1999).

6. Chamberlayne, *Ham Chamberlayne*, 134. For other critical evaluations of Pendleton, see David Gregg McIntosh to Jennings C. Wise, June 8, 1916, David Gregg McIntosh Papers, Civil War Miscellaneous Collection, United States Army Military History Institute, Carlisle, Pa. [repository hereafter cited as USAMHI]; Walter Herron Taylor, *Lee's Adjutant: The Wartime Letters of Colonel Walter Herron Taylor, 1862–1865*, ed. R. Lockwood Tower (Columbia: Univ. of South Carolina Press, 1995), 186.

7. On the close ties between Pendleton and Davis, see Jefferson Davis, *The Rise and Fall of the Confederate Government*, 2 vols. (New York: D. Appleton, 1881), 2:148; Robert E. Lee, *Lee's Dispatches: Unpublished Letters of General Robert E. Lee, C.S.A. to Jefferson Davis and the War Department of the Confederate States of America, 1862–65*, ed. Douglas Southall Freeman, with additional dispatches by Grady McWhiney (1957; reprint, Baton Rouge: Louisiana State Univ. Press, 1994), 79, 242.

8. On the problems of individual batteries assigned to brigades, see Edward Porter Alexander, "Confederate Artillery Service," in J. William Jones and others, eds., *Southern Historical Society Papers*, 52 vols. (1876–1959; reprint, Wilmington, N.C: Broadfoot, 1900–1992), 11:98–102 [set hereafter cited as SHSP].

9. Alexander, "Confederate Artillery Service," in SHSP 11:102.

10. Henry J. Hunt, "The Third Day at Gettysburg," in *Battles and Leaders of the Civil War*, ed. Robert Underwood Johnson and Clarence Clough Buel, 4 vols. (1887–1888; reprint, Edison, N.J.: Castle, 1995), 3:373–74 [set hereafter cited as B&L].

11. Wise, *Long Arm of Lee* 2:667–68.

12. On the unreliability of Confederate shells, see Edward Porter Alexander, *Fighting for the Confederacy: The Personal Recollections of General Edward Porter Alexander*, ed. Gary W. Gallagher (Chapel Hill: Univ. of North Carolina Press, 1989), 122, 246, 248, 323.

13. Charles S. Wainwright, *A Diary of Battle: The Personal Journals of Colonel Charles S. Wainwright, 1861–1865*, ed. Allan Nevins (New York: Harcourt, Brace & World, 1962), 249.

14. Alexander, *Fighting for the Confederacy*, 251. For similar criticism regarding the misuse of Ewell's artillery, see Edward Porter Alexander, "The Great Charge and Artillery Fighting at Gettysburg," in B&L 3: 363; Wise, *Long Arm of Lee* 2:666–68.

15. Alexander, *Fighting for the Confederacy*, 251; U.S. War Department, *The War of the Rebellion: A Compilation of the Official Records of the Union and Confederate Armies*, 128 vols. (Washington, D.C.: GPO, 1880–1901), ser. 1, vol. 27, pt. 1:706 [hereafter cited as OR; all references are to series 1]; Wise, *Long Arm of Lee* 2:668–69.

16. OR, vol. 27, pt. 2:320.

17. Carol Reardon correctly asserts that "since Pickett and Pettigrew would march forth on different axes of advance, cooperation was essential to success, but history is relatively silent on measures taken by any senior leader to assure that troops from two different corps could coordinate their actions in the heat of battle." (Carol Reardon, *Pickett's Charge in History and Memory* [Chapel Hill: Univ. of North Carolina Press, 1997], 8.)

18. Alexander, *Fighting For the Confederacy*, 280; James Longstreet, *From Manassas to Appomattox: Memoirs of the Civil War in America* (1896; reprint, Secaucus, N.J.: Blue and Grey, 1984), 388. For a narrative of Alexander's actions at Gettysburg, see Jay Jorgensen, "Edward Porter Alexander: Confederate Cannoneer at Gettysburg," *Gettysburg Magazine* 17:41–53.

19. Edward Porter Alexander, "Causes of Confederate Defeat at Gettysburg," in SHSP 4:102; Alexander, "The Great Charge and Artillery Fighting at Gettysburg," in B&L 3:363.

20. Walker's Gettysburg report lacks important specifics regarding the actions of the Third Corps artillery or his communication with the army's high command; see OR, vol. 27, pt. 2:610. For Hill's report, which also failed to detail the actions of his corps artillery, see OR, vol. 27, pt. 2:608.

21. Alexander, *Fighting For the Confederacy*, 246.

22. Ibid., 250–51.

23. Ibid., 254.

24. Ibid.

25. *Supplement to the Official Records of the Union and Confederate Armies*, ed. Janet B. Hewett and others, 98 vols. to date (Wilmington, N.C.: Broadfoot, 1994–), 5:354 [hereafter cited as ORS].

26. Alexander, *Fighting for the Confederacy*, 255; Fitzhugh Lee, *General Lee* (1894; reprint, Wilmington, N.C.: Broadfoot, 1989), 293.

27. Alexander, *Fighting for the Confederacy*, 247.

28. Ibid., 249; Edward Porter Alexander to John B. Bachelder, May 3, 1876, in *The Bachelder Papers: Gettysburg in Their Own Words*, ed. David L. and Audrey J. Ladd, 3 vols. (Dayton, Ohio: Morningside, 1994), 1:488.

29. Stewart, *Pickett's Charge*, 153–54; Coddington, *The Gettysburg Campaign*, 499.

30. ORS 5:341; Robert A. Bright, "Our Confederate Column—Pickett's Charge," *Richmond Times-Dispatch*, February 7, 1904.

31. Alexander, "The Great Charge and Artillery Fighting at Gettysburg," in B&L 3:357; Coddington, *The Gettysburg Campaign*, 501; Alexander, *Fighting for the Confederacy*, 261.

32. OR, vol. 27, pt. 2:321; ORS 5:310; "The Battle of Gettysburg," *Richmond Enquirer*, July 23, 1863.

33. ORS 5:355. On the advance of Alexander's eighteen guns, see Alexander, *Fighting for the Confederacy*, 262–63; ORS 5:361–62.

34. William T. Poague, *Gunner With Stonewall: Reminiscences of William Thomas Poague*, ed. Monroe F. Cockrell (1957; reprint, Wilmington, N.C.: Broadfoot, 1987), 74. For a critical assessment of Lindsay Walker, see Wise, *Long Arm of Lee* 2:685.

35. OR, vol. 27, pt. 2:321.

36. Thomas J. Goree, *Longstreet's Aide: The Civil War Letters of Major Thomas J. Goree*, ed. Thomas W. Cutrer (Charlottesville: Univ. Press of Virginia, 1995), 159. Jennings C. Wise commented on Goree's contention that Pendleton spent most of his time behind the lines on July 3, noting that the army's chief of artillery supervised "the convenient placing of the ordnance trains" but seemed "to have failed for some reason to verify personally the posting of the batteries." Wise, *Long Arm of Lee* 2:666.

"I Do Not Believe That Pickett's Divison Would Have Reached Our Line":
Henry J. Hunt and the Union Artillery on July 3

1. The only modern biography of Hunt is Edward G. Longacre, *The Man behind the Guns: A Biography of General Henry J. Hunt, Commander of Artillery, Army of the Potomac* (Cranberry, N.J.:

A. S. Barnes, 1977). See page 11 for a summary of Hunt's attributes and accomplishments as an artillerist.

2. Ezra J. Warner, *Generals in Blue: Lives of the Union Commanders* (Baton Rouge: Louisiana State Univ. Press, 1964), 242; Francis B. Heitman, *Historical Register and Dictionary of the United States Army, from Its Organization, September 29, 1789, to March 2, 1903,* 2 vols. (Washington, D.C.: GPO, 1903), 1:556.

3. The best narrative history of the Army of the Potomac remains Bruce Catton's trilogy, *Mr. Lincoln's Army, Glory Road,* and *A Stillness at Appomattox* (Garden City, N.Y.: Doubleday, 1951–53).

4. James K. P. Scott, "The Story of the Battles at Gettysburg," vol. 3, p. 46, unpublished manuscript in author's collection. Scott included a chapter titled "Artillery at Gettysburg" in the final volume of his planned trilogy on the battle.

5. Ibid., 47.

6. Ibid.

7. Longacre, *Man behind the Guns,* 13; *Report of the Joint Committee on the Conduct of the War, at the Second Session Thirty–eighth Congress. Army of the Potomac. Battle of Petersburg* (Washington, D.C.: GPO, 1865), 448 [hereafter cited as *CCW*]; David Shultz and Richard Rollins, "A Combined and Concentrated Fire: The Deployment of the Federal Artillery on July 3rd.," manuscript article, p. 9. Shultz and Rollins observe that "during the battle of Antietam on Sept. 17, Hunt had under his direct command 322 various cannons in 55 batteries, of which 285 became engaged."

8. Shultz and Rollins, "Combined and Concentrated Fire," 10.

9. Scott, "Battles at Gettysburg," vol. 3, p. 48; Shultz & Rollins, "Combined and Concentrated Fire," 13; Special Orders No. 129, May 12, 1863, in U.S. War Department, *The War of the Rebellion: A Compilation of the Official Records of the Union and Confederate Armies,* 128 vols. (Washington, D.C.: GPO, 1880–1901), ser. 1, vol. 25, pt. 2:471–72 [hereafter cited as *OR*; all references are to volumes in series 1].

10. Shultz and Rollins, "Combined and Concentrated Fire," 13 [footnoted material]. See also *OR,* vol. 25, pt. 2:574–84.

11. For Hancock's and Hunt's arguments after the war, which continued until the mid-1880s, see their correspondence with John B. Bachelder in David L. Ladd and Audrey J. Ladd, eds., *The Bachelder Papers: Gettysburg in Their Own Words,* 3 vols. (Dayton, Ohio: Morningside, 1994–1995) [hereafter cited as *Bachelder Papers*]. See also Francis P. Walker, "General Hancock and the Artillery at Gettysburg," and Henry J. Hunt, "Rejoinder by Henry J. Hunt, Brevet Major-General, U.S.A.," in Robert Underwood Johnson and Clarence Clough Buel, eds., *Battles and Leaders of the Civil War,* 4 vols. (New York: Century, 1887–1888), 3:385–87 [hereafter cited as *B&L*].

12. Henry J. Hunt, "Journal of Siege Operations, April, 1864–March, 1865," p. 13 [Gettysburg National Military Park historian Kathleen Georg Harrison identified this part of the journal as having been written February 1, 1884, from notes of the operation], copy of selections from the original in Hunt File, Vertical File, Gettysburg National Military Park Library, Gettysburg, Pa. [repository hereafter cited as GNMPL].

13. Henry J. Hunt to his wife, July 28, 1863, Stanley H. Ford Papers, U.S. Army Military History Institute, Carlisle Barracks, Pa. [repository hereafter cited as USAMHI].

14. *CCW,* 447–48.

15. Ibid., 448.

16. Shultz & Rollins, "Combined and Concentrated Fire," 16.

17. *CCW,* 449; *OR,* vol. 27, pt. 1:234. Hunt's official report stated that it was about 2:00 P.M. when "General Sickles formed his corps in line."

18. For Hancock's description of his role in bringing reinforcements to crucial areas on July 2, see OR, vol. 27, pt. 1:369–72.

19. CCW, 464; OR, vol. 27, pt. 1:237.

20. Longacre, Man behind the Guns, 170.

21. OR, vol. 27, pt. 1:237–38. Hunt indicated that he placed Edward D. Muhlenberg's and David H. Kinzie's batteries at 1:00 A.M. and that they opened fire at 4:30 A.M.

22. Henry J. Hunt, Three Days at Gettysburg: July 1st, 2nd, and 3rd, 1863, by Henry J. Hunt, Chief of Artillery, Army of the Potomac, ed. Kathleen R. Georg (Golden, Colo.: Outbooks, 1981), 48–49. Hunt's account first appeared as a three-part series in Century Magazine (1886–1887) and later as three articles in B&L, 3:255–84, 290–313, 369–85.

23. "Account of Brig. Gen. Henry Hunt, Chief of Artillery, Army of the Potomac, with his Additions in Margins," January 20, 1873, Bachelder Papers, 1:429.

24. Hunt, Three Days at Gettysburg, 48 n. 35. In her note, Kathleen R. Georg observes that "Hazard's Brigade brought the total of Union guns from the Ziegler's Grove southward to the George Weikert lane to 77."

25. Capt. Andrew Cowan to John B. Bachelder, August 26, 1866, in Bachelder Papers, 1:282. Cowan described Union infantry "a half dozen yards in front of my guns, lying down."

26. Association of Licensed Guides, seminar titled "The Third Day at Gettysburg: Desperate Valor," October 15–17, 1993, comments by Hans Henzel, Licensed Battlefield Guide.

27. Hunt, Three Days at Gettysburg, 48 n. 35. Georg's note states that "[Hunt] does not mention the other 45 cannon which participated in the cannonade from other points along the line." There were nineteen cannons on Cemetery Hill off the right flank of the Second Corps.

28. Hunt, Three Days at Gettysburg, 49.

29. Henry J. Hunt to William T. Sherman, February [?], 1882, in Bachelder Papers, 2:821 [quoting paragraph 727 of Army Regulations, 1861–63]; OR, vol. 27, pt. 1:238.

30. Hunt, "Journal of Siege Operations," 25 [entry for May 20, 1864; handwritten note down the right margin], Hunt File, Vertical File, GNMPL.

31. Ibid., 26–27. "At Gettysburg again the 3rd Corps left all the Amm wagons behind," wrote Hunt. "The 2nd Corps half of its trains, and the others were deficient."

32. Elwood Christ, The Struggle for the Bliss Farm at Gettysburg, July 2nd and 3rd 1863: "Over a Wide, Hot . . . Crimson Plain" (Baltimore: Butternut and Blue, 1993), 57.

33. Warner, Generals in Blue, 171–72.

34. Hunt, Three Days at Gettysburg, 49–51. The estimate of the depth of the Union target is based on the author's personal observation.

35. "Account of Brig. Gen. Henry Hunt, Chief of Artillery, Army of the Potomac, with his Additions in Margins," January 20, 1873, Bachelder Papers, 1:432–33.

36. OR, vol. 27, pt. 1:239; Henry J. Hunt, "The Third Day at Gettysburg," in B&L 3:374.

37. Dallas County, Alabama, newspaper account, 1863, Reese's Battery File, Vertical File, GNMPL [neither the specific date nor the name of the newspaper is identified]. "Think of it men and women of Dallas," wrote the author of this account, "four guns silenced 19."

38. The following two paragraphs are based on John Gibbon, The Artillerist's Manual 1860, Compiled from Various Sources and Adapted to the Service of the United States (New York: n.p., 1860), 267, 255, 268.

39. Herb S. Crumb, ed., The Eleventh Corps Artillery at Gettysburg: The Papers of Major Thomas Osborn, Chief of Artillery (Hamilton, N.Y.: Edmonston Publishing, 1991), 40.

40. Ibid., 40–42.

41. Ibid., 42.

42. Ibid., 42–43.

43. Hunt, Three Days at Gettysburg, 52–53.

44. Henry J. Hunt to John B. Bachelder, January 6, 1866, *Bachelder Papers*, 1:230.

45. Longacre, *Man behind the Guns*, 177.

46. Ibid., 176; Captain Andrew Cowan to John B. Bachelder, August 26, 1866, *Bachelder Papers*, 1: 282.

47. Perry D. Jamieson, *Crossing the Deadly Ground: United States Army Tactics, 1865–1899* (Tuscaloosa: Univ. of Alabama Press, 1994), 2.

48. Shultz and Rollins, "Combined and Concentrated Fire," 9; "Account of Brig. Gen. Henry Hunt, Chief of Artillery, Army of the Potomac, with his Additions in Margins," January 20, 1873, *Bachelder Papers*, 1:433. (All references to McGilvery's testimony are based on conversations between Hunt and McGilvery and are Hunt's retelling of events. For corroboration, see the excerpt from a letter Capt. John Bigelow of the 9th Massachusetts Battery wrote to Hunt on November 4, 1875, quoted in Hunt to William T. Sherman, February [?], 1882, *Bachelder Papers*, 2:826.) Most artillery manuals indicate that each gun could fire a hundred hurried or thirty carefully aimed shots per hour. The Confederate advance lasted approximately eighteen minutes.

49. Victor A Coulter, "Smoke at Gettysburg," 2–3, manuscript article [written for the *Infantry Journal* (March–April 1937)], USAMHI.

50. Ibid., 4. Coulter reached his conclusions based on a hot and humid day with "hardly a breath of air stirring anywhere."

51. Shultz and Rollins, "Combined and Concentrated Fire," 1.

52. Coulter, "Smoke at Gettysburg," 1.

53. Henry J. Hunt to his wife, July 28, 1863, Stanley H. Ford Papers, USAMHI.

54. Hunt died at the Soldier's Home in Washington, D.C., on February 11, 1889 (Warner, *Generals in Blue*, 242–43).

Bibliographic Essay

READERS CAN LOCATE THE SOURCES ON WHICH THE AUTHORS BASED their essays by perusing the notes. For those interested in exploring other facets of the operations in Pennsylvania during June and July 1863, the best bibliography is Richard A. Sauers, Jr., comp., *The Gettysburg Campaign, June 3–August 1, 1863: A Comprehensive, Selectively Annotated Bibliography* (Westport, Conn.: Greenwood, 1982). Sauers listed more than 2,500 items, but more than fifteen years of additional scholarship has contributed a wealth of new works to the literature. Although the following books represent only a fraction of that mountain of material, they provide a range of narrative approaches, firsthand testimony, and interpretive insights.

The basic published collection of primary evidence is U.S. War Department, *The War of the Rebellion: A Compilation of the Official Records of the Union and Confederate Armies* (128 vols., index, and atlas, Washington, D.C.: GPO, 1880–1901). Series 1, vol. 27, pts. 1–3 of the *Official Records* (more popularly known as the OR) include nearly 3,500 pages of official reports, correspondence, orders, and other items pertinent to Gettysburg. Part 1, vol. 5, of Janet B. Hewett and others, eds., *Supplement to the Official Records of the Union and Confederate Armies* (98 vols. to date, Wilmington, N.C.: Broadfoot, 1994–), offer an additional five hundred pages of material about both armies, including a number of Confederate reports that shed light on Pickett's Charge. *Report of the Joint Committee on the Conduct of the War, at the Second Session Thirty-eighth Congress. Army of the Potomac. Battle of Petersburg* (Washington, D.C.: GPO, 1865) contains extensive comments about the campaign by various important Union officers and illuminates the politically charged atmosphere that often surrounded the Army of the Potomac's high command.

For important postwar accounts, see David L. Ladd and Audrey J. Ladd, eds., *The Bachelder Papers: Gettysburg in Their Own Words* (3 vols., Dayton, Ohio: Morningside, 1994–1995), which contains extensive correspondence between Bachelder and numerous veterans of the battle; vol. 3 of *Papers of the Military Historical Society of Massachusetts* (1895–1918; reprinted in 15 vols. with a general index, Wilmington, N.C.: Broadfoot, 1989–1990); *Papers of the Military Order of the Loyal Legion of the*

United States (66 vols. and 3-vol. index, Wilmington, N.C.: Broadfoot, 1991–1998); Ken Bandy and Florence Freeland, eds., *The Gettysburg Papers* (2 vols., Dayton, Ohio: Morningside, 1978), which reprints important items from the two preceding titles; and James L. McLean, Jr., and Judy W. McLean, eds., *Gettysburg Sources* (3 vols., Baltimore, Md.: Butternut and Blue, 1986–1990). Four essential collections with a Confederate focus are J. William Jones and others, eds., *Southern Historical Society Papers* (1877–1959; reprint, 52 vols. and 3-vol. index, Wilmington, N.C.: Broadfoot, 1990–1992); Walter Clark, ed., *Histories of the Several Regiments and Battalions from North Carolina in the Great War 1861–'65* (1901; reprint, 5 vols., Wilmington, N.C.: Broadfoot, 1991–1992); *The Southern Bivouac* (1882–1887; reprint, 5 vols. and one-vol. index, Wilmington, N.C.: Broadfoot, 1992–1993); and *Confederate Veteran* (1893–1932; reprint, 40 vols. and 3-vol. index, Wilmington, N.C.: Broadfoot, 1990).

Among monographs on the battle, the most comprehensive remains Edwin B. Coddington's deeply researched *The Gettysburg Campaign: A Study in Command* (New York: Scribner's, 1968). Also useful are David L. Ladd and Audrey J. Ladd, eds., *John Bachelder's History of the Battle of Gettysburg* (Dayton, Ohio: Morningside, 1997), which the editors constructed from the papers of the greatest nineteenth-century student of the battle; Clifford Dowdey's *Death of a Nation: The Story of Lee and His Men at Gettysburg* (New York: Knopf, 1958), which follows an interpretive trail blazed by Lost Cause writers; and Glenn Tucker's *High Tide at Gettysburg: The Campaign in Pennsylvania* (Indianapolis: Bobbs-Merrill, 1958), which sometimes sacrifices accuracy for the sake of literary drama. *Gettysburg: Historical Articles of Lasting Interest* (Dayton, Ohio, 1989–), a biannual scholarly magazine, publishes material on the battle and its aftermath. For visitors to the battlefield, Jay Luvaas and Harold W. Nelson, eds., *The U.S. Army War College Guide to the Battle of Gettysburg* (Carlisle, Pa.: South Mountain Press, 1986), is invaluable.

Michael Shaara's novel *The Killer Angels* (New York: McKay, 1974), among the most popular books ever written on the battle, explores the roles of R. E. Lee, James Longstreet, Joshua L. Chamberlain, John Buford, and other participants in fascinating and sometimes controversial portraits. Champ Clark and the Editors of Time-Life Books, *Gettysburg: The Confederate High Tide* (Alexandria, Va.: Time-Life, 1985), is an excellent pictorial treatment, and Editors of Time-Life Books, *Voices of the Civil War: Gettysburg* (Alexandria, Va.: Time-Life, 1995), effectively combines illustrations and testimony from participants in the battle. *Gettysburg: A Journey in Time* (New York: Scribner's, 1975), by William A. Frassanito, permits students to compare modern photographs of the field with those taken in the nineteenth century; Jack McLaughlin's *Gettysburg: The Long Encampment* (New York: Appleton-Century, 1963) allocates several dozen pages and numerous photographs to the history of the battlefield after 1863.

Several monographs deal with specific days of the battle. Warren W. Hassler's *Crisis at the Crossroads: The First Day at Gettysburg* (Tuscaloosa: Univ. of Alabama Press, 1970) offers a brief narrative based largely on printed sources. David G. Martin's much longer *Gettysburg: July 1* (revised ed., Conshohocken, Pa.: Combined Books, 1996) delves a bit more deeply into manuscript materials. Lance J. Herdegen and

William J. K. Beaudot's massively detailed *In the Bloody Railroad Cut at Gettysburg* (Dayton, Ohio: Morningside, 1990) and James L. McLean, Jr.'s *Cutler's Brigade at Gettysburg* (Baltimore: Butternut and Blue, 1987) explore the fighting west of Gettysburg on July 1. Harry W. Pfanz's *Gettysburg: The Second Day* (Chapel Hill: Univ. of North Carolina Press, 1987) is an exceptionally thorough and judicious treatment of the fighting along the southern end of the battlefield on July 2. Other notable works on the second day's action include Oliver W. Norton's *The Attack and Defense of Little Round Top: Gettysburg, July 2, 1863* (1913; reprint, Dayton, Ohio: Morningside, 1983) and Richard A. Sauers's *A Caspian Sea of Ink: The Meade-Sickles Controversy* (Baltimore: Butternut and Blue, 1989). Harry W. Pfanz's *Gettysburg: Cemetery Hill and Culp's Hill* (Chapel Hill: Univ. of North Carolina Press, 1993) covers action on the northern end of the field during all three days and serves as a worthy companion to his earlier discussion of the second day's fighting.

There are no monographs devoted to the third day as a whole, but several address specific elements of the fighting. George R. Stewart's *Pickett's Charge: A Microhistory of the Final Attack at Gettysburg, July 3, 1863* (Cambridge, Mass.: Houghton Mifflin, 1959) remains the best narrative treatment of Longstreet's final assault, while *Nothing But Glory: Pickett's Division at Gettysburg*, by Kathleen R. Georg and John W. Busey (Hightstown, N.J.: Longstreet House, 1987), provides great detail on the most famous command in the attack. John Michael Priest's *Into the Fight: Pickett's Charge at Gettysburg* (Shippensburg, Pa.: White Mane, 1998) is a starkly revisionist treatment of the great Confederate assault. Carol Reardon's *Pickett's Charge in History and Memory* (Chapel Hill: Univ. of North Carolina Press, 1997) explores what happened on the afternoon of July 3 and, more especially, how veterans of the assault sought to shape public memory of the event. As its title suggests, Richard Rollins, ed., *Pickett's Charge! Eyewitness Accounts* (revised ed., Redondo Beach, Calif.: Rank and File, 1996), collects an array of testimony about the famous attack.

A handful of personal accounts, diaries, and printed letters stand out in the voluminous literature by participants. The most famous collection of such narratives relating to Gettysburg is in the third volume of Robert Underwood Johnson and Clarence Clough Buel, eds., *Battles and Leaders of the Civil War* (4 vols., New York: Century, 1887). Written in the 1880s and often intended to settle old scores, these articles include important contributions from George G. Meade, James Longstreet, Daniel E. Sickles, Henry J. Hunt, Edward Porter Alexander, John Gibbon, Evander M. Law, and John D. Imboden. For additional testimony from Longstreet, Walter H. Taylor of Lee's staff, James C. Biddle of Meade's staff, and others, see [Alexander K. McClure, ed.], *The Annals of the War Written by Leading Participants North and South. Originally Published in the Philadelphia Weekly Times* (1879; reprint, Dayton, Ohio: Morningside, 1988).

Among Confederate primary accounts, Lee's crucial letters from June and July 1863 are conveniently gathered in *The Wartime Papers of R. E. Lee* (Boston: Little, Brown, 1961), ed. Clifford Dowdey and Louis H. Manarin. James Longstreet defends his conduct at Gettysburg in *From Manassas to Appomattox: Memoirs of the Civil War in America* (Philadelphia: Lippincott, 1896); Jubal A. Early's *Lieutenant General*

Jubal Anderson Early, C.S.A.: Autobiographical Sketch and Narrative of the War between the States (1912; reprint, Wilmington, N.C.: Broadfoot, 1989) displays a moderate tenor at odds with its author's reputation as a fierce Confederate partisan; William C. Oates's The War between the Union and the Confederacy (1905; reprint, Dayton, Ohio: Morningside, 1974) presents a Southern perspective on the fighting at Little Round Top on July 2; and Edward Porter Alexander's Fighting for the Confederacy: The Personal Recollections of General Edward Porter Alexander, ed. Gary W. Gallagher (Chapel Hill: Univ. of North Carolina Press, 1989) and Military Memoirs of a Confederate: A Critical Narrative (New York: Scribner's, 1907) offer more sophisticated analysis than the writings of any other soldier in either army. In contrast to Alexander's books, John B. Gordon's highly readable Reminiscences of the Civil War (New York: Scribner's, 1904) should be used with caution.

Necessary Union titles include Life and Letters of George Gordon Meade (2 vols., New York: Scribner's, 1913), a superior source on the Federal commander put together largely by his son George Meade, and Alpheus S. Williams's richly rewarding From the Cannon's Mouth: The Civil War Letters of General Alpheus S. Williams, ed. Milo M. Quaife (Detroit: Wayne State Univ. Press, 1959). Three other Union commanders wrote substantial accounts. Abner Doubleday's Chancellorsville and Gettysburg (1882; reprint, Wilmington, N.C.: Broadfoot, 1989) betrays the bitterness of a man who believed his services at Gettysburg on July 1 went largely unappreciated; both special pleading and essential information mark O. O. Howard's Autobiography of Oliver Otis Howard (2 vols., New York: Baker and Taylor, 1907) and Carl Schurz's ponderous Reminiscences of Carl Schurz (3 vols., New York: McClure, 1907–1908). For perspectives from lower in the Union chain of command, see Frank Haskell's classic description of Pickett's Charge titled The Battle of Gettysburg (Madison, Wisc.: Wisconsin History Commission, 1908); Rufus Dawes's Service with the Sixth Wisconsin Volunteers (Marietta, Ohio: E. R. Alderman, 1890); and Stephen Minot Weld's War Diary and Letters of Stephen Minot Weld, 1861–1865 (1912; reprint, Boston: Massachusetts Historical Society, 1979).

A pair of superb accounts by foreign observers are FitzGerald Ross, Cities and Camps of the Confederate States, ed. Richard Barksdale Harwell (1865; reprint, Urbana: Univ. of Illinois Press, 1958), and A. J. L. Fremantle, Three Months in the Southern States: April–June, 1863 (1863; reprint, Lincoln: Univ. of Nebraska Press, 1991). Officers in the Austrian and British armies respectively, Ross and Fremantle accompanied Longstreet's headquarters as observers; their keen, descriptive, and analytical passages possess enduring value for students of Gettysburg.

Among essential Confederate biographical studies are Douglas Southall Freeman's R. E. Lee: A Biography (4 vols., New York: Scribner's, 1934–1935), which renders harsh judgments about Longstreet on July 3, 1863, and Lee's Lieutenants: A Study in Command (3 vols., New York: Scribner's, 1942–1944), a more evenhanded treatment of Lee and his principal subordinates. Alan T. Nolan's Lee Considered: General Robert E. Lee and Civil War History (Chapel Hill: Univ. of North Carolina Press, 1991) criticizes Lee's decision to press the tactical offensive at Gettysburg. On Lee's senior corps commander, William Garrett Piston's Lee's Tarnished Lieutenant: James

Longstreet and His Place in Southern History (Athens: Univ. of Georgia Press, 1987), which focuses on the postwar years, and Jeffry D. Wert's General James Longstreet (New York: Simon and Schuster, 1993), with its wartime emphasis, provide careful and largely favorable assessments of their subject. Donald C. Pfanz's exhaustive Richard S. Ewell: A Soldier's Life (Chapel Hill: Univ. of North Carolina Press, 1998) and James I. Robertson, Jr.'s General A. P. Hill: The Story of a Southern Warrior (New York: Random House, 1987) are easily the best treatments of the chiefs of the Confederate Second and Third corps respectively. Reader's interested in division commander George E. Pickett should be warned that all of LaSalle Corbell Pickett's writings—especially The Heart of a Soldier as Revealed in the Intimate Letters of Genl. George E. Pickett, C.S.A. (New York: Seth Moyle, 1913), which purports to print part of the general's wartime correspondence—should be used with great care. The most revealing biography is Lesley J. Gordon, General George E. Pickett in Life and Legend (Chapel Hill: Univ. of North Carolina Press, 1998).

Freeman Cleaves's generally appreciative Meade of Gettysburg (Norman: Univ. of Oklahoma Press, 1960) is the best examination of the Federal chief. Good studies of Meade's subordinates include David M. Jordan's Winfield Scott Hancock: A Soldier's Life (Bloomington: Indiana Univ. Press, 1988); W. A. Swanberg's engagingly written Sickles the Incredible (New York: Scribner's, 1956); Charles Elihu Slocum's laudatory The Life and Services of Major-General Henry Warner Slocum (Toledo, Ohio: Slocum, 1913); Edward J. Nichols's straightforward Toward Gettysburg: A Biography of General John F. Reynolds (University Park: Penn State Univ. Press, 1958); and John A. Carpenter's Sword and Olive Branch: Oliver Otis Howard (Pittsburgh: Univ. of Pittsburgh Press, 1964). Edward G. Longacre's The Man behind the Guns: A Biography of General Henry J. Hunt, Commander of Artillery, Army of the Potomac (South Brunswick, N.J.: A. S. Barnes, 1977) is the only full-scale life of the able Union artillerist.

Any listing of books on Gettysburg must mention three landmark multivolume works. Shelby Foote's The Civil War: A Narrative (3 vols., New York: Random House, 1958–1974), the second volume of which covers Gettysburg, sets a standard for sheer literary power that no other author has matched. A close second to Foote in terms of narrative skill is Bruce Catton's Glory Road (Garden City, N.Y.: Doubleday, 1952), part of Catton's Army of the Potomac trilogy; less engagingly written but valuable for its analytical contribution is Kenneth P. Williams's Lincoln Finds a General (5 vols., New York: Macmillan, 1949–1959), volume 2 of which deals with Gettysburg.

Contributors

PETER S. CARMICHAEL is a member of the Department of History at Western Carolina University. The author of *Lee's Young Artillerist: William R. J. Pegram*, as well as several essays and articles in popular and scholarly journals, he is completing a study of Virginia slaveholders' sons and the formation of southern identity in the late antebellum years.

GARY W. GALLAGHER is a member of the Department of History at the University of Virginia. He is the author of *Stephen Dodson Ramseur: Lee's Gallant General, Lee and His Generals in War and Memory*, and *The Confederate War*, and editor of *Antietam: Essays on the 1862 Maryland Campaign* and *Struggle for the Shenandoah: Essays on the 1864 Valley Campaign*.

A. WILSON GREENE, who holds degrees in history from Florida State University and Louisiana State University, is executive director of Pamplin Park Civil War Site and former president of the Association for the Preservation of Civil War Sites. He is the author of *Whatever You Resolve to Be: Essays on Stonewall Jackson* and coauthor of *The National Geographic Guide to the National Civil War Battlefields*.

D. SCOTT HARTWIG, who studied under E. B. Long at the University of Wyoming, has published several articles and essays on Civil War military history as well as *The Battle of Antietam and the Maryland Campaign of 1862: A Bibliography*. He currently is completing a full-scale study of the 1862 Maryland campaign.

ROBERT K. KRICK grew up in California but has lived and worked on the Virginia battlefields for more than twenty-five years. He has written dozens of articles and ten books, the most recent being *Stonewall Jackson at Cedar Mountain* and *Conquering the Valley: Stonewall Jackson at Port Republic*.

GARY M. KROSS attended Marquette University and has been a Licensed Battlefield Guide at Gettysburg for a dozen years. His publications include numerous articles on Gettysburg for *Blue & Gray Magazine*.

ALAN T. NOLAN, an Indianapolis lawyer, is a graduate of Indiana University and the Harvard Law School. He is chairman of the Board of Trustees of the Indiana Historical Society and a member of the Indianapolis Civil War Round Table. His books include *The Iron Brigade: A Military History* and *Lee Considered: General Robert E. Lee and Civil War History*.

CAROL REARDON is a member of the Department of History at Pennsylvania State University and a former holder of the Harold Keith Johnson Visiting Professorship in Military History at the U.S. Army Military History Institute and U.S. Army War College. She is the author of *Soldiers and Scholars: The U.S. Army and the Uses of Military History, 1865–1920*, *Pickett's Charge in History and Memory*, and numerous essays in the fields of Civil War and military history.

WILLIAM GLENN ROBERTSON is a member of the faculty at the Combat Studies Institute of the U.S. Army Command and General Staff College. He has published *Back Door to Richmond: The Bermuda Hundred Campaign* and *The Petersburg Campaign: The Battle of Old Men and Young Boys*.

RICHARD A. SAUERS, who did his graduate work at Pennsylvania State University, is curator of Soldiers and Sailors Memorial Hall in Pittsburgh, Pennsylvania. His publications include *The Gettysburg Campaign, June 3–August 1, 1863: A Comprehensive, Selectively Annotated Bibliography*, *Advance the Colors! Pennsylvania Civil War Battleflags*, and *A Succession of Honorable Victories: The Burnside Expedition in North Carolina*.

Index

Page numbers for illustrations are in italics.

Blackford, Minor, 247
Blackford, W. W., 148
Blocher's Knoll, 60, 63, 70
Breastworks: on Cemetery Hill, 65, 69;
    on Culp's Hill, 184–86, 195–98
Brewster, William R., 210
Bright, Robert A., 262–63, 265
British observers, 37, 110
Brockenbrough, John M., 77, 88
Brooke, John R., 207–8, 212, 220–23,
    221, 226
Brooks, John Stanley, 100
Brown, Edmund R., 175
Brown, George Campbell, 39–41, 124
Bruce, George A., 9
Buchanan, James, 133
Buford, John, 34, 56, 62, 65, 169
Burnside, Ambrose E., 72, 75, 131, 135,
    165, 287
Buschbeck, Adolphus, 49
Butler, Benjamin F., 131, 133
Butterfield, Daniel, 135–36, 143, 232–33,
    240
Bynum, G. W., 85
Bynum, William P., 100

Caldwell, John C., 204–28, 207
Campaigns of the Army of the Potomac
    (Swinton), 111
Candy, Charles, 172, 178, 180, 192–93, 202
Carlisle Road, 56, 61–62, 70
Carter, Thomas Hill, 91–92
Cashtown, Pa., 33–34, 88
Cemetery Hill, 294; bombardment of,
    186–87, 297–98; and Ewell, 21–24,
    25–26, 28–29, 32, 39–43, 122–23; and
    Howard, 54, 57, 63–64, 66–68; retreat to,
    39–41, 65, 70; strength of, 39, 41, 68–69
Cemetery Ridge, 54, 138, 139, 145–46, 302,
    304; artillery on, 291–92; bombardment
    of, 237–41, 273–74, 277, 294
Chamberlain, Joshua L., 169
Chamberlayne, John H., 271
Chambersburg, Pa., 33, 39
Chambersburg Pike, 73–74, 77, 81, 89
Chambliss, John R., Jr., 14
Chancellorsville, Va., 287; Army of the
    Potomac at, 44–46, 135, 170; artillery at,
    270, 273; casualties at, 8, 231; effects of,
    44, 101; Heth at, 76–77; Jackson at,
    162–63; Lee at, 7, 270; Lee's options
    after, 3–5

Christie, Daniel Harvey, 104
Clausewitz, Carl von, 4
Cobham, George A., 173, 179–81, 185,
    201–2
Cocke, William, 246
Coddington, Edwin B., 28, 30, 45, 57, 178,
    199, 243, 281; on Lee, 18–20, 120
Colgrove, Silas, 184, 190, 200, 202
Confederacy: grand strategies of, 4–6,
    8–12; manpower disadvantage of, 7–10,
    12, 128
Confederate units, 79–80; First Corps,
    122–23, 167, 245–46, 252, 274, 282;
    Jeff Davis Artillery, 297–98; Second
    Corps, 26, 37, 38, 89, 121–25, 274, 283;
    Third Corps, 26, 246, 252, 282
Connally, John Kerr, 82, 88
Connecticut units: 5th Infantry, 181, 200;
    20th Infantry, 181, 185, 200
Connelly, Thomas L., 254
Conrad, Bryan, 120
Cooper, Samuel, 100, 129
Cope, Emmor B., 81
Coster, Charles Robert, 49, 59, 62–63
Couch, Darius N., 236
Coulter, Victor A., 303
Cowan, Andrew, 301–2
Coy, L. R., 190–91
Crane, Nirom M., 181
Crisis at the Crossroads (Hassler), 28
Crocker, James, 262
Crook, George, 76
Cross, Daniel F., 212
Cross, Edward E., 207–8, 212–17, 215, 220,
    222, 226
Crutchfield, Stapleton, 272
Culp, E. C., 60, 64
Culp's Hill, 54, 139, 179–82, 200;
    earthworks on, 65, 184–86, 195–98;
    and Ewell, 21–26, 28–29, 41; and
    Johnson, 186–87, 194–99; and
    Twelfth Corps, 188–203
Curtin, Andrew G., 126–27
Cushing, Alonzo H., 293, 301

Da Ponte, Lorenzo, 131–33
Daniel, Junius, 90, 92–93, 95–97, 105
Davis, Jefferson, 76, 78, 88–89, 272;
    correspondence with Lee, 6–8, 13, 29, 32,
    37, 94–95, 115–16
Davis, Joseph R., 35, 73, 77–82, 78, 87–88,
    106

Dawes, Rufus R., 84–85, 88
De Trobriand, Regis, 210–11
Dearing, James, 246
Defensive vs. offensive: by Lee, 3–9, 11–12, 109–15, 117–29; and Longstreet, 155–56, 164, 166
Delaware units: 1st Infantry, 181; 2d Infantry, 221
Devil's Den, 210, 224
Dilger, Hubert, 55, 59, 62
Doles, George, 60–62, 90–92, 95, 98, 105
Doubleday, Abner, 56–57, 59, 62–65, 69–70, 143, 177, 256–57
Douglas, Henry Kyd, 29, 31
Dowdey, Clifford, 30, 119, 166

Early, Jubal A., 19, 70, 92, 105, 123, 123–24, 126, 260; desire to attack, 29, 122; and Ewell, 38–42; and Longstreet, 124, 252; and Lost Cause tradition, 25, 31, 112–13, 250
Eckenrode, H. J., 120
Edwards, LeRoy Summerfield, 109
Egan, John, 293
Egan, Jonathan, 241
Emmitsburg, Md., 51–52, 138, 139
Emmitsburg Road, 138, 140–42, 210–11, 225
Emmitsburg-Gettysburg Road, 53
Emmittsburg Pike, 157, 159
Eustis, Henry L., 239
Ewell, Richard Stoddert, 13, 39, 57, 89, 90, 118, 161; arrival in Gettysburg, 18–19, 121; and artillery, 274–75, 283; and Cemetery Hill, 65, 114, 122–23, 178; criticism of, 20–26, 28–30, 38–43, 119; and Culp's Hill, 186, 194, 199; and Lee, 14–16, 122–24, 159; personality of, 106, 164

Fairview, 273
Favill, Josiah M., 208–9, 212, 218
Felser, John R., 184
Field, Charles, 261
First Bull Run, 284–85
First Manassas, 271
First Virginia Infantry Association, 258–59
Food/forage, 33–34; and Heth, 28; as Lee's motivation for offensive, 4, 20, 125–26; and Lee's orders to Stuart, 14–15
Forney farm, 91–92, 101–5
Fort Sanders, 164–66
Foster, John G., 164–65

Fredericksburg, Va., 72, 134–35, 272, 287
Freeman, Douglas Southall, 28; on Ewell, 23, 30, 43; on Longstreet, 118, 153, 268
Fremantle, A. J. L., 37, 110, 128; on Lee, 115, 122
French, William H., 235–36
Freudenburg, C. G., 219
From Manassass to Appomattox (Longstreet), 263
Fry, Burkett D., 255
Fry, Charles W., 91–92
Fuller, Charles A., 211, 215
Fuller, J. F. C., 12, 119

Garfield, James A., 149
Geary, John (Lt.), 187
Geary, John White, 139–40, 145, 172, 173; and Culp's Hill, 179–80, 182, 200; and Greene, 184–85; march to Gettysburg, 22, 174, 177–78; and Williams, 182, 188–90, 199, 201–2
Georgia units: Dole's brigade, 60–61, 92; 15th Infantry, 221; 50th Infantry, 222
German-Americans, 173–74; in Eleventh Corps, 45–47, 49
Gerrish, Theodore, 256–57
Gibbon, John, 208, 232–37, 293–94
Gilbreath, F. W., 52
Gordon, John B., 23, 94, 261; attack by, 60–62, 68, 70; and Ewell, 29, 40–41; memoirs criticized, 31, 41
Goree, Thomas J., 116, 283
Granite Schoolhouse Lane, 191
Grant, Ulysses S., 149, 305
Greene, George Sears, 173, 178, 180, 184–85, 189–90, 202–3
Guin, George, 54
Guindon, Eugene W., 175

Hale, Charles, 209–10, 213–14
Hall, Daniel, 53–54
Hall, J., 83
Halleck, Henry W., 66, 127, 142–43
Halsey, Don P., 104
Halstead, Eminel P., 66–67
Hampton, Wade, 14, 110
Hancock, Winfield Scott, 32, 139, 169, 209, 211, 216, 256, 296, 297, 299–300; and artillery, 287–88, 290, 293–96, 300–301; command of, 177–78, 232; and First Division, 205–6, 207, 226–27; and Howard, 66–68, 71; and Hunt, 305;

Latrobe, Osmun, 261
Law, Evander M., 80, 118, 156–57, 163, 165–66
Lee, Alfred E., 51, 56
Lee, Cassius, 30
Lee, Fitzhugh, 14, 25, 153–55, 163, 260, 261, 279
Lee, G. W. C., 79
Lee, Robert E., 5, 32, 186, 236–37, 270; and artillery, 275–78, 281–83, 297–98; criticism of, 16–18, 25, 109–15, 268; defense of, 31, 249, 251–56, 267; and Ewell, 23–24, 29, 38–42, 194; grand strategy of, 6–10; and Heth, 34–35, 75–76; and initiation of battle, 34–36; and Longstreet, 121–26, 150–51, 155, 159–60, 164, 167, 263, 268; motivation for offensive, 3–5, 10–12, 125–26; and O'Neal, 94–95; and Pendleton, 271–72, 275; praise for, 109–10, 260–61, 265; response to Gettysburg, 113–16, 128–29; on South's manpower disadvantage, 7–8; and Stuart, 14–17; and subordinates, 20–24, 32, 52, 106, 123; weaknesses of, 12–17, 20, 73
Lee, W. H. F., 14
Lee's Lieutenants (Freeman), 23, 30
Leister house, 189, 232, 237–40, 243
Lewisburg, Va., 76
Life and Campaigns of General Robert E. Lee (McCabe), 111–12
Lincoln, Abraham, 49, 136
Little Round Top, 118, 139–40; Federals on, 158, 208, 210, 239, 242, 294; and Sickles, 142, 145–46
Littlestown, Pa., 174, 182
Lockwood, Henry Hayes, 181–82, 184, 190–92, 200–202
Long, Armistead L., 19, 122, 250, 252, 273
Longstreet, Helen Dortch, 266
Longstreet, James, 13, 128, 149, 186–88, 253; and artillery, 275, 281–83; attack by, 114, 209–10; criticism of, 25, 118, 156–57, 245, 251–53; criticism of Lee by, 25, 111, 114–15; and Lee, 14, 121–26; at Peach Orchard, 142, 145–46; personality of, 147–50, 152, 155–56, 165; and Pickett, 261–62, 265–67; and Pickett's Charge, 245–47, 277, 280; and Pickett's men, 245–49, 253–54, 258–65, 269; poor leadership by, 164–66, 278–79; in postwar controversy, 113, 116–17,

167–68, 249, 251–56, 259–60, 267–69; strategy of, 117–19
Lost Cause tradition, 31, 124, 250, 263; blame of Lee subordinates in, 21, 116–17, 249; blame of Longstreet in, 245–46, 252–56; defense of Lee in, 112–13, 251–52, 258–59, 263; and Pickett's men, 253–59, 261–62
Louisiana units, 186, 196

McAllister's Hill, 201
McAllister's Woods, 181–82, 185, 200
McCabe, James D., Jr., 111
McCandless, William, 242
McClellan, George, 8, 285–88
McDougall, Archibald L., 172, 180–81, 190, 200, 202
McGilvery, Freeman, 191, 291–92, 294–95, 300, 302
Magruder, William Thomas, 79
McGuire, Hunter Holmes, 168
Mahone, William, 164
McIntosh, David Gregg, 125–26
McKay, Charles W., 63
McKeen, Boyd, 220
McKim, Randolph H., 110
McLaws, Lafayette, 118, 122, 154, 155, 160–62, 165–66, 252–53, 255–56; and Longstreet, 152–53, 158–60
McLean, Nathaniel C., 47
Maine units: 2d Battery, 83
Mansfield, J. K. F., 171
Marksmanship, 75–76
Marshall, Charles, 4, 11–13
Marshall, James K., 265
Martin, Rawley, 257
Maryland units: 1st Eastern Shore Regiment, 181–82; 1st Potomac Home Guard, 181–82, 191–92; 3d Infantry, 181, 200
Mason, Addison G., 178
Massachusetts units: Bigelow's Battery, 192; 2d Infantry, 181, 200; 12th Infantry, 97; 28th Infantry, 219; 33d Infantry, 51, 64
Maulsby, William Pinckney, 182, 191–92
Maurice, Frederick, 15
Mayo, Joseph C., 265
Meade, George (Capt.), 139, 240–42
Meade, George (Gen.), 51–52, 124–27, 135–36, 144, 233; and artillery, 281, 293; decision making by, 182–84, 201; and Hancock, 66–68, 178–79, 293; and

Meade, George (Gen.) (*cont.*)
Howard, 52, 59, 66–68, 71; and Hunt,
288–90, 304–5; and Pipe Creek Circular,
175–76; pressure on, 117–18, 120, 127;
and Sickles, 136–38, 140–46, 209, 211;
and Slocum, 177–79, 188–90; surveying
line, 139–40, 231–44; and Twelfth Corps,
201–2
Mechanicsville, Va., 33
Meysenburg, T. A., 54
Middleburg, Pa., 34
Milroy, Robert H., 89
Mississippi units, 225; 2d Infantry, 79–82,
83–86; 11th Infantry, 79–80, 106; 42d
Infantry, 79–82, 84–86
Morgan, Charles H., 178–79, 226–27
Morgan, John T., 94
Mosby, John S., 27, 51, 263
Moses, Raphael J., 122, 125, 262
Mudge, Charles R., 200
Mulholland, St. Clair, 209, 211, 218, 222
Mummasburg Road, 57, 60, 95, 97, 102

Neill, Thomas H., 199
Nepotism, 78
New Hampshire units: 5th Infantry, 215,
220–23
New Jersey units: 13th Infantry, 181, 200
New York Herald, 143
New York Times, 46
New York units: 1st Artillery Battery, 208;
1st Light Artillery Battery, 211; Excelsior
Brigade, 134; 27th Infantry, 171; 28th
Infantry, 172; 60th Infantry, 180, 187,
195, 198; 61st Infantry, 220; 64th Infantry,
221; 76th Infantry, 81–82, 89; 78th
Infantry, 180, 187, 195; 84th Infantry,
83, 85; 95th Infantry, 83, 85; 102d
Infantry, 180, 195; 107th Infantry, 181,
200; 123d Infantry, 181, 185, 200;
137th Infantry, 180, 195, 197–98,
201; 145th Infantry, 181, 200; 147th
Infantry, 81, 83; 149th Infantry, 180,
195, 198, 201; 150th Infantry, 182,
192
Newspapers: blame for Pickett's Charge,
247–48; on Eleventh Corps, 45–46;
Longstreet in, 267
Newton, John, 232–34, 237
Nicholls, Francis T., 186
Nichols, G. W., 61
Nolan, Alan T., 120

North Carolina units: 2d Infantry, 95; 5th
Infantry, 101–2; 12th Infantry, 101–2,
104–5; 20th Infantry, 99–101; 23d
Infantry, 101–4; 55th Infantry, 79–82,
84–86, 88–89

Oak Hill, 56, 59–60, 70
Oak Ridge, 73–74, 90–91, 95, 105–6
Official Records, 6, 8
Ohio units: First Artillery, 55, 59, 62–63;
5th Infantry, 178; 61st Infantry, 196;
66th Infantry, 174; 82d Infantry, 68
O'Neal, Edward A., Jr., 90–96, 93, 98–101,
106
Osborn, Thomas W., 55, 65, 298–99
Osborne, Stephen A., 221–22, 226

Page, R. C. M, 98
Paine, William H., 238, 240
Park, Robert E., 97–98
Parmlee, Uriah N., 225
Paul, Gabriel R., 92, 101
Peach Orchard, 140–42, 210–11, 225,
227, 282
Pender, William Dorsey, 32, 33–38, 76,
78, 90
Pendleton, William Nelson, 19, 272,
279–80; incompetence of, 264, 271–75,
280–81, 283; in Lost Cause tradition, 156,
250, 253, 264
Peninsula campaign, 6, 46, 134–35
Pennsylvania units, 127–28; Knap's Battery,
187; 26th Militia, 126; 28th Infantry, 180;
29th Infantry, 180, 201; 46th Infantry,
181, 185, 200; 56th Infantry, 81–82;
71st Infantry, 197–98; 75th Infantry,
68; 81st Infantry, 220; 88th Infantry, 97;
106th Infantry, 197; 109th Infantry,
180; 111th Infantry, 180; 116th Infantry,
218; 128th Infantry, 172; 147th
Infantry, 178; 148th Infantry, 215,
220–23
Permeus, J. J., 226
Perrin, Abner, 37
Pettigrew, James Johnston, 77, 88;
encounter with Buford, 18, 33–34, 74;
and Pickett's Charge, 246, 247, 248–49,
265, 282
Peyton, Charles S., 246
Pfanz, Harry W., 120
Pickens, Samuel Bonneau, 92, 97
Pickett, Charles, 262–63

Pickett, George E., 250–51, 260, 261; and
    Longstreet, 151, 261, 263, 265–66;
    Longstreet and men of, 253–56, 268–69;
    publicity by men, 257–62, 264–65;
    silencing of men, 256–57
Pickett, LaSalle Corbell, 261, 264–67
Pickett and His Men (LaSalle Pickett), 264
Pickett's Charge: artillery against, 298–305;
    Confederate artillery for, 270–83
Pickett's Division Association, 259–60
Pickett's Men: A Fragment of War History
    (Harrison), 248–49
Pipe Creek Circular, 138, 175–76
Piston, William Garrett, 245, 254
Pleasonton, Alfred, 232, 237
Poague, William T., 282
Pollard, Edward A., 111
Pope, John, 45, 48–49
Powell, William H., 225
Power's Hill, 182, 188, 191, 201, 240
Proskauer, Adolph, 97–98

Railroad, unfinished, 83–87
Ramseur, S. Dodson, 90, 93, 102, 105–6,
    110
Randolph, George E., 139
Reconnaissance, 33–34, 157, 183, 288;
    around Emmitsburg Road, 140–42;
    in force, 28, 33–36; by Howard, 54,
    59; lack of, 37–38, 77; and Lee's
    decisions, 12–17, 20, 33, 37–38, 120,
    122
Redington, John O., 195
Reese, Chauncey B., 238
Reese, William, 297–98
Reserve Artillery, 271
Reynolds, John F., 51, 88, 136–38, 176, 231;
    command of, 52–53; death of, 54–55,
    177, 178
Richardson, Charles, 279–80
Richardson, Israel B., 205
Richmond, Va., 4, 7
Ripley, Rowell S., 151
Roberts, A. K., 82
Robertson, Beverly H., 14
Robertson, Jerome B., 165, 222
Robinson, John C., 92, 172, 238–39
Rock Creek, 181, 185–86, 189–90, 193–94,
    200
Rodes, Robert E., 37, 89–98, 90, 100, 106,
    122; approach to Gettysburg, 38–39; and
    Cemetery Hill, 39–42; and Iverson, 90,

92, 100–101, 104–5; and Oak Hill, 61, 70;
    and Oak Ridge, 39, 91, 95; and O'Neal,
    90, 92–96; at onset of battle, 19–20;
    praise for, 89–90
Rodgers, Hiram C., 189–90
Rorty, James, 208
Rose Woods, 210–11, 218, 222, 224, 226
Round Top, 160
Ruger, Thomas H., 172, 177, 180–81, 184,
    189, 199–200, 202

Salomon, Edward, 52
Sauers, Richard, 131
Scales, Alfred Moore, 100
Schimmelfennig, Alexander, 49, 55–57,
    59–60, 62–64, 70–71, 169
Schurz, Carl, 55, 67, 68, 70; and Barlow,
    59–60; on Chancellorsville, 45–46;
    holding line, 56–57, 62–63; moving to
    Gettysburg, 52–53; praise for, 49–50, 50;
    retreat by, 63–65
Scotland, Pa., 38
Second Bull Run, 6–8, 134
Second Fredericksburg, 271
Second Manassas, 155
Seddon, John, 115
Sedgwick, John, 139, 232–33, 235–37, 243
Seminary Ridge, 37–39, 57, 274–75,
    282, 297
Semmes, 215, 218, 222
Seven Days campaign, 6, 271
Seven Pines, Va., 153, 166
Shaler, Alexander, 235, 239
Shallenberger, W. S., 209
Sharpe, George H., 234–35
Sharpsburg, Md., 6–7, 8, 46, 81, 271–72,
    285–87
Sheridan, Philip H., 170
Sickles, Daniel E., 131–46, 132, 227;
    advance of, 142–46, 159, 188, 208–10;
    criticism of, 143, 169, 225; and Hooker,
    134–36; and Howard, 55, 57; and Hunt,
    139–40, 289; and Meade, 136–40, 142,
    144–46, 211, 232, 234; postwar activities,
    142–44, 259; prewar career, 131–34;
    wound of, 142, 145, 231
Sickles, Mrs. Teresa Bagioli, 133–34
Sigel, Franz, 46
Skelly, D. A., 54
Slocum, Henry W., 22, 170, 185; approach
    to Gettysburg, 55–57, 59, 62, 174–78,
    178; command of, 177–79, 184, 232;

Three Days at Gettysburg
was designed by Will Underwood;
composed by The Book Page, Inc.,
in 10.2/13.5 Quadraat on a Macintosh
Power PC system using Quark XPress;
printed by sheet-fed offset lithography
on 50-pound Turin Book natural stock
(an acid-free, totally chlorine-free paper),
Smyth sewn and bound over binder's
boards in Arrestox B clot!., and wrapped
with dust jackets printed in three colors finished
with polypropylene matte film lamination
by Thomson-Shore, Inc.;
and published by
The Kent State University Press
KENT, OHIO 44242